Deep Dive Python

Techniques and Best Practices for Developers

Adarsh Divakaran

Apress®

Deep Dive Python: Techniques and Best Practices for Developers

Adarsh Divakaran ⓘ
Kannur, Kerala, India

ISBN-13 (pbk): 979-8-8688-1260-6   ISBN-13 (electronic): 979-8-8688-1261-3
https://doi.org/10.1007/979-8-8688-1261-3

Managing Director, Apress Media LLC: Welmoed Spahr
Acquisitions Editor: Celestin Suresh John
Desk Editor: James Markham
Editorial Project Manager: Gryffin Winkler

Cover designed by eStudioCalamar

Cover image designed by Aixklusiv from Pixabay

Distributed to the book trade worldwide by Springer Science+Business Media New York, 1 New York Plaza, New York, NY 10004. Phone 1-800-SPRINGER, fax (201) 348-4505, e-mail orders-ny@springer-sbm.com, or visit www.springeronline.com. Apress Media, LLC is a Delaware LLC and the sole member (owner) is Springer Science + Business Media Finance Inc (SSBM Finance Inc). SSBM Finance Inc is a **Delaware** corporation.

For information on translations, please e-mail booktranslations@springernature.com; for reprint, paperback, or audio rights, please e-mail bookpermissions@springernature.com.

Apress titles may be purchased in bulk for academic, corporate, or promotional use. eBook versions and licenses are also available for most titles. For more information, reference our Print and eBook Bulk Sales web page at http://www.apress.com/bulk-sales.

Any source code or other supplementary material referenced by the author in this book is available to readers on GitHub. For more detailed information, please visit https://www.apress.com/gp/services/source-code.

If disposing of this product, please recycle the paper

Table of Contents

xiii

About the Author

Adarsh Divakaran is a seasoned Python programmer with extensive experience in the Python ecosystem. He is the co-founder of Digievo Labs, which provides Python and software development consulting to global clients and works on building multiple SaaS products. Python serves as the foundation for his work, encompassing the development and integration of APIs, web applications, data scraping, data analysis, and a range of automation tasks. Adarsh has also been a speaker at various global technology conferences, including the GraphQL Summit, PyCascades, EuroPython, DjangoCon US, FlaskCon, and PiterPy.

About the Technical Reviewer

Andrea Gavana has been programming Python for more than 20 years, dabbling with other languages since the late 1990s. He graduated from university with a master's degree in Chemical Engineering, and he is now Master Development Planning Architect working for TotalEnergies in Copenhagen, Denmark.

Andrea enjoys programming at work and for fun, and he has been involved in multiple open source projects, all Python-based. One of his favorite hobbies is Python coding, but he is also fond of cycling, swimming, and cozy dinners with family and friends. This is his fifth book as a technical reviewer.

Acknowledgments

This book wouldn't have come to life without the support and inspiration of many people along the way.

To my family and friends: thank you for your unwavering encouragement, patience, and belief in me through the long nights and shifting deadlines.

To my teachers who sparked my curiosity about computers and programming: your early influence shaped the way I think and learn even today.

To the open source community: your tireless efforts, code contributions, and documentation helped me learn, grow, and build. This book is deeply inspired by your work.

To the Python community, especially those who share knowledge freely—whether through blog posts, talks, or code: your generosity continues to amaze me.

And to every reader picking up this book: thank you. You're the reason it exists.

Introduction

Deep Dive Python is a cookbook-style guide for intermediate to advanced Python developers. You don't have to read this book from cover to cover. Each chapter stands on its own, so you can pick the ones most relevant to what you're working on and start there.

This book was born out of a simple idea: we learn better when we see real code solving real problems. Rather than relying on textbook examples, I've focused on how concepts actually show up in open source projects. More than 80% of the code snippets in this book are taken from real codebases on GitHub. These are the same tools and patterns developers use every day.

You won't find detailed introductions to basic Python topics here. The goal is not to explain what a variable is or how a for loop works. Instead, we'll explore how slightly more complex ideas are used in practice. Things like dunder methods, descriptors, iterators, decorators, and advanced function patterns—all shown through examples from the Python ecosystem.

The focus is to go one level deeper than most tutorials and to do it in a way that's simple and clear. If a concept confused me at first, I've made sure to explain it the way I wish someone had explained it to me.

You can treat this book as a reference, a guide, or a companion for your daily Python work. I hope it helps you connect the dots and write better code.

CHAPTER 1

Lists

`list` is a mutable sequence that can store heterogeneous data. In Python, lists are fundamental and special; Python has its dedicated syntactical sugar for creating lists—comprehensions, which we will explore in detail.

An interesting aspect of the `list` class in Python is its naming convention. Despite being a class, it is named in lowercase, following a pattern more commonly associated with functions. This naming style is consistent with other fundamental Python classes, such as `tuple` and `str`, aligning with the general convention for Python built-ins, which are predominantly lowercase. This consistent lowercase naming across built-in types underscores Python's emphasis on simplicity and readability.

Initializing Empty Lists

We can initialize an empty list using square brackets (`[]`) or by calling the `list()` constructor. Among these, using the square bracket syntax is faster.

Benchmark the time taken for initializing an empty list:

```python
import timeit
import dis

# Using square brackets
time1 = timeit.timeit("[]", number=1000000)

# Using list() constructor
time2 = timeit.timeit("list()", number=1000000)

print("Using []:", time1)  # Output: Using []: 0.013635800000000003
print("Using list():", time2)  # Output: Using list(): 0.0319226
```

© Adarsh Divakaran 2025
A. Divakaran, *Deep Dive Python*, https://doi.org/10.1007/979-8-8688-1261-3_1

```
dis.dis("[]")
"""
1            0 BUILD_LIST              0
             2 RETURN_VALUE
"""

dis.dis("list()")
"""
  1            0 LOAD_NAME              0 (list)
               2 CALL_FUNCTION          0
               4 RETURN_VALUE
"""
```

The output generated by the dis module provides a human-readable representation of the Python bytecode instructions.

Here, we can see the disassembled code for each initialization statement.

It can be seen that the square bracket syntax is more optimized without the need to load and call the list constructor. This justifies its faster performance. Though slower for creating empty lists, the list() constructor is useful when constructing a list from an iterable using list(iterable).

Indexing

Since list indices start from 0, for a list named lst, lst[0] will return the first member of the list. To fetch elements from the end of the list, we commonly use negative indices. lst[-1] returns the last element from the list.

Index 0: Returns the first element

Index -1: Returns the first element from the list's end

What if we need a consistent behavior in this case? We can use the bitwise not (~) operator for indexing.

Index 0: Returns the first element

Index ~0: Returns the first element from the list's end

Index 1: Returns the second element

Index ~1: Returns the second element from the list's end

```
numbers = [1, 2, 3, 4, 5]

print(numbers[0])   # Output: 1
print(numbers[~0])  # Output: 5
print(numbers[-1])  # Output: 5
print(numbers[-0])  # Output: 1

print(numbers[-2] == numbers[~1])  # Output: True
```

Slicing

A slice operation on a list returns a subset of its members matching the slicing criteria. A slice operation can take `start`, `stop`, and `step` index values as its arguments.

From Python docs:

- The slice of *s* from *i* to *j* is defined as the sequence of items with index *k* such that i <= k < j. If *i* or *j* is greater than len(s), use len(s). If *i* is omitted or None, use 0. If *j* is omitted or None, use len(s). If *i* is greater than or equal to *j*, the slice is empty.

- The slice of *s* from *i* to *j* with step *k* is defined as the sequence of items with index x = i + n*k such that 0 <= n < (j-i)/k. In other words, the indices are i, i+k, i+2*k, i+3*k and so on, stopping when *j* is reached (but never including *j*). When *k* is positive, *i* and *j* are reduced to len(s) if they are greater. When *k* is negative, *i* and *j* are reduced to len(s) - 1 if they are greater. If *i* and *j* are omitted or None, they become "end" values (which end depends on the sign of *k*). Note, *k* cannot be zero. If *k* is None, it is treated like 1.

Below are a few examples of slicing a list using the subscript notation:

```
numbers = [0, 1, 2, 3, 4, 5, 6]

numbers_copy = numbers[:]  # Creates a copy of the full list
print(numbers_copy)  # Output: [0, 1, 2, 3, 4, 5, 6]
```

```
natural_numbers = numbers[1:]
print(natural_numbers)  # Output: [1, 2, 3, 4, 5, 6]

# Stop index can overflow safely
natural_numbers = numbers[1:100]
print(natural_numbers)  # Output: [1, 2, 3, 4, 5, 6]

# On specifying stop, the element at the stop index is excluded.
natural_numbers_upto_5 = numbers[1:6]
print(natural_numbers_upto_5)  # Output: [1, 2, 3, 4, 5]

odd_numbers = numbers[1::2]
print(odd_numbers)  # Output: [1, 3, 5]

reversed_numbers = numbers[::-1]
print(reversed_numbers)  # Output: [6, 5, 4, 3, 2, 1, 0]

reversed_even_numbers = numbers[-1::-2]
print(reversed_even_numbers)  # Output: [6, 4, 2, 0]

reversed_even_numbers = numbers[~0::-2]  # Indices -1 (used above) and ~0
are equivalent
print(reversed_even_numbers)  # Output: [6, 4, 2, 0]
```

A slice operation works on sequences. In addition to lists, which are mutable sequences, all slice operations work on immutable sequences, including tuples and strings. Generalizing, slicing can be extended to any Python class that implements the __getitem__ (to retrieve elements using slicing syntax) and __setitem__ (to modify elements using slicing syntax) dunder methods.

What if we need to create dynamic slices? We can pass around the start, stop, and step variable values, but things can get complex when we need to omit some of these values. The subscript syntax for slicing lists does not accept None.

For dynamic applications, we can leverage the built-in slice function (it is a class in reality). Below is the type annotation for slice. It can be seen that slice either accepts a single argument (the stop) or three arguments (start, stop, and the optional step).

```
# File: typeshed/stdlib/builtins.pyi

class slice:
    @overload
    def __new__(cls, __stop: Any) -> Self:
        ...

    @overload
    def __new__(cls, __start: Any, __stop: Any, __step: Any = ...) -> Self:
        ...
```

From Python docs:

> A slice is an object usually containing a portion of a sequence.
> A slice is created using the subscript notation, [ ], with colons
> between numbers when several are given, such as in `variable_`
> `name[1:3:5]`. The bracket (subscript) notation uses `slice` objects
> internally.

Below is an example of slicing using the `slice` built-in and its equivalent using the subscript notation:

```
numbers = [0, 1, 2, 3, 4, 5, 6]

s = slice(~0, None, -2)

print(numbers[~0::-2] == numbers[s])
# Output: True
```

Dynamic Slices

We can create slice objects and pass them around for dynamic use cases. In the coming sections, we will see a few examples of slice objects used in open source projects.

Example from scikit-learn

scikit-learn, a popular machine learning library, generates slices dynamically to split sequences into batches.

```
# File: scikit-learn/sklearn/utils/__init__.py

def gen_batches(n, batch_size, *, min_batch_size=0):
    """Generator to create slices containing `batch_size` elements from
    0 to `n`.

    The last slice may contain less than `batch_size` elements, when
    `batch_size` does not divide `n`.

    Yields
    ------
    slice of `batch_size` elements

    """
    start = 0
    for _ in range(int(n // batch_size)):
        end = start + batch_size
        if end + min_batch_size > n:
            continue
        yield slice(start, end)
        start = end
    if start < n:
        yield slice(start, n)
```

The code creates a generator, which returns slices corresponding to each batch one by one.

This is used as seen below in scikit-learn tests:

```
# File: scikit-learn/sklearn/utils/tests/test_extmath.py

def test_incremental_weighted_mean_and_variance(
    mean, var, weight_loc, weight_scale, rng
):
    # Testing of correctness and numerical stability
    def _assert(X, sample_weight, expected_mean, expected_var):
        n = X.shape[0]
        for chunk_size in [1, n // 10 + 1, n // 4 + 1, n // 2 + 1, n]:
            last_mean, last_weight_sum, last_var = 0, 0, 0
            for batch in gen_batches(n, chunk_size):
```

```
        last_mean, last_var, last_weight_sum = _incremental_mean_
        and_var(
            X[batch],
            last_mean,
            last_var,
            last_weight_sum,
            sample_weight=sample_weight[batch],
        )
    assert_allclose(last_mean, expected_mean)
```

The loop variable batch is a slice object, and the expression X[batch] will perform slicing on the sequence X.

Snippet from IPython

IPython is an interactive Python shell. It uses the slice function to select lines from an input file based on the arguments supplied to the command-line interface (CLI).

```
# File: ipython/IPython/core/magics/code.py

# To match, e.g. 8-10 1:5 :10 3-
range_re = re.compile(r"""
(?P<start>\d+)?
((?P<sep>[\-:])
 (?P<end>\d+)?)?
$""", re.VERBOSE)

def extract_code_ranges(ranges_str):
    """Turn a string of range for %%load into 2-tuples of (start, stop)
    ready to use as a slice of the content split by lines.

    Examples
    --------
    list(extract_input_ranges("5-10 2"))
    [(4, 10), (1, 2)]
    """
    for range_str in ranges_str.split():
        rmatch = range_re.match(range_str)
```

```python
        if not rmatch:
            continue
        sep = rmatch.group("sep")
        start = rmatch.group("start")
        end = rmatch.group("end")

        if sep == '-':
            start = int(start) - 1 if start else None
            end = int(end) if end else None
        elif sep == ':':
            start = int(start) - 1 if start else None
            end = int(end) - 1 if end else None
        else:
            end = int(start)
            start = int(start) - 1
        yield (start, end)

@magics_class
class CodeMagics(Magics):
    """Magics related to code management (loading, saving, editing, ...)."""

    @line_magic
    def load(self, arg_s):
        """Load code into the current frontend.
        ...
        Options:
          -r <lines>: Specify lines or ranges of lines to load from
          the source.
          Ranges could be specified as x-y (x..y) or in python-style x:y
          (x..(y-1)). Both limits x and y can be left blank (meaning the
          beginning and end of the file, respectively).
        ...
        """
        opts, args = self.parse_options(arg_s, 'yns:r:')
        search_ns = 'n' in opts
        contents = self.shell.find_user_code(args, search_ns=search_ns)

        ...
```

```
if 'r' in opts:
    ranges = opts['r'].replace(',', ' ')
    lines = contents.split('\n')
    slices = extract_code_ranges(ranges)
    contents = [lines[slice(*slc)] for slc in slices]  # <-- slice
    called with tuple unpacking
    contents = '\n'.join(strip_initial_indent(chain.from_
    iterable(contents)))

...

contents = "# %load {}\n".format(arg_s) + contents

self.shell.set_next_input(contents, replace=True)
```

The load method of the CodeMagics class loads the input file contents, and if the range (r) argument is specified in the command, file contents are split line by line and saved to the list named lines. The variable slices is a generator object, and it returns tuples corresponding to the start and end line numbers to be selected.

lines[slice(*slc)] slices the lines list based on the current range tuple returned from the slices generator object.

Full Slice

A full slice (e.g., numbers[:] or numbers[::]) returns a copy of the entire list. A full slice can be obtained using slice(None) when using the "slice" function.

Example from Pandas

Added below is an example of creating a full slice, from the Pandas library:

```
# File: pandas/pandas/core/arrays/arrow/array.py

class ArrowExtensionArray(
    OpsMixin,
    ExtensionArraySupportsAnyAll,
    ArrowStringArrayMixin,
    BaseStringArrayMethods,
):
```

```python
    """
    Pandas ExtensionArray backed by a PyArrow ChunkedArray.
    """

    _pa_array: pa.ChunkedArray
    _dtype: ArrowDtype

    def __getitem__(self, item: PositionalIndexer):
        item = check_array_indexer(self, item)

        ...

        if item is Ellipsis:
            item = slice(None)  # <-- Full slice

        if is_scalar(item) and not is_integer(item):
            # e.g. "foo" or 2.5
            # exception message copied from numpy
            raise IndexError(
                r"only integers, slices (`:`), ellipsis (`...`), numpy."
                newaxis "
                r"(`None`) and integer or boolean arrays are valid indices"
            )

        if isinstance(item, slice):
            if item.start == item.stop:
                pass
            elif (
                    item.stop is not None
                    and item.stop < -len(self)
                    and item.step is not None
                    and item.step < 0
            ):
                item = slice(item.start, None, item.step)

        value = self._pa_array[item]

        ...
```

A full slice is created above to return a copy of the array whenever Ellipsis is passed as the item index for the __getitem__ method.

In the above example, the class ArrowExtensionArray stores the actual array data inside the attribute _pa_array. The expression array[...] will result in a call to the __getitem__ method of the ArrowExtensionArray with Ellipsis (...) as the item argument value. Since the condition item is Ellipsis is satisfied, item is reassigned as slice(None).

Finally, the "value" variable is calculated as value = self._pa_array[item]. This way, the statement can support both normal slicing and full slicing.

Consider this example:

```
array: ArrowExtensionArray # Assume array as an instance of
ArrowExtensionArray

array[...] # Will return a copy of the array

array[0:3] # Will return the slice
```

List Comprehensions

List comprehensions are Python's syntactic sugar for creating list objects. In the following examples, we will see some real-world uses of list comprehensions.

With Conditional Filtering

1. The below code from PyTorch uses list comprehension to create a list of missing dependencies:

```
# File: pytorch/torch/hub.py

def _check_module_exists(name):
    import importlib.util

    return importlib.util.find_spec(name) is not None

def _check_dependencies(m):
    dependencies = _load_attr_from_module(m, VAR_DEPENDENCY)
```

```python
if dependencies is not None:
    missing_deps = [pkg for pkg in dependencies if not _check_
    module_exists(pkg)]
    if len(missing_deps):
        raise RuntimeError(f"Missing dependencies: {',
        '.join(missing_deps)}")
```

The `missing_deps` list is populated based on calls to the `_check_module_exists` function.

2. The homeassistant library leverages comprehension to build a stringified list of subcodes:

   # File: core/homeassistant/components/onvif/util.py

   ```python
   def extract_subcodes_as_strings(subcodes: Any) -> list[str]:
       """Stringify ONVIF subcodes."""
       if isinstance(subcodes, list):
           return [code.text if hasattr(code, "text") else str(code)
           for code in subcodes]
       return [str(subcodes)]
   ```

   If the subcode has a `text` attribute, it is given preference over `str(code)`.

3. Beets, an audio library manager, uses list comprehensions in its `move_items` function:

   # File: beets/ui/commands.py

   ```python
   def move_items(lib, dest, query, copy, album, pretend,
   confirm=False, export=False):
       """Moves or copies items to a new base directory, given by
       dest. If
       dest is None, then the library's base directory is used,
       making the
       command "consolidate" files.
       """
       items, albums = _do_query(lib, query, album, False)
   ```

```
    objs = albums if album else items
    num_objs = len(objs)

    # Filter out files that don't need to be moved.
    def isitemmoved(item):
        return item.path != item.destination(basedir=dest)

    def isalbummoved(album):
        return any(isitemmoved(i) for i in album.items())

    objs = [o for o in objs if (isalbummoved if album else
    isitemmoved)(o)]
    num_unmoved = num_objs - len(objs)   # number of objects that
do not need to be moved
        ...
```

The code works as follows:

- Based on the `album` argument, the variable `objs` initially contains a list of albums or individual songs (items).

- The expression (`isalbummoved if album else isitemmoved`) dynamically selects a function based on the `album` flag. `isalbummoved` is chosen for albums and `isitemmoved` for individual items.

- The list comprehension iterates over `objs`, applying the selected function to each object. It keeps only those objects that the function identifies as needing to be moved.

With Tuple Unpacking

Django uses tuple unpacking with comprehension in its `BaseForm` class.

```
# File: django/forms/boundfield.py
class BoundField(RenderableFieldMixin):
    "A Field plus data"

    def _has_changed(self):
        field = self.field
        ...
        return field.has_changed(initial_value, self.data)
```

13

```python
# File: django/forms/forms.py
class BaseForm(RenderableFormMixin):
    def _bound_items(self):
        """Yield (name, bf) pairs, where bf is a BoundField object."""
        for name in self.fields:
            yield name, self[name]

    @cached_property
    def changed_data(self):
        return [name for name, bf in self._bound_items() if bf._has_
        changed()]
```

The return from self._bound_items() is unpacked into name and bf variables, and a list of names with changed bound fields is returned using the comprehension.

Nested Comprehensions

scikit-learn uses list comprehensions for calculating the max_time and max_inertia values.

```python
# File:  scikit-learn/benchmarks/bench_plot_fastkmeans.py

def compute_bench(samples_range, features_range):

    results = defaultdict(lambda: [])
    ...

    for n_samples in samples_range:
        for n_features in features_range:
            ...
            kmeans = KMeans(init="k-means++", n_clusters=10).fit(data)
            ...
            delta = time() - tstart
            results["kmeans_speed"].append(delta)
            results["kmeans_quality"].append(kmeans.inertia_)

            mbkmeans = MiniBatchKMeans(
                init="k-means++", n_clusters=10, batch_size=chunk
            )
```

```
        ...
        delta = time() - tstart
        results["MiniBatchKMeans Speed"].append(delta)
        results["MiniBatchKMeans Quality"].append(mbkmeans.inertia_)

if __name__ == "__main__":
    ...

    samples_range = np.linspace(50, 150, 5).astype(int)
    features_range = np.linspace(150, 50000, 5).astype(int)
    chunks = np.linspace(500, 10000, 15).astype(int)

    results = compute_bench(samples_range, features_range)
    results_2 = compute_bench_2(chunks)

    max_time = max(
        [max(i) for i in [t for (label, t) in results.items() if "speed"
        in label]]
    )
    max_inertia = max(
        [max(i) for i in [t for (label, t) in results.items() if "speed"
        not in label]]
    )
    ...
```

Considering the example of max_time calculation

1. The inner list comprehension [t for (label, t) in results.
    items() if "speed" in label] iterates over the results.
    items() (which are key-value tuples from the results dictionary).
    It unpacks each item into label and t and includes t in the list if
    the label contains the string speed. Note that the loop variable t
    holds a list and we now have a list of lists.

2. The outer list comprehension [max(i) for i in [...]] then
    iterates over the list produced by the inner comprehension. For
    each sublist i, it finds the maximum value with max(i). This list is
    then fed to the max built-in function to return the largest member.

Nested Loops

When working with collections of collections (e.g., list of lists or list of custom objects), nested for loops within list comprehensions can significantly simplify the code, as seen below:

```
# File: llama.cpp/convert.py

@dataclass
class ModelPlus:
    model: LazyModel
    paths: list[Path]   # Where this was read from.
    format: Literal["ggml", "torch", "safetensors", "none"]
    vocab: Vocab | None   # For GGML models (which have vocab built in),
    the vocab.

...


def merge_multifile_models(models_plus: list[ModelPlus]) -> ModelPlus:
    formats = set(mp.format for mp in models_plus)
    assert len(formats) == 1, "different formats?"
    format = formats.pop()
    paths = [path for mp in models_plus for path in mp.paths]   # <--

    ...
```

ModelPlus is a dataclass that stores a list of paths in its paths attribute.

Here, list comprehension is used to flatten these paths from a list of ModelPlus objects. The snippet above creates a single, combined list of all paths from all ModelPlus objects. This is a common pattern in data processing, where we need to aggregate or transform data from a structured format into a simpler, flat structure for further processing or analysis.

Multidimensional Lists

Python's list comprehensions go beyond just simple one-dimensional cases. They can be extended to create multidimensional lists.

Below is an example from wttr.in (a console-oriented weather app), which transforms data from a screen buffer into a two-dimensional (2D) array:

```
# File: wttr.in/lib/fmt/png.py

def render_ansi(text, options=None):
    """Render `text` (terminal sequence) in a PNG file
    paying attention to passed command line `options`.

    Return: file content
    """

    screen = pyte.screens.Screen(COLS, ROWS)
    screen.set_mode(pyte.modes.LNM)
    stream = pyte.Stream(screen)

    ...

    buf = sorted(screen.buffer.items(), key=lambda x: x[0])
    buf = [[x[1] for x in sorted(line[1].items(), key=lambda x: x[0])] for
    line in buf]

    ...
```

The snippet transforms buf, a dictionary representing a screen buffer where each key–value pair corresponds to a line on the screen. The value of each line is another dictionary where each key–value pair represents a character position and the character itself. For clarity, the type annotation of the buffer attribute is given below:

```
screen.buffer: Dict[int, StaticDefaultDict[int, Char]]
```

- *Outer comprehension*:
  - for line in buf: This iterates over each item in buf. Each line is a tuple with two elements, where line[0] is the line number and line[1] is the dictionary of characters in that line.
  - This outer loop forms the first dimension of the new list, representing each line of the screen.

- *Inner comprehension*:

    - `[x[1] for x in sorted(line[1].items(), key=lambda x: x[0])]`: This is nested within the outer comprehension and operates on `line[1]`, which is the dictionary of characters for that specific line.

    - `sorted(line[1].items(), key=lambda x: x[0])`: This sorts the items (key–value pairs) of the characters dictionary based on the keys (which are character positions), ensuring that characters are processed in the correct order.

    - `[x[1] for x in ...]`: This list comprehension extracts the second element of each sorted tuple (which is the character itself) from the line's dictionary.

- *Result*: The final result `buf` is a two-dimensional list. Each sublist within `buf` represents a line of the screen, and each element within a sublist is a character from that line, arranged in the correct order.

Copying Lists

In Python, variable assignment statements are used to bind a name (the variable) to a value. Consider the below example:

```
original_list = [1, 2, 3]
new_list = original_list

new_list[1] = 10

print(f"{new_list=}")  # Output: new_list=[1, 10, 3]
print(f"{original_list=}")  # Output: original_list=[1, 10, 3]
```

The statement `new_list = original_list` did not create a copy of the original list. It just created a new name, pointing to an existing value.

```
original_list = [1, 2, 3]
new_list = original_list
print(id(original_list))  # Output: 2462103902016
print(id(new_list))  # Output: 2462103902016
```

In CPython, the id function returns the memory address of an object. If two different objects return the same id value, they both point to the same location in memory, and a change in one will reflect in the other name.

It can be seen that both original_list and new_list point to the same location in memory.

The behavior is similar to variables passed as function arguments. Python uses a mechanism called "pass-by-object-reference" for function calls. So function arguments get the same object reference when the arguments are passed.

```python
def prepend_and_print_list(input_list):
    input_list[0] = 0
    print(f"{input_list=}")  # Output: input_list=[0, 6, 7]
    print(f"{id(input_list)=}")  # Output: id(input_list)=2280139985088

numbers = [5, 6, 7]
prepend_and_print_list(numbers)

print(f"{numbers=}")  # Output: input_list=[0, 6, 7]
print(f"{id(numbers)=}")  # Output: id(numbers)=2280139985088
```

We must be extra careful when assigning mutable objects to new names and passing them around to functions to prevent accidental modifications.

Shallow Copy

From Python docs: Assignment statements in Python do not copy objects; they create bindings between a target and an object. For collections that are mutable or contain mutable items, a copy is sometimes needed so one can change one copy without changing the other.

A shallow copy can be created using the copy function imported from the copy module:

```python
import copy

def prepend_and_print_list(input_list):
    input_list[0] = 0
    print(f"{input_list=}")  # Output: input_list=[0, 2, 3]
    print(f"{id(input_list)=}")  # Output: id(input_list)=2105927466432

original_list = [1, 2, 3]
new_list = copy.copy(original_list)

print(f"{id(original_list)=}")  # Output: id(original_list)=2105927466176
print(f"{id(new_list)=}")  # Output: id(new_list)=2105927471296

new_list[1] = 10

print(f"{new_list=}")  # Output: new_list=[1, 10, 3]
print(f"{original_list=}")  # Output: original_list=[1, 2, 3]

prepend_and_print_list(copy.copy(original_list))
print(f"{original_list=}")  # Output: original_list=[1, 2, 3]
```

In the above example, a copy of the original list is assigned to new_list, and another copy is created and passed to the prepend_and_print_list function. It can be seen the original_list, new_list, and input_list all occupy different memory locations, and change in one won't affect another.

But there is a catch:

```python
import copy

original_list = [1, [1, 2, 3], {"key": "value"}]

copy_list = copy.copy(original_list)

copy_list.append(10)
copy_list[0] = 0

print(f"{copy_list=}")
# Output: copy_list=[0, [1, 2, 3], {'key': 'value'}, 10]

print(f"{original_list=}")
# Output: original_list=[1, [1, 2, 3], {'key': 'value'}]
```

```
copy_list[1].append(100)
copy_list[2]["key"] = "new_value"

print(f"{copy_list=}")
# Output: copy_list=[0, [1, 2, 3, 100], {'key': 'new_value'}, 10]

print(f"{original_list=}")
# Output: original_list=[1, [1, 2, 3, 100], {'key': 'new_value'}]{'key':
'new_value'}]
```

copy.copy() creates a shallow copy. In the case of lists, copy creates a new list and populates it with the references of the child objects present in the original.

This creates a problem with mutable list members, as seen in the above example. Change in a mutable member of the copied list affects the members of the original list.

The below snippet explains this behavior:

```
import copy

original_list = [1, [1, 2, 3], {"key": "value"}]
copy_list = copy.copy(original_list)

print(f"{id(copy_list)=}")
# Output: id(copy_list)=1968377371200

print(f"{id(original_list)=}")
# Output: id(original_list)=1968377363456

print(f"{id(copy_list[1])=}")
# Output: id(copy_list[1])=1968377369408

print(f"{id(original_list[1])=}")
# Output: id(original_list[1])=1968377369408
```

As expected, copy_list and original_list point to different addresses in memory. But the members at index 1 of both lists hold the same reference.

Deep Copy

Deep copies are required when we need to copy the list as well as its members recursively.

The issue we have seen above with shallow copies is not present when using `copy.deepcopy()`:

```python
import copy

original_list = [1, [1, 2, 3], {"key": ["value1", "value2"]}]
copy_list = copy.deepcopy(original_list)

print(f"{id(copy_list[1])=}")
# Output: id(copy_list[1])=2853180478528

print(f"{id(original_list[1])=}")
# Output: id(original_list[1])=2853180473152

print(f"{id(copy_list[2]['key'])=}")
# Output: id(copy_list[2]['key'])=2853180471872

print(f"{id(original_list[2]['key'])=}")
# Output: id(original_list[2]['key'])=2853180472320
```

It can be seen that every list member is now copied when the `deepcopy` function is used, owing to their different `id` values.

Points to keep in mind:

- For a list with immutable members, shallow and deep copies behave the same.

- Apart from lists, similar assignment and copy behavior applies for other mutables including dicts and sets.

Sorting Lists

Lists come with a `sort` method, which modifies the list in place (without returning anything). To return a sorted copy of the list without modifying the original, the `sorted` built-in function can be called. The `sorted` function can be applied to other iterables also, apart from lists.

Below are the type annotations for sort and sorted functions from the Python typeshed library:

```
# File: typeshed/stdlib/builtins.pyi

@overload
def sorted(
    __iterable: Iterable[SupportsRichComparisonT],
    *,
    key: None = None,
    reverse: bool = False
) -> list[SupportsRichComparisonT]:
    ...

@overload
def sorted(
    __iterable: Iterable[_T],
    *,
    key: Callable[[_T], SupportsRichComparison],
    reverse: bool = False
) -> list[_T]:
    ...

class list(MutableSequence[_T]):
    @overload
    def sort(
        self: list[SupportsRichComparisonT], *, key: None = None, reverse:
        bool = False
    ) -> None:
        ...

    @overload
    def sort(
        self, *, key: Callable[[_T], SupportsRichComparison], reverse:
        bool = False
    ) -> None:
        ...
```

Both sort and sorted accept an optional argument key function, which, if supplied, will be used to calculate the comparison key.

From Python docs:

> *key* specifies a function of one argument that is used to extract a comparison key from each list element (e.g., key=str.lower). The key corresponding to each item in the list is calculated once and then used for the entire sorting process.

Lambda functions can be used as key functions in sorting operations. Lambdas allow us to specify a simple expression that determines the sorting criteria. This approach is ideal for quick, inline sorting logic where defining a separate function might be unnecessarily verbose.

The snippet from the "youtube-dl" library illustrates the usage of lambdas:

```python
# File: youtube_dl/youtube_dl/YoutubeDL.py

class YoutubeDL(object):
    def process_video_result(self, info_dict, download=True):
        ...
        thumbnails = info_dict.get("thumbnails")
        ...

        if thumbnails:
            thumbnails.sort(
                key=lambda t: (
                    t.get("preference") if t.get("preference") is not None
                    else -1,
                    t.get("width") if t.get("width") is not None else -1,
                    t.get("height") if t.get("height") is not None else -1,
                    t.get("id") if t.get("id") is not None else "",
                    t.get("url"),
                )
            )
        ...
```

This particular example sorts the list of thumbnails based on multiple criteria, prioritizing preference, width, height, id, and URL in that order.

Built-In Key Functions

Python provides various standard library functions that can be used as sort keys. The coming sections cover examples using these in sorting operations.

The attrgetter Function

The attrgetter function from the operator module can come in handy as a sort key in sorting operations, particularly when we need to sort objects based on one or more of their attributes.

attrgetter creates a callable that fetches the specified attribute(s) from its operand. An example snippet showcasing the same is added below:

```python
from operator import attrgetter

class Vehicle:
    def __init__(self, make, model, year):
        self.make = make
        self.model = model
        self.year = year

vehicle = Vehicle("Manufacturer X", "Model Y", 2022)

make_getter = attrgetter('make')
print(make_getter(vehicle))  # Output: Manufacturer X

make_and_model_getter = attrgetter('make', 'model')
print(type(make_and_model_getter))  # Output: <class 'operator.attrgetter'>
print(make_and_model_getter(vehicle))  # Output: ('Manufacturer X', 'Model Y')
```

Let's see attrgetter in action for sorting lists in the below example from AWS X-Ray SDK for Python, which is the Python interface to AWS's distributed tracing solution:

```python
# File: aws-xray-sdk-python/aws_xray_sdk/core/sampling/rule_cache.py

class RuleCache:
    """

    Cache sampling rules and quota retrieved by ``TargetPoller``
    and ``RulePoller``. It will not return anything if it expires.
    """
```

```python
def __init__(self):
    self._last_updated = None
    self._rules = []
    self._lock = threading.Lock()

def get_matched_rule(self, sampling_req, now):
    return matched_rule

def load_rules(self, rules):
    # Record the old rules for later merging.
    with self._lock:
        self._load_rules(rules)

def _load_rules(self, rules):
    oldRules = {}
    for rule in self.rules:
        oldRules[rule.name] = rule

    # Update the rules in the cache.
    self.rules = rules

    # Transfer state information to refreshed rules.
    for rule in self.rules:
        old = oldRules.get(rule.name, None)
        if old:
            rule.merge(old)

    # The cache should maintain the order of the rules based on
    # priority. If priority is the same we sort name by alphabet
    # as rule name is unique.
    self.rules.sort(key=attrgetter("priority", "name"))
```

The attrgetter("priority", "name") key directs Python to sort the rules list first by the priority attribute and then, in cases of equal priority, by the name attribute.

The itemgetter Function

The itemgetter function from the operator module is a concise and efficient tool for retrieving specific items from a collection. itemgetter is perfect for cases where we need to access items from sequences like lists, tuples, or even dictionaries using keys.

As we have seen above, `attrgetter` dynamically fetches attributes (similar to using the dot notation) from an object, whereas `itemgetter` fetches items using the subscript (`[]`) notation.

Below is an example usage of `itemgetter` seen in the source code of the Wagtail CMS:

```python
# File: wagtail/wagtail/admin/forms/account.py

def _get_time_zone_choices():
    time_zones = [
        (tz, str(l18n.tz_fullnames.get(tz, tz)))
        for tz in get_available_admin_time_zones()
    ]
    time_zones.sort(key=itemgetter(1))
    return BLANK_CHOICE_DASH + time_zones
```

In the example, `itemgetter(1)` is employed to sort the `time_zones` list based on the second element of each tuple, which represents the time zone's name.

The `itemgetter` function can also be used to sort a list of dictionaries based on a specific key value since dictionaries also use the subscript notation to fetch items with keys.

The methodcaller Function

The `methodcaller` function, also from Python's `operator` module, returns a callable that can invoke the methods on objects. This function is especially useful for scenarios where we need to call the same method on a series of objects and use the return value as the sort key.

The below example calls the `strip` method of strings and uses the whitespace-removed strings as the sort key:

```python
from operator import methodcaller

# List of strings with leading and trailing spaces
fruits = ["apple", "banana", " cherry", "  date", "fig"]

fruits.sort()
print(fruits)  # Output: ['  date', ' cherry', 'apple', 'banana', 'fig']

fruits.sort(key=methodcaller('strip'))
print(fruits)  # Output: ['apple', 'banana', ' cherry', '  date', 'fig']
```

Note that the original list items are not modified in this case. The result of the method call is used just to calculate the key value for sorting.

The cmp_to_key Function

> "Unlike key functions that return an absolute value for sorting,
> a comparison function computes the relative ordering for two
> inputs."

In Python 2, sorting functions like sorted() and the .sort() had a cmp parameter that allowed specifying a comparison function. This comparison function cmp took two arguments and returned a negative number for less than, zero for equality, and a positive number for greater than.

In Python 3, the cmp parameter for sorting was removed. If we have a comparison function (which takes two arguments and returns their comparison result), this can be converted to a sort key by using the cmp_to_key function, provided in the functools module.

The below example from pretty_midi, a MIDI processing library, illustrates the use of cmp_to_key:

```
# File: pretty_midi/pretty_midi.py

class PrettyMIDI(object):
    """A container for MIDI data in an easily-manipulable format."""

    ...

    def write(self, filename):
        """Write the MIDI data out to a .mid file."""

        def event_compare(event1, event2):
            """Compares two events for sorting.

            Events are sorted by tick time ascending. Events with the
            same tick time are sorted by event type. Some events are
            sorted by additional values. For example, Note On events are
            sorted by pitch then velocity, ensuring that a Note Off (Note
            On with velocity 0) will never follow a Note On with the
            same pitch.
```

```
Parameters
----------
event1, event2 : mido.Message
    Two events to be compared.
"""

secondary_sort = {
    "set_tempo": lambda e: (1 * 256 * 256),
    "time_signature": lambda e: (2 * 256 * 256),
    "key_signature": lambda e: (3 * 256 * 256),
    "lyrics": lambda e: (4 * 256 * 256),
    "text_events": lambda e: (5 * 256 * 256),
    "program_change": lambda e: (6 * 256 * 256),
    "pitchwheel": lambda e: ((7 * 256 * 256) + e.pitch),
    "control_change": lambda e: (
        (8 * 256 * 256) + (e.control * 256) + e.value
    ),
    "note_off": lambda e: ((9 * 256 * 256) + (e.note * 256)),
    "note_on": lambda e: ((10 * 256 * 256) + (e.note * 256) +
    e.velocity),
    "end_of_track": lambda e: (11 * 256 * 256),
}
# If the events have the same tick, and both events have types
# which appear in the secondary_sort dictionary, use the dictionary
# to determine their ordering.
if (
    event1.time == event2.time
    and event1.type in secondary_sort
    and event2.type in secondary_sort
):
    return (secondary_sort[event1.type](event1) -
            secondary_sort[event2.type](event2))
```

```
        # Otherwise, just return the difference of their ticks.
        return event1.time - event2.time

    # Create track 0 with timing information
    timing_track = mido.MidiTrack()

    ...    # Code processing the timing_track

    # Sort the (absolute-tick-timed) events.
    timing_track.sort(key=functools.cmp_to_key(event_compare))

    ...
```

The event_compare function provides a specific comparison logic for MIDI events, ensuring they are sorted correctly by their tick time and type, along with additional criteria for certain event types. Then, functools.cmp_to_key is used to convert this comparison function into a key function. This is useful when we already have a comparison function defined, as it eliminates the need to create an additional function to define sort keys.

Stability of sort

Python's sorting is guaranteed to be stable. This means that the relative order of equal elements remains unchanged after sorting. If two elements have the same key value, the sort method and sorted built-in function guarantee that their original order is preserved in the sorted output.

This is useful when performing multiple sorts on the same data. The below snippet performs two stages of sorting to rank students based on their scores and the number of wrong answers. If two students have the same score, the one with the lowest number of wrong answers will be ranked first:

```
# Code for tie-breaking. If two students have the same marks,
# the student with the smallest number of wrong answers gets the
better rank

# list of tuples containing (student_name, wrong_answers, score)
students = [
    ("Alice", 25, 90),
    ("Bob", 30, 85),
```

```
        ("Carol", 35, 90),
        ("David", 30, 80),
        ("Eve", 25, 85),
]

# sort by the number of wrong answers (ascending)
students.sort(key=lambda x: (x[1]))
print(students)  # Output:
# [('Alice', 25, 90), ('Eve', 25, 85), ('Bob', 30, 85), ('David', 30, 80),
('Carol', 35, 90)]

# sort by score, descending
students.sort(key=lambda x: (x[2]), reverse=True)
print(students)  # Output:
# [('Alice', 25, 90), ('Carol', 35, 90), ('Eve', 25, 85), ('Bob', 30, 85),
('David', 30, 80)]

# The two-step sorting can be simplified into a single step as:
# students.sort(key=lambda x: (-x[2], x[1]))
```

In the above example, after the second sort stage (sort by score), even though Alice and Carol have the same score, Alice comes first since the previous list order is maintained for equal key values.

Custom List Classes

Sometimes, we need custom lists or list-like classes that modify or extend some functionality of lists tailored to our requirements. Three main ways of doing that are

1. Inheriting from list to create a custom list class

2. Inheriting from UserList—a specialized class to make customizing lists easier

3. Using the MutableSequence abstract base class (ABC) to build a list-like class

We will look at each of them one by one with their real-world examples.

Inheriting from the list Class

SQLAlchemy

SQLAlchemy is a popular Python ORM for connecting to various SQL databases (DBs). OrderingList exists as a part of extension modules in SQLAlchemy, which are used to extend core ORM functionality and are usually tailored for a niche functionality. It is used to implement automatic ordering to relationships (e.g., foreign key). This will be clearer once we look into its implementation and usage examples.

SQLAlchemy's OrderingList is created by inheriting from typing.List.

> For creating custom list classes, inheriting from typing.List is equivalent to inheriting from the built-in list.

Now let's take a look at the source code. The source file includes a function ordering_list that acts as a factory to generate OrderingList objects:

```python
# File: sqlalchemy/lib/sqlalchemy/ext/orderinglist.py

def ordering_list(
        attr: str,
        count_from: Optional[int] = None,
        ordering_func: Optional[OrderingFunc] = None,
        reorder_on_append: bool = False,
) -> Callable[[], OrderingList]:
    """Prepares an :class:`OrderingList` factory for use in mapper
    definitions.

    Returns an object suitable for use as an argument to a Mapper
    relationship's ``collection_class`` option.

    Additional arguments are passed to the :class:`.OrderingList`
    constructor.

    """

    kw = _unsugar_count_from(
        count_from=count_from,
        ordering_func=ordering_func,
        reorder_on_append=reorder_on_append,
```

```
    )
    return lambda: OrderingList(attr, **kw)

...

class OrderingList(List[_T]):
    """A custom list that manages position information for its children.

    The :class:`.OrderingList` object is normally set up using the
    :func:`.ordering_list` factory function, used in conjunction with
    the :func:`_orm.relationship` function.

    """

    ordering_attr: str
    ordering_func: OrderingFunc
    reorder_on_append: bool

    def __init__(
            self,
            ordering_attr: Optional[str] = None,
            ordering_func: Optional[OrderingFunc] = None,
            reorder_on_append: bool = False,
    ):
        """A custom list that manages position information for its
        children.

        ``OrderingList`` is a ``collection_class`` list implementation that
        syncs position in a Python list with a position attribute on the
        mapped objects.

        """
        self.ordering_attr = ordering_attr
        if ordering_func is None:
            ordering_func = count_from_0
        self.ordering_func = ordering_func
        self.reorder_on_append = reorder_on_append
```

```python
    # More complex serialization schemes (multi column, e.g.) are
    possible by
    # subclassing and reimplementing these two methods.
    def _get_order_value(self, entity):
        return getattr(entity, self.ordering_attr)

    def _set_order_value(self, entity, value):
        setattr(entity, self.ordering_attr, value)

    def reorder(self) -> None:
        """Synchronize ordering for the entire collection.

        Sweeps through the list and ensures that each object has accurate
        ordering information set.

        ...

        """
        for index, entity in enumerate(self):
            self._order_entity(index, entity, True)

    # As of 0.5, _reorder is no longer semi-private
    _reorder = reorder

    def _order_entity(self, index, entity, reorder=True):
        have = self._get_order_value(entity)

        # Don't disturb existing ordering if reorder is False
        if have is not None and not reorder:
            return

        should_be = self.ordering_func(index, self)
        if have != should_be:
            self._set_order_value(entity, should_be)

    def append(self, entity):
        super().append(entity)
        self._order_entity(len(self) - 1, entity, self.reorder_on_append)

    ...
```

```
def insert(self, index, entity):
    super().insert(index, entity)
    self._reorder()

def __delitem__(self, index):
    super().__delitem__(index)
    self._reorder()
```

OrderingList can be used to automatically keep track of the insertion order of the members in a related (think of foreign keys) list and preserve the order in the database.

It can be seen that the __init__ dunder is overridden to get some additional inputs. We can see the _get_order_value and _reorder methods, which will help with the ordering of the members. Standard list methods such as insert are overridden, and a call to _reorder is made on every insert operation.

Consider a blogging application where each blog post has multiple images associated with it that need to be ordered. We are interested in displaying images in a specific order.

The below code using OrderingList can be used for the same:

```
class BlogPost(Base):
    __tablename__ = 'blog_post'

    id = Column(Integer, primary_key=True)
    title = Column(String)

    # Images in the gallery are ordered
    images = relationship("Image", order_by="Image.position",
                          collection_class=ordering_list('position'))

class Image(Base):
    __tablename__ = 'image'

    id = Column(Integer, primary_key=True)
    blog_post_id = Column(Integer, ForeignKey('blog_post.id'))
    url = Column(String)

    position = Column(Integer)  # This determines the order in the
    image gallery
```

```
# Create a blog post
post = BlogPost(title="My Travel Adventures")

# Add images in a specific order
post.images.append(Image(url="path/to/image1.jpg"))
post.images.append(Image(url="path/to/image2.jpg"))
post.images.insert(1, Image(url="path/to/image3.jpg"))  # This will be the
second image

# The images will be automatically ordered by their position
for image in post.images:
    print(image.position, image.url)

# Output :
# 0 path/to/image1.jpg
# 1 path/to/image3.jpg
# 2 path/to/image2.jpg
```

We can see that even though we are not explicitly specifying the position attribute for each image, it is auto-managed by OrderingList.

Inheriting from UserList

> *Python docs (collections.UserList)*: This class acts as a wrapper around list objects. It is a useful base class for your own list-like classes, which can inherit from them and override existing methods or add new ones. In this way, one can add new behaviors to lists. The need for this class has been partially supplanted by the ability to subclass directly from list; however, this class can be easier to work with because the underlying list is accessible as an attribute.

UserList offers a data attribute that will get modified when operations are performed on the child classes. This makes it easier to operate on the data without using super class calls.

Let's consider an example:

```python
from collections import UserList

class FixedSizeList(UserList):
    def append(self, item):
        del self.data[0]
        self.data.append(item)

l = FixedSizeList((1, 2, 3, 4))
print(l)  # Output: [1, 2, 3, 4]

l.append(5)
print(l)  # Output: [2, 3, 4, 5]
l.append(6)
print(l)  # Output: [3, 4, 5, 6]

# Note that the example used above is incomplete, since other methods like
insert can modify the list size.
```

UserList stores its members under the data attribute, providing easier access for modifying various list operations.

Androguard

UserList works best when we just have to extend the list functionality without any modifications. The below example is from Androguard, a library that helps reverse engineer Android apps. In the example, the FilterSet class inherits from UserList:

```python
# File: androguard/androguard/ui/filter.py

class FilterSet(UserList[_T]):

    def passes(self, interface=None, method=None, call_type=None):
        """Return True if all filters in the set pass, False otherwise."""
        return all([f.passes(interface, method, call_type) for f in
        self.data])
```

Objects of `FilterSet` behave like normal lists, the only difference being having a `passes` method that returns true if all the filters added in this custom class pass. It calls the `passes` method of all the list members and returns true if all of them are truthy. For doing this, the implementation iterates through `self.data` members, i.e., the underlying list members.

OpenMMLab mmrazor

```python
# File:  mmrazor/mmrazor/structures/subnet/candidate.py

class Candidates(UserList):
    """The data structure of sampled candidate. The format is
    Union[Dict[str,
    Dict], List[Dict[str, Dict]]].
    """

    _indicators = ('score', 'flops', 'params', 'latency')

    def __init__(self, initdata: Optional[_format_input] = None):
        self.data = []
        if initdata is not None:
            initdata = self._format(initdata)
            if isinstance(initdata, list):
                self.data = initdata
            else:
                self.data.append(initdata)

    def _format(self, data: _format_input) -> _format_return:
        """Transform [Dict, ...] to Union[Dict[str, Dict], List[Dict[str,
        Dict]]].

        Args:
            data: Four types of input are supported:
                1. Dict: only include network information.
                2. List[Dict]: multiple candidates only include network
                    information.
                3. Dict[str, Dict]: network information and the
                    corresponding resources.
```

      4. List[Dict[str, Dict]]: multiple candidate information.
Returns:
    Union[Dict[str, Dict], UserList[Dict[str, Dict]]]:
        A dict or a list of dict that contains a pair of network
        information and the corresponding Score | FLOPs | Params |
        Latency results in each candidate.
"""

```python
def _format_item(
        cond: Union[Dict, Dict[str, Dict]]) -> Dict[str, Dict]:
    """Transform Dict to Dict[str, Dict]."""
    if isinstance(list(cond.values())[0], dict):
        for value in list(cond.values()):
            for key in list(self._indicators):
                value.setdefault(key, 0.)
        return cond
    else:
        return {str(cond): {}.fromkeys(self._indicators, -1)}

if isinstance(data, UserList):
    return [_format_item(i) for i in data.data]

elif isinstance(data, list):
    return [_format_item(i) for i in data]

else:
    return _format_item(data)

def append(self, item: _format_input) -> None:
    """Append operation."""
    item = self._format(item)
    if isinstance(item, list):
        self.data = self.data + item
    else:
        self.data.append(item)
```

```python
    def insert(self, i: int, item: _format_input) -> None:
        """Insert operation."""
        item = self._format(item)
        self.data.insert(i, item)

    def extend(self, other: Any) -> None:
        """Extend operation."""
        other = self._format(other)
        if isinstance(other, list):
            self.data.extend(other)
        else:
            self.data.extend([other])

    def set_score(self, i: int, score: float) -> None:
        """Set score to the specified subnet by index."""
        self.set_resource(i, score, 'score')

    def set_resource(self,
                     i: int,
                     resources: float,
                     key_indicator: str = 'flops') -> None:
        """Set resources to the specified subnet by index."""
        assert key_indicator in ['score', 'flops', 'params', 'latency']
        for _, value in self.data[i].items():
            value[key_indicator] = resources

    @property
    def scores(self) -> List[float]:
        """The scores of candidates."""
        return [
            round(value.get('score', 0.), 2) for item in self.data
            for _, value in item.items()
        ]
```

In this example, every member of the Candidates list is formatted before adding it to the list using the _format method. We can see that append, insert, and extend are overridden to format the list item before adding it to the data attribute. This is done so as to associate each input items together with their resource values and scores.

The below snippet showcases sample operations on the Candidates objects:

```
candidates = Candidates()
subnet_1 = {'1': 'choice1', '2': 'choice2'}
candidates.append(subnet_1)
print(candidates)
# Output: [{"{'1': 'choice1', '2': 'choice2'}": {'score': -1, 'flops': -1,
'params': -1, 'latency': -1}}]

candidates.set_resource(0, 49.9, 'flops')
candidates.set_score(0, 100.)
print(candidates)
# Output: [{"{'1': 'choice1', '2': 'choice2'}": {'score': 100.0, 'flops':
49.9, 'params': -1, 'latency': -1}}]

subnet_2 = {'choice_3': 'layer_3', 'choice_4': 'layer_4'}
candidates.append(subnet_2)
print(candidates.scores)  # Output: [100.0, -1]
print(candidates)
# Output [{"{'1': 'choice1', '2': 'choice2'}": {'score': 100.0, 'flops':
49.9, 'params': -1, 'latency': -1}},
# {"{'choice_3': 'layer_3', 'choice_4': 'layer_4'}": {'score': -1, 'flops':
-1, 'params': -1, 'latency': -1}}]
```

MutableSequence from collections.abc

In Python, lists fully conform to the Sequence protocol, specifically the MutableSequence protocol defined in the collections module.

For a class to conform to the Sequence protocol, it should allow indexing, iteration, slicing, length calculation, and other methods specified by the Sequence protocol. MutableSequence requires __getitem__, __setitem__, __delitem__, and __len__ dunder methods and the insert method to be defined in its concrete implementations.

A custom class can be created by inheriting from typing.MutableSequence or collections.abc.MutableSequence:

```
# File: robotframework/src/robot/model/itemlist.py

from typing import MutableSequence

class ItemList(MutableSequence[T]):
    """List of items of a certain enforced type.

    New items can be created using the :meth:`create` method and
    existing items
    added using the common list methods like :meth:`append` or
    :meth:`insert`.

    """

    __slots__ = ["_item_class", "_common_attrs", "_items"]

    def __init__(
        self,
        item_class: Type[T],
        common_attrs: "dict[str, Any]|None" = None,
        items: "Iterable[T|DataDict]" = (),
    ):
        self._item_class = item_class
        self._common_attrs = common_attrs
        self._items: "list[T]" = []
        if items:
            self.extend(items)

    def append(self, item: "T|DataDict") -> T:
        item = self._check_type_and_set_attrs(item)
        self._items.append(item)
        return item

    def _check_type_and_set_attrs(self, item: "T|DataDict") -> T:
        if not isinstance(item, self._item_class):
            if isinstance(item, dict):
                item = self._item_from_dict(item)
```

```python
        else:
            raise TypeError(
                f"Only {type_name(self._item_class)} objects "
                f"accepted, got {type_name(item)}."
            )
    if self._common_attrs:
        for attr, value in self._common_attrs.items():
            setattr(item, attr, value)
    return item

def extend(self, items: "Iterable[T|DataDict]"):
    self._items.extend(self._check_type_and_set_attrs(i) for i
    in items)

def insert(self, index: int, item: "T|DataDict"):
    item = self._check_type_and_set_attrs(item)
    self._items.insert(index, item)

def __delitem__(self, index: "int|slice"):
    del self._items[index]

def __contains__(self, item: object) -> bool:
    return item in self._items

def __len__(self) -> int:
    return len(self._items)

def __getitem__(self, index):
    if isinstance(index, slice):
        return self._create_new_from(self._items[index])
    return self._items[index]

def __setitem__(self, index, item):
    if isinstance(index, slice):
        self._items[index] = [self._check_type_and_set_attrs(i) for i
        in item]
    else:
        self._items[index] = self._check_type_and_set_attrs(item)
...
```

In choosing `MutableSequence`, we need to implement the abstract methods from scratch, and this gives us full control over the source code.

In the above example, for every insert and modify-related operation, an additional call to `_check_type_and_set_attrs` is made for preprocessing and validation (enforcing homogeneity) of the list members.

Choosing Between list, UserList, and MutableSequence

- Inheriting directly from `list` is recommended for performance-critical applications. However, this comes with a maintenance cost. The `list` class was not designed with inheritance in mind, and its underlying code might be duplicated across multiple dunder (double underscore) methods. If you choose this option, thorough testing is required to ensure consistency. For example, if validation is added to the child class, the validation logic should be replicated across its methods, such as `append`, `insert`, and `__setitem__`, to ensure consistent behavior.

- `UserList` was introduced at a time when the built-in `list` was not inheritable. It acts as a convenient wrapper and simplifies the customization process by exposing the underlying list in a separate `data` attribute. This is the easiest option among the three and should be preferred for adding a few extra methods or for slight modifications.

- Using `MutableSequence` can be the most challenging option to implement since it requires implementing multiple abstract methods from scratch. Overriding `abc.MutableSequence` by writing pure Python code won't be as performant as the built-in list, as the latter is heavily optimized for performance. However, this is the go-to option if complete control over the implementation of a custom sequence is needed.

Conclusion

Lists are a fundamental Python data structure for storing mutable sequences. They are flexible and versatile for heterogeneous data and come with many useful methods like append, insert, pop, sort, etc. Python's slicing and comprehensions provide powerful workflows for the creation as well as modification of lists.

While lists are ideal for various applications due to their dynamic nature and ability to hold mixed data types, they may not always be the most efficient choice. For instance, `array.array()` is more suitable for large sequences of uniform data types, offering better performance and memory efficiency. Similarly, `deque` from the collections module is optimal for queue-like data structures where we need fast appends and pops from both ends. If mutability is not desired, `tuple`, an immutable sequence, can be used.

In summary, data types of members, performance constraints, and customization needs must be kept in mind when choosing between these sequence types. Lists strike a great balance for general use, but tuples, arrays, and deques shine in certain specific use cases.

CHAPTER 2

Tuples

The previous chapter introduced lists, which are mutable sequences commonly used for storing homogeneous data. Tuples are immutable sequences. This means like lists, they support item access using integer indices. They also support membership checks, iterations, and length checks since all sequences are a superset of collections.

They can store heterogeneous data and are typically used for the same. An example can be seen in the built-in enumerate function. It returns an iterator that produces tuples (containing the item's index and the item) from the input iterable:

```
colors = ["red", "green", "blue"]

print(list(enumerate(colors)))
# Output: [(0, 'red'), (1, 'green'), (2, 'blue')]
```

In this chapter, we will explore various tuple operations and usage examples.

Initializing Tuples

Tuples can be initialized by specifying comma-separated member values or from an iterable using the tuple constructor. Parentheses (()) can be used to initialize empty tuples. Optionally, parentheses can be used to wrap the tuple members, to enhance readability.

```
empty = ()
print(type(empty))  # Output: <class 'tuple'>

numbers = tuple(range(10))  # Tuple from an iterable
print(numbers)  # Output: (0, 1, 2, 3, 4, 5, 6, 7, 8, 9)

student_data = 1, "John", "PhD", 2024
print(type(student_data))  # Output: <class 'tuple'>
```

© Adarsh Divakaran 2025
A. Divakaran, *Deep Dive Python*, https://doi.org/10.1007/979-8-8688-1261-3_2

```
print(student_data == 1, "John", "PhD", 2024)  # Output: False John
PhD 2024
# The tuple should be wrapped in parentheses in the above expression for
the expected behavior.
```

```
print(student_data == (1, "John", "PhD", 2024))  # Output: True
```

```
singleton = (1)
print(type(singleton))  # Output: <class 'int'>
# Parentheses are also used to denote precedence in an expression.
# This makes singleton tuples a special case, and they should have a
trailing comma.
```

```
singleton = (1,)  # Equivalent to singleton = 1,
print(type(singleton))  # Output: <class 'tuple'>
```

Note the special syntax required for singleton tuples. Singleton tuples can be created as 1, or (1,). Python treats comma-separated values as tuples by default, which simplifies use cases such as returning multiple values from functions.

Immutability

Tuples are immutable and raise an error when tried to be modified.

```
card_pack = (3, 5, 7)
```

```
card_pack[1] = 10
```

```
# Error output:
#   File "...\mutate.py", line 3, in <module>
#     card_pack[1] = 10
#     ~~~~~~~~~^^^
# TypeError: 'tuple' object does not support item assignment
```

Tuples store a reference for their members and do not create a copy. This should be kept in mind while working with container types as tuple members.

```
guest_list = ["G1", "G2"]  # List of guests (IDs)
menu_items = ["M3", "M7", "M6"]  # List of menu items (IDs)
```

```
party_plan = (guest_list, menu_items)
```

```
print(f"{party_plan=}")   # Output: party_plan=(['G1', 'G2'], ['M3',
'M7', 'M6'])

guest_list.clear()
print(f"{party_plan=}")   # Output: party_plan=([], ['M3', 'M7', 'M6'])

print(f"{id(party_plan[0])=}")   # id(party_plan[0])=2917449798848
print(f"{id(guest_list)=}")   # id(guest_list)=2917449798848
```

The change to the guest_list is reflected on the party_plan tuple also. It can be seen that both guest_list and party_plan[0] point to the same location in memory since the id value returned for both of them is the same.

Lists vs. Tuples

Tuples and lists are similar in supporting indexing, slicing, and iteration. However, the main difference between them is that tuples are immutable, meaning their values cannot be changed after initialization, making them ideal for use cases where a sequence of values should not be modified after initialization.

From Python docs:

> Though tuples may seem similar to lists, they are often used in different situations and for different purposes. Tuples are immutable and usually contain a heterogeneous sequence of elements that are accessed via unpacking (see later in this section) or indexing (or even by attribute in the case of namedtuples). Lists are mutable, and their elements are usually homogeneous and are accessed by iterating over the list.

Tuple initialization is faster compared with lists. For data access, both of them have comparable access times.

```
import sys
import timeit

tuple_inst_time = timeit.timeit("x=(1,2,3,4,5)", number=1000000)
list_inst_time = timeit.timeit("y=[1,2,3,4,5]", number=1000000)
```

```
print("Tuple Instantiation Time:", tuple_inst_time)
print("List Instantiation Time:", list_inst_time)

# Output:
# Tuple Instantiation Time: 0.008451200000000006
# List Instantiation Time: 0.034034
```

Also, tuples take up less space in memory.

```
my_list = [i for i in range(100)]
my_tuple = tuple(i for i in range(100))
print("List memory usage:", sys.getsizeof(my_list))
print("Tuple memory usage:", sys.getsizeof(my_tuple))

# Output:
# List memory usage: 920
# Tuple memory usage: 840
```

Lists take up more memory because they are over-allocated a bit to make append operations efficient.

Summarizing, tuples should be opted for when data integrity, performance, and hashability are priorities. We will see more on the hashability part going forward in this chapter, where we use tuples as dictionary keys.

> Tuples support slice operations and indexing similar to lists. For examples of various slicing operations, refer to section "Slicing" in Chapter 1 (list slicing).

Tuple Packing and Unpacking

Tuple Packing

Tuple packing is a Python feature where multiple values are packed together into a tuple. It is commonly seen in return statements of functions returning multiple values.

```
def function(*args):
    print(f"{type(args)=}")
    return 1, True
```

```
result = function(1, 2, 3)
print(f"{type(result)=}")

# Output:
# type(args)=<class 'tuple'>
# type(result)=<class 'tuple'>
```

An arbitrary number of positional arguments can be supplied to the function, which will be packed into the args tuple.

This usage is common in wrapper functions such as decorators, where an intermediatory will supply arguments to the wrapped function. The below snippet is from the CPython functools module:

```
# File: CPython/Lib/functools.py

def _lru_cache_wrapper(user_function, maxsize, typed, _CacheInfo):
    # Constants shared by all lru cache instances:
    sentinel = object()            # unique object used to signal
                                   #    cache misses
    make_key = _make_key           # build a key from the function arguments
    PREV, NEXT, KEY, RESULT = 0, 1, 2, 3   # names for the link fields

    cache = {}
    hits = misses = 0

    ...

    if maxsize == 0:
        def wrapper(*args, **kwds):
            # No caching -- just a statistics update
            nonlocal misses
            misses += 1
            result = user_function(*args, **kwds)
            return result
    ...
```

This is a wrapper function used for lru_cache, provided by the functools module, which calls the decorated/wrapped function and updates the result of the call in the cache before returning.

Tuple Unpacking

Tuple unpacking allows us to assign each tuple member to a separate variable in a readable and convenient way.

Variable-Length Assignment

The example below from Pyglet showcases the tuple `color` being unpacked:

```python
# File: pyglet/text/__init__.py

class DocumentLabel(layout.TextLayout):
    @property
    def color(self):
        """Text color.

        Color is a 4-tuple of RGBA components, each in range [0, 255].

        :type: (int, int, int, int)
        """
        return self.document.get_style("color")

    @color.setter
    def color(self, color):
        r, g, b, *a = color
        color = r, g, b, a[0] if a else 255
        self.document.set_style(0, len(self.document.text),
        {"color": color})
```

The tuple `color` may contain three or four elements. The fourth element, which denotes alpha/transparency, can be omitted.

The variables r, g, and b will get the corresponding color values in all cases.

- If an alpha element is present in the tuple, "a" will be a single-membered list containing the alpha value.

- If the tuple has only three elements, "a" will become an empty list.

```python
r, g, b, *a = (255, 255, 255)
print(a)   # Output: []

r, g, b, *a = (255, 255, 255, 0)
```

```
print(a)  # Output: [0]
r, g, b, *a = (255, 255, 255, 0, 100)
print(a)  # Output: [0, 100]
```

The example showcases variable-length assignments. Here, the tuple elements are unpacked, and the total number of tuple elements can vary.

This can be extended to other use cases, such as to fetch only the last member of the tuple or the first and last members, as showcased below:

```
data = (1, 2, 3, 4, 5)

*_, last = data
print(last)  # Output: 5

first, *_, last = data
print(first, last)  # Output: 1 5

first, second, *_, last = data
print(first, second, last)  # Output: 1 2 5
```

This way, unpacking allows us to unpack desired members from the tuple.

Unpacking in Loops

The below snippet from the node runtime showcases tuple unpacking and its usage as the loop variable:

```
# File: node/tools/install.py

def package_files(action, name, bins):
  target_path = 'lib/node_modules/' + name + '/'

  ...

  root = 'deps/' + name
  for dirname, subdirs, basenames in os.walk(root, topdown=True):

    subdirs[:] = [subdir for subdir in subdirs if subdir != 'test']
    paths = [os.path.join(dirname, basename) for basename in basenames]

    ...
```

The os.walk function returns a three-membered tuple (dirpath, dirnames, filenames). This tuple is unpacked into dirname, subdirs, and basenames variables in each iteration.

Ignoring Values

By convention, underscores are used to denote ignored values in code. Though they are valid variable names and store the assigned value just like any other variable, underscores are also used in tuple unpacking to denote ignored values.

The below code from Flask ignores the partition element value using an _:

```
# File: src/flask/app.py

def run(
    self,
    host: str | None = None,
    port: int | None = None,
    debug: bool | None = None,
    load_dotenv: bool = True,
    **options: t.Any,
) -> None:
    ...

    server_name = self.config.get("SERVER_NAME")
    sn_host = sn_port = None

    if server_name:
        sn_host, _, sn_port = server_name.partition(":")

    ...
```

This pattern is commonly seen together with the partition method of strings, which returns three-membered tuples as its output.

```
server_name = "localhost:5000"
print(server_name.partition(":"))  # Output: ('localhost', ':', '5000')

server_name = "localhost"
print(server_name.partition(":"))  # Output: ('localhost', '', '')
```

```
server_name = ""
print(server_name.partition(":"))  # Output: ('', '', '')

server_name = "localhost:5000:invalid"
print(server_name.partition(":"))  # Output:  ('localhost', ':',
'5000:invalid')
```

In the example from Flask, the server hostname and port are unpacked from the partitioned tuple, and the separator (:) is ignored.

> Unpacking is not just limited to tuples. Though unpacking is commonly seen with tuples, it can be generalized to any iterables.

Comparisons and Sorting

Tuples are compared lexicographically, element by element. When two elements are found to be equal, the comparison proceeds to the next element until an inequality is found.

Due to this property, they come in handy for various comparison operations.

Version Checking

Example 1: **TensorFlow**

```
# File: tensorflow/python/types/core.py

import sys

if sys.version_info >= (3, 8):
    from typing import Protocol
    from typing import runtime_checkable
else:
    from typing_extensions import Protocol
    from typing_extensions import runtime_checkable
```

The Protocol class and runtime_checkable decorator were added to the typing module from Python 3.8. For earlier versions, they should be imported from the typing_extensions library.

sys.version_info returns a tuple containing the five components of the version number: major, minor, micro, release level, and serial (the version_info value corresponding to the Python version 2.0 is (2, 0, 0, 'final', 0)). This tuple is compared with the tuple (3, 8) to import the Protocol and runtime_checkable from the right source.

Example 2: **Django**

```
# File: django/db/backends/mysql/features.py

class DatabaseFeatures(BaseDatabaseFeatures):
    @cached_property
    def has_select_for_update_skip_locked(self):
        if self.connection.mysql_is_mariadb:
            return self.connection.mysql_version >= (10, 6)
        return True

    @cached_property
    def supports_explain_analyze(self):
        return self.connection.mysql_is_mariadb or self.connection.mysql_
        version >= (
            8,
            0,
            18,
        )
```

Django uses a similar version check to determine the supported features based on the connected database version.

As Sort Keys

The comparison behavior makes tuples suited for use as sort keys.

```
# File: tensorflow/python/tools/api/generator/create_python_api.py

def get_canonical_import(import_set):
    """Obtain one single import from a set of possible sources of a symbol.

    One symbol might come from multiple places as it is being imported and
    reexported. To simplify API changes, we always use the same import for the
```

same module, and give preference based on higher priority and
alphabetical ordering.

Args:
  import_set: (set) Imports providing the same symbol. This is a set of
  tuples in the form (import, priority). We want to pick an import with
  highest priority.
"""
 # Here we sort by priority (higher preferred) and
then alphabetically by
 # import string.

```
import_list = sorted(
    import_set,
    key=lambda imp_and_priority: (-imp_and_priority[1], imp_and_
    priority[0]),
)
return import_list[0][0]
```

The argument import_set is a set of tuples of the form (import, priority). The
above snippet from TensorFlow uses a tuple in the key lambda function to sort imports
based on priority (descending) and then by name.

Sorting Tuples

Since tuples are immutable, there is no in-place sorting solution for tuples. The sorted
built-in function should be used for sorting tuples. sorted returns a list with sorted
values from the tuple in its output.

```
# File: mars/tensor/merge/concatenate.py

def _norm_axis(axis):
    if isinstance(axis, int):
        return axis, True
    if isinstance(axis, Iterable):
        axis = sorted(tuple(axis))
```

```
    if len(axis) == 1:
        return axis[0], True
    return axis, False
```

   ...

In cases where we need a sorted tuple, the return of sorted should be explicitly cast to a tuple using the tuple constructor.

Tuples as Dict Keys

The immutable nature of tuples makes them hashable. They can be readily used as dictionary keys.

```
landmark_map = {}

# GPS coordinates as a tuple (latitude, longitude)
coordinates_key = (27.1751, 78.0421)

coordinates_key_hash = hash(coordinates_key)
print(f"{coordinates_key_hash=}")  # Output: coordinates_key_
hash=-6404387799400299302

landmark_map[coordinates_key] = "Taj Mahal"
```

The coordinates_key tuple can be used as the key for the landmark_map dictionary. But the case is different for tuples with mutable members.

```
student_club_membership_status = {}

student_info = ("Alex", ["Chess Club", "Science Club"])
try:
    student_club_membership_status[student_info] = "Active Member"
except TypeError as e:
    print(f"{e=}")  # Output: e=TypeError("unhashable type: 'list'")
```

For a tuple to be hashable, its members should also be hashable. Tuples having mutable members will lead to an error when used as a dict key.

The below example from Django shows a cache implementation using tuples as the cache key:

```python
# File: django/utils/formats.py

# format_cache is a mapping from (format_type, lang) to the format string.
# By using the cache, it is possible to avoid running get_format_modules
# repeatedly.
_format_cache = {}

def get_format(format_type, lang=None, use_l10n=None):
    """

    For a specific format type, return the format for the current
    language (locale). Default to the format in the settings.
    format_type is the name of the format, e.g. 'DATE_FORMAT'.

    """

    ...

    format_type = str(format_type)  # format_type may be lazy.
    cache_key = (format_type, lang)
    try:
        return _format_cache[cache_key]
    except KeyError:
        pass

    # The requested format_type has not been cached yet.
    ...

    val = None
    if use_l10n:
        for module in get_format_modules(lang):
            val = getattr(module, format_type, None)
            if val is not None:
                break
    ...

    _format_cache[cache_key] = val
    return val
```

When the get_format function is called, it initially checks the dictionary _format_ cache for the presence of a member corresponding to the requested cache_key, which is a tuple (format_type, lang). If the key is not found, the format_type value is calculated, added to the cache, and returned.

namedtuple (collections.namedtuple)

Tuples are typically used to store heterogeneous data. In some cases, accessing attributes by name would be more convenient. namedtuple from the collections module can be used in such cases.

The signature of namedtuple is as follows:

```
collections.namedtuple(typename, field_names, *, rename=False,
defaults=None, module=None)
```

If the rename parameter is set to True, any invalid field names are automatically replaced with positional names. The defaults parameter can be set to None or an iterable of default values. It's important to note that fields with a default value must come after any fields without a default. This is because the defaults are applied to the rightmost parameters.

Python's dis module contains a namedtuple Positions:

```
# File: cpython/Lib/dis.py

Positions = collections.namedtuple(
    'Positions',
    [
        'lineno',
        'end_lineno',
        'col_offset',
        'end_col_offset',
    ],
    defaults=[None] * 4
)
```

This namedtuple is populated and is added to the positions attribute of the frame info returned by the inspect module:

```
import inspect

def get_frame_info():
    frame = inspect.currentframe()
    return (inspect.
            getframeinfo(frame))

current_frame_info = get_frame_info()
position = current_frame_info.positions

print(f"Line Number: {position.lineno}")
print(f"End Line Number: {position[1]}")
print(f"Column Offset: {position.col_offset}")
print(f"End Column Offset: {position[3]}")

# Line Number: 6
# End Line Number: 7
# Column Offset: 12
# End Column Offset: 31
```

As seen in the above example, the namedtuple attributes are accessible via named attributes as well as the indices. In the snippet above, the position namedtuple stores the positions (line numbers, column offsets) of the inspect.getframeinfo function call.

typing.NamedTuple

typing.NamedTuple is the type-annotated version of namedtuple. Its definition follows an inheritance model.

```
from typing import NamedTuple

class Product(NamedTuple):
    name: str
    category: str
    price: float = 0.0   # Default price
    stock: int = 0       # Default available stock
```

61

The equivalent `collections.namedtuple` definition for the above is

```python
from collections import namedtuple

Product = namedtuple('Product', 'name category price stock',
defaults=[0.0, 0])
```

The below example from the Neural Network Intelligence library showcases the usage of NamedTuple to store algorithm metadata:

```python
# File: nni/tools/package_utils/common.py

from typing import NamedTuple

from typing_extensions import Literal

class AlgoMeta(NamedTuple):
    name: str
    alias: str | None
    class_name: str | None
    accept_class_args: bool
    class_args: dict | None
    validator_class_name: str | None
    algo_type: Literal["tuner", "assessor"]
    is_advisor: bool
    is_builtin: bool
    nni_version: str | None

    @staticmethod
    def load(
        meta: dict, algo_type: Literal["tuner", "assessor", "advisor"] |
        None = None
    ) -> AlgoMeta:
        if algo_type is None:
            algo_type = meta["algoType"]  # type: ignore
        return AlgoMeta(
            name=meta["builtinName"],
            alias=meta.get("alias"),
            class_name=meta["className"],
```

```
            accept_class_args=meta.get("acceptClassArgs", True),
            class_args=meta.get("classArgs"),
            validator_class_name=meta.get("classArgsValidator"),
            algo_type=("assessor" if algo_type == "assessor" else "tuner"),
            is_advisor=meta.get("isAdvisor", algo_type == "advisor"),
            is_builtin=(meta.get("source") == "nni"),
            nni_version=meta.get("nniVo, algo_type))  # type: ignore
    return algos
```

This NamedTuple is used, as seen below, to load algorithms from the config file and return their metadata:

```
# File: nni/tools/package_utils/config_manager.py

def _load_config_file(path):
    with open(path, encoding="utf_8") as f:
        config = yaml.safe_load(f)
    algos = []
    for algo_type in ["tuner", "assessor", "advisor"]:
        for algo in config.get(algo_type + "s", []):
            algos.append(AlgoMeta.load(algo, algo_type))  # type: ignore
    return algos
```

A NamedTuple is used here to ensure that the AlgoMeta objects (stored inside the algo list) should not be mutated at runtime.

Evident from the above example, a NamedTuple may look similar to dataclasses. Though visually similar, dataclasses are mutable and more customizable (as well as heavier) compared with namedtuples.

Conclusion

Tuples are a fundamental data structure in Python known for their immutability. They can be indexed and iterated over, just like lists, but differ significantly due to their immutable nature. This immutability makes tuples a reliable choice for storing data that must remain constant, ensuring stability and consistency when data is passed across various parts of a program. The immutable nature of tuples allows them to be hashable, making them suitable for use as keys in dictionaries.

Additionally, tuples support comparison operations, which is advantageous for data sorting and organization tasks. When tuples are compared in Python, it's done element by element, which is particularly effective for structured data comparisons.

Python further extends the utility of tuples with namedtuples, which provide clearer, more readable code, especially in scenarios where tuples contain numerous elements or have a complex structure. namedtuples allow for elements to be accessed by names, reducing the likelihood of errors and enhancing code maintainability.

## CHAPTER 3

Set and Dictionary

In the previous chapter, we looked at tuples, which are immutable, ordered collections that are often used to group related pieces of data. We saw how tuples differ from lists in terms of mutability and how they play a role in functions that return multiple values. Building on that understanding of sequences and immutability, we now turn our attention to two more collection types: dictionaries and sets.

In Python, dictionaries and sets are fundamental data structures used to store and manipulate collections in ways that differ significantly from sequences. A dictionary, commonly referred to as a "dict," is an unordered collection of key–value pairs, where each key is unique and maps to a specific value. Dictionaries are especially useful for fast lookups, flexible data modeling, and dynamic updates.

Sets, on the other hand, are unordered collections of unique elements. They are ideal for checking membership, eliminating duplicates, and performing operations based on set theory—like unions, intersections, and differences.

In this chapter, we'll dive into the core behavior of dictionaries and sets, explore the operations they support, and learn practical techniques to use them effectively in real-world Python programs.

Set in Python

Sets are unordered collections of unique elements. Sets are mutable, but the elements in a set should be hashable. This means that the set members should be immutable.

Basic initialization:

Sets can be initialized using the set constructor or by using curly braces with comma-separated elements.

© Adarsh Divakaran 2025
A. Divakaran, *Deep Dive Python*, https://doi.org/10.1007/979-8-8688-1261-3_3

```
# Using curly braces
fruits = {"apple", "banana", "cherry"}

# Using the set() constructor
numbers = set([1, 2, 3, 4, 5])

print(f"{numbers=}")
print(f"{fruits=}")

"""Output:
numbers={1, 2, 3, 4, 5}
fruits={'cherry', 'apple', 'banana'}
"""
```

Adding and removing elements:

Members can be added to a set using the add method. For removing elements

1. The remove method removes an element from a set, and it raises a KeyError when an element is not found.

2. The discard method removes an element if present; otherwise, no error is raised.

```
fruits = {"cherry", "apple", "banana"}
fruits.add("orange")

fruits.remove("banana")  # Raises KeyError if not found
fruits.discard("grape")  # No error if not found

print(f"{fruits=}")
# Output: fruits={'cherry', 'apple', 'orange'}
```

Checking membership:

Similar to other container datatypes, the in keyword can be used to check set membership.

```
fruits = {"cherry", "apple", "banana"}
print("apple" in fruits)  # True
print("other" in fruits)  # False
```

Basic set operations:

Sets support basic mathematical set operations such as union, intersection, and set difference.

```
set1 = {1, 2, 3}
set2 = {3, 4, 5}

# Union
union_set = set1 | set2
print(f"Union set: {union_set}")
# Output:  {1, 2, 3, 4, 5}

# Intersection
intersection_set = set1 & set2
print(f"Intersection: {intersection_set}")
# Output: {3}

# Difference
difference_set = set1 - set2
print(f"Difference: {difference_set}")
# Output:  {1, 2}
```

The key characteristics of sets are as follows:

- Sets allow for fast membership testing.

- Sets support mathematical set operations.

- Sets do not contain duplicated elements. Each element appears only one time.

```
example_set = set()

example_set.add(1)
example_set.add(2)
example_set.add(1)
print(example_set)  # Output: {1, 2}
```

Due to this property, sets are commonly used to remove duplicates from lists.

```
example_list = [1, 3, 2, 1]
print(set(example_list))
# Output: {1, 2, 3}
```

Dict in Python

Dictionaries in Python, referred to as "dicts," are collections of key–value pairs. Each key in a dictionary should be hashable and map to a specific value. Dictionaries are highly efficient for data retrieval, insertion, and deletion operations.

Dictionary initialization:

We can create a dictionary using curly braces {} with key-value pairs separated by colons or by using the dict() function.

```
# Creating a dictionary with curly braces
person = {"name": "Alice", "age": 30, "city": "New York"}
print(person)
# Output: {'name': 'Alice', 'age': 30, 'city': 'New York'}

# Creating a dictionary with the dict() function
person = dict(name="Alice", age=30, city="New York")
print(person)
# Output: {'name': 'Alice', 'age': 30, 'city': 'New York'}
```

Accessing values:

We can access the value associated with a specific key using square brackets [ ] or the get() method.

```
person = {"name": "Alice", "age": 30, "city": "New York"}
# Using square brackets
print(person["name"]) # Output: Alice

# Using the get() method
print(person.get("age")) # Output: 30
```

Adding and updating key-value pairs:

We can add a new key-value pair or update an existing key's value by using square brackets [ ].

```
person = {"name": "Alice", "age": 30, "city": "New York"}

# Adding a new key-value pair
person["email"] = "alice@example.com"
print(person)
# Output: {'name': 'Alice', 'age': 30, 'city': 'New York', 'email': 'alice@
example.com'}

# Updating an existing key's value
person["age"] = 31
print(person)
# Output: {'name': 'Alice', 'age': 31, 'city': 'New York', 'email': 'alice@
example.com'}
```

Removing key-value pairs:

We can remove a key-value pair using the del statement or the pop( ) method.

```
person = {"name": "Alice", "age": 30, "city": "New York", "email": "alice@
example.com"}

# Using the del statement
del person["city"]
print(person)  # Output: {'name': 'Alice', 'age': 31, 'email': 'alice@
example.com'}

# Using the pop() method
email = person.pop("email")
print(email)
# Output: alice@example.com

print(person)
# Output: {'name': 'Alice', 'age': 31}
```

Checking for keys:

We can check if a key exists in a dictionary using the in keyword.

```
person = {"name": "Alice", "age": 30}

print("name" in person)  # Output: True
print("city" in person)  # Output: False
```

Iterating through a dictionary:

We can iterate through a dictionary's keys, values, or key–value pairs using loops.

```
person = {"name": "Alice", "age": 30}

# Iterating through keys for key in person:
for key in person:
    print(key)

""" Output:
name
age
"""

# Iterating through values for value in person.values():
for value in person.values():
    print(value)

""" Output:
Alice
30
"""

# Iterating through key-value pairs
for key, value in person.items():
    print(key, value)

""" Output:
name Alice
age 30
"""
```

Dictionary methods:

Dictionaries come with several useful methods for various operations:

- *keys()*: Returns a view object of all keys

```
person = {"name": "Alice", "age": 30}
print(person.keys())
# Output: dict_keys(['name', 'age'])
```

- *values()*: Returns a view object of all values

```
person = {"name": "Alice", "age": 30}
print(person.values())
# Output: dict_values(['Alice', 30])
```

- *items()*: Returns a view object of all key–value pairs

```
person = {"name": "Alice", "age": 30}
print(person.items())
# Output: dict_items([('name', 'Alice'), ('age', 30)])
```

- *clear()*: Removes all key-value pairs from the dictionary

```
person = {"name": "Alice", "age": 30}
person.clear()
print(person)
# Output: {}
```

Comprehensions

Comprehensions provide a concise way to create dictionaries and sets in Python. Comprehensions can make the code more readable and efficient by combining the creation and population of these data structures into a single, readable line.

Dictionary Comprehensions

Dictionary comprehensions allow us to create dictionaries in a single line of code. The syntax is similar to list comprehensions but uses curly braces {} and a colon to separate keys and values.

Basic syntax:

```
{key: value for item in iterable}
```

Examples:

1. Creating a dictionary from a list of tuples:

    ```
    pairs = [("name", "Alice"), ("age", 30), ("city", "New York")]
    person = {key: value for key, value in pairs}
    print(person)  # Output: {'name': 'Alice', 'age': 30, 'city':
    'New York'}
    ```

2. Creating a dictionary with squares of numbers:

    ```
    squares = {x: x**2 for x in range(1, 6)}
    print(squares)
    # Output: {1: 1, 2: 4, 3: 9, 4: 16, 5: 25}
    ```

3. Filtering items:

    ```
    original = {"a": 1, "b": 2, "c": 3, "d": 4}
    filtered = {k: v for k, v in original.items() if v % 2 == 0}
    print(filtered)  # Output: {'b': 2, 'd': 4}
    ```

Set Comprehensions

Set comprehensions allow us to create sets in a single line of code. The syntax is similar to dict comprehensions, but it contains an expression resulting in a single set element rather than key and value pairs.

Basic syntax:

```
{expression for item in iterable}
```

Examples:

1. Creating a set of squares:

    ```
    squares = {x**2 for x in range(1, 6)}
    print(squares)
    # Output: {1, 4, 9, 16, 25}
    ```

2. Creating a set from a list with duplicates:

```
numbers = [1, 2, 2, 3, 4, 4, 5]
unique_numbers = {x for x in numbers}
print(unique_numbers)
# Output: {1, 2, 3, 4, 5}
```

Commonly, deduplication is done more easily using
`set(numbers)`.

3. Filtering items in a set comprehension:

```
original = [1, 2, 3, 4, 5, 6]
evens = {x for x in original if x % 2 == 0}
print(evens)
# Output: {2, 4, 6}
```

By using dictionary and set comprehensions, we can write more concise and readable code, making it easier to create and manipulate these data structures efficiently.

Hashability

Hashability is a fundamental concept in Python that determines whether an object can be used as a key in a dictionary or as an element in a set. An object is considered hashable if it has a hash value that remains constant during its lifetime and can be compared to other objects. Hashable objects must implement the __hash__() and __eq__() methods.

Sets and dicts work based on the concept of hashability:

- *Sets*: Sets use hash values to quickly determine if an element is present, ensuring that each element is unique.

- *Dictionaries*: Dictionaries use hash values to store and retrieve key-value pairs efficiently.

Hashability in Sets

Set elements must be hashable. This means when an unhashable element is tried to be added to a set, it should raise an error.

```
valid_set = {1, "a", (1, 2)}  # Valid

invalid_set = {[1, 2], {3, 4}}  # TypeError: unhashable type: 'list'`
```

Sets can include hashable members such as strings, tuples, etc. Adding a mutable element will result in a TypeError.

Hashability in Dictionaries

Dictionary keys must be hashable. Similar to set elements, only hashable/immutable objects can act as dict keys.

```
valid_dict = {1: "one", "two": 2, (3, 4): "tuple"}  # Valid #
invalid_dict = {[1, 2]: "list"}  # TypeError: unhashable type: 'list'`
```

Hash Collisions

Hash collisions occur when two different objects have the same hash value. In dictionaries, this can lead to one key replacing another if they are considered equal.

For example, both the integer 1 and boolean True have the same hash value.

```
print(hash(1))  # Output: 1
print(hash(True))  # Output: 1
```

When these are used as dictionary keys, both are considered equal for storing and retrieving dict members.

```
example_dict = {1: "one", True: "true"}
print(example_dict)  # Output: {1: 'true'}
```

In this case, the value provided by the key 1 is replaced by True because both these keys have the same hash value.

```
print(example_dict[1])  # Output: 'true'
print(example_dict[True])  # Output: 'true'`
```

Since the dict values are mapped based on the hash value of the keys, 1 and True can both be used to fetch the corresponding value.

Custom Hashable Objects

We can create custom objects and define their hash behavior by implementing the __hash__() and __eq__() methods. This will allow us to use the instances of custom classes as keys in dictionaries or elements in sets.

```python
class Person:
    def __init__(self, name, age):
        self.name = name
        self.age = age

    def __hash__(self):
        return hash((self.name, self.age))

    def __eq__(self, other):
        if not isinstance(other, Person):
            return False
        return self.name == other.name and self.age == other.age

    def __repr__(self):
        return f"Person({self.name}, {self.age})"

person1 = Person("Alice", 30)
person2 = Person("Bob", 25)
employee_dict = {person1: "Employee 1", person2: "Employee 2"}

print(employee_dict[Person("Alice", 30)])
# Output: Employee 1

example_set = {person1, person2}
print(example_set)
# Output: {Person(Bob, 25), Person(Alice, 30)}
```

We have defined a custom hash method for the Person class. When the objects of this class are used as set elements or dict keys, this custom hash function will be used.

More Set Operations

In addition to the basic operations, Python sets offer a variety of advanced methods and operations that allow for more complex manipulations and queries. These operations can help us perform tasks such as finding subsets, supersets, and symmetric differences, as well as updating sets with new elements.

Symmetric Difference

We can use the symmetric_difference() method or the ^ operator to find elements that are in either of the sets but not in both.

```
set1 = {1, 2, 3, 4}
set2 = {3, 4, 5, 6}
sym_diff = set1 ^ set2  # {1, 2, 5, 6}
```

Subset and Superset Checks

Subset: We can use the `issubset()` method to check if a set is a subset of another set. A set *Set1* is a subset of *Set2* if all elements of *Set1* are also in *Set2*.

Superset: We can use the `issuperset()` method to check if a set is a superset of another set. A set *Set1* is a superset of *Set2* if it contains all elements of *Set2*.

```
set1 = {1, 2}
set2 = {1, 2, 3, 4}
is_subset = set1.issubset(set2)   # True
is_superset = set2.issuperset(set1)   # True
```

Disjoint Set Check

The `isdisjoint()` method returns true if the set has no common elements with the other set passed as the argument to the method call.

```
set1 = {1, 2}
set2 = {3, 4}
are_disjoint = set1.isdisjoint(set2)   # True
```

Clearing a Set

We can use the `clear()` method to remove all elements from the set.

```
my_set = {1, 2, 3}
my_set.clear()
print(my_set)  # Output: set()
```

The pop Method

The pop method of a set removes and returns a random element from the set.

```
my_set = {1, 2, 3}

element = my_set.pop()  # Removes and returns a random element
print(f"{element} was removed")  # 1 was removed
print(my_set)  # {2, 3}

element = my_set.pop()
print(f"{element} was removed")  # 2 was removed
print(my_set)  # {3}
```

Update Methods

The update methods on a set can be used for in-place updation of a set. Most of these methods take an arbitrary number of iterables as the argument and update the set based on performing the specified operation with the provided iterable members.

The update Method

The `update()` method on a set accepts a number of iterables and updates the set, adding elements from all others.

```
set1 = {1, 2, 3}
set1.update([3, 4], {5, 6})
print(set1)  # {1, 2, 3, 4, 5, 6}
```

The update call is equivalent to set |= other.

Intersection Update

The `intersection_update()` method keeps only the elements that are present in both sets.

```
set1 = {1, 2, 3, 4}
set2 = {3, 4, 5, 6}
set1.intersection_update(set2)
print(set1)  # {3, 4}
```

The intersection update is equivalent to `set &= other`.

Difference Update

The `difference_update()` method updates a set by removing elements found in the other set.

```
set1 = {1, 2, 3, 4}
set2 = {3, 4, 5, 6}
set1.difference_update(set2)
print(set1)  # {1, 2}
```

The difference update is equivalent to `set -= other`.

Symmetric Difference Update

The `symmetric_difference_update()` method updates the set with elements that are in either set but not in both. It only accepts a single iterable as the argument.

```
set1 = {1, 2, 3, 4}
set2 = {3, 4, 5, 6}
set1.symmetric_difference_update(set2)
print(set1)  # {1, 2, 5, 6}
```

This operation is equivalent to `set ^= other`.

More Dictionary Operations

In addition to basic operations, Python dictionaries offer a variety of advanced methods and functionalities that allow for more complex manipulations and queries. These advanced operations can help us perform tasks such as setting default values, merging dictionaries, and working with dictionary view objects.

The **setdefault()** Method

The setdefault() method returns the value of a key if it is in the dictionary. If not, it inserts the key with a specified default value and returns it.

```
person = {
    "name": "Alice",
    "age": 30,
}

# Using setdefault() to get the value of an existing key
print(person.setdefault("name", "Unknown"))  # Output: Alice

# Using setdefault() to insert a new key with a default value
print(person.setdefault("city", "New York"))  # Output: New York

print(person)  # Output: {'name': 'Alice', 'age': 30, 'city': 'New York'}
```

In the above snippet, the key *city* is set using the setdefault() method. The key *name* was already present in the dict. So it was retrieved and returned.

The **popitem()** Method

The popitem() method removes and returns the last key–value pair inserted into the dictionary. This method is useful for implementing LIFO (last-in, first-out) order.

```
person = {
    "name": "Alice",
    "age": 30,
    "city": "New York",
}
```

```
# Using popitem() to remove the last key-value pair
last_item = person.popitem()

print(last_item)  # Output: ('city', 'New York')
print(person)  # Output: {'name': 'Alice', 'age': 30}
```

The **update()** Method

The update() method updates the dictionary with elements from another dictionary or an iterable of key–value pairs.

```
person = {"name": "Alice", "age": 30}
person.update({"email": "alice@example.com", "age": 31})

print(person)
# Output: {'name': 'Alice', 'age': 31, 'email': 'alice@example.com'}
```

The **fromkeys()** Method

The fromkeys() class method on the dict class creates a new dictionary with keys from an iterable and values set to a specified default.

```
keys = ["name", "age", "city"]
example_dict = dict.fromkeys(keys, "Unknown")

print(example_dict)
# Output: {'name': 'Unknown', 'age': 'Unknown', 'city': 'Unknown'}
```

Dictionary View Objects

Dictionary view objects provide a dynamic view of the dictionary's entries, which means that when the dictionary changes, the view reflects these changes.

There are three types of view objects—keys, values, and items:

- *keys()*: Returns a view object of all keys

  ```
  person = {"name": "Alice", "age": 30}
  keys_view = person.keys()
  ```

```
print(keys_view)
# Output: dict_keys(['name', 'age'])
```

- *values()*: Returns a view object of all values

```
values_view = person.values()
print(values_view)
# Output: dict_values(['Alice', 30])
```

- *items()*: Returns a view object of all key-value pairs

```
items_view = person.items()
print(items_view)
# Output: dict_items([('name', 'Alice'), ('age', 30)])
```

These view objects are dynamic and reflect changes made to the dictionary.

```
person["city"] = "New York"
print(keys_view)
# Output: dict_keys(['name', 'age', 'city'])

print(values_view)
# Output: dict_values(['Alice', 30, 'New York'])

print(items_view)
# Output: dict_items([('name', 'Alice'), ('age', 30), ('city',
'New York')])
```

Here, the addition of the *city* key to the dictionary is reflected in all the dictionary view objects.

Dictionary Packing and Unpacking

In Python, dictionary packing and unpacking are commonly used when dealing with functions that accept a variable number of keyword arguments.

Packing **kwargs into a Dictionary

We can also pack keyword arguments into a dictionary using the **kwargs syntax in the function definition. This allows the function to accept an arbitrary number of keyword arguments.

```python
def print_info(**kwargs):
    for key, value in kwargs.items():
        print(f"{key}: {value}")

# Calling the function with keyword arguments
print_info(name="Bob", age=25, city="Los Angeles", profession="Engineer")

""" Output:
name: Bob
age: 25
city: Los Angeles
profession: Engineer
"""
```

In this example, the print_info() will accept any number of keyword arguments. Using **kwargs in the function argument will make the passed arguments get packed into a dictionary named kwargs.

Dictionary Unpacking

We can use a dictionary to pass keyword arguments to a function using the ** operator. This is known as dictionary unpacking.

```python
def greet(name, city, age):
    print(f"Hello, my name is {name}, I'm {age} years old and I live in
    {city}.")

# Dictionary containing the arguments
person_info = {"name": "Alice", "age": 30, "city": "New York"}

# Unpacking the dictionary to pass as keyword arguments
greet(**person_info)

# Output:
# Hello, my name is Alice, I'm 30 years old and I live in New York.
```

In this example, the person_info dictionary is used to pass arguments to the greet() function. Notice here that the dictionary keys and the function arguments are the same. This is required for the unpacking to work when calling functions using keyword arguments.

The snippet below from *FastAPI* showcases a real-world dict unpacking example:

```python
# File: fastapi/utils.py

def create_response_field(
    name: str,
    type_: Type[Any],
    class_validators: Optional[Dict[str, Validator]] = None,
    default: Optional[Any] = Undefined,
    required: Union[bool, UndefinedType] = Undefined,
    model_config: Type[BaseConfig] = BaseConfig,
    field_info: Optional[FieldInfo] = None,
    alias: Optional[str] = None,
    mode: Literal["validation", "serialization"] = "validation",
) -> ModelField:
    """
    Create a new response field. Raises if type_ is invalid.
    """
    class_validators = class_validators or {}
    if PYDANTIC_V2:
        field_info = field_info or FieldInfo(
            annotation=type_, default=default, alias=alias
        )
    else:
        field_info = field_info or FieldInfo()
    kwargs = {"name": name, "field_info": field_info}
    if PYDANTIC_V2:
        kwargs.update({"mode": mode})
    else:
        kwargs.update(
            {
                "type_": type_,
                "class_validators": class_validators,
```

```
                "default": default,
                "required": required,
                "model_config": model_config,
                "alias": alias,
            }
        )
    try:
        return ModelField(**kwargs)  # type: ignore[arg-type]
    except (RuntimeError, PydanticSchemaGenerationError):
        raise fastapi.exceptions.FastAPIError(
            "Invalid args for response field! Hint: "
            f"check that {type_} is a valid Pydantic field type. "
            "If you are using a return type annotation that is not a valid
            Pydantic "
            "field (e.g. Union[Response, dict, None]) you can disable
            generating the "
            "response model from the type annotation with the path
            operation decorator "
            "parameter response_model=None. Read more: "
            "https://fastapi.tiangolo.com/tutorial/response-model/"
        ) from None
```

In this example, a kwargs dictionary is created and populated with various parameters. The content of this dictionary depends on whether the code is running with Pydantic v2 or an earlier version. Depending on the Pydantic version and other conditions, different sets of parameters are included in the kwargs dictionary.

The **kwargs syntax in ModelField(**kwargs) unpacks the kwargs dictionary into keyword arguments for the ModelField constructor. By using dictionary unpacking, the code can handle different versions of Pydantic without needing separate function calls or complex if-else structures.

Dictionary Merging and Unpacking

Python 3.5 (with the PEP 448) introduced a new way to merge dictionaries using the ** unpacking operator. This allows for more concise and readable code when combining dictionaries.

```
dict1 = {"a": 1, "b": 2}
dict2 = {"c": 3, "d": 4}
merged = {**dict1, **dict2, "e": 5}

print(merged)
# Output: {'a': 1, 'b': 2, 'c': 3, 'd': 4, 'e': 5}
```

In the snippet, the ** dictionary unpacking operator is used to create the merged dictionary by combining two dictionaries (*dict1* and *dict2*).

Set Variant: frozenset

A frozenset is an immutable version of a set in Python. It's a built-in class that creates an unchangeable set of unique elements. Once created, a frozenset cannot be modified. We cannot add or remove elements.

Unlike regular sets, frozensets are hashable. This means they can be used as dictionary keys or as elements of other sets. frozensets can be created using the frozenset constructor.

In the snippet below from Django, a frozenset is used to define a fixed set of format settings:

```
# File: django/utils/formats.py

FORMAT_SETTINGS = frozenset(
    [
        "DECIMAL_SEPARATOR",
        "THOUSAND_SEPARATOR",
        "NUMBER_GROUPING",
        "FIRST_DAY_OF_WEEK",
        "MONTH_DAY_FORMAT",
        "TIME_FORMAT",
        "DATE_FORMAT",
        "DATETIME_FORMAT",
        "SHORT_DATE_FORMAT",
        "SHORT_DATETIME_FORMAT",
        "YEAR_MONTH_FORMAT",
```

```
        "DATE_INPUT_FORMATS",
        "TIME_INPUT_FORMATS",
        "DATETIME_INPUT_FORMATS",
    ]
)
```

Using a frozenset here ensures that the `FORMAT_SETTINGS` set is protected from accidental modifications.

Dictionary: Variants

The Python standard library contains a number of specialized dict-like classes for various operations. We will explore some of them in the coming sections.

collections.defaultdict

A defaultdict is a subclass of Python's dict that automatically handles missing keys. When a key is accessed that doesn't exist, it calls a factory function to create a default value for that key, instead of raising a KeyError. This behavior simplifies code in scenarios involving data accumulation or grouping.

The signature of defaultdict is as follows:

```
class collections.defaultdict(default_factory=None, /[, ...])
```

The `default_factory` is a callable that returns the default value when a key is not found. If not provided, defaultdict behaves like a regular dictionary for missing keys.

The snippet below from Django showcases a defaultdict usage:

```
# File: django/utils/cache.py

def patch_cache_control(response, **kwargs):
    """

    Patch the Cache-Control header by adding all keyword arguments to it.
    The transformation is as follows:

    * All keyword parameter names are turned to lowercase, and underscores
      are converted to hyphens.
```

* If the value of a parameter is True (exactly True, not just a
  true value), only the parameter name is added to the header.
* All other parameters are added with their value, after applying
  str() to it.
"""

```python
def dictitem(s):
    t = s.split("=", 1)
    if len(t) > 1:
        return (t[0].lower(), t[1])
    else:
        return (t[0].lower(), True)

...

cc = defaultdict(set)
if response.get("Cache-Control"):
    for field in cc_delim_re.split(response.headers["Cache-Control"]):
        directive, value = dictitem(field)
        if directive == "no-cache":
            # no-cache supports multiple field names.
            cc[directive].add(value)
        else:
            cc[directive] = value
```

The defaultdict is used here to simplify handling of Cache-Control directives.

- cc = defaultdict(set) creates a dictionary that automatically
  initializes new keys with an empty set. When accessing a non-
  existent key, instead of raising a KeyError, it creates a new empty set
  for that key.

- For the "no-cache" directive, which can have multiple values, it
  allows easy addition of values to a set. It removes the need to check if
  the key exists first.

In the below code from *homeassistant*, defaultdict is used to efficiently track and accumulate setup times for different integrations:

```python
# File: homeassistant/bootstrap.py
class _WatchPendingSetups:
    """Periodic log and dispatch of setups that are pending."""

    def _async_watch(self) -> None:
        """Periodic log of setups that are pending."""
        now = monotonic()
        self._duration_count += SLOW_STARTUP_CHECK_INTERVAL

        remaining_with_setup_started: defaultdict[str, float] =
        defaultdict(float)

        for integration_group, start_time in self._setup_started.items():
            domain, _ = integration_group
            remaining_with_setup_started[domain] += now - start_time

        if remaining_with_setup_started:
            _LOGGER.debug("Integration remaining: %s", remaining_with_
            setup_started)
        elif waiting_tasks := self._hass._active_tasks:  # noqa: SLF001
            _LOGGER.debug("Waiting on tasks: %s", waiting_tasks)
        self._async_dispatch(remaining_with_setup_started)

        ...
```

In this code

- remaining_with_setup_started = defaultdict(float) creates a dictionary that automatically initializes new keys with 0.0 (as the call float() returns 0.0).

- remaining_with_setup_started[domain] += now - start_time adds the elapsed time to the total for each domain without needing to check if the domain exists in the dictionary first.

collections.OrderedDict

The OrderedDict dictionary subclass remembers the order in which keys were inserted. It combines the functionality of a dictionary with the ability to maintain key order. It also contains a specialized method move_to_end to move a key to the left or right end of the dictionary.

Note that from Python 3.7 onward, the built-in dict type preserves insertion order by default. collections.OrderedDict was originally introduced in Python 2.7 and 3.1 to provide **a dictionary that remembers the insertion order of keys**, which regular dict didn't guarantee back then. The main difference between OrderedDict and a regular dict in modern Python is that OrderedDict lets us explicitly reorder keys using .move_to_end(), while dict does not.

The below code from *godot* showcases a usage example of OrderedDict:

```
# File: godot/SConstruct

modules_enabled = OrderedDict()

env.module_dependencies = {}
env.module_icons_paths = []
env.doc_class_path = platform_doc_class_path

for name, path in modules_detected.items():

    sys.path.insert(0, path)
    env.current_module = name
    import config

    if config.can_build(env, env["platform"]):
        # Disable it if a required dependency is missing.
        if not env.module_check_dependencies(name):
            continue

        ...
        modules_enabled[name] = path

    sys.path.remove(path)
    sys.modules.pop("config")
```

```
env.module_list = modules_enabled

...

def sort_module_list(env):
    deps = {
        k: v[0] + list(filter(lambda x: x in env.module_list, v[1]))
        for k, v in env.module_dependencies.items()
    }

    frontier = list(env.module_list.keys())
    explored = []
    while len(frontier):
        cur = frontier.pop()
        deps_list = deps[cur] if cur in deps else []
        if len(deps_list) and any([d not in explored for d in deps_list]):
            # Will explore later, after its dependencies
            frontier.insert(0, cur)
            continue
        explored.append(cur)
    for k in explored:
        env.module_list.move_to_end(k)
```

In this code, OrderedDict is used to manage a list of enabled modules while preserving their order. Here

1. `modules_enabled = OrderedDict()` creates an empty OrderedDict to store enabled modules.

2. As modules are processed and enabled, they are added to `modules_enabled` in the order they are detected and validated.

3. Each entry in `modules_enabled` has the module name as the key and its path as the value. The `OrderedDict` maintains the order in which these entries were inserted.

4. In the `sort_module_list` function, the `move_to_end` method of the OrderedDict is called (`env.module_list.move_to_end(k)`) to reorder modules based on their dependencies.

5.   OrderedDict allows for consistent iteration order, which is important when processing modules in a specific sequence. The ordered nature of the dictionary is crucial here for the dependency sorting algorithm, ensuring that modules are processed in the correct order.

collections.Counter

Counter is a dict subclass for counting hashable objects. It's a collection where elements are stored as dictionary keys and their counts as dictionary values.

The snippet below from the Hugging Face transformers library exemplifies the usage of Counter:

```python
# File: transformers/scripts/check_tokenizers.py
from collections import Counter

def check_details(line, spm_ids, tok_ids, slow, fast):
    # Encoding can be the same with same result AAA -> A + AA vs AA + A
    # We can check that we use at least exactly the same number of tokens.
    for i, (spm_id, tok_id) in enumerate(zip(spm_ids, tok_ids)):
        if spm_id != tok_id:
            break
    first = i
    for i, (spm_id, tok_id) in enumerate(zip(reversed(spm_ids),
    reversed(tok_ids))):
        if spm_id != tok_id:
            break
    last = len(spm_ids) - i

    ...

    if last - first > 5:
        # We might have twice a single problem, attempt to subdivide the
        disjointed tokens into smaller problems
        spms = Counter(spm_ids[first:last])
        toks = Counter(tok_ids[first:last])
```

```
removable_tokens = {spm_ for (spm_, si) in spms.items() if toks.
get(spm_, 0) == si}
min_width = 3

...
```

In this code, Counter is used to efficiently compare the frequency of tokens in two different tokenization results:

- `spms = Counter(spm_ids[first:last])` and `toks = Counter(tok_ids[first:last])` create frequency dictionaries for tokens in the mismatched sections.

- These Counters are used to identify tokens that appear with the same frequency in both tokenizations:

  ```
  removable_tokens = {spm_ for (spm_, si) in spms.items() if toks.
  get(spm_, 0) == si}
  ```

Using a `Counter` object here simplifies the process of counting and comparing token frequencies, making it easy to identify tokens that are common to both tokenizations or unique to one.

Below is another usage example of the `Counter` object from the same library, *transformers*:

```
# File: transformers/utils/get_ci_error_statistics.py
from collections import Counter

def reduce_by_error(logs, error_filter=None):
    """count each error"""

    counter = Counter()
    counter.update([x[1] for x in logs])
    counts = counter.most_common()
    r = {}
    for error, count in counts:
        if error_filter is None or error not in error_filter:
            r[error] = {
                "count": count,
```

```
            "failed_tests": [(x[2], x[0]) for x in logs if x[1]
            == error],
        }
    r = dict(sorted(r.items(), key=lambda item: item[1]["count"],
    reverse=True))
    return r
```

In the snippet, an empty Counter object is created to store error frequencies.

- The statement counter.update([x[1] for x in logs]) counts occurrences of each error type. It assumes x[1] in each log entry contains the error type.

- The statement counts = counter.most_common() returns a list of (error, count) tuples, sorted by count in descending order.

- The code then iterates over these counts to create a detailed dictionary of errors, including their count and associated failed tests.

collections.ChainMap

ChainMap is a class that provides the ability to link multiple mappings together to create a single, updateable view. The mappings are stored in a list, with lookups searching through them in order. It is different from the normal dictionary union in that ChainMap is a dynamic view, while union creates a static new dictionary.

The below snippet from *streamlit* showcases the usage of ChainMap:

```
# File: lib/streamlit/connections/sql_connection.py
from collections import ChainMap

class SQLConnection(BaseConnection["Engine"]):
    """A connection to a SQL database using a SQLAlchemy Engine. Initialize
    using ``st.connection("<name>", type="sql")``"""

    def _connect(self, autocommit: bool = False, **kwargs) -> Engine:
        import sqlalchemy

        kwargs = deepcopy(kwargs)
```

```
conn_param_kwargs = extract_from_dict(_ALL_CONNECTION_
PARAMS, kwargs)
conn_params = ChainMap(conn_param_kwargs, self._secrets.to_
dict())  # (1)

if not len(conn_params):
    raise StreamlitAPIException(
        "Missing SQL DB connection configuration. "
        "Did you forget to set this in `secrets.toml` or as kwargs "
        "to `st.connection`?"
    )

if "url" in conn_params:
    url = sqlalchemy.engine.make_url(conn_params["url"])
else:
    for p in _REQUIRED_CONNECTION_PARAMS:
        if p not in conn_params:
            raise StreamlitAPIException(f"Missing SQL DB connection
            param: {p}")

    drivername = conn_params["dialect"] + (
        f"+{conn_params['driver']}" if "driver" in conn_
        params else ""
    )

    url = sqlalchemy.engine.URL.create(
        drivername=drivername,
        username=conn_params["username"],
        password=conn_params.get("password"),
        host=conn_params["host"],
        port=int(conn_params["port"]) if "port" in conn_params
        else None,
        database=conn_params.get("database"),
        query=conn_params["query"] if "query" in conn_params
        else None,
    )
```

```
create_engine_kwargs = ChainMap(
    kwargs, self._secrets.get("create_engine_kwargs", {})
) # (2)
eng = sqlalchemy.create_engine(url, **create_engine_kwargs)

...
```

In this code, ChainMap is used twice to combine multiple dictionaries in a specific order of precedence:

1. *In the line marked by the comment* (1):

   conn_params = ChainMap(conn_param_kwargs, self._secrets. to_dict()) creates a view that prioritizes conn_param_kwargs over self._secrets. It allows looking up connection parameters first in the explicitly provided kwargs and then falling back to the secrets if not found.

2. *In the line marked as* (2):

   create_engine_kwargs = ChainMap(kwargs, self._secrets. get("create_engine_kwargs", {})) combines additional kwargs with engine-specific secrets, prioritizing the explicitly provided kwargs.

Custom Dictionary Classes

In this section, we will explore the methods to create custom dict or dict-like classes.

From the Built-In `dict`

Inheriting directly from Python's built-in dict class is the simplest method for building custom dict classes. It provides all standard dictionary functionality out of the box, allowing us to override or extend specific methods as needed. This approach is suitable for minor modifications to dictionary behavior.

In the snippet below from Django, `CountsDict` inherits from the built-in dict class:

```python
# File: django/utils/html.py

class CountsDict(dict):
    def __init__(self, *args, word, **kwargs):
        super().__init__(*args, *kwargs)
        self.word = word

    def __missing__(self, key):
        self[key] = self.word.count(key)
        return self[key]
```

By inheriting from dict, CountsDict automatically gets all standard dictionary functionality.

- The __init__ method is overridden to accept an additional "word" parameter, which is stored as an instance attribute.

- The key customization, in this case, is done on the __missing__ dunder, which is called when a key is not found in the dictionary. Here, it's used to automatically calculate and store the count of a character in the word.

- The dictionary populates itself with counts as keys are accessed.

From MutableMapping

For more control and flexibility, we can create a custom dictionary class by inheriting from `collections.abc.MutableMapping`. Inheriting from this abstract base class requires implementing all abstract methods (__getitem__, __setitem__, __delitem__, __iter__, and __len__). This approach offers more flexibility and control over the underlying data structure and behavior but requires more implementation work.

Inheriting from `typing.MutableMapping` is also equivalent to inheriting from the built-in `collections.abc.MutableMapping`. Inheriting from the typing module version will provide better type hinting and static type-checking support.

The below snippet from *protobuf* showcases a custom dict-like mapping class created by inheriting from `MutableMapping`:

```python
# File: python/google/protobuf/internal/containers.py
from typing import MutableMapping, TypeVar

_K = TypeVar('_K')
_V = TypeVar('_V')

class ScalarMap(MutableMapping[_K, _V]):
    """Simple, type-checked, dict-like container for holding repeated
    scalars."""

    # Disallows assignment to other attributes.
    __slots__ = [
        "_key_checker",
        "_value_checker",
        "_values",
        "_message_listener",
        "_entry_descriptor",
    ]

    def __init__(
        self,
        message_listener: Any,
        key_checker: Any,
        value_checker: Any,
        entry_descriptor: Any,
    ) -> None:
        """

        Args:
          message_listener: A MessageListener implementation.
            The ScalarMap will call this object's Modified() method when it
            is modified.
          key_checker: A type_checkers.ValueChecker instance to run on keys
          inserted into this container.
          value_checker: A type_checkers.ValueChecker instance to run on
          values inserted into this container.
          entry_descriptor: The MessageDescriptor of a map entry: key
          and value.
```

```
    """
        self._message_listener = message_listener
        self._key_checker = key_checker
        self._value_checker = value_checker
        self._entry_descriptor = entry_descriptor
        self._values = {}

    def __getitem__(self, key: _K) -> _V:
        try:
            return self._values[key]
        except KeyError:
            key = self._key_checker.CheckValue(key)
            val = self._value_checker.DefaultValue()
            self._values[key] = val
            return val

    def __contains__(self, item: _K) -> bool:
        # We check the key's type to match the strong-typing flavor of
        the API.
        # Also this makes it easier to match the behavior of the C++
        implementation.
        self._key_checker.CheckValue(item)
        return item in self._values

    @overload
    def get(self, key: _K) -> Optional[_V]:
        ...

    @overload
    def get(self, key: _K, default: _T) -> Union[_V, _T]:
        ...

    # We need to override this explicitly, because our defaultdict-like
    behavior
    # will make the default implementation (from our base class)
    always insert
    # the key.
    def get(self, key, default=None):
```

98

```
        if key in self:
            return self[key]
        else:
            return default

    def __setitem__(self, key: _K, value: _V) -> _T:
        checked_key = self._key_checker.CheckValue(key)
        checked_value = self._value_checker.CheckValue(value)
        self._values[checked_key] = checked_value
        self._message_listener.Modified()

    def __delitem__(self, key: _K) -> None:
        del self._values[key]
        self._message_listener.Modified()

    def MergeFrom(self, other: "ScalarMap[_K, _V]") -> None:
        self._values.update(other._values)
        self._message_listener.Modified()

    # This is defined in the abstract base, but we can do it much more
    cheaply.
    def clear(self) -> None:
        self._values.clear()
        self._message_listener.Modified()

    ...
```

Here, the required abstract methods are implemented along with custom implementations for get(), clear(), etc. Using MutableMapping as a base class allows for a custom underlying data structure (_values attribute in this case). Also, ScalarMap is defined here as a slotted class to make it more efficient.

From UserDict

The collections.UserDict class provides a wrapper around the built-in dictionary, making it easier to create custom dictionary classes. By inheriting from UserDict, we can avoid directly subclassing dict and instead work with an internal dictionary attribute (data). This approach simplifies the process of extending dictionary behavior, allowing easy customization of specific behaviors while maintaining most standard dictionary functionality.

The snippet below from Apache Spark defines a custom dict class by inheriting from UserDict:

```python
# File: spark/python/pyspark/sql/datasource.py

from collections import UserDict

class CaseInsensitiveDict(UserDict):
    """
    A case-insensitive map of string keys to values.

    This is used by Python data source options to ensure consistent case
    insensitivity.
    """

    def __init__(self, *args: Any, **kwargs: Any) -> None:
        super().__init__(*args, **kwargs)
        self.update(*args, **kwargs)

    def __setitem__(self, key: str, value: Any) -> None:
        super().__setitem__(key.lower(), value)

    def __getitem__(self, key: str) -> Any:
        return super().__getitem__(key.lower())

    def __delitem__(self, key: str) -> None:
        super().__delitem__(key.lower())

    def __contains__(self, key: object) -> bool:
        if isinstance(key, str):
            return super().__contains__(key.lower())
        return False
```

```python
    def update(self, *args: Any, **kwargs: Any) -> None:
        for k, v in dict(*args, **kwargs).items():
            self[k] = v

    def copy(self) -> "CaseInsensitiveDict":
        return type(self)(self)
```

In this code, CaseInsensitiveDict inherits from collections.UserDict to create a custom dictionary class with case-insensitive key handling. The class overrides key dict methods to implement case-insensitive behavior. All keys are first converted to lowercase before performing operations.

Custom Set Class: MutableSet

Custom set classes derived from MutableSet allow us to create specialized set-like objects with tailored behavior. The collections.abc.MutableSet abstract base class provides a foundation for implementing custom set types in Python. Implementing classes must define __contains__, __iter__, __len__, add, and discard abstract methods.

The below snippet from *sympy* defines a custom OrderedSet by inheriting from MutableSet:

```python
# File: sympy/core/containers.py
from collections.abc import MutableSet

class OrderedSet(MutableSet):
    def __init__(self, iterable=None):
        if iterable:
            self.map = OrderedDict((item, None) for item in iterable)
        else:
            self.map = OrderedDict()

    def __len__(self):
        return len(self.map)

    def __contains__(self, key):
        return key in self.map
```

```python
def add(self, key):
    self.map[key] = None

def discard(self, key):
    self.map.pop(key)

def pop(self, last=True):
    return self.map.popitem(last=last)[0]

def __iter__(self):
    yield from self.map.keys()

def __repr__(self):
    if not self.map:
        return "%s()" % (self.__class__.__name__,)
    return "%s(%r)" % (self.__class__.__name__, list(self.map.keys()))

def intersection(self, other):
    return self.__class__([val for val in self if val in other])

def difference(self, other):
    return self.__class__([val for val in self if val not in other])

def update(self, iterable):
    for val in iterable:
        self.add(val)
```

The OrderedSet object maintains the order of insertion, which is not a feature of Python's built-in set by using OrderedDict as the underlying data structure (the .map attribute). Inheriting from MutableSet ensures that OrderedSet behaves like a standard Python set, making it interoperable with code expecting set-like objects.

Typing Sets and Dicts

Python's typing module provides a way to specify the types of elements in dictionaries and sets, which can help with code readability and type checking.

Typing Dictionaries

To specify the types of keys and values in a dictionary, we can use the `dict` built-in type with a subscript notation. The first member inside the [ ] denotes the key type, and the second one is the value type. The typing module also has a "Dict" class, which can be used to annotate dictionaries, but it has been deprecated since Python 3.9.

Example:

```python
# Dictionary with string keys and integer values
scores: dict[str, int] = {"Alice": 95, "Bob": 87}

# Dictionary with any type of key and value
mixed_dict: dict[Any, Any] = {1: "one", "two": 2, (3, 4): [5, 6]}
```

We can also use more complex types, such as dictionaries with tuple keys or nested dictionaries:

```python
nested_dict: dict[str, dict[str, int]] = {
    "Alice": {"math": 95, "science": 92},
    "Bob": {"math": 87, "science": 89},
}

# A dictionary with tuple keys and string values
coordinates: dict[tuple[int, int], str] = {
    (0, 0): "Origin",
    (1, 2): "Point A",
    (3, 4): "Point B",
}
```

Typing Sets

To specify the type of elements in a set, we can use the `set` built-in and specify the set element type using subscript notation.

Example:

```python
# set of integers
int_set: set[int] = {1, 2, 3, 4, 5}

# set of strings
str_set: set[str] = {"apple", "banana", "cherry"}
```

A set of tuples can be annotated as

```
points: set[tuple[int, int]] = {(0, 0), (1, 2), (3, 4)}
```

TypedDict

typing.TypedDict, introduced in Python 3.8, is a special type hint class that allows us to define dictionaries with a fixed set of keys, each associated with a specific value type. It's part of the typing module and provides a way to create more strongly typed dictionaries in Python. It is useful in scenarios where we need to work with dictionaries that have a predetermined structure, such as configuration objects, API responses, or data transfer objects.

The below snippet defines a TypedDict named Record using its constructor:

```python
from typing import TypedDict
from datetime import timedelta

Record = TypedDict("Record", {"count": int, "total": timedelta})

timer: dict[str, Record] = {}

def add_record(
    timer: dict[str, Record], key: str, count: int, total: timedelta
) -> None:
    timer[key] = {"count": count, "total": total}

def get_record(timer: dict[str, Record], key: str) -> Record:
    return timer[key]

# Adding records
add_record(timer, "task1", 5, timedelta(hours=2))
add_record(timer, "task2", 3, timedelta(hours=1, minutes=30))

# Retrieving and printing records
record1 = get_record(timer, "task1")
record2 = get_record(timer, "task2")
```

In this code

- timer: Dict[str, Record] = {} initializes an empty dictionary timer where the keys are strings and the values are of type Record.

- The code snippet passes a static type check.

- When new keys are introduced in the timer dict values, type check will fail.

For example:

```
timer[key] = {"count": count, "total": total}
```

If a new key is added along with "count" and "total" without updating the Record TypedDict, static type checkers will flag it as an error.

TypedDicts can also be defined using inheritance. The Record TypedDict can also be defined using inheritance as below:

```
from typing import TypedDict
from datetime import timedelta

class Record(TypedDict):
    count: int
    total: timedelta
```

The code below from *homeassistant* exemplifies the usage of TypedDicts:

```
# File: homeassistant/core.py

from typing import TypedDict, NotRequired, Any
from .const import (
    COMPRESSED_STATE_ATTRIBUTES,
    COMPRESSED_STATE_CONTEXT,
    COMPRESSED_STATE_LAST_CHANGED,
    COMPRESSED_STATE_LAST_UPDATED,
    COMPRESSED_STATE_STATE
)
```

```python
class CompressedState(TypedDict):
    """Compressed dict of a state."""

    s: str  # COMPRESSED_STATE_STATE
    a: ReadOnlyDict[str, Any]  # COMPRESSED_STATE_ATTRIBUTES
    c: str | dict[str, Any]  # COMPRESSED_STATE_CONTEXT
    lc: float  # COMPRESSED_STATE_LAST_CHANGED
    lu: NotRequired[float]  # COMPRESSED_STATE_LAST_UPDATED

class State:
    """Object to represent a state within the state machine."""

    ...

    @cached_property
    def as_compressed_state(self) -> CompressedState:
        """Build a compressed dict of a state for adds.

        Omits the lu (last_updated) if it matches (lc) last_changed.

        Sends c (context) as a string if it only contains an id.
        """
        state_context = self.context
        if state_context.parent_id is None and state_context.user_id
        is None:
            context: dict[str, Any] | str = state_context.id
        else:
            # _as_dict is marked as protected
            # to avoid callers outside of this module
            # from misusing it by mistake.
            context = state_context._as_dict  # noqa: SLF001
        compressed_state: CompressedState = {
            COMPRESSED_STATE_STATE: self.state,
            COMPRESSED_STATE_ATTRIBUTES: self.attributes,
            COMPRESSED_STATE_CONTEXT: context,
            COMPRESSED_STATE_LAST_CHANGED: self.last_changed_timestamp,
        }
```

```
    if self.last_changed != self.last_updated:
        compressed_state[
            COMPRESSED_STATE_LAST_UPDATED
        ] = self.last_updated_timestamp
    return compressed_state
```

In this code, TypedDict is used to define a structured dictionary type called CompressedState.

- Each key in the TypedDict is associated with a specific type:

  - "s" (state) is a string.

  - "a" (attributes) is a ReadOnlyDict of string keys to Any values.

  - "c" (context) can be either a string or a dictionary.

  - "lc" (last changed) is a float.

  - "lu" (last updated) is an optional float.

- The "lu" field is marked as NotRequired, indicating it may be omitted from the dictionary.

- This definition as a TypedDict allows static type checkers to verify that CompressedState dictionaries are used correctly throughout the code.

- In the as_compressed_state method, CompressedState is used as the return type annotation, ensuring the method returns a dictionary conforming to the defined structure.

Using TypedDict in this context provides a clear, enforceable contract for the structure of compressed state dictionaries. It enhances code readability, helps catch errors early through static type checking, and improves developer experience.

Conclusion

In this chapter, we've explored the powerful and versatile data structures of dictionaries and sets in Python. We've covered a wide range of topics, including

1. Basic operations and methods for both dictionaries and sets

2. Advanced operations like dictionary merging, view objects, and set operations

3. The concept of hashability and its importance in these data structures

4. Creating custom dictionary and set classes

5. Dictionary and set variants like frozenset, defaultdict, and OrderedDict

6. Typing dict and set objects for improved code clarity and reliability

When writing code, we should select the most suitable data structures based on the data storage, retrieval, and modification requirements.

We should use dictionaries when the requirements are

- *Key-value pairs*: We need to associate unique keys with specific values.

  - *Example*: Storing user information where the user ID is the key and the user details are the value.

- *Fast lookups by key*: We need to quickly retrieve values based on unique keys.

  - *Example*: Look up a user's email address by their username.

- *Dynamic data*: We need to frequently add, update, or remove key-value pairs.

  - *Example*: Managing a cache of recently accessed data.

- *Complex data structures*: We need to store more complex data structures, such as nested dictionaries.

  - *Example*: Storing configuration settings for an application.

We should use sets when the requirements are

- *Uniqueness*: We need to store unique elements and automatically handle duplicates.

    – *Example*: Storing a collection of unique email addresses.

- *Membership testing*: We need to frequently check if an element is present in the collection.

    – *Example*: Checking if a product is in a user's wishlist.

- *Set operations*: We need to perform mathematical set operations like union, intersection, and difference.

    – *Example*: Finding common items in two shopping carts.

- *Unordered collection*: The order of elements does not matter.

    – *Example*: Storing a collection of unique tags.

CHAPTER 4

Logging

In the last few chapters, we explored Python's core data structures like lists, tuples, sets, and dictionaries—tools that help us organize and manipulate data. Now, we shift focus from data structures to understanding how we can monitor what our programs are doing in real time using logging.

Logging is essential in software development for monitoring, debugging, and ensuring the reliability of applications. Logging involves recording the events and data during a program execution, thus providing a history of application events. Python's built-in `logging` module contains powerful tools catered to diverse use cases. In the following sections, we will go through Python's logging functionalities in detail.

Configuration

Python gives us multiple ways to configure the logging behavior. We can use some of the logging configuration functions, or we can make the necessary setup by directly calling the logging module functions.

Using logging.basicConfig

It simplifies the initial setup of logging configuration. It allows us to specify basic logging parameters like the threshold log level, format, output stream to use, etc.

Below is an example of `basicConfig` usage from opencv:

```python
# File: opencv/modules/objc/generator/gen_objc.py

if __name__ == "__main__":
    # initialize logger
    logging.basicConfig(
```

© Adarsh Divakaran 2025
A. Divakaran, *Deep Dive Python*, https://doi.org/10.1007/979-8-8688-1261-3_4

```
        filename="gen_objc.log", format=None, filemode="w",
        level=logging.INFO
    )
    handler = logging.StreamHandler()
    handler.setLevel(os.environ.get("LOG_LEVEL", logging.WARNING))
    logging.getLogger().addHandler(handler)
```

Python's `logging.config` module allows for further configuration by the usage of `FileConfig` and `DictConfig` methods in the module. These can be leveraged in more complex scenarios.

DictConfig

`DictConfig` allows configuring the logging system using a dictionary. It allows us to define loggers, formatters, handlers, and filters using a nested dict format.

The below example from `locust`, a load testing library, uses a dict-based config for logging:

 # File: locust/log.py

```
import logging
import logging.config

...

def setup_logging(loglevel, logfile=None):
    loglevel = loglevel.upper()

    LOGGING_CONFIG = {
        "version": 1,
        "disable_existing_loggers": False,
        "formatters": {
            "default": {
                "format": f"[%(asctime)s] {HOSTNAME}/%(levelname)s/%(name)
                s: %(message)s",
            },
```

```
            "plain": {
                "format": "%(message)s",
            },
        },
        "handlers": {
            "console": {
                "class": "logging.StreamHandler",
                "formatter": "default",
            },
            "console_plain": {
                "class": "logging.StreamHandler",
                "formatter": "plain",
            },
            "log_reader": {"class": "locust.log.LogReader", "formatter":
            "default"},
        },
        "loggers": {
            "locust": {
                "handlers": ["console", "log_reader"],
                "level": loglevel,
                "propagate": False,
            },
            "locust.stats_logger": {
                "handlers": ["console_plain", "log_reader"],
                "level": "INFO",
                "propagate": False,
            },
        },
        "root": {
            "handlers": ["console", "log_reader"],
            "level": loglevel,
        },
}
```

```
if logfile:
    # if a file has been specified add a file logging handler and set
    # the locust and root loggers to use it
    LOGGING_CONFIG["handlers"]["file"] = {
        "class": "logging.FileHandler",
        "filename": logfile,
        "formatter": "default",
    }
    LOGGING_CONFIG["loggers"]["locust"]["handlers"] = ["file",
    "log_reader"]
    LOGGING_CONFIG["root"]["handlers"] = ["file", "log_reader"]

logging.config.dictConfig(LOGGING_CONFIG)
```

Using a dictionary configuration allows for dynamic updates of the configuration at runtime. It also allows us to define configuration using formats like JSON (JavaScript Object Notation), which can be converted to dictionaries.

FileConfig

FileConfig allows configuring the logging system using a configuration file that conforms to Python's configparser file format.

The below code from *amazon-redshift-utils* uses file-based configuration using the logging.conf file:

```
# File: amazon-redshift-utils/src/UserLastLogin/config/logging.conf
```

[loggers]
keys=root

[handlers]
keys=stream_handler

[formatters]
keys=formatter

[logger_root]
level=INFO
handlers=stream_handler

114

[handler_stream_handler]
```
class=StreamHandler
level=INFO
formatter=formatter
args=(sys.stdout,)
```

[formatter_formatter]
```
format=%(asctime)s %(levelname)-5s %(message)s
#format=%(asctime)s %(levelname)-5s %(module)-20s %(funcName)-15s
%(message)s
```

The filepath is specified in the code for setting up logging according to the configuration:

```
# File: amazon-redshift-utils/src/UserLastLogin/lib/utils.py

...
import logging.config

logging.config.fileConfig("config/logging.conf")
logger = logging.getLogger()
```

File-based config is helpful to update the logging configuration without making changes to the code.

Log Levels

Log levels indicate the severity or importance of a log message. They help in filtering log messages so that only relevant information is recorded and monitored. The default log levels include

1. *DEBUG*: Used for detailed diagnostic information useful during development. *Example*: Track variable values or function calls to troubleshoot issues during development.

2. *INFO*: Reports events that occur during normal operation. *Example*: Log successful startup or shutdown of services to monitor the application's status.

3. *WARNING*: Indicates a potential problem or important event that might not be immediately critical but needs attention. *Example*: Notify when a deprecated function is used or when an API call takes longer than expected.

4. *ERROR*: Logs events when an issue occurs that prevents part of the application from functioning correctly. *Example*: Capture exceptions or errors when a file fails to load or a database connection cannot be established.

5. *CRITICAL*: Reserved for severe error conditions that require immediate attention. *Example*: Alert on system failures or data corruption that necessitates immediate intervention to prevent complete application failure.

Log levels have associated numerical values that determine their severity and control whether a message gets logged based on a specified threshold. Here are the log levels and their corresponding numerical values:

- *DEBUG*: 10

- *INFO*: 20

- *WARNING*: 30

- *ERROR*: 40

- *CRITICAL*: 50

The logging system compares the numerical value of each log message's level against the threshold level set for the logger or handler. A log message gets logged only if its level is greater than or equal to the threshold. These numerical values are useful when we need to define custom log levels in our application.

Also, there is a `logging.NOTSET` level (numeric value 0), which acts as the default level for loggers and handlers when no specific level is set. It signifies that no specific logging level is set for a logger or handler, allowing them to inherit the level from their parent logger.

The below snippets from Zulip, an open source Slack alternative, show the usage of various log levels:

```
# File: zulip/zerver/management/commands/process_queue.py

class ThreadedWorker(threading.Thread):
    def __init__(self, queue_name: str, logger: logging.Logger) -> None:
        ...

    @override
    def run(self) -> None:
        with configure_scope() as scope, log_and_exit_if_exception(
            self.logger, self.queue_name, threaded=True
        ):
            worker = get_worker(self.queue_name, threaded=True)
            worker.setup()
            logging.debug("starting consuming %s", self.queue_name)
            worker.start()
```

Here, the status of workers consuming the queue is logged with a debug level. The debug level is used since these logs are not critical for monitoring the application and are only useful for the developers to debug issues.

```
# File: zulip/zerver/apps.py

def flush_cache(sender: Optional[AppConfig], **kwargs: Any) -> None:
    logging.info("Clearing memcached cache after migrations")
    cache.clear()
```

The info level is used to log messages that confirm that the program is working as expected. In this case, an info message is logged after cache migration.

```
# File: zulip/zerver/views/auth.py

@log_view_func
def log_into_subdomain(request: HttpRequest, token: str) -> HttpResponse:

    # The tokens are intended to have the same format as API keys.
    if not has_api_key_format(token):
        logging.warning("log_into_subdomain: Malformed token given:
        %s", token)
        return HttpResponse(status=400)
```

117

The log message uses the `warning` level to alert developers about the usage of a malformed token.

```python
# File: zulip/zerver/views/zephyr.py
```

```python
def webathena_kerberos_login(
    request: HttpRequest,
    user_profile: UserProfile,
    cred: Optional[str] = REQ(default=None),
) -> HttpResponse:
    ...

    if settings.PERSONAL_ZMIRROR_SERVER is None:
        logging.error(
            "PERSONAL_ZMIRROR_SERVER is not properly configured", stack_
            info=True
        )
        raise JsonableError(_("We were unable to set up mirroring for you"))
```

The error level is used to indicate that a function cannot be performed successfully (due to a configuration issue in this case).

```python
# File: zulip/scripts/lib/check-database-compatibility
```

```python
if os.path.exists("/etc/init.d/postgresql") and os.path.exists("/etc/zulip/
zulip.conf"):
    postgresql_version = int(
        get_config(get_config_file(), "postgresql", "version", "0")
    )
    if postgresql_version == 0:
        ...
    elif postgresql_version != django_pg_version:
        logging.critical(
            "PostgreSQL version mismatch: %d (running) vs %d (configured)",
            django_pg_version,
            postgresql_version,
        )
        ...
        sys.exit(1)
```

A critical level is used when the application cannot continue and is exiting execution.

Using logging.error vs. logging.exception

Both `logging.error` and `logging.exception` are used for logging error messages (ERROR log level). The difference between them is that `logging.error` writes a simple error message, while `logging.exception` captures exception information along with the specified error message and logs them.

```python
import logging

try:
    result = 10 / 0
except ZeroDivisionError:
    logging.error("An error occurred")
    """

    ERROR:root:An error occurred
    """

    logging.exception("Exception occurred")
    """

    ERROR:root:Exception occurred
    Traceback (most recent call last):
      File "../file.py", line 4, in <module>
        result = 10 / 0
                 ~~~^~~

    ZeroDivisionError: division by zero
    """
```

It can be seen that `logging.exception` automatically adds traceback information to the log. `logging.exception` should be used within an except block to capture and log exception details.

Loggers

The `logging.Logger` class in Python is the primary interface for logging events. It provides methods to log messages at different severity levels and manage the overall logging flow.

Attributes of logging.Logger:

1. *name*:

   – The name of the logger. Used to identify the logger, often hierarchical (e.g., "module.submodule").

2. *level*:

   – The threshold level for the logger (messages below this level are ignored).

3. *parent*:

   – The parent logger in the hierarchy.

4. *propagate*:

   – A boolean indicating if the log messages should be passed to the parent logger. The default is `True`.

5. *handlers*:

   – A list of handler objects attached to the logger.

6. *disabled*:

   – A boolean indicating if the logger is disabled. When `True`, the logger will not process any messages.

These attributes control the behavior, output, and management of log messages and are often accessed and modified using the `Logger` class's methods.

The `logging.getLogger(name)` function in Python's logging module is used to create or retrieve a logger instance. If a logger with the specified name already exists, `getLogger` returns the existing logger. If no name is provided, it returns the root logger.

Creating Logger objects:

Logger objects can be created by directly instantiating the Logger class specifying the necessary attributes such as the name and threshold level:

```
logger = logging.Logger('main_logger', level='DEBUG')
```

The below usage creates a new logger with the name of the current module. This allows for module-specific logging configurations as well as easier identification of log messages:

```
logger = logging.Logger(__name__)
```

The getLogger can be also used to create a logger object (or retrieve if one already exists):

```
LOGGER: Final[logging.Logger] = logging.getLogger(__package__)
```

Here, getLogger retrieves or creates a logger named after the current package. This can be used to ensure a consistent logger configuration across the entire package.

Formatters

Formatters determine how the log record attributes are present in the final output. They allow customization of the message format, including timestamp, log level, logger name, and the actual log message.

The below snippet shows a formatter used by the pytorch library:

```
# File: torch/distributed/checkpoint/_dedup_tensors.py

def init_logger() -> logging.Logger:
    logger = logging.getLogger(__name__)
    level = logging.INFO
    logger.setLevel(level)
    console = logging.StreamHandler()
    formatter = logging.Formatter(
        "%(asctime)s %(filename)s:%(lineno)s %(levelname)s p:%(processName)
        s t:%(threadName)s: %(message)s"
    )
    console.setFormatter(formatter)
    console.setLevel(level)
    logger.addHandler(console)
    logger.propagate = False
    return logger

logger = init_logger()
```

The formatter used here includes the following information:

- `%(asctime)s`: The timestamp of when the log message was generated

- `%(filename)s`: The name of the file where the logging call was made

- `%(lineno)s`: The line number in the file where the logging call was made

- `%(levelname)s`: The log level (e.g., INFO, DEBUG, ERROR)

- `p:%(processName)s`: The name of the process generating the log message (preceded by a "p:")

- `t:%(threadName)s`: The name of the thread generating the log message (preceded by a "t:")

- `%(message)s`: The actual log message

Below is a sample logging output that can be generated by using this formatter:

```
2024-05-20 15:45:12,555 _dedup_tensors.py:25 INFO p:MainProcess
t:MainThread: Deduplication process started successfully.
```

In the below snippet from pupy, different formatters are chosen based on the logging handler used:

```
# File: pupy/pupysh.py

if __name__ == "__main__":
    ...

    root_logger = logging.getLogger()

    if args.logfile:
        logging_stream = logging.FileHandler(args.logfile)
        logging_stream.setFormatter(
            logging.Formatter(
                "%(asctime)-15s|%(levelname)-5s|%(relativeCreated)6d|%(thread
                Name)s|%(name)s| %(message)s"
            )
        )
```

```
else:
    logging_stream = logging.StreamHandler()
    logging_stream.setFormatter(logging.Formatter("%(asctime)-15s|
    %(message)s"))

logging_stream.setLevel(logging.DEBUG)
```

Considering the formatter attached to FileHandler, it can be broken down into the below components:

- `%(asctime)-15s`: The timestamp of when the log message was generated, left-aligned and padded to 15 characters

- `%(levelname)-5s`: The log level (e.g., INFO, DEBUG, ERROR), left-aligned and padded to five characters

- `%(relativeCreated)6d`: The time in milliseconds since the logging module was loaded, right-aligned and padded to six characters

- `%(threadName)s`: The name of the thread generating the log message

- `%(name)s`: The name of the logger that generated the log message

- `%(message)s`: The actual log message

An example log message from the formatter will look like

```
2024-05-20 19:19:17,159|INFO |  1234|MainThread|root| Process started
successfully.
```

The above examples use printf-style formatting to structure log messages. There are other formatting styles available, such as `str.format`, which can be specified in the formatter's constructor.

Handlers

Handlers are the components that determine where the log messages are output. They can be used to route log messages to their desired destinations, like consoles, files, etc.

Examples of built-in handlers include

- *FileHandler*: Writes logging messages to a file

- *NullHandler*: Discards all logging messages

- *WatchedFileHandler*: Similar to FileHandler, but watches for file changes and reopens it if needed

- *BaseRotatingHandler*: Base class for handlers that can automatically rotate log files based on size or time

- *SocketHandler*: Sends logging messages over a network socket

- *DatagramHandler*: Similar to SocketHandler, but uses UDP for datagram-based messages

- *SysLogHandler*: Sends logging messages to a syslog server

- *NTEventLogHandler*: Writes logging messages to the Windows NT Event Log (only available on Windows)

- *MemoryHandler*: Stores logging messages in memory

- *HTTPHandler*: Sends logging messages over an HTTP request

- *QueueHandler*: Puts logging messages in a queue for asynchronous processing

In the coming sections, we will explore some common built-in handlers as well as designing custom handlers.

SMTPHandler

The SMTPHandler class in Python's `logging.handlers` module is used to send logging messages over SMTP (Simple Mail Transfer Protocol), which is the protocol used for sending emails.

In the below code from *flaskbb*, an instance of SMTPHandler is created and configured to send emails:

```python
# File: flaskbb/app.py

def configure_mail_logs(app, formatter):
    from logging.handlers import SMTPHandler

    formatter = logging.Formatter("%(asctime)s %(levelname)-7s %(name)-25s %(message)s")
```

```
mail_handler = SMTPHandler(
    app.config["MAIL_SERVER"],
    app.config["MAIL_DEFAULT_SENDER"],
    app.config["ADMINS"],
    "application error, no admins specified",
    (app.config["MAIL_USERNAME"], app.config["MAIL_PASSWORD"]),
)

mail_handler.setLevel(logging.ERROR)
mail_handler.setFormatter(formatter)
app.logger.addHandler(mail_handler)
```

The arguments passed in the SMTPHandler init are as follows:

- mailhost: The host address of the mail server to use for sending the email. Here app.config["MAIL_SERVER"].

- fromaddr: The email address that the email will be sent from.

- toaddrs: A list of recipients for the email. Taken from the config value app.config["ADMINS"].

- subject: The subject line of the email.

- credentials: If specified, this should be a tuple of the form (username, password) for the account to use when sending the email. Here mail username and password config variables are passed in a tuple.

SMTPHandler can be utilized, as seen above, when we want to be notified of any errors that occur via email. The configure_mail_logs function would be called during the application's initialization process to add the handler to the app logger.

StreamHandler

StreamHandler writes log messages to a stream (which can be a file-like object or any object supporting write() and flush() methods).

In the below snippet from *ray*, StreamHandler is initialized with sys.stderr as the stream:

```
# File: ray/release/ray_release/logger.py

import logging
import sys

logger = logging.getLogger()
logger.setLevel(logging.INFO)

def add_handlers(logger: logging.Logger):
    handler = logging.StreamHandler(stream=sys.stderr)
    formatter = logging.Formatter(
        fmt="[%(levelname)s %(asctime)s] %(filename)s: %(lineno)
        d  %(message)s"
    )
    handler.setFormatter(formatter)
    logger.addHandler(handler)

if not logger.hasHandlers():
    add_handlers(logger)
```

sys.stderr is the standard error stream, which is used for the output of error messages. Whenever a log message is passed to the logger, it will be handled by this handler and outputted to the standard error stream in the specified format.

Log Rotation and Timed File Handlers

Log rotation is a process that helps in managing log files generated by a system. It works by renaming and moving the log files when they reach a certain size or age. This is crucial in preventing log files from consuming too much disk space, which can lead to system crashes or slow performance.

RotatingFileHandler

RotatingFileHandler from the logging.handlers can be used to implement log rotation. This class ensures that the output is directed to a log file on the disk. When the log file reaches a certain size, it is closed, and a new log file is opened for output.

The below snippet from *griddb* uses RotatingFileHandler for managing the log output:

```python
# File: griddb/bin/log.py

...

def logger(binfile, level):
    logdir = os.environ["GS_LOG"]
    filebase = os.path.basename(binfile)
    logFile = os.path.join(logdir, filebase + ".log")
    log = logging.getLogger()
    handler = logging.handlers.RotatingFileHandler(
        logFile, maxBytes=(5 * 1024 * 1024), backupCount=10
    )
    handler.setFormatter(
        logging.Formatter(
            "%(asctime)s [%(process)d] [%(levelname)s] %(funcName)
            s(%(lineno)d) %(message)s"
        )
    )
    log.addHandler(handler)
    log.sctLevel(level)
    return log
```

In this code, RotatingFileHandler is initialized with a log filename, a maximum log file size (5MB in this case), and a backup count of 10. This means that when the current log file reaches 5MB, it will be closed, and a new log file will be opened. The old log file will be kept as a backup. This process will repeat until there are ten backup files. When there are ten backup files and the current log file reaches 5MB, the oldest backup file will be deleted, and the current log file will be closed and kept as a new backup file.

TimedRotatingFileHandler

TimedRotatingFileHandler is used to create log files that rotates (i.e., creates a new log file) at certain timed intervals.

```python
# File: luigi/luigi/process.py

def get_log_format():
    return "%(asctime)s %(name)s[%(process)s] %(levelname)s: %(message)s"

def get_spool_handler(filename):
    handler = logging.handlers.TimedRotatingFileHandler(
        filename=filename,
        when="d",
        encoding="utf8",
        backupCount=7,  # keep one week of historical logs
    )
    formatter = logging.Formatter(get_log_format())
    handler.setFormatter(formatter)
    return handler
```

Here's a breakdown of the parameters used in the `TimedRotatingFileHandler`:

- `filename`: This is the name of the log file. The logs will be written to this file until it is time for the file to be rotated.

- `when`: This parameter determines how often the log file is rotated. In this case, "d" means the log file is rotated every day.

- `encoding`: This is the encoding to use when writing to the file. In this case, "utf8" is used.

- `backupCount`: This is the number of backup files to keep. In this case, seven backup files are kept, which means one week of logs are kept.

Custom Handlers

We can define custom logging handlers for custom logging needs beyond those provided by built-in handlers. This is done by inheriting from the `logging.Handler` base class and overriding methods, such as emit, that control the output of the log record.

The below example from `autogpt` defines `TTSHandler`, which sends the log messages to a text-to-speech engine:

```
# File: autogpts/autogpt/autogpt/logs/handlers.py

class TTSHandler(logging.Handler):
    """Output messages to the configured TTS engine (if any)"""

    def __init__(self, config: TTSConfig):
        super().__init__()
        self.config = config
        self.tts_provider = TextToSpeechProvider(config)

    def format(self, record: logging.LogRecord) -> str:
        if getattr(record, "title", ""):
            msg = f"{getattr(record, 'title')} {record.msg}"
        else:
            msg = f"{record.msg}"

        return remove_color_codes(msg)

    def emit(self, record: logging.LogRecord) -> None:
        if not self.config.speak_mode:
            return

        message = self.format(record)
        self.tts_provider.say(message)
```

The methods overridden here are

1. *The* format *method*: It formats the log record. In this case, if the log record has a title attribute, it prepends the title to the message. The remove_color_codes function is used to remove any color codes from the message.

2. *The* emit *method*: It is responsible for emitting the log record. In this case, if the speak_mode in the config is not enabled, it returns without doing anything. Otherwise, it formats the log record and passes the formatted message to the say method of the text-to-speech engine, which will speak out the log message.

LogRecord

A LogRecord is the object used by the logging system to represent an event being logged. It contains all the information related to the event, such as the message, log level, timestamp, filename, etc. It is created automatically by the logging methods (such as debug, info, etc.).

The below code from waflib uses various attributes of the LogRecord (which is passed into the emit method of the handler) to modify the log handling behavior:

```python
# File: waflib/Logs.py

class log_handler(logging.StreamHandler):
    """"Dispatches messages to stderr/stdout depending on the severity
    level"""

    def emit(self, record):
        """
        Delegates the functionality to :py:meth:`waflib.Log.log_handler.
        emit_override`
        """
        # default implementation
        try:
            try:
                self.stream = record.stream
            except AttributeError:
                if record.levelno >= logging.WARNING:
                    record.stream = self.stream = sys.stderr
                else:
                    record.stream = self.stream = sys.stdout
            self.emit_override(record)
            self.flush()
        except (KeyboardInterrupt, SystemExit):
            raise
        except:  # from the python library -_-
            self.handleError(record)
```

LogRecord is normally auto-created with various logging operations. As seen in the above snippet, it gets passed onto the emit method of the handler as the record argument. Various LogRecord attributes such as the levelno and stream can be accessed to get the meta-information or can be modified to customize its behavior, as seen in the above snippet.

Filters

Filters can be applied to loggers as well as handlers to further customize the logging behavior. They allow fine-grained control over the logging output, enabling the inclusion or exclusion of log records based on specific criteria.

Custom filter classes can be created by inheriting from logging.Filter and then overriding its filter method. The filter method is called with a log record, and it should return True if the record is to be processed and False if the record should be discarded.

In the below code from *discord.py*, a custom filter class NitpickFileIgnorer is created by inheriting from the logging.Filter class:

```python
# File: discord.py/docs/extensions/nitpick_file_ignorer.py

import logging

from sphinx.application import Sphinx
from sphinx.util import logging as sphinx_logging

class NitpickFileIgnorer(logging.Filter):
    def __init__(self, app: Sphinx) -> None:
        self.app = app
        super().__init__()

    def filter(self, record: sphinx_logging.SphinxLogRecord) -> bool:
        if getattr(record, "type", None) == "ref":
            return (
                record.location.get("refdoc")
                not in self.app.config.nitpick_ignore_files
            )
        return True
```

```
def setup(app: Sphinx):
    app.add_config_value("nitpick_ignore_files", [], "")
    f = NitpickFileIgnorer(app)
        sphinx_logging.getLogger("sphinx.transforms.
          post_transforms").logger.addFilter(f)
    return {"parallel_read_safe": True}
```

In the filter method of NitpickFileIgnorer, it checks if the type attribute of the record is "ref". If it is, it checks if the refdoc attribute of the record.location is not in the nitpick_ignore_files list of the Sphinx application. The log record passes the filter only if it is not present in the ignored files list.

The below code from *mlflow* defines LoggerMessageFilter, which is used to filter out log messages from a specified module matching a regular expression pattern:

```
# File: mlflow/utils/logging_utils.py

class LoggerMessageFilter(logging.Filter):
    def __init__(self, module: str, filter_regex: re.Pattern):
        super().__init__()
        self._pattern = filter_regex
        self._module = module

    def filter(self, record):
        if record.name == self._module and self._pattern.
        search(record.msg):
            return False
        return True

@contextlib.contextmanager
def suppress_logs(module: str, filter_regex: re.Pattern):
    """

    Context manager that suppresses log messages from the specified module
    that match the specified regular expression. This is useful for
    suppressing expected log messages from third-party
    libraries that are not relevant to the current test.
    """

    logger = logging.getLogger(module)
```

```
filter = LoggerMessageFilter(module=module, filter_regex=filter_regex)
logger.addFilter(filter)
try:
    yield
finally:
    logger.removeFilter(filter)
```

The overridden `filter` method here checks if the name of the record matches the specified module and if the message in the record matches the regular expression pattern. If both conditions are met, the method returns `False`, indicating that the log message should be suppressed.

The `suppress_logs` function is a context manager that uses this filter to suppress log messages from a specified module that matches a specified regular expression. When the context manager is entered, it gets the logger for the specified module, creates a new instance of `LoggerMessageFilter` with the specified module and regular expression, and adds the filter to the logger.

LoggerAdapter

`LoggerAdapter` allows us to add contextual information to log records without modifying the application's main logging logic. It wraps a logger and supplements log records with additional context (typically as extra keyword arguments). This is useful for adding information such as user IDs, session IDs, or any other contextual data to the log messages.

Logger adapters are designed by subclassing the `logging.LoggerAdapter` class and overriding the `process` method.

The below snippet from *mkdocs* defines a `PrefixedLoggerAdapter`, which adds a prefix to every log message:

```
# File: mkdocs/plugins.py

class PrefixedLogger(logging.LoggerAdapter):
    """A logger adapter to prefix log messages."""

    def __init__(self, prefix: str, logger: logging.Logger) -> None:
        """

        Initialize the logger adapter.
```

```
    Arguments:
        prefix: The string to insert in front of every message.
        logger: The logger instance.
    """

    super().__init__(logger, {})
    self.prefix = prefix

def process(self, msg: str, kwargs: MutableMapping[str, Any]) ->
tuple[str, Any]:
    """

    Process the message.

    Arguments:
        msg: The message:
        kwargs: Remaining arguments.

    Returns:
        The processed message.
    """

    return f"{self.prefix}: {msg}", kwargs
```

The prefix to add is passed when initializing the PrefixedLogger instance. This can be used as per the below snippet, replacing the default logger:

```
import logging

logger = logging.getLogger(__name__)

prefixed_logger = PrefixedLogger("MyPrefix", logger)

prefixed_logger.info("This is an info message")
```

The logging output produced by the adapter will include the prefix added with each log message as seen below:

```
MyPrefix: This is an info message
```

The *Digits* library from Nvidia uses JobIdLoggerAdapter, as seen in the snippet below, to augment log messages with job IDs:

```
# File: digits/log.py

class JobIdLoggerAdapter(logging.LoggerAdapter):
    """

    Accepts an optional keyword argument: 'job_id'

    You can use this in 2 ways:
        1. On class initialization
            adapter = JobIdLoggerAdapter(logger, {'job_id': job_id})
            adapter.debug(msg)
        2. On method invocation
            adapter = JobIdLoggerAdapter(logger, {})
            adapter.debug(msg, job_id=id)
    """

    def process(self, msg, kwargs):
        if "job_id" in kwargs:
            if "extra" not in kwargs:
                kwargs["extra"] = {}
            kwargs["extra"]["job_id"] = " [%s]" % kwargs["job_id"]
            del kwargs["job_id"]
        elif "job_id" in self.extra:
            if "extra" not in kwargs:
                kwargs["extra"] = {}
            kwargs["extra"]["job_id"] = " [%s]" % self.extra["job_id"]
        return msg, kwargs
```

The overridden process method checks if a job_id is passed in the kwargs of the logging method or in the extra dictionary during initialization. If a job_id is found, it is added to the extra dictionary in kwargs, which can then be used by the formatter to add it to the log record. This can be used to track specific jobs from the log output.

Log Propagation

In Python logging, propagation refers to the ability of logging messages to travel up the logger hierarchy. Loggers are organized in a tree-like structure, with the root logger at the top. By default, a logger's message is sent to its own handlers and then also "propagates"

135

up the hierarchy. This means its parent logger (and potentially loggers all the way up to the root) also gets a chance to handle the message with their handlers. Log propagation continues up the hierarchy until the record reaches the root logger or a logger with propagate set to False.

```python
import logging

# Define handler and logger for the parent

handler = logging.StreamHandler()
handler.setLevel(logging.WARNING)  # Set higher level for parent logger.
handler.setFormatter(
    logging.Formatter("Parent logger| %(name)-20s |%(levelname)-5s|
    %(message)s")
)

root_logger = logging.getLogger("myapp")
root_logger.addHandler(handler)

# Define handler and logger for the child module
child_handler = logging.StreamHandler()
child_handler.setFormatter(
    logging.Formatter("Child logger | %(name)-20s |%(levelname)-5s|
    %(message)s")
)

child_logger = logging.getLogger("myapp.childmodule")
child_logger.addHandler(child_handler)
child_logger.setLevel(logging.DEBUG)

child_logger.debug("This is a debug message.")
child_logger.info("This is an info message.")
child_logger.warning("This is a warning message.")
```

In the above logging snippet, there are two loggers defined: a parent logger ("myapp") and a child logger ("myapp.childmodule"). The parent logger is set to handle only WARNING-level messages and above, while the child logger is set to handle all levels of messages, including DEBUG, INFO, and WARNING.

When a message is logged through the child logger, it is first handled by the child logger's handler, which formats and outputs the message. After this, the message is also propagated up to the parent logger due to the default setting of propagate = True for all loggers in Python's logging module. The parent logger then handles the message if its level is WARNING or above.

```
Child logger | myapp.childmodule     |DEBUG| This is a debug message.
Child logger | myapp.childmodule     |INFO | This is an info message.
Child logger | myapp.childmodule     |WARNING| This is a warning message.
Parent logger| myapp.childmodule     |WARNING| This is a warning message.
```

In the output, we can see that the debug and info messages from the child logger are not handled by the parent logger because their levels are below WARNING. However, the warning message from the child logger is handled by both the child and parent loggers.

Setting child_logger.propagate = False would prevent the message from reaching the parent logger. This means that if this line were added to the code, only the child logger would handle the messages, regardless of their level.

The Logging Flow

The entire logging process is summarized below, integrating the concepts we discussed.

Logger Flow

1. *Logging call*: A logging call is made in the user code, e.g., logger.info(...).

2. *Logger enabled check*: The logger checks if it is enabled for the specific log level of the call. If not enabled, the process stops.

3. *Create LogRecord*: If the logger is enabled for the log level, a LogRecord is created to hold the log message and associated metadata.

4. *Filter attached to logger*: The logger checks if any filters attached to it reject the LogRecord. If a filter rejects it, the process stops.

5. *Pass to handlers*: If the LogRecord passes the filter check, it is passed to the handlers of the current logger.

6. *Handler flow initiation*: The handler flow is initiated, where the LogRecord is passed to the handler.

Handler Flow

1. *Handler enabled check*: The handler checks if it is enabled for the level of the LogRecord. If not enabled, the process stops.

2. *Filter attached to handler*: The handler checks if any filters attached to it reject the LogRecord. If a filter rejects it, the process stops.

3. *Emit*: If the LogRecord passes the filter check, the handler emits the log record, which includes formatting and outputting the log message.

Logger Propagation

1. propagate *check*: After passing the LogRecord to its handlers, the logger checks if the propagate attribute is set to True.

2. *Parent logger check*: If propagate is True, the logger checks if there is a parent logger.

3. *Set logger to parent*: If a parent logger exists, the current logger is set to its parent, and the process repeats from the step of passing the LogRecord to the handlers of the current logger.

4. *End of flow*: If there are no parent loggers, the process stops.

This flow ensures that log messages are processed efficiently, filtered, and formatted correctly before being outputted to the desired destinations.

Logging in Libraries

Applications are responsible for configuring logging. Libraries should only create loggers and leave configuration tasks to the application. This separation of responsibilities ensures that the library's logging can be easily integrated into any application's logging system.

If we are developing a library that will be used by others in their applications, there are a few things to keep in mind:

- *Use __name__ for loggers*: Create loggers using the module's __name__ to ensure unique loggers for each module. This helps in distinguishing logs from different parts of the library.

- *Avoid adding handlers*: Configuring logging (adding handlers, formatters, and filters) should be the responsibility of the application developer. As a library developer, you should avoid adding handlers to your loggers. Instead, attach a NullHandler to prevent "No handler found" warnings and leave the configuration to the application.

Conclusion

We have explored various components of Python's logging system and covered their interactions, from the creation of the log record to its output by handlers.

1. *Loggers*: Primary objects used to generate log messages. They are named and can have multiple handlers attached to them.

2. *LogRecord*: Object that contains all the information about a logging event, such as message, level, and timestamp.

3. *Formatters*: Define the structure and content of log messages, making them readable and consistent.

4. *Filters*: Provide granular control over which log records are processed by allowing or denying log records based on specific criteria.

5. *LoggerAdapter*: Enhances log records with additional contextual information.

6. *Logging handlers*: Direct log messages to various destinations like files, consoles, or external systems.

7. *Log propagation*: Mechanism by which log messages generated by a logger are passed up to its parent loggers, ensuring centralized logging control.

These components work together to create a robust logging system. Loggers emit log records, which are formatted according to the configured formatters. Filters then decide whether to send the record to any handlers based on defined criteria. Finally, handlers write the formatted log messages to their designated destinations.

CHAPTER 5

Exceptions

In the previous chapter, we explored Python's logging module and saw how to record useful runtime information to help monitor and debug our applications.

Now, we turn our attention to another key aspect of building reliable software: handling exceptions. In Python programming, exceptions and tracebacks are essential concepts that enable us to deal with errors gracefully and debug our code effectively. Exceptions are events that disrupt the normal flow of a program, often caused by invalid operations or unexpected conditions. When an exception occurs, Python generates a traceback—a detailed report showing the call stack and the exact line where the error was raised.

In this chapter, we'll learn how to raise, catch, and handle exceptions, how tracebacks work, and how to use them to pinpoint and fix bugs. Understanding these concepts will help us write more robust and fault-tolerant code.

Exceptions in Python

Exceptions are events that disrupt the normal program execution flow. They occur when the program encounters an error or an unexpected condition that it cannot handle. In Python, exceptions are a powerful mechanism for managing errors and other exceptional events. They allow us to write robust and fault-tolerant code by providing a way to handle errors rather than letting the program crash with an error. By using exceptions, we can ensure that our program can recover from unexpected situations and continue to operate smoothly.

© Adarsh Divakaran 2025
A. Divakaran, *Deep Dive Python*, https://doi.org/10.1007/979-8-8688-1261-3_5

Built-In Exceptions

Python includes a variety of built-in exceptions to handle different error situations. Here are some common built-in exceptions:

- *TypeError*: Raised when an operation or function is applied to an object of an inappropriate type

- *ValueError*: Raised when an operation or function receives an argument of the correct type but an inappropriate value

- *NameError*: Raised when a local or global name is not found

- *IndexError*: Raised when a sequence subscript is out of range

- *KeyError*: Raised when a mapping key is not found

- *ZeroDivisionError*: Raised when the second argument of a division or modulo operation is zero

- *FileNotFoundError*: Raised when a file or directory is requested but cannot be found

Tracebacks

A traceback is a report that provides information about the sequence of events leading up to an error in a program. When an exception occurs, Python generates a traceback to help developers understand where and why the error happened. The traceback includes details about the call stack, showing the lines of code that were executed before the error occurred. This information is invaluable for debugging and fixing issues in the code.

The below snippet creates a ZeroDivisionError:

```python
def divide(a, b):
  return a / b

def main():
  result = divide(10, 0)
  print(result)

main()
```

Running the above code leads to a traceback output similar to the one below:

```
Traceback (most recent call last):
  File "...\traceback_example.py", line 8, in <module>
    main()
  File "...\traceback_example.py", line 5, in main
    result = divide(10, 0)
             ^^^^^^^^^^^^^
  File "...\traceback_example.py", line 2, in divide
    return a / b
           ~~^~~
ZeroDivisionError: division by zero
```

The traceback shows the sequence of function calls that led to the error, making it easier for us to identify and fix the problem.

Exception Base Classes and Exception Hierarchy

The BaseException and Exception Classes

BaseException

BaseException is the root class for all built-in exceptions in Python. It's the top-level parent class in the exception hierarchy. All exceptions in Python must be instances of a class that derives from BaseException.

- BaseException has a few parameters that it can accept:
  - args: A tuple of arguments passed to the exception constructor
  - with_traceback(tb): A method to set a new traceback for the exception

- System-exiting exceptions like SystemExit, KeyboardInterrupt, and GeneratorExit are direct subclasses of BaseException.

Exception

Exception is a direct subclass of BaseException. All built-in, non-system-exiting exceptions are derived from this class.

Below are a few pointers about the Exception class and its usage:

1. All user-defined exceptions should be derived from the Exception class or one of its subclasses, not directly from BaseException.

    From CPython docs:

    The built-in exception classes can be subclassed to define new exceptions; programmers are encouraged to derive new exceptions from the Exception class or one of its subclasses and not from BaseException.

2. When we use a try–except block to catch Exception, we will catch most errors and exceptions, but not system-exiting ones.

3. The Exception class inherits all the parameters and methods from BaseException.

4. Many built-in exception classes like ValueError, TypeError, and RuntimeError are subclasses of Exception.

Built-In Exception Hierarchy

The inheritance hierarchy of built-in exceptions as of Python 3.12 is given below as per the CPython documentation:

```
BaseException
 ├─── BaseExceptionGroup
 ├─── GeneratorExit
 ├─── KeyboardInterrupt
 ├─── SystemExit
 └─── Exception
       ├─── ArithmeticError
       │     ├─── FloatingPointError
       │     ├─── OverflowError
       │     └─── ZeroDivisionError
       ├─── AssertionError
       ├─── AttributeError
       ├─── BufferError
       ├─── EOFError
```

```
├── ExceptionGroup [BaseExceptionGroup]
├── ImportError
│       └── ModuleNotFoundError
├── LookupError
│       ├── IndexError
│       └── KeyError
├── MemoryError
├── NameError
│       └── UnboundLocalError
├── OSError
│       ├── BlockingIOError
│       ├── ChildProcessError
│       ├── ConnectionError
│       │       ├── BrokenPipeError
│       │       ├── ConnectionAbortedError
│       │       ├── ConnectionRefusedError
│       │       └── ConnectionResetError
│       ├── FileExistsError
│       ├── FileNotFoundError
│       ├── InterruptedError
│       ├── IsADirectoryError
│       ├── NotADircctoryError
│       ├── PermissionError
│       ├── ProcessLookupError
│       └── TimeoutError
├── ReferenceError
├── RuntimeError
│       ├── NotImplementedError
│       └── RecursionError
├── StopAsyncIteration
├── StopIteration
├── SyntaxError
│       └── IndentationError
│               └── TabError
├── SystemError
```

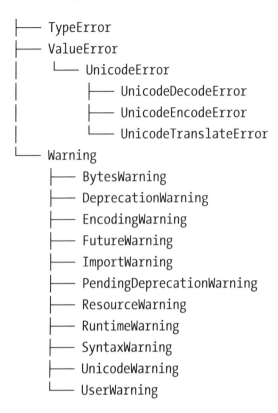

```
├──── TypeError
├──── ValueError
│        └──── UnicodeError
│                 ├──── UnicodeDecodeError
│                 ├──── UnicodeEncodeError
│                 └──── UnicodeTranslateError
└──── Warning
         ├──── BytesWarning
         ├──── DeprecationWarning
         ├──── EncodingWarning
         ├──── FutureWarning
         ├──── ImportWarning
         ├──── PendingDeprecationWarning
         ├──── ResourceWarning
         ├──── RuntimeWarning
         ├──── SyntaxWarning
         ├──── UnicodeWarning
         └──── UserWarning
```

At the top of the hierarchy is BaseException, the root class from which all exceptions derive. Directly under BaseException are critical system-related exceptions like SystemExit, KeyboardInterrupt, and GeneratorExit, as well as BaseExceptionGroup, which is used for grouping exceptions (introduced in Python 3.12). The Exception class, a subclass of BaseException, serves as the base for most user-defined and built-in exceptions. It branches into various specific exception classes, such as ArithmeticError for numerical issues, LookupError for indexing problems, and OSError for operating system–related errors. Each of these categories further subdivides into more granular exceptions, like ZeroDivisionError under ArithmeticError and FileNotFoundError under OSError, allowing for more precise error handling.

Handling Exceptions: The **try** Block

The try block in Python is a fundamental construct used for exception handling. It allows us to test a block of code for errors and handle them gracefully without crashing the program. When an exception occurs within the try block, the control is immediately transferred to the corresponding except block, where the error can be managed. The try block can also be paired with else and finally blocks to execute code that should run if no exceptions occur or to perform cleanup actions, respectively.

Here are some key points to consider when working with exceptions using the try block:

1. *Multiple except blocks*

    Python allows the use of multiple except blocks following a single try block. The interpreter checks these blocks sequentially until it finds a matching exception type.

2. *Exception inheritance*

    Except blocks can handle not only the specified exception but also its child exceptions. Due to this, except Exception catches almost all of the exceptions (other than system-exit exceptions, which are inherited from BaseException).

3. *Exception re-raising*

    Within an except block, we can re-raise a caught exception using a simple "raise" statement without arguments. This is useful for adding context or logging before propagating the exception.

4. *Catching* BaseException

    While it's possible to catch BaseException to handle all possible exceptions, this practice is generally discouraged. It can inadvertently mask critical errors and make debugging more challenging.

5. *Catching* Exception

    Using Exception as a catch-all in a try–except block will handle most errors and exceptions, excluding system-exiting ones. However, it is advisable to catch specific exception classes individually whenever possible. This approach minimizes the risk of masking unknown exceptions, which can complicate debugging and hinder the identification of the root cause of issues.

6. *Custom exception creation*

When developing custom exceptions, it's recommended to subclass Exception or one of its existing subclasses. This practice ensures proper integration with Python's exception-handling system and maintains consistency with built-in exceptions.

In this section, we will explore various usage examples of the try block:

1. *Single* except *block*

This configuration is used to catch a specific type of exception. If the exception matches the type specified, the code within the except block is executed. Other exceptions occurring with the block remain unhandled and will be raised.

```python
# File: llama-index-core/llama_index/core/utils.py

class GlobalsHelper:

    @property
    def stopwords(self) -> List[str]:
        """Get stopwords."""
        if self._stopwords is None:
            try:
                import nltk
                from nltk.corpus import stopwords
            except ImportError:
                raise ImportError(
                    "`nltk` package not found, please run `pip
                    install nltk`"
                )

            try:
                nltk.data.find("corpora/stopwords",
                paths=[self._nltk_data_dir])
            except LookupError:
                nltk.download("stopwords", download_dir=self._
                nltk_data_dir)
            self._stopwords = stopwords.words("english")
        return self._stopwords
```

The snippet above from *llamaindex* contains two try blocks, both with a single except. In the first case, the statement handles an ImportError by raising a custom exception message. All other exceptions encountered when executing the code within the block remain unhandled.

2. *Multiple* except *blocks*

Multiple except blocks can be used to handle different types of exceptions separately. Each except block specifies a different exception type, allowing for customized handling based on the exception raised.

```
# File: celery/worker/worker.py

class WorkController:
 def start(self):
    try:
        self.blueprint.start(self)
    except WorkerTerminate:
        self.terminate()
    except Exception as exc:
        logger.critical("Unrecoverable error: %r", exc, exc_
        info=True)
        self.stop(exitcode=EX_FAILURE)
    except SystemExit as exc:
        self.stop(exitcode=exc.code)
    except KeyboardInterrupt:
        self.stop(exitcode=EX_FAILURE)
```

The snippet above from *Celery* performs appropriate actions based on the type of the encountered exception.

3. except *block with an exceptions tuple*

A single except block can match multiple exception types when the types are specified as a tuple. This can be used when a group of exceptions needs to be handled in a similar manner.

```
# File: src/transformers/trainer.py

class Trainer:

    ...

    def num_examples(self, dataloader: DataLoader) -> int:
        """
        Helper to get number of samples in a [`~torch.utils.data.
        DataLoader`] by accessing its dataset. When
        dataloader.dataset does not exist or has no length,
        estimates as best it can
        """
        try:
            dataset = dataloader.dataset
            # Special case for IterableDatasetShard, we need to
            dig deeper
            if isinstance(dataset, IterableDatasetShard):
                return len(dataloader.dataset.dataset)
            return len(dataloader.dataset)
        except (
            NameError,
            AttributeError,
            TypeError,
        ):  # no dataset or length, estimate by length of dataloader
            return len(dataloader) * self.args.per_device_train_
            batch_size
```

In the above snippet from *transformers,* multiple expected errors
are grouped and handled inside a single except block.

4. else *block*

The else block is optional and follows the except blocks. It is
executed only if no exceptions were raised in the try block. This is
useful for code that should run only if the try block succeeds.

```
# File: src/sentry/utils/safe.py

def safe_execute(func: Callable[P, R], *args: P.args, **kwargs:
P.kwargs) -> R | None:
    try:
        result = func(*args, **kwargs)
    except Exception as e:
        if hasattr(func, "im_class"):
            cls = func.im_class
        else:
            cls = func.__class__

        func_name = getattr(func, "__name__", str(func))
        cls_name = cls.__name__
        logger = logging.getLogger(f"sentry.safe.{cls_name.
        lower()}")

        logger.exception("%s.process_error", func_name,
        extra={"exception": e})
        return None
    else:
        return result
```

The snippet above from *sentry* is used to safely execute a function, making sure it won't raise any exceptions. The `else` block is used here to return the actual return value of the function call, in case no exceptions occur during the call.

5. finally *block*

    The `finally` block is also optional and is executed regardless of whether an exception was raised or not. It is typically used for cleanup actions, such as closing files or releasing resources.

```
# File: epr.py

def open_media(scr, epub, src):

    sfx = os.path.splitext(src)[1]
    fd, path = tempfile.mkstemp(suffix=sfx)
```

```
try:
    with os.fdopen(fd, "wb") as tmp:
        tmp.write(epub.file.read(src))
    # run(VWR +" "+ path, shell=True)
    subprocess.call(
        VWR + [path],
        # shell=True,
        stdout=subprocess.DEVNULL,
        stderr=subprocess.DEVNULL
    )
    k = scr.getch()
finally:
    os.remove(path)
return k
```

In the above example, the `finally` block is used to remove
a temporary file created by the parent function regardless of
whether an exception occurs during execution or not.

Exception Chaining

In Python, when an exception occurs while handling another exception, it can lead to
exception chaining.

When raising a new exception while another exception is already being handled, the
new exception's `__context__` attribute is automatically set to the handled exception.
This implicit exception context can be supplemented with an explicit cause by using
`from` with `raise` like `raise new_exc from original_exc`.

The expression following `from` must be an exception or None.

The `cause`, `context`, and `suppress_context` attributes of exception objects provide
additional information about the relationships between exceptions, which can be useful
for debugging and understanding the flow of errors.

The __cause__, __context__, and __suppress_context__ Attributes

__cause__

The __cause__ attribute on an exception object is used for explicit exception chaining. It's set when we raise a new exception from within an except block using the raise ... from ... syntax.

```
try:
  1 / 0
except ZeroDivisionError as e:
  raise ValueError("Can't divide by zero!") from e
```

Executing the above snippet will give the below traceback output:

```
Traceback (most recent call last):
  File "...\cause.py", line 2, in <module>
    1 / 0
    ~~^~~
ZeroDivisionError: division by zero
```

The above exception was the direct cause of the following exception:

```
Traceback (most recent call last):
  File "...\cause.py", line 4, in <module>
    raise ValueError("Can't divide by zero!") from e
ValueError: Can't divide by zero!
```

In this case, the ValueError object's __cause__ would point to the original ZeroDivisionError.

__context__

The **context** attribute is used for implicit exception chaining. It's automatically set by Python when a new exception is raised while handling another exception.

```
try:
    try:
        1 / 0
    except ZeroDivisionError:
        int('not a number')
except ValueError as e:
    print(f"Caught: {e}")
    print(f"Context: {e.__context__}")
    raise
```

The snippet will produce a traceback similar to the one shown below:

```
Caught: invalid literal for int() with base 10: 'not a number'
Context: division by zero

Traceback (most recent call last):
  File "...\context.py", line 3, in <module>
    1 / 0
    ~~^~~
ZeroDivisionError: division by zero

During handling of the above exception, another exception occurred:

Traceback (most recent call last):
  File "...\context.py", line 5, in <module>
    int('not a number')
ValueError: invalid literal for int() with base 10: 'not a number'
```

Here, the ValueError object's (e) __context__ points to the ZeroDivisionError that was being handled when the ValueError occurred.

__suppress_context__

The __suppress_context__ attribute of an exception object is a boolean that controls whether the exception context should be displayed. Setting __cause__ implicitly sets the __suppress_context__ attribute to True.

```python
try:
    1 / 0
except ZeroDivisionError:
    try:
        raise ValueError("A custom error message") from None
    except ValueError as e:
        print(f"Suppress context: {e.__suppress_context__}")
        raise
```

The code will produce the following traceback:

```
Suppress context: True
Traceback (most recent call last):
  File "...suppress_context.py", line 5, in <module>
    raise ValueError("A custom error message") from None
ValueError: A custom error message
```

In this example, __suppress_context__ is True, so the original ZeroDivisionError context is not displayed in the traceback.

Raise from Exception

Below is a snippet from the *homeassistant* library showcasing an example of providing an explicit exception context:

```python
# File: homeassistant/helpers/http.py

class HomeAssistantView:
    """Base view for all views."""

    url: str | None = None
    extra_urls: list[str] = []
    # Views inheriting from this class can override this
    requires_auth = True
    cors_allowed = False
```

```python
    @staticmethod
    def json(
        result: Any,
        status_code: HTTPStatus | int = HTTPStatus.OK,
        headers: LooseHeaders | None = None,
    ) -> web.Response:
        """Return a JSON response."""
        try:
            msg = json_bytes(result)
        except JSON_ENCODE_EXCEPTIONS as err:
            _LOGGER.error(
                "Unable to serialize to JSON. Bad data found at %s",
                format_unserializable_data(
                    find_paths_unserializable_data(result, dump=json_dumps)
                ),
            )
            raise HTTPInternalServerError from err   # (1)

        response = web.Response(
            body=msg,
            content_type=CONTENT_TYPE_JSON,
            status=int(status_code),
            headers=headers,
            zlib_executor_size=32768,
        )
        ...
```

This snippet demonstrates exception handling and re-raising in a Python web application context. The raise from statement is marked as (1).

The code attempts to serialize a result to JSON. If this fails due to JSON encoding exceptions, it logs an error with details about the unserializable data. Then, instead of letting the original exception propagate, it raises a new HTTPInternalServerError exception using raise from. The raise from syntax explicitly chains the new exception to the original one, preserving the full context of the error. This approach allows the application to convert a low-level serialization error into a more appropriate HTTP-level error while maintaining the original error information for debugging purposes.

Raise from None

The below snippet showcases the Cython definition of an auth function from *edgedb* and illustrates the usage of raise ... from None:

```
# File: edgedb/edb/server/protocol/auth_helpers.pyx

cdef auth_jwt(tenant, prefixed_token: str, user: str, dbname: str):
    ...

    try:
        token = jwt.JWT(
            key=skey,
            algs=["RS256", "ES256"],
            jwt=encoded_token,
        )
    except jwt.JWException as e:
        logger.debug('authentication failure', exc_info=True)
        raise errors.AuthenticationError(
            f'authentication failed: {e.args[0]}'
        ) from None
    except Exception as e:
        logger.debug('authentication failure', exc_info=True)
        raise errors.AuthenticationError(
            f'authentication failed: cannot decode JWT'
        ) from None

    try:
        claims = json.loads(token.claims)
    except Exception as e:
        raise errors.AuthenticationError(
            f'authentication failed: malformed claims section in JWT'
        ) from None
```

The code attempts to decode and validate a JWT. If specific JWT-related exceptions occur, or if there's any other exception during token processing, it logs the error and raises a new AuthenticationError with a custom message. The raise from None syntax is used to raise these new exceptions.

`raise from None` explicitly breaks the exception chain, suppressing the original exception's traceback. This approach is used here to abstract away the low-level details of the authentication failure, presenting only a high-level authentication error to the caller.

The same pattern is repeated when parsing the JWT claims, ensuring that any issues during this process also result in a generic `AuthenticationError` without exposing the underlying exception details.

Exceptions in Threads and Processes

In multithreaded and multiprocess Python applications, exception handling takes on additional complexity. This section explores the nuances of exception handling in threads and processes, highlighting key differences from single-threaded execution.

Exceptions in Threads

When working with threads in Python, it should be kept in mind that exceptions raised in threads other than the main thread behave differently from those in the main execution context. These exceptions do not propagate to the main thread by default. Instead, when an unhandled exception occurs in a secondary thread, Python logs the error to stderr and allows the thread to exit silently. This behavior can lead to subtle bugs if not properly managed, as the main program may continue execution unaware of failures in its threads.

```python
from threading import Thread

def thread_function():
    raise Exception("Error occurred")

t = Thread(target=thread_function)
t.start()
t.join()
print("Script completed successfully")
```

Even though the thread_function raises an exception, it won't interrupt the main thread. The program will print the message "Script completed successfully" and end normally.

Handling Exceptions in ThreadPoolExecutor

For more controlled exception handling in threaded environments, the ThreadPoolExecutor class can be used. When using a ThreadPoolExecutor, exceptions can be managed through the future objects returned by the submit() method. By calling future.result(), we can retrieve the result of the thread's execution or re-raise any exception that occurred within the thread. This approach allows for centralized error handling and provides a mechanism to propagate exceptions from worker threads back to the main execution context.

The below snippet shows an example where the exceptions of the tasks submitted to the thread pool are handled from the main thread:

```python
# File: audius-protocol/packages/discovery-provider/src/tasks/index_spl_
token.py
def parse_sol_tx_batch(
    db, solana_client_manager, redis, tx_sig_batch_records, retries=10
):
    """

    Parse a batch of solana transactions in parallel by calling
    parse_sol_play_transaction with a ThreaPoolExecutor

    """

    ...

    last_tx_in_batch = tx_sig_batch_records[0]
    challenge_bus = index_solana_plays.challenge_event_bus

    # Process each batch in parallel
    with concurrent.futures.ThreadPoolExecutor() as executor:
        parse_sol_tx_futures = {
            executor.submit(
                parse_sol_play_transaction, solana_client_manager, tx_
                sig, redis
            ): tx_sig
            for tx_sig in tx_sig_batch_records
        }
        try:
```

```
    for future in concurrent.futures.as_completed(
        parse_sol_tx_futures, timeout=45
    ):
        result = future.result()
        ...

except Exception as exc:
    logger.error(
        f"index_solana_plays.py | Error parsing sol play
        transaction: {exc}"
    )
    # timeout in a ThreadPoolExecutor doesn't actually stop
    execution of the underlying thread
    # in order to do that we need to actually clear the queue which
    we do here to force this
    # task to stop execution
    executor._threads.clear()
    concurrent.futures.thread._threads_queues.clear()

    # if we have retries left, recursively call this function again
    if retries > 0:
        return parse_sol_tx_batch(
            db, solana_client_manager, redis, tx_sig_batch_records,
            retries - 1
        )

    # if no more retries, raise
    raise exc
```

The function above (parse_sol_tx_batch) uses a ThreadPoolExecutor to process a batch of Solana transactions in parallel. The code uses concurrent.futures.as_completed() to iterate over the futures as they complete, with a timeout of 45 seconds. If any exception occurs during the execution (including timeouts), it's caught in the except block.

When an exception is caught

1.   The code logs the error.

2.   It clears the executor's thread queue (executor._threads.clear())
     and the global thread queue (concurrent.futures.thread._threads_
     queues.clear()). This is a forceful way to stop all running threads,
     as the normal timeout mechanism doesn't actually stop thread
     execution.

3.   If there are retries left, it recursively calls the function again with
     one less retry.

4.   If no retries are left, it re-raises the exception.

Exceptions in Multiprocessing and ProcessPoolExecutor

Exception behavior in multiprocessing is similar to that of multithreading. Individual
Process exceptions will not affect the main program execution. Also, the behavior
of exceptions in process pools is analogous to that in thread pools. When using a
ProcessPoolExecutor, exceptions in worker processes are captured and can be accessed
through the future objects, similar to ThreadPoolExecutor.

Custom Exception Classes

When writing our own application or library, we can define specific exception classes
that the application developers (or library users) can handle specifically. For example, a
web application framework can have exceptions specific to each HTTP error code.

The below snippet from *werkzeug* showcases the definition of some HTTP
exceptions:

```
# File: src/werkzeug/exceptions.py

class HTTPException(Exception):
    """The base class for all HTTP exceptions. This exception can be called
    as a WSGI application to render a default error page or you can catch
    the subclasses of it independently and render nicer error messages.
    """
```

```python
    code: int | None = None
    description: str | None = None

    def __init__(
        self,
        description: str | None = None,
        response: Response | None = None,
    ) -> None:
        super().__init__()
        if description is not None:
            self.description = description
        self.response = response

    @property
    def name(self) -> str:
        """The status name."""
        from .http import HTTP_STATUS_CODES

        return HTTP_STATUS_CODES.get(self.code, "Unknown Error")
        # type: ignore

    def get_body(
        self,
        environ: WSGIEnvironment | None = None,
        scope: dict[str, t.Any] | None = None,
    ) -> str:
        """Get the HTML body."""
        return (
            "<!doctype html>\n"
            "<html lang=en>\n"
            f"<title>{self.code} {escape(self.name)}</title>\n"
            f"<h1>{escape(self.name)}</h1>\n"
            f"{self.get_description(environ)}\n"
        )
```

```python
    def get_headers(
        self,
        environ: WSGIEnvironment | None = None,
        scope: dict[str, t.Any] | None = None,
    ) -> list[tuple[str, str]]:
        """Get a list of headers."""
        return [("Content-Type", "text/html; charset=utf-8")]

    ...

    def __str__(self) -> str:
        code = self.code if self.code is not None else "???"
        return f"{code} {self.name}: {self.description}"

    def __repr__(self) -> str:
        code = self.code if self.code is not None else "???"
        return f"<{type(self).__name__} '{code}: {self.name}'>"


class Unauthorized(HTTPException):
    """*401* ``Unauthorized``

    Raise if the user is not authorized to access a resource.

    The ``www_authenticate`` argument should be used to set the
    ``WWW-Authenticate`` header.
    """

    code = 401
    description = (
        "The server could not verify that you are authorized to access"
        " the URL requested. You either supplied the wrong credentials"
        " (e.g. a bad password), or your browser doesn't understand"
        " how to supply the credentials required."
    )

    def __init__(
        self,
        description: str | None = None,
        response: Response | None = None,
```

```
        www_authenticate: None | (WWWAuthenticate |
        t.Iterable[WWWAuthenticate]) = None,
    ) -> None:
        super().__init__(description, response)

        from .datastructures import WWWAuthenticate

        if isinstance(www_authenticate, WWWAuthenticate):
            www_authenticate = (www_authenticate,)

        self.www_authenticate = www_authenticate

    def get_headers(
        self,
        environ: WSGIEnvironment | None = None,
        scope: dict[str, t.Any] | None = None,
    ) -> list[tuple[str, str]]:
        headers = super().get_headers(environ, scope)
        if self.www_authenticate:
            headers.extend(("WWW-Authenticate", str(x)) for x in self.www_
            authenticate)
        return headers

class Forbidden(HTTPException):
    """*403* `Forbidden`

    Raise if the user doesn't have the permission for the requested
    resource
    but was authenticated.
    """

    code = 403
    description = (
        "You don't have the permission to access the requested"
        " resource. It is either read-protected or not readable by the"
        " server."
    )
```

Here, the base HTTPException class is derived from the built-in Exception class and is augmented with custom attributes (such as code and description) as well as custom methods (such as get_headers). These can be used to access exception info when these exception objects are being handled. The HTTPException is subclassed again for more specific error classes, such as Unauthorized and Forbidden.

The below snippet from *Flask* uses the HTTPException we saw above:

```
# File: src/flask/ctx.py
class RequestContext:
    def match_request(self) -> None:
        """Can be overridden by a subclass to hook into the matching
        of the request.
        """
        try:
            result = self.url_adapter.match(return_rule=True)
            # type: ignore
            self.request.url_rule, self.request.view_args = result
            # type: ignore
        except HTTPException as e:
            self.request.routing_exception = e
```

This match_request checks for routes matching an incoming request. If an HTTPException or any of its child classes, such as Forbidden, is encountered while doing this, it is saved to the routing_exception attribute of self.request to handle it later.

The user-defined exceptions can be organized into an exception hierarchy similar to the one we have seen in the standard library. When defined this way, we can use the parent exception classes to catch a set of related child exceptions.

The below code from *Celery* showcases the exception hierarchy defined by Celery and a few of its exception classes:

```
# File: celery/exceptions.py

"""Celery error types.

Error Hierarchy
===============
```

- :exc:`Exception`
    - :exc:`celery.exceptions.CeleryError`
        - :exc:`~celery.exceptions.ImproperlyConfigured`
        - :exc:`~celery.exceptions.SecurityError`
        - :exc:`~celery.exceptions.TaskPredicate`
            - :exc:`~celery.exceptions.Ignore`
            - :exc:`~celery.exceptions.Reject`
            - :exc:`~celery.exceptions.Retry`
        - :exc:`~celery.exceptions.TaskError`
            - :exc:`~celery.exceptions.QueueNotFound`
            - :exc:`~celery.exceptions.IncompleteStream`
            - :exc:`~celery.exceptions.NotRegistered`
            - :exc:`~celery.exceptions.AlreadyRegistered`
            - :exc:`~celery.exceptions.TimeoutError`
            - :exc:`~celery.exceptions.MaxRetriesExceededError`
            - :exc:`~celery.exceptions.TaskRevokedError`
            - :exc:`~celery.exceptions.InvalidTaskError`
            - :exc:`~celery.exceptions.ChordError`
        - :exc:`~celery.exceptions.BackendError`
            - :exc:`~celery.exceptions.BackendGetMetaError`
            - :exc:`~celery.exceptions.BackendStoreError`
    - :class:`kombu.exceptions.KombuError`
        - :exc:`~celery.exceptions.OperationalError`

            Raised when a transport connection error occurs while
            sending a message (be it a task, remote control command error).

        .. note::
            This exception does not inherit from
            :exc:`~celery.exceptions.CeleryError`.
    - **billiard errors** (prefork pool)
        - :exc:`~celery.exceptions.SoftTimeLimitExceeded`
        - :exc:`~celery.exceptions.TimeLimitExceeded`
        - :exc:`~celery.exceptions.WorkerLostError`
        - :exc:`~celery.exceptions.Terminated`

```
- :class:`UserWarning`
    - :class:`~celery.exceptions.CeleryWarning`
        - :class:`~celery.exceptions.AlwaysEagerIgnored`
        - :class:`~celery.exceptions.DuplicateNodenameWarning`
        - :class:`~celery.exceptions.FixupWarning`
        - :class:`~celery.exceptions.NotConfigured`
        - :class:`~celery.exceptions.SecurityWarning`
- :exc:`BaseException`
    - :exc:`SystemExit`
        - :exc:`~celery.exceptions.WorkerTerminate`
        - :exc:`~celery.exceptions.WorkerShutdown`
"""

...

class CeleryError(Exception):
    """Base class for all Celery errors."""

class TaskPredicate(CeleryError):
    """Base class for task-related semi-predicates."""

class Retry(TaskPredicate):
    """The task is to be retried later."""

    #: Optional message describing context of retry.
    message = None

    #: Exception (if any) that caused the retry to happen.
    exc = None

    #: Time of retry (ETA), either :class:`numbers.Real` or
    #: :class:`~datetime.datetime`.
    when = None

    def __init__(
        self, message=None, exc=None, when=None, is_eager=False, sig=None,
        **kwargs
    ):
```

```
        from kombu.utils.encoding import safe_repr

        self.message = message
        if isinstance(exc, str):
            self.exc, self.excs = None, exc
        else:
            self.exc, self.excs = (
                get_pickleable_exception(exc),
                safe_repr(exc) if exc else None,
            )
        self.when = when
        self.is_eager = is_eager
        self.sig = sig
        super().__init__(self, exc, when, **kwargs)

    def humanize(self):
        if isinstance(self.when, numbers.Number):
            return f"in {self.when}s"
        return f"at {self.when}"

    def __str__(self):
        if self.message:
            return self.message
        if self.excs:
            return f"Retry {self.humanize()}: {self.excs}"
        return f"Retry {self.humanize()}"

    def __reduce__(self):
        return self.__class__, (self.message, self.exc, self.when)
```

...

The defined exceptions start with a base CeleryError class that inherits from Python's built-in Exception class. From there, it branches out into various specialized exception types like TaskPredicate, TaskError, and BackendError, each representing different categories of errors that can occur within Celery. The structure also includes a Retry class, which is a special type of exception used to indicate that a task should be retried, with additional attributes to specify retry details such as timing and reason.

The traceback Module

The traceback module in Python is a powerful tool for working with and manipulating the stack traces of exceptions. When an exception occurs, Python generates a stack trace that provides a detailed report of the call stack at the point where the exception was raised. This information is invaluable for debugging, as it helps developers understand the sequence of function calls that led to the error.

The traceback module provides several functions to extract, format, and print stack traces, making it easier to diagnose and fix issues in code. Here's an introduction to some of the key features and functions of the traceback module.

traceback.print_stack

traceback.print_stack() is a function in Python's traceback module that prints the current call stack to the specified file. It's a useful tool for debugging and understanding the execution flow of a program. This function allows developers to see the sequence of function calls that led to the current point of execution.

Its signature is given below:

```
traceback.print_stack(f=None, limit=None, file=None)
```

It accepts the below arguments:

- f: The stack frame to start from (default is the current frame)

- limit: The maximum number of stack frames to print (default is all frames)

- file: The file-like object to which the stack trace is printed (default is sys.stderr)

Alternatives:

- traceback.format_stack: Returns the stack trace as a list of strings, which can be useful for logging or further processing

- traceback.extract_stack: Extracts the raw traceback information from the current frame as a list of FrameSummary objects, which can be formatted or manipulated as needed

The below snippet from CPython logging code illustrates the usage of print_
stack():

```python
# File: cpython/Lib/logging/__init__.py

class Logger(Filterer):
    """

    Instances of the Logger class represent a single logging channel.
    """

    def findCaller(self, stack_info=False, stacklevel=1):
        """
        Find the stack frame of the caller so that we can note
        the source
        file name, line number and function name.
        """
        f = currentframe()
        #On some versions of IronPython, currentframe() returns None if
        #IronPython isn't run with -X:Frames.
        if f is None:
            return "(unknown file)", 0, "(unknown function)", None
        while stacklevel > 0:
            next_f = f.f_back
            if next_f is None:
                ## We've got options here.
                ## If we want to use the last (deepest) frame:
                break
                ## If we want to mimic the warnings module:
                #return ("sys", 1, "(unknown function)", None)
                ## If we want to be pedantic:
                #raise ValueError("call stack is not deep enough")
            f = next_f
            if not _is_internal_frame(f):
                stacklevel -= 1
        co = f.f_code
        sinfo = None
```

```
    if stack_info:
        with io.StringIO() as sio:
            sio.write("Stack (most recent call last):\n")
            traceback.print_stack(f, file=sio)
            sinfo = sio.getvalue()
            if sinfo[-1] == '\n':
                sinfo = sinfo[:-1]
    return co.co_filename, f.f_lineno, co.co_name, sinfo
```

In this code snippet from Python's logging module, traceback.print_stack() is used within the findCaller method of the Logger class. This usage demonstrates a practical application of stack tracing in a logging context. Here's a breakdown of how it's being used:

1. The findCaller method is responsible for identifying the caller's information (filename, line number, function name) in the stack.

2. When stack_info is set to True, the method provides additional stack trace information.

3. Inside a conditional block, a StringIO object is created to capture the stack trace as a string.

4. traceback.print_stack(f, file=sio) is called, which prints the stack trace starting from the frame f to the StringIO object sio.

5. The resulting stack trace is stored in the sinfo variable, with the trailing newline removed if present.

This usage of print_stack() allows the logging system to include detailed stack information when needed without directly printing it to standard output or error streams. Instead, it captures the stack trace as a string, which can then be included in log messages or used for further processing.

traceback.print_exc

traceback.print_exc is a function in Python's traceback module that prints the stack trace of the most recent exception caught by an except block. This function is useful for debugging, as it provides detailed information about the exception, including the type, value, and traceback.

```
traceback.print_exc(limit=None, file=None, chain=True)
```

- `limit`: The maximum number of stack frames to print (default is all frames) if *limit* is positive. Otherwise, print the last `abs(limit)` entries.

- `file`: The file-like object to which the stack trace is printed (default is `sys.stderr`).

- `chain`: Whether to print the chain of exceptions (default is `True`).

This function is a shorthand for the `print_exception` function in the traceback module.

The snippet below from *localstack* uses the `print_exc()`:

```python
# File: localstack-core/localstack/runtime/main.py

def print_runtime_information(in_docker: bool = False):
    # FIXME: this is legacy code from the old CLI, reconcile with new CLI
    # and runtime output
    from localstack.utils.container_networking import get_main_
    container_name
    from localstack.utils.container_utils.container_client import
    ContainerException
    from localstack.utils.docker_utils import DOCKER_CLIENT

    print()
    print(f"LocalStack version: {constants.VERSION}")
    if in_docker:
        try:
            container_name = get_main_container_name()
            print("LocalStack Docker container name: %s" % container_name)
            inspect_result = DOCKER_CLIENT.inspect_
            container(container_name)
            container_id = inspect_result["Id"]
            print("LocalStack Docker container id: %s" % container_id[:12])
            image_details = DOCKER_CLIENT.inspect_image(inspect_
            result["Image"])
            digests = image_details.get("RepoDigests") or ["Unavailable"]
            print("LocalStack Docker image sha: %s" % digests[0])
```

```python
    except ContainerException:
        print(
            "LocalStack Docker container info: Failed to inspect the
            LocalStack docker container. "
            "This is likely because the docker socket was not mounted
            into the container. "
            "Without access to the docker socket, LocalStack will not
            function properly. Please "
            "consult the LocalStack documentation on how to correctly
            start up LocalStack. ",
            end="",
        )
        if config.DEBUG:
            print("Docker debug information:")
            traceback.print_exc()  # <--(1)
        else:
            print(
                "You can run LocalStack with `DEBUG=1` to get more
                information about the error."
            )
```

Here traceback.print_exc() is used within a conditional block that checks if debugging is enabled (if config.DEBUG:).

1. When an exception occurs while trying to inspect the Docker container (caught by the except ContainerException: block), and debugging is enabled, print_exc() is called to provide detailed error information.

2. By default, print_exc() prints the full stack trace of the most recent exception, including

   – The type of the exception

   – The exception message

   – The sequence of function calls that led to the exception

   In this case, it's used without arguments, which means it will print the entire stack trace.

3. The use of print_exc() here provides developers with detailed debugging information about why the Docker container inspection failed, which can be crucial for troubleshooting in complex environments.

traceback.format_exc

traceback.format_exc returns a string representation of the stack trace for the most recent exception caught by an except block. This is similar to the print_exc() function, but returns a string instead of printing to a file. It accepts the limit and chain arguments, which are also present in print_exc.

The snippet below from *pulumi* showcases a usage of format_exc:

```
# File: pulumi/sdk/python/cmd/pulumi-language-python-exec

def _get_user_stacktrace(user_program_abspath: str) -> str:
    '''grabs the current stacktrace and truncates it to show the only
    stacks pertaining to a user's program'''
    tb = traceback.extract_tb(sys.exc_info()[2])

    for frame_index, frame in enumerate(tb):
        # loop over stack frames until we reach the main program
        # then return the traceback truncated to the user's code
        cur_module = frame[0]
        if get_abs_module_path(user_program_abspath) == get_abs_module_
        path(cur_module):
            # we have detected the start of a user's stack trace
            remaining_frames = len(tb)-frame_index

            # include remaining frames from the bottom by negating
            return traceback.format_exc(limit=-remaining_frames)

    # we did not detect a __main__ program, return normal traceback
    return traceback.format_exc()
```

This function, _get_user_stacktrace, is designed to provide a custom stack trace that focuses on the user's code rather than including the entire stack trace, which might include internal library calls. Here's an explanation of how it uses traceback.format_exc():

1. The function first extracts the full traceback using traceback.extract_tb(sys.exc_info()[2]).

2. It then iterates through the stack frames, looking for the frame that corresponds to the user's main program (identified by user_program_abspath).

3. Once it finds the user's main program frame, it calculates how many frames are left from that point to the end of the traceback (remaining_frames).

4. The key usage of format_exc() here is when the user's main program is found in the stack:

   ```
   return traceback.format_exc(limit=-remaining_frames)
   ```

   Here, format_exc() is called with a negative limit. This tells format_exc() to include only the last remaining_frames number of frames in the formatted traceback. This effectively trims the traceback to only show frames from the user's code onward.

traceback.format_exception_only

The traceback.format_exception_only function returns a list of strings representing the exception type and value. This function is useful when we need a concise representation of the exception without the full traceback.

The function signature can be simplified as follows:

traceback.format_exception_only(etype, value)

- etype: The exception type
- value: The exception value

Since Python 3.10, instead of passing *value*, an exception object can be passed as the first argument. If *value* is provided, the first argument is ignored in order to provide backward compatibility.

traceback.format_exception_only returns a list of strings, each representing a line of the formatted exception type and value.

The snippet below from *certbot* uses traceback.format_exception_only in its logging code:

```python
# File: certbot/certbot/_internal/log.py

def post_arg_parse_except_hook(
    exc_type: Type[BaseException],
    exc_value: BaseException,
    trace: TracebackType,
    debug: bool,
    quiet: bool,
    log_path: str,
) -> None:
    """Logs fatal exceptions and reports them to the user.

    If debug is True, the full exception and traceback is shown to the
    user, otherwise, it is suppressed. sys.exit is always called with a
    nonzero status.

    :param type exc_type: type of the raised exception
    :param BaseException exc_value: raised exception
    :param traceback trace: traceback of where the exception was raised
    :param bool debug: True if the traceback should be shown to the user
    :param bool quiet: True if Certbot is running in quiet mode
    :param str log_path: path to file or directory containing the log

    """
    exc_info = (exc_type, exc_value, trace)

    # Only print human advice if not running under --quiet
    def exit_func() -> None:
        if quiet:
            sys.exit(1)
        else:
            exit_with_advice(log_path)
```

```python
# constants.QUIET_LOGGING_LEVEL or higher should be used to
# display message the user, otherwise, a lower level like
# logger.DEBUG should be used
if debug or not issubclass(exc_type, Exception):
    assert constants.QUIET_LOGGING_LEVEL <= logging.ERROR
    if exc_type is KeyboardInterrupt:
        logger.error("Exiting due to user request.")
        sys.exit(1)
    logger.error("Exiting abnormally:", exc_info=exc_info)
else:
    logger.debug("Exiting abnormally:", exc_info=exc_info)
    # Use logger to print the error message to take advantage of
    # our logger printing warnings and errors in red text.
    if issubclass(exc_type, errors.Error):
        logger.error(str(exc_value))
        exit_func()
    logger.error("An unexpected error occurred:")
    if messages.is_acme_error(exc_value):
        logger.error(
            display_util.describe_acme_error(cast(messages.Error,
            exc_value))
        )
    else:
        output = traceback.format_exception_only(exc_type, exc_
        value)  # <--(1)
        # format_exception_only returns a list of strings each
        # terminated by a newline. We combine them into one string
        # and remove the final newline before passing it to
        # logger.error.
        logger.error("".join(output).rstrip())
exit_func()
```

In the code here, format_exception_only is called in non-debug environments since it returns only the exception type and message without the stack trace.

The call is marked in the comment (1) in the snippet. The `format_exception_only` function returns a list of strings, each representing a line of the formatted exception. In this case, it's typically just one or two lines: the exception type and the exception message. The code below then joins these lines, removes the trailing newline, and writes to stderr:

```
logger.error("".join(output).rstrip())
```

This usage of `format_exception_only()` serves several purposes:

1. *Conciseness*: It provides a brief, to-the-point description of the exception without the potentially lengthy stack trace.

2. For non-debug modes, it gives users just enough information about what went wrong without overwhelming them with technical details.

sys module: **excepthook** and **exc_info**

sys.exc_info

`sys.exc_info` is a function that returns information about the current exception being handled. It provides access to the type, value, and traceback of the most recently raised exception. This function returns the old-style representation of the handled exception. If an exception e is currently handled (so `exception()` would return e), `exc_info()` returns the tuple (`type(e)`, `e`, `e.__traceback__`). This is useful in scenarios where detailed exception information is required for logging, debugging, or custom error-handling routines.

The below snippet from CPython's code module illustrates the usage of `exc_info`:

```
# File: cpython/Lib/code.py

class InteractiveInterpreter:
    """Base class for InteractiveConsole.

    This class deals with parsing and interpreter state (the user's
    namespace); it doesn't deal with input buffering or prompting or
    input file naming (the filename is always passed in explicitly).
```

```
    """

def showsyntaxerror(self, filename=None, **kwargs):
    """Display the syntax error that just occurred.

    This doesn't display a stack trace because there isn't one.

    """
    colorize = kwargs.pop("colorize", False)
    type, value, tb = sys.exc_info()
    sys.last_exc = value
    sys.last_type = type
    sys.last_value = value
    sys.last_traceback = tb
    if filename and type is SyntaxError:
        # Work hard to stuff the correct filename in the exception
        try:
            msg, (dummy_filename, lineno, offset, line) = value.args
        except ValueError:
            # Not the format we expect; leave it alone
            pass
        else:
            # Stuff in the right filename
            value = SyntaxError(msg, (filename, lineno, offset, line))
            sys.last_exc = sys.last_value = value
    if sys.excepthook is sys.__excepthook__:
        lines = traceback.format_exception_only(type, value,
        colorize=colorize)
        self.write("".join(lines))
    else:
        # If someone has set sys.excepthook, we let that take
        precedence
        # over self.write
        sys.excepthook(type, value, tb)
```

In this code snippet, `sys.exc_info()` is used to retrieve information about the current exception. Its usage is as follows:

```
type, value, tb = sys.exc_info()
```

- This line calls `sys.exc_info()` and unpacks its return values into three variables:

  - type: The exception type

  - value: The exception instance

  - tb: The traceback object

- This info is used to handle `SyntaxErrors` specially, modifying the filename if necessary.

- Finally, the exception information is used to format and display the error:

  The use of `sys.exc_info()` here allows the `InteractiveInterpreter` to access and manipulate exception information without interfering with the normal exception-handling process.

sys.excepthook

When an exception other than `SystemExit` is raised and uncaught, the interpreter calls `sys.excepthook` with three arguments, the exception class, the exception instance, and a traceback object. The default `excepthook` function prints out a given traceback and exception to `sys.stderr`.

It has a signature as follows:

```
sys.excepthook(type, value, traceback)
```

It serves as a global exception handler, providing developers with a mechanism to intercept and process unhandled exceptions before they terminate the program. This function allows for customized error reporting, logging, or even attempts at recovery when exceptions occur outside of try–except blocks.

The below snippet from *Ruff* defines a custom excepthook:

```python
# File: python/ruff-ecosystem/ruff_ecosystem/cli.py

def excepthook(type, value, tb):
    if hasattr(sys, "ps1") or not sys.stderr.isatty():
        # we are in interactive mode or we don't have a tty so call
        # the default
        sys.__excepthook__(type, value, tb)
    else:
        import pdb
        import traceback

        traceback.print_exception(type, value, tb)
        print()
        pdb.post_mortem(tb)

def entrypoint():
    args = parse_args()

    if args.pdb:
        sys.excepthook = excepthook

    if args.verbose:
        logging.basicConfig(level=logging.DEBUG)
    else:
        logging.basicConfig(level=logging.INFO)
```

The snippet works as follows:

- In the entrypoint function, the custom excepthook is conditionally set as sys.excepthook = excepthook.

- excepthook checks if the program is in interactive mode (hasattr(sys, "ps1")) or if the standard error is not connected to a terminal (not sys.stderr.isatty()). In these cases, it falls back to the default exception-handling behavior using sys.__excepthook__.

- If the program is not in interactive mode and stderr is connected to a terminal, it provides enhanced exception handling:

  - It imports the pdb (Python Debugger) and `traceback` modules.

  - It prints the exception traceback using `traceback.print_exception`.

  - It then starts a postmortem debugging session using `pdb.post_mortem(tb)`.

Zero-Cost Exceptions

In programming, "zero-cost" typically means that a feature doesn't add any overhead when it's not being used. Python 3.11 introduced a significant performance enhancement for exception handling known as "zero-cost exceptions." This feature makes exception handling in Python much more efficient, especially in code that doesn't raise exceptions. Let's dive into what this means and why it's important.

When working with exception handling, in the case of Python version 3.11 and later, we can expect the following things:

1. *No (significant) performance penalty*: Code that doesn't raise exceptions now runs just as fast as if there were no exception handling at all.

2. *Faster normal execution*: The presence of try–except blocks no longer slows down the execution of the code inside them when no exception occurs.

Traditionally, the overhead of setting up exception handling in Python could impact performance, even if no exceptions were actually raised. This was due to the need to maintain additional state and stack frames to manage potential exceptions.

In Python, two common programming styles for handling potential errors are "Look Before You Leap" (LBYL) and "Easier to Ask for Forgiveness than Permission" (EAFP). LBYL involves checking for conditions that might cause an error before performing an operation, typically using `if` statements. For example, before accessing a dictionary key, we might check if the key exists. On the other hand, EAFP embraces the use of exception handling, where we perform the operation directly and handle any exceptions that arise.

With Python's efficient exception handling, especially after the introduction of zero-cost exceptions, the EAFP style has become even more attractive. It often leads to cleaner, more readable code, and now, with zero-cost exceptions, it doesn't come with a performance penalty when exceptions don't occur. This improvement reinforces Python's philosophy of preferring EAFP in many situations, as it aligns well with Python's goal of writing clear, expressive code without sacrificing performance. However, the choice between LBYL and EAFP still depends on the specific context and the developer's judgment about which style makes the code more readable and maintainable in each particular case.

Conclusion

In this chapter, we have explored the exception-handling landscape in Python and looked into concepts such as built-in exceptions, exception chaining, base classes, tracebacks, and the creation of custom exceptions. By leveraging Python's rich exception-handling mechanisms, we can ensure that our programs are resilient, provide meaningful error messages, and maintain a smooth user experience even in the face of errors. By thoughtfully implementing try–except blocks, utilizing specific exception classes, and creating custom exceptions where necessary, we can build libraries and applications that are both user-friendly and developer-friendly.

## CHAPTER 6

Functions and Functools

In the previous chapter, we looked at how Python handles errors using exceptions and tracebacks, helping us write safer and more predictable code.

Now, we turn our focus to functions—the core building blocks of any Python program. Functions let us break down complex logic into smaller, reusable parts, making our code easier to understand and maintain. In this chapter, we'll explore how Python functions work under the hood, from definition to invocation, and cover function behaviors like default arguments, closures, and variable scopes. We'll also dive into the `functools` module, which offers tools to enhance, wrap, and manipulate functions more effectively.

Positional and Keyword Arguments

Arguments can be passed to functions when called as positional or keyword arguments. Keyword arguments allow us to pass arguments to a function by explicitly specifying the name of the parameter, regardless of their order in the function definition. This can improve the code's readability. We can restrict the argument passing as positional only or keyword only.

Positional-Only Arguments

Positional-only arguments are specified in a function definition by a / symbol after all positional-only parameters. The arguments prior to the / must be supplied only by position.

```python
def greet(name, /, greeting):
    return f"{greeting}, {name}!"

print(greet("Alice", greeting="Hello"))
```

© Adarsh Divakaran 2025
A. Divakaran, *Deep Dive Python*, https://doi.org/10.1007/979-8-8688-1261-3_6

In this function, the argument name must be given by position, whereas the argument greeting can be given by position or keyword.

These are to be used when

- The meaning of the arguments is clear from the context and argument names won't add value to the readability of the code.

- The function parameters have names that are meant to be used internally only.

Keyword-Only Arguments

Keyword-only arguments are specified by an * symbol in the function's parameters, which forces any parameters following it to be provided as keyword arguments.

```python
def greet(*, name, greeting):
    return f"{greeting}, {name}!"

print(greet(name="Alice", greeting="Hello"))
```

Here, both name and greeting must be specified by their names, and it is not possible to pass them as positional arguments.

These are to be used when

- The function is complex and has a large number of arguments; thus, readability is a concern.

- The function performs critical business logic operations and it is better to let the caller know the parameters they are passing explicitly to avoid mix-ups.

Argument-Passing Model in Python

Python uses a model called "pass-by-assignment" or "pass-by-object-reference" for argument passing.

Passing Immutable Objects

When an immutable object (like an integer, float, tuple, or string) is passed to a function, any changes to that object within the function do not affect the original object outside the function.

```python
def modify(x):
    x = 15
    print("Inside modify():", x)

a = 10
modify(a)
print("Outside modify():", a)

""" Output:
Inside modify(): 15
Outside modify(): 10
"""
```

The variable a in the outer scope remains unchanged.

Passing Mutable Objects

When a mutable object (like a list, dictionary, or set) is passed, the function receives a reference to the same object.

```python
def modify(lst):
    lst.append(4)
    print("Inside modify():", lst)

my_list = [1, 2, 3]
modify(my_list)
print("Outside modify():", my_list)

""" Output:
Inside modify(): [1, 2, 3, 4]
Outside modify(): [1, 2, 3, 4]
"""
```

Here, the changes to my_list inside the function also affect my_list outside the function.

The behavior of passing arguments in Python is consistent with how normal assignment statements work in the language (hence called pass-by-assignment).

Argument Unpacking and Packing

Argument unpacking allows a function to receive arguments dynamically from sequences (like lists or tuples) or dictionaries.

Argument Unpacking

We can use the * operator to unpack a sequence (such as a list or tuple) into positional arguments for a function.

```python
def add(a, b, c):
    return a + b + c

numbers = [1, 2, 3]
print(add(*numbers))  # Output: 6
```

In this example, the list numbers is unpacked into the function add. Each element of the list corresponds to one of the function's parameters.

The ** operator allows us to unpack a dictionary into keyword arguments for a function. The keys must match the parameter names of the function.

```python
def describe_pet(name, species):
    print(f"{name} is a {species}.")

pet_info = {"name": "Baxter", "species": "dog"}
describe_pet(**pet_info)

# Output: Baxter is a dog.
```

Here, pet_info is a dictionary whose keys correspond to the parameter names of the describe_pet function.

We can also combine * and ** in a single function call to unpack positional and keyword arguments simultaneously.

```
def greet(name, punctuation, greeting):
    print(f"{greeting}, {name}{punctuation}")

args = ["Alice"]
kwargs = {"greeting": "Hello", "punctuation": "!"}
greet(*args, **kwargs)

# Output: Hello, Alice!
```

This example demonstrates how to unpack both a list and a dictionary to pass arguments to a function.

Argument Packing

Argument packing can be used in function definitions to accept an arbitrary number of positional or keyword arguments.

- *args collects all the positional arguments passed to the function into a tuple.

- **kwargs collects all the keyword arguments passed to the function into a dictionary.

  ```
  def do_something(*args, **kwargs):
      print("Positional arguments:", args)
      print("Keyword arguments:", kwargs)

  # Calling the function with a mix of positional and keyword
  arguments
  do_something(1, 2, "three", first="apple", second="banana")

  """ Output:
  Positional arguments: (1, 2, 'three')
  Keyword arguments: {'first': 'apple', 'second': 'banana'}
  """
  ```

Argument packing is useful when

- The number of inputs can vary case by case. In this scenario, variable-length arguments can be used instead of overloading for simplicity.

- The function acts as a wrapper and passes around arguments to wrapped functions.

Also, in object-oriented programming, **kwargs can be used in constructors to set attributes of an object dynamically.

Recursion

Recursion in programming is a technique where a function calls itself as a part of its execution. It is often used to solve problems that can be broken down into simpler, smaller problems of the same type. Python supports recursion, but there is a limit on the depth of recursion to prevent stack overflow errors.

The below recursive example for calculating the factorial of a number works for smaller numbers but will lead to an error when the recursion limit is reached:

```python
def factorial(n):
    if n == 0:
        return 1
    else:
        return n * factorial(n - 1)

print(factorial(5)) # Output: 120

print(factorial(3000))
""" Stack trace
  ...
  File "...\recursion.py", line 5, in factorial
    return n * factorial(n - 1)
               ^^^^^^^^^^^^^^^^
  [Previous line repeated 996 more times]
RecursionError: maximum recursion depth exceeded
"""
```

When the recursion depth goes over the limit, a `RecursionError` is raised.

For manually overriding the default limit, the `sys` module provides the `setrecursionlimit(limit)` function to set the maximum recursion depth to `limit`, which must be a positive integer.

Default Arguments

Default arguments allow a function to be called with fewer arguments than it is defined to accept. The missing argument values will be substituted with the defined defaults.

Default values are evaluated and assigned only once when the function is defined, not each time the function is called. Due to this, providing mutables as the default arguments can lead to confusing bugs. If a mutable object like a list or dictionary is used as a default argument, and if it is modified during the function execution, the default value is altered permanently. The future calls to the function will refer to the modified value.

The below snippet illustrates a scenario where using mutable defaults results in confusing behavior:

```python
def append_to(element, my_list=[]):
    my_list.append(element)
    return my_list

print(append_to(1))  # Output: [1]
print(append_to(2))  # Output: [1, 2]
```

After the first call to the `append_to` function, `my_list` has become `[1]`, and the subsequent calls to the function will take this new value of `my_list` as default.

Instead of using mutable defaults, a non-mutable value, such as None, should be used in such cases. The below example showcases the corrected approach:

```python
def append_to(element, my_list=None):
    if my_list is None:
        my_list = []
    my_list.append(element)
    return my_list

print(append_to(1))  # Output: [1]
print(append_to(2))  # Output: [2]
```

Nested Functions/Closures

Nested functions in Python are functions defined inside other functions. They are commonly used for organizational purposes, to encapsulate a particular piece of logic within another function. Nested functions can access variables from the enclosing function's scope. This is known as a "closure" when the nested function remembers the values from the enclosing scope even after that scope has finished execution.

Decorators leverage closures to achieve their functionality. This will be explored more in detail in Chapter 9 on decorators.

The nonlocal Keyword

The nonlocal keyword is most commonly used within nested functions where we need to modify a variable defined in an outer function. It is similar to the global keyword in that it allows for the modification of variables defined in outer scope.

The below code from sentry, which is used to write the dependency tree to a file, uses the nonlocal keyword to modify the indentation variable from inside the nested function:

```python
# File: src/sentry/_importchecker.py

def emit_ascii_tree(filename):
    dependencies: dict[str, set[str]] = {}

    for from_name, to_name in observations:
        dependencies.setdefault(from_name, set()).add(to_name)

    indentation = 0

    def _write_dep(f: IO[str], name: str, seen: dict[str, int]) -> None:
        nonlocal indentation  # (1) variable `indentation` is declared
        nonlocal

        marker = f"{indentation:02}"
        children = dependencies.get(name) or set()

        if name in seen:
            count = seen[name]
            seen[name] = count + 1
```

```python
            f.write(f"{'  ' * indentation}-{marker} {name} ({count})\n")
            return

        seen[name] = 1
        f.write(f"{'  ' * indentation}-{marker} {name}:\n")
        indentation += 1

        for child in sorted(children):
            _write_dep(f, child, seen=seen) # (3)
        indentation -= 1

    seen: dict[str, int] = {}
    with open(filename, "w") as f:
        for name in import_order:
            _write_dep(f, name, seen=seen) # (2)

        top_n = sorted(seen.items(), key=lambda x: x[1], reverse=True)
        f.write("\nTop dependencies:\n")
        for name, count in top_n[:30]:
            f.write(f"  - {name}: {count}\n")
```

In the above code, the nonlocal keyword is used to declare that the variable indentation is not local to the function _write_dep. Thus, when indentation is modified inside _write_dep, the change will be reflected in the outer function emit_ascii_tree as well.

The use of nonlocal here is for maintaining the state of indentation across multiple recursive calls to _write_dep. It can be seen in comment # (2) that the _write_dep function is called multiple times in the loop. Each call to _write_dep can either increase the indentation before making recursive calls for child dependencies (seen in comment # (3)) or decrease it once all children are processed, ensuring the output file has a correctly indented tree structure of module dependencies. If nonlocal wasn't used, the currently processed indentation value would get lost after the lifecycle of the _write_dep function completes, i.e., after every single execution.

Higher-Order Functions

A higher-order function is a function that takes either one or more functions as its arguments or returns a function as its result. In Python, the built-in map and `filter` functions are examples of higher-order functions.

map

The signature of the built-in map is as follows:

map(*function, iterable, *iterables*)

map takes a function and an iterable as its arguments and returns an iterator that applies the function to each member of the iterable, yielding results.

```
# File: pysnooper/pycompat.py

def timedelta_parse(s):
    hours, minutes, seconds, microseconds = map(int, s.replace(".", ":").
    split(":"))
```

The code above uses map to convert a string input containing timedelta value to hours, minutes, seconds, and microseconds as integers. If the string 05:01:23.023 is received as the input, it is converted to [05, 01, 23, 03] using the replace and split methods. The map function then applies int() to each, returning an iterator that yields the list members cast to int one by one.

map also accepts an arbitrary number of iterables as arguments after the first two arguments seen above. In such a case, members from these iterables are passed in as function arguments one by one.

```
def multiply(x, y):
    return x * y

list1 = [1, 2, 3, 4]
list2 = [10, 20, 30, 40]

# map with two iterables
result = map(multiply, list1, list2)

print(list(result))  # Output: [10, 40, 90, 160]
```

The result of the map operation gives an iterator that yields 1*10 (first members of list1 and list2) as the first member, followed by 2*20, 3*30, etc.

filter

The signature of filter is as below:

> filter(*function*, *iterable*)

Similar to map, filter accepts a function and an iterable as its arguments. It constructs an iterator from elements of the iterable for which the function returns True. It is used to filter out elements from the iterable.

In the below code from the Pyspider library, the filter() function is used to filter out None values from the result of the map() function:

```python
# File: pyspider/database/mongodb/taskdb.py

def status_count(self, project):
    if project not in self.projects:
        self._list_project()
    if project not in self.projects:
        return {}
    collection_name = self._collection_name(project)

    ...

    def _count_for_status(collection, status):
        total = collection.find({"status": status}).count()
        return {"total": total, "_id": status} if total else None

    c = self.database[collection_name]
    ret = filter(
        lambda x: x,
        map(
            lambda s: _count_for_status(c, s), [self.ACTIVE, self.SUCCESS,
            self.FAILED]
        ),
    )
    ...
```

The `map()` function applies the `_count_for_status(c, s)` function to each element in the list `[self.ACTIVE, self.SUCCESS, self.FAILED]`. This function returns None if the total count for a status is zero.

The `filter()` function is used with a lambda function `lambda x: x`. This filters out any None results from the `map()` function, leaving only the counts for statuses that are not zero in the `ret` iterator.

Function Introspection

Function introspection will allow us to examine various properties of functions at runtime. Introspection is useful for debugging, building development tools, and implementing dynamic features.

Accessing Function Signature

The inspect module in Python provides several tools for inspecting live objects, including functions. The `inspect.signature()` function returns a `Signature` object that includes information about the parameters the function takes.

```python
import inspect

def sample_function(x, y=2, *, z=3):
    pass

sig = inspect.signature(sample_function)
print(sig)
# Output: (x, y=2, *, z=3)

for name, param in sig.parameters.items():
    print(f"{name}: {param.kind}, default={param.default}")

"""Output:
x: POSITIONAL_OR_KEYWORD, default=<class 'inspect._empty'>
y: POSITIONAL_OR_KEYWORD, default=2
z: KEYWORD_ONLY, default=3
"""
```

The above snippet uses the signature objects to dynamically fetch information regarding `sample_function` arguments.

Accessing Annotations

Argument type and return type annotations are accessible via the function's `__annotations__` attribute, which is a dictionary where keys are parameter names and values are the annotations.

```python
def annotated_function(x: int, y: str = "default") -> bool:
    return True

print(annotated_function.__annotations__)
# Output: {'x': <class 'int'>, 'y': <class 'str'>, 'return': <class 'bool'>}
```

It can be seen that the return type of the function is added in the `return` key of the annotations dictionary.

Function Attributes and Docstring

Every function carries a set of attributes that can provide insights into its properties. Some of these attributes are listed below:

      `__name__`: The name of the function

      `__qualname__`: A qualified name to show the function's scope

      `__module__`: The name of the module in which the function is defined

      `__doc__`: Holds the function's documentation string, which is written as the first unassigned string in a function body

```python
def outer_function():
    def my_function():
        """This is a simple function."""
        pass
```

```
        print(my_function.__name__)  # Output: 'my_function'
        print(my_function.__qualname__)  # Output: 'outer_
        function.<locals>.my_function'
        print(my_function.__module__)  # Output: '__main__'
        print(my_function.__doc__)  # Output: 'This is a simple
        function.'

    outer_function()
```

The functools Module

The functools module in Python is a collection of higher-order functions that act on or return other functions. We will explore some of the functools members in the coming sections.

partial

The partial function from functools allows us to freeze a certain number of arguments of a function and generate a new function with fewer parameters.

The below code from setuptools uses partial to create a new function make_rel from os.path.relpath:

```
# File: setuptools/_distutils/filelist.py

def findall(dir=os.curdir):
    """
    Find all files under 'dir' and return the list of full filenames.
    Unless dir is '.', return full filenames with dir prepended.
    """
    files = _find_all_simple(dir)
    if dir == os.curdir:
        make_rel = functools.partial(os.path.relpath, start=dir)
        files = map(make_rel, files)
    return list(files)
```

The signature of os.path.relpath is as below:

> os.path.relpath(*path*, *start=os.curdir*)

In the given code, functools.partial(os.path.relpath, start=dir) is used to create a new function make_rel that behaves like the os.path.relpath function, but with the start argument already set to dir.

When make_rel is called with a file (e.g., make_rel(files[0]), it returns the file's relative filepath from the specified start directory (i.e., dir).

The below code from textual uses partial to bind arguments to a method called _animate, so that it can be passed as a callback function:

```
# File: src/textual/_animator.py

class Animator:
    """An object to manage updates to a given attribute over a period of
    time."""
    def animate(
        self,
        obj: object,
        attribute: str,
        value: Any,
        *,
        final_value: object = ...,
        duration: float | None = None,
        speed: float | None = None,
        easing: EasingFunction | str = DEFAULT_EASING,
        delay: float = 0.0,
        on_complete: CallbackType | None = None,
        level: AnimationLevel = "full",
    ) -> None:
        """Animate an attribute to a new value.

        Args:
            obj: The object containing the attribute.
            attribute: The name of the attribute.
            value: The destination value of the attribute.
```

```
        final_value: The final value, or ellipsis if it is the same as
        ``value``.
        duration: The duration of the animation, or ``None`` to
        use speed.
        speed: The speed of the animation.
        easing: An easing function.
        delay: Number of seconds to delay the start of the
        animation by.
        on_complete: Callback to run after the animation completes.
        level: Minimum level required for the animation to take place
        (inclusive).
    """

    animate_callback = partial(
        self._animate,
        obj,
        attribute,
        value,
        final_value=final_value,
        duration=duration,
        speed=speed,
        easing=easing,
        on_complete=on_complete,
        level=level,
    )
    if delay:
        self._complete_event.clear()
        self._scheduled[(id(obj), attribute)] = self.app.set_timer(
            delay, animate_callback
        )
    else:
        animate_callback()
```

In the provided code, partial is used to create a new function animate_callback from the method self._animate. The arguments obj, attribute, value, final_value, duration, speed, easing, on_complete, and level are fixed for the new function. When animate_callback is called, it doesn't need any arguments because they are already provided by partial.

The newly created function is used as a callback for a timer. When the timer expires, it calls the function without any arguments. By using `partial`, the necessary arguments are provided in advance.

partialmethod

partialmethod from functools allows us to create new methods by freezing arguments from existing method definitions. It is different from `partial` in that the `partialmethod` output is designed to be used as a method definition rather than being directly callable.

The below example from `aim`, an experiment tracking library, uses partialmethod to define new methods from the existing function, _log_message:

```python
# File: aim/sdk/run.py

class BasicRun(BaseRun, StructuredRunMixin):
    ...

    # logging API
    def _log_message(self, level: int, msg: str, **params):
        frame_info = getframeinfo(currentframe().f_back)
        logger_info = (frame_info.filename, frame_info.lineno)
        self.track(
            LogRecord(msg, level, logger_info=logger_info, **params),
            name="__log_records",
        )
        block = level > logging.WARNING
        self._checkins.check_in(flag_name="new_logs", block=block)

    log_error = partialmethod(_log_message, logging.ERROR)
    log_warning = partialmethod(_log_message, logging.WARNING)
    log_info = partialmethod(_log_message, logging.INFO)
    log_debug = partialmethod(_log_message, logging.DEBUG)
```

Here partialmethod is used to define functions such as `log_error` where the first argument (`level`) is fixed with the supplied `logging.ERROR` level.

lru_cache

The lru_cache is an in-memory cache decorator that is used to cache expensive function calls. It can be used to speed up operations when a costly or I/O bound function is called multiple times with the same arguments.

The maximum cache size can be passed using the maxsize argument. "LRU" stands for Least Recently Used, indicating that the caching strategy removes the least recently accessed items first when the cache becomes full.

In the below snippet from Wagtail, lru_cache is used to cache the results of the get_content_languages and get_supported_content_language_variant functions:

```python
# File: wagtail/coreutils.py

@functools.lru_cache(maxsize=None)
def get_content_languages():
    """
    Cache of settings.WAGTAIL_CONTENT_LANGUAGES in a dictionary for easy
    lookups by key.
    """
    content_languages = getattr(settings, "WAGTAIL_CONTENT_
    LANGUAGES", None)
    languages = dict(settings.LANGUAGES)

    if content_languages is None:
        # Default to a single language based on LANGUAGE_CODE
        default_language_code = get_supported_language_variant(settings.
        LANGUAGE_CODE)

        ...

    # Check that each content language is in LANGUAGES
    for language_code, name in content_languages:
        if language_code not in languages:
            raise ImproperlyConfigured(
                "The language {} is specified in WAGTAIL_CONTENT_LANGUAGES
                but not LANGUAGES. "
                "WAGTAIL_CONTENT_LANGUAGES must be a subset of
                LANGUAGES.".format(
                    language_code
```

```
            )
        )

    return dict(content_languages)

@functools.lru_cache(maxsize=1000)
def get_supported_content_language_variant(lang_code, strict=False):
    """

    Return the language code that's listed in supported languages, possibly
    selecting a more generic variant. Raise LookupError if nothing
    is found.
    If `strict` is False (the default), look for a country-specific variant
    when neither the language code nor its generic variant is found.
    lru_cache should have a maxsize to prevent from memory exhaustion
    attacks, as the provided language codes are taken from the HTTP
    request. See also <https://www.djangoproject.com/weblog/2007/oct/26/
    security-fix/>.

    """

    if lang_code:
        # If 'fr-ca' is not supported, try special fallback or language-
        only 'fr'.
        possible_lang_codes = [lang_code]
        try:
            possible_lang_codes.extend(LANG_INFO[lang_code]["fallback"])
        except KeyError:
            pass
        generic_lang_code = lang_code.split("-")[0]
        possible_lang_codes.append(generic_lang_code)
        supported_lang_codes = get_content_languages()

        for code in possible_lang_codes:
            if code in supported_lang_codes and check_for_language(code):
                return code
        if not strict:
```

203

```
        # if fr-fr is not supported, try fr-ca.
        for supported_code in supported_lang_codes:
            if supported_code.startswith(generic_lang_code + "-"):
                return supported_code
    raise LookupError(lang_code)
```

In the get_content_languages function, maxsize is set to None. Since the function does not take any arguments, there will be only a single entry at maximum in the cache since argument combinations are not possible.

In the get_supported_content_language_variant function, lru_cache is used to memoize the language variant data and reuse the result when multiple users supplying the same language codes request for the supported language variants. Here maxsize is set to 1000 to prevent memory exhaustion attacks. This is because the language codes that this function works with are taken from HTTP requests from the user side, and an attacker could potentially send a large number of unique language codes in an attempt to exhaust the server's memory.

When working with lru_cache, it should be noted that

- The positional and keyword arguments provided to the function should be hashable for the cache to work since a dictionary is used to store the cached results.

- The max_size should be chosen carefully so as not to overload the system memory when the cache grows too large.

- Distinct argument patterns may be considered to be distinct by the cache. f(a=0, b=1) and f(b=1, a=0) differ in their keyword argument order and may have two separate cache entries.

The functools module has a simple cache() function also, which is equivalent to lru_cache(max_size=None) in behavior.

cached_property

The cached_property decorator was introduced in Python 3.8 as part of the functools module. It is useful for creating properties (from methods of classes) whose values are computed once and then cached for subsequent use.

This caching approach is beneficial for properties requiring expensive computational tasks or data retrieval operations when accessed, and this computation needs to be executed only once per object instance.

The below snippet from `mkdocs` uses `cached_property` to cache a few of its property methods:

```python
# File: mkdocs/structure/files.py

class File:
    """

    A MkDocs File object.
    """

    src_dir: str | None
    """The OS path of the top-level directory that the source file
    originates from.

    Assumed to be the *docs_dir*; not populated for generated files."""

    dest_dir: str
    """The OS path of the destination directory (top-level site_dir) that
    the file should be copied to."""

    def _get_url(self, use_directory_urls: bool | None = None) -> str:
        """Soft-deprecated, do not use."""
        url = self.dest_uri
        dirname, filename = posixpath.split(url)
        if use_directory_urls is None:
            use_directory_urls = self.use_directory_urls
        if use_directory_urls and filename == "index.html":
            url = (dirname or ".") + "/"
        return urlquote(url)

    url = cached_property(_get_url)
    """The URI of the destination file relative to the destination
    directory as a string."""

    @cached_property
    def abs_src_path(self) -> str | None:
```

```
    """
    The absolute concrete path of the source file. Will use backslashes
    on Windows.

    Note: do not use this path to read the file, prefer `content_
    bytes`/`content_string`.
    """
    if self.src_dir is None:
        return None
    return os.path.normpath(os.path.join(self.src_dir, self.src_uri))

@cached_property
def abs_dest_path(self) -> str:
    The absolute concrete path of the destination file. Will use
    backslashes on Windows."""
    return os.path.normpath(os.path.join(self.dest_dir, self.dest_uri))
```

In the snippet, url, abs_src_path, and abs_dest_path are cached_properties. This is because, by design, the attributes used in the computation of these properties are not expected to change for a File object. Thus, using cached_property will help avoid the computation process each time the property is accessed.

total_ordering

When we need to support comparison-related (equality checks, sorting, etc.) operations on custom classes, we may need to implement the rich comparison operators for the class. The total_ordering decorator simplifies the implementation of ordering methods in classes. It provides a way to define all comparison operations (<, <=, >, >=) based on just two methods, the __eq__ method and one other (__lt__, __le__, __gt__, or __ge__) method. This avoids the need to define each comparison method explicitly.

In the below example from quay, the DataType class has only defined two comparison methods __eq__ and __lt__:

```
# File: quay/data/registry_model/datatype.py

def datatype(name, static_fields):
    """
```

Defines a base class for a datatype that will represent a row from the database, in an abstracted form.
    """

```
@total_ordering
class DataType(object):
    __name__ = name

    def __init__(self, **kwargs):
        self._db_id = kwargs.pop("db_id", None)
        self._inputs = kwargs.pop("inputs", None)
        self._fields = kwargs

        for name in static_fields:
            assert name in self._fields, "Missing field %s" % name

    def __eq__(self, other):
        return self._db_id == other._db_id

    def __lt__(self, other):
        return self._db_id < other._db_id

    ...

return DataType
```

The DataType class is decorated with the total_ordering decorator, and the decorator will supply the rest of the comparison methods.

reduce

The reduce function from functools allows us to apply a particular function to all items in an iterable in order to reduce it to a single value.

reduce has the below syntax:

        reduce(function, iterable[, initializer])

reduce works by taking two items from the iterable at a time and applying the function to them, then using the result along with the next item from the iterable, and repeating this process until all items have been processed.

If the optional `initializer` is present, it is placed before the items of the iterable in the calculation.

In the below snippet from `redash`, the `reduce` function is used to check if a user has all required permissions:

```python
# File: redash/models/users.py

from functools import reduce

class PermissionsCheckMixin(object):
    def has_permission(self, permission):
        return self.has_permissions((permission,))

    def has_permissions(self, permissions):
        has_permissions = reduce(
            lambda a, b: a and b,
            [permission in self.permissions for permission in permissions],
            True,
        )

        return has_permissions
```

The iterable to be passed to `reduce` is created by using a list comprehension, generating a list of boolean values. Each boolean indicates whether a specific permission is included in `self.permissions`.

The `reduce` applies a lambda function (`lambda a, b: a and b`) that performs a logical AND between each pair of elements. This ensures that the final result is `True` only if all items in the list are `True`. The `initializer` value `True` is used to start the reduction process. This is because if `permissions` is empty, the result of the reduction should logically be `True` (i.e., no permissions needed means no permissions to check).

singledispatch

The `singledispatch` decorator allows us to implement function overloading in Python. It allows us to define functions that behave differently based on the type of the first argument it receives.

When a function is decorated with @singledispatch, it is transformed into a generic function. This base function handles the default case. We can then add other cases by using the register() method of the generic function to associate other types with other functions.

The below snippet from OpenMetaData uses singledispatch to initialize SSL for different kinds of database connections:

```python
# File: OpenMetaData/ingestion/src/metadata/utils/ssl_manager.py

from functools import singledispatch

@singledispatch
def check_ssl_and_init(_):
    return None

@check_ssl_and_init.register(MysqlConnection)
@check_ssl_and_init.register(DorisConnection)
def _(connection):
    service_connection = cast(Union[MysqlConnection, DorisConnection],
    connection)
    ssl: Optional[verifySSLConfig.SslConfig] = service_connection.sslConfig
    if ssl and (
        ssl.__root__.caCertificate or ssl.__root__.sslCertificate or ssl.__
        root__.sslKey
    ):
        return SSLManager(
            ca=ssl.__root__.caCertificate,
            cert=ssl.__root__.sslCertificate,
            key=ssl.__root__.sslKey,
        )
    return None

@check_ssl_and_init.register(PostgresConnection)
@check_ssl_and_init.register(RedshiftConnection)
@check_ssl_and_init.register(GreenplumConnection)
```

```python
def _(connection):
    connection = cast(
        Union[PostgresConnection, RedshiftConnection, GreenplumConnection],
        connection,
    )
    if connection.sslMode:
        return SSLManager(
            ca=connection.sslConfig.__root__.caCertificate
            if connection.sslConfig
            else None
        )
    return None
```

Here, the generic function is check_ssl_and_init. Two variants are defined based on the first argument, which denotes the database connection class. Since different database classes have different ways of storing SSL attributes, the overloading here helps to group similar connection classes together and dispatch the call to check_ssl_and_init based on the connection class type.

For type-annotated functions, we can omit specifying the type of the first argument in the register decorator, and that will be inferred from the annotation.

singledispatchmethod

The @singledispatchmethod decorator, introduced in Python 3.8, extends the functionality of @singledispatch to class methods.

The below example from OpenMetaData uses singledispatchmethod to overload functions based on the next argument after self, which is connection in this case:

```python
# File: OpenMetaData/ingestion/src/metadata/utils/ssl_manager.py

class SSLManager:
    "SSL Manager to manage SSL certificates for service connections"

    ...

    @singledispatchmethod
    def setup_ssl(self, connection):
```

```python
    raise NotImplementedError(f"Connection {type(connection)} type not
    supported")

@setup_ssl.register(MysqlConnection)
@setup_ssl.register(DorisConnection)
def _(self, connection):
    # Use the temporary file paths for SSL configuration
    connection = cast(Union[MysqlConnection, DorisConnection],
    connection)
    connection.connectionArguments = (
        connection.connectionArguments or init_empty_connection_
        arguments()
    )
    ssl_args = connection.connectionArguments.__root__.get("ssl", {})
    if connection.sslConfig.__root__.caCertificate:
        ssl_args["ssl_ca"] = self.ca_file_path
    if connection.sslConfig.__root__.sslCertificate:
        ssl_args["ssl_cert"] = self.cert_file_path
    if connection.sslConfig.__root__.sslKey:
        ssl_args["ssl_key"] = self.key_file_path
    connection.connectionArguments.__root__["ssl"] = ssl_args
    return connection

@setup_ssl.register(QlikSenseConnection)
def _(self, connection):
    return {
        "ca_certs": self.ca_file_path,
        "certfile": self.cert_file_path,
        "keyfile": self.key_file_path,
        "check_hostname": connection.validateHostName,
    }

@setup_ssl.register(KafkaConnection)
def _(self, connection):
    connection = cast(KafkaConnection, connection)
    connection.schemaRegistryConfig["ssl.ca.location"] = self.ca_
    file_path
```

```
connection.schemaRegistryConfig["ssl.key.location"] = self.key_
file_path
connection.schemaRegistryConfig[
    "ssl.certificate.location"
] = self.cert_file_path
return connection
```

In this case, the setup_ssl method of the SSLManager class is overridden. Similar to the example seen in the case of singledispatch, the dispatch happens based on the connection argument, which receives the database connection class for SSL setup.

Conclusion

In this chapter, we have explored various functionalities/concepts related to Python functions. We explored the concepts of higher-order functions, nested functions and function introspection, argument packing and unpacking, etc. We also went through some of the useful higher-order functions provided by the functools module.

In addition, we will see more concepts closely related to functions in the upcoming chapters.

1. *Chapter 9 on decorators*: Decorators are (commonly) special functions in Python that modify the behavior of other functions or methods.

2. *Chapter 12 covering generators*: Generators are specialized stateful functions that create iterables using the yield statement.

CHAPTER 7

Classes and Object-Oriented Programming

In the previous chapter, we explored how functions help us structure code in a modular and reusable way.

Building on that foundation, this chapter introduces object-oriented programming in Python using classes. Classes allow us to model real-world entities by grouping related data and behavior together. We'll learn how to define classes, create instances, and organize code using methods and attributes. We'll also explore inheritance and how to design class hierarchies to promote reuse and extensibility in our programs.

Class Methods

The `classmethod` decorator is used to mark a class's method as a class method. A class method is a method that is bound to the class and not the instance of the class. The class method will get access to the class state instead of the objects.

In the below snippet from Apache Airflow, `init` and `reset` are made class methods:

```
# File: airflow/secrets/cache.py

class SecretCache:
    """A static class to manage the global secret cache."""

    __manager: multiprocessing.managers.SyncManager | None = None
    _cache: dict[str, _CacheValue] | None = None
    _ttl: datetime.timedelta

    ...
```

© Adarsh Divakaran 2025
A. Divakaran, *Deep Dive Python*, https://doi.org/10.1007/979-8-8688-1261-3_7

```python
@classmethod
def init(cls):
    """

    Initialize the cache, provided the configuration allows it.

    Safe to call several times.
    """

    if cls._cache is not None:
        return
    use_cache = conf.getboolean(section="secrets", key="use_cache",
    fallback=False)
    if not use_cache:
        return
    if cls.__manager is None:
        # it is not really necessary to save the manager, but doing so
        allows to reuse it between tests,
        # making them run a lot faster because this operation takes
        ~300ms each time
        cls.__manager = multiprocessing.Manager()
    cls._cache = cls.__manager.dict()
    ttl_seconds = conf.getint(section="secrets", key="cache_ttl_
    seconds", fallback=15 * 60)
    cls._ttl = datetime.timedelta(seconds=ttl_seconds)

@classmethod
def reset(cls):
    """Use for test purposes only."""
    cls._cache = None
```

These methods are made class methods instead of instance methods because they are operating on class-level data, not instance-level data. In the provided code, the _cache, __manager, and _ttl are class variables, meaning they are shared across all instances of the class. The init method initializes the class-level cache, and the reset method resets the class-level cache. These operations should affect all instances of the class, not just one, so class methods are used instead of normal methods.

Static Method

The staticmethod decorator is used to define methods that don't access or modify the instance or class data. These methods are not bound to an instance or class. These can be called on the class itself.

Static methods are suitable for

- Utility functions that do not need to access or modify class or instance-specific data.

- Functions that are related to the class logically but do not require access to the class or instance variables. Keeping them as static methods makes the code easier to read and maintain since related functions are grouped within the class structure.

The below code from Bitcoin Core marks build_request and response_is_error methods as static methods:

```
# File: bitcoin/contrib/linearize/linearize-hashes.py

from http.client import HTTPConnection
import json
import base64

settings = {}

class BitcoinRPC:
    def __init__(self, host, port, username, password):
        authpair = "%s:%s" % (username, password)
        authpair = authpair.encode('utf-8')
        self.authhdr = b"Basic " + base64.b64encode(authpair)
        self.conn = HTTPConnection(host, port=port, timeout=30)

    def execute(self, obj):
        try:
            self.conn.request('POST', '/', json.dumps(obj),
                { 'Authorization' : self.authhdr,
                  'Content-type' : 'application/json' })
        except ConnectionRefusedError:
            ...
```

```python
    @staticmethod
    def build_request(idx, method, params):
        obj = { 'version' : '1.1',
            'method' : method,
            'id' : idx }
        if params is None:
            obj['params'] = []
        else:
            obj['params'] = params
        return obj

    @staticmethod
    def response_is_error(resp_obj):
        return 'error' in resp_obj and resp_obj['error'] is not None
```

Both the methods build_request and response_is_error are independent of the class state but are related logically to the BitcoinRPC class. Hence, these are defined as static methods.

Namespace Dictionary

Every class in Python maintains its namespace as a dictionary (excluding slotted classes). This dictionary is accessible using the __dict__ attribute of the class.

```python
from pprint import pprint

class Car:
    wheels = 4  # Class variable

    def __init__(self, make):
        self.make = make  # Instance variable

    def display_info(self):
        print(f"The {self.make} car has {Car.wheels} wheels.")

pprint(Car.__dict__)
""" Output:
mappingproxy({'__dict__': <attribute '__dict__' of 'Car' objects>,
```

```
      '__doc__': None,
      '__init__': <function Car.__init__ at 0x00000238195651C0>,
      '__module__': '__main__',
      '__weakref__': <attribute '__weakref__' of 'Car' objects>,
      'display_info': <function Car.display_info at
      0x0000023819840860>,
      'wheels': 4})
"""
```

The class variables and methods are stored in the class's namespace dictionary.

The namespace dictionary is commonly used for introspecting the class during debugging and to assign dynamic attributes and methods to the class.

Property

The property built-in allows us to define managed attributes of a class. The property attribute behaves similarly to a normal attribute outside the class, but we can define functions that will get run each time the property attribute is accessed, assigned, or deleted.

Below is the signature of the property callable:

class property(*fget=None, fset=None, fdel=None, doc=None*)

A property can have up to four methods associated with it:

1. *Getter*: Retrieves the value of the attribute

2. *Setter*: Sets the value of the attribute

3. *Deleter*: Deletes the attribute

4. *Docstring*: Provides a documentation string for the property

Typically, a property is defined by using the @property decorator.

The example below from Scrapy showcases a read-only decorator. In such a case, setter and deleter definitions are omitted, and the @property decorator is used to decorate the getter method:

```python
# File: scrapy/commands/parse.py

class Command(BaseRunSpiderCommand):
    requires_project = True

    spider = None
    items: Dict[int, List[Any]] = {}
    requests: Dict[int, List[Request]] = {}

    @property
    def max_level(self) -> int:
        max_items, max_requests = 0, 0
        if self.items:
            max_items = max(self.items)
        if self.requests:
            max_requests = max(self.requests)
        return max(max_items, max_requests)
```

The max_level property attribute value is calculated on the fly based on the items and requests attributes of the class, every time the property is accessed. If we try to assign a value to this max_level property, this will lead to an AttributeError.

To define properties with setter and deleter in addition to the getter method, we will need to use their corresponding property decorators. Once the initial method (with a sample name method1) is decorated with @property, we will be using decorator functions method1.setter to decorate the setter method and method1.deleter to decorate the deleter.

The code below from the urllib module of CPython shows the usage of the property attribute with getter, setter, and deleter methods defined:

```python
# File: cpython/Lib/urllib/request.py

class Request:

    ...

    @property
    def full_url(self):
        if self.fragment:
            return '{}#{}'.format(self._full_url, self.fragment)
        return self._full_url
```

```python
@full_url.setter
def full_url(self, url):
    # unwrap('<URL:type://host/path>') --> 'type://host/path'
    self._full_url = unwrap(url)
    self._full_url, self.fragment = _splittag(self._full_url)
    self._parse()

@full_url.deleter
def full_url(self):
    self._full_url = None
    self.fragment = None
    self.selector = ''

@property
def data(self):
    return self._data

@data.setter
def data(self, data):
    if data != self._data:
        self._data = data
        # issue 16464
        # if we change data we need to remove content-length header
        # (cause it's most probably calculated for previous value)
        if self.has_header("Content-length"):
            self.remove_header("Content-length")

@data.deleter
def data(self):
    self.data = None
```

The class Request has two property attributes: full_url and data. Property methods are used here to perform related operations in the class when these are accessed, set, or deleted. In the case of the data attribute, its value is stored in the _data attribute, and whenever it is modified, the Content-length HTTP header is also cleared.

Properties are used when we need to support dynamic operations (such as validation or computations based on the latest state of the class) during operations on the property attribute. These are also used for backward compatibility reasons when we need to give a normal attribute method-like properties.

Private Attributes and Name Mangling

Unlike other popular object-oriented languages, Python objects do not have private attributes, which can only be accessed inside the class's methods. Every object attribute can be accessed from outside of the class as well. Attributes meant to be used internally are prepended by an underscore (_), and it is the developer's responsibility to honor this convention. Many static analysis tools and IDEs also warn developers not to use these attributes (prepended by a single underscore) outside of the class. The example snippet from property that we have discussed already showcases the same:

```python
# File: cpython/Lib/urllib/request.py

class Request:
    ...

    @property
    def data(self):
        return self._data

    @data.setter
    def data(self, data):
        if data != self._data:
            self._data = data
            # issue 16464
            # if we change data we need to remove content-length header
            # (cause it's most probably calculated for previous value)
            if self.has_header("Content-length"):
                self.remove_header("Content-length")

    ...
```

Here, the _data attribute is meant to be private and is not designed to be modified directly. Access and modification for this attribute is proxied by using the data property attribute.

This convention is outlined in the CPython docs:

> "Private" instance variables that cannot be accessed except from inside an object don't exist in Python. However, there is a convention that is followed by most Python code: a name prefixed with an underscore (e.g., _spam) should be treated as a non-public part of the API (whether it is a function, a method, or a data member). It should be considered an implementation detail and subject to change without notice.

Name Mangling

Name mangling is a technique that is used to protect class-private attributes from being unintentionally overridden or accessed. Mangling is applied to identifiers that start with two underscore characters (__) and do not end with more than one underscore. The Python interpreter automatically changes the name of these by adding _ClassName to the beginning of the identifier.

From Python docs:

> Since there is a valid use case for class-private members (namely, to avoid name clashes of names with names defined by subclasses), there is limited support for such a mechanism, called name mangling. Any identifier of the form __spam (at least two leading underscores, at most one trailing underscore) is textually replaced with _classname__spam, where classname is the current class name with leading underscore(s) stripped. This mangling is done without regard to the syntactic position of the identifier, as long as it occurs within the definition of a class.

The below example illustrates name mangling using a private attribute and private method with mangling applied:

```python
class MyClass:
    def __init__(self):
        self.__private_attr = "I am private"

    def __private_method(self):
        return "This is a private method"

    def access_private_method(self):
        return self.__private_method()

obj = MyClass()
```

When the private attribute and method are tried to be accessed directly, an AttributeError is raised as if such a name doesn't exist in the class.

```python
print(obj.__private_attr)  # This will raise an AttributeError
print(obj.__private_method())  # This will also raise an AttributeError
```

However, to access these identifiers, we can either use the access_private_method method or can use the mangled names directly:

```python
# Accessing the private method through a public method
print(obj.access_private_method())  # Output: This is a private method
```

```python
# Accessing private method & attribute using the mangled names
print(obj._MyClass__private_method())  # Output: This is a private method
print(obj._MyClass__private_attr)  # Output: I am private
```

Mangling is designed mostly to avoid accidental modifications, and the attributes can still be accessed by using mangled names.

In the case of inheritance, mangling helps prevent accidental overrides of private attributes:

```python
class BaseClass:
    def __init__(self):
        self.__private_attr = "Base private attribute"

    def __private_method(self):
        return "Base private method"

    def access_private_method(self):
        return self.__private_method()
```

```python
class SubClass(BaseClass):
    def __init__(self):
        super().__init__()
        self.__private_attr = "Subclass private attribute"

    def __private_method(self):
        return "Subclass private method"

    def access_subclass_private_method(self):
        return self.__private_method()

# Instantiate the subclass
obj = SubClass()

# Attempt to access private attributes and methods
print(obj.access_private_method())  # Output: Base private method
print(obj.access_subclass_private_method())  # Output: Subclass
private method

# Accessing the mangled names directly
print(obj._BaseClass__private_attr)  # Output: Base private attribute
print(obj._SubClass__private_attr)  # Output: Subclass private attribute
```

Using mangling helps us to keep the private attributes and methods of the base class and the subclasses separately. Each of the base and subclasses stores its own copy of the private attributes. Let's see the behavior without using mangling.

The snippet below shows a similar inheritance pattern to the one above, with the only difference being that the private attribute names are not mangled (since they start with single underscores only):

```python
class BaseClass:
    def __init__(self):
        self._private_attr = "Base private attribute"

    def _private_method(self):
        return "Base private method"

    def access_private_method(self):
        return self._private_method()
```

```python
class SubClass(BaseClass):
    def __init__(self):
        super().__init__()
        self._private_attr = "Subclass private attribute"

    def _private_method(self):
        return "Subclass private method"

    def access_subclass_private_method(self):
        return self._private_method()

obj = SubClass()

print(obj.access_private_method())  # Output: Subclass private method
print(obj.access_subclass_private_method())  # Output: Subclass
private method
print(obj._private_attr)  # Output: Subclass private attribute
```

Here, a private attribute and method from the base class are overridden by their definitions in the subclass. Mangling is useful when developing large or complex systems where subclasses might unknowingly redefine private attributes or methods.

Note that name mangling is not applied if a name starts and ends with double underscores (like in the case of dunder methods).

Slotted Classes

In Python, __slots__ is a class attribute that is used to define a fixed set of attributes for a class.

From CPython docs:

> __slots__ allows us to explicitly declare data members (like properties) and deny the creation of __dict__ and __weakref__ (unless explicitly declared in __slots__ or available in a parent.)

> The space saved over using **dict** can be significant. Attribute lookup speed can be significantly improved as well.

If the __dict__ variable is not present inside slots, instances cannot be assigned any new variables other than those defined in slots.

The below code is from Scrapy, a web scraping library. The class Link is defined as a slotted class:

```
# File: scrapy/link.py

from typing import Any

class Link:
    """Link objects represent an extracted link by the LinkExtractor.

    Using the anchor tag sample below to illustrate the parameters::

            <a href="https://example.com/nofollow.html#foo"
            rel="nofollow">Dont follow this one</a>

    :param url: the absolute url being linked to in the anchor tag.
            From the sample, this is ``https://example.com/
            nofollow.html``.

    :param text: the text in the anchor tag. From the sample, this is
    ``Dont follow this one``.

    :param fragment: the part of the url after the hash symbol. From the
    sample, this is ``foo``.

    :param nofollow: an indication of the presence or absence of a nofollow
    valuc in the ``rel`` attribute of the anchor tag.
    """

    __slots__ = ["url", "text", "fragment", "nofollow"]

    def __init__(
        self, url: str, text: str = "", fragment: str = "", nofollow:
        bool = False
    ):
        if not isinstance(url, str):
            got = url.__class__.__name__
            raise TypeError(f"Link urls must be str objects, got {got}")
        self.url: str = url
        self.text: str = text
```

```python
        self.fragment: str = fragment
        self.nofollow: bool = nofollow

    def __eq__(self, other: Any) -> bool:
        if not isinstance(other, Link):
            raise NotImplementedError
        return (
            self.url == other.url
            and self.text == other.text
            and self.fragment == other.fragment
            and self.nofollow == other.nofollow
        )

    def __hash__(self) -> int:
        return (
            hash(self.url) ^ hash(self.text) ^ hash(self.fragment) ^
            hash(self.nofollow)
        )

    def __repr__(self) -> str:
        return (
            f"Link(url={self.url!r}, text={self.text!r}, "
            f"fragment={self.fragment!r}, nofollow={self.nofollow!r})"
        )
```

In the Link class, __slots__ is defined as ["url", "text", "fragment", "nofollow"]. Due to this, the instances of the Link class can only have these four attributes. Scrapy is used for web scraping, and a large number of its use cases may involve creating a large number of Link class instances. Since Link is defined as a slotted class, the memory footprint of the program is reduced when compared with using normal classes.

Attribute Access Using __getattr__ and __getattribute__

Python provides several built-in methods to control how the attributes of a class are accessed:

1. __getattribute__:

    The __getattribute__ special method of a class is automatically called when an attribute of a class is accessed. It intercepts every attempt to access any attribute, regardless of whether it actually exists on the object or not. It can be overridden to implement custom behavior every time an attribute is accessed.

2. __getattr__:

    Unlike __getattribute__, __getattr__ is called only when the attribute being accessed does not exist in the object. It acts as a fallback method to handle attribute lookups that would otherwise raise an AttributeError.

The example below illustrates __getattribute__ usage from Ray, a library that helps scale AI workloads and applications:

```
# File: python/ray/tune/tuner.py

class Tuner:
    ...

    @classmethod
    def restore(
        cls,
        path: str,
        trainable: Union[str, Callable, Type[Trainable], "BaseTrainer"],
        resume_unfinished: bool = True,
        resume_errored: bool = False,
        restart_errored: bool = False,
        param_space: Optional[Dict[str, Any]] = None,
        storage_filesystem: Optional[pyarrow.fs.FileSystem] = None,
        _resume_config: Optional[ResumeConfig] = None,
```

```
    ) -> "Tuner":
        """Restores Tuner after a previously failed run."""
        ...

    def __getattribute__(self, item):
        if item == "restore":
            raise AttributeError(
                "`Tuner.restore()` is a classmethod and cannot be
                called on an "
                "instance. Use `tuner = Tuner.restore(...)` to
                instantiate the "
                "Tuner instead."
            )
        return super().__getattribute__(item)
```

Here __getattribute__ is used to inspect attribute access from objects and raise an error in case the restore method is tried to be accessed.

Overriding __getattribute__ requires careful handling to avoid infinite recursion and other issues. Typically, to access other attributes of the instance safely without recursion, we can use super().__getattribute__(attr_name) within the custom __getattribute__, as seen in the above snippet.

```
# File: gym/core.py

class Wrapper(Env[ObsType, ActType]):

    def __init__(self, env: Env):
        """Wraps an environment to allow a modular transformation of the
        :meth:`step` and :meth:`reset` methods.

        Args:
            env: The environment to wrap
        """
        self.env = env

        ...

        self._metadata: Optional[dict] = None
```

```
def __getattr__(self, name):
    """Returns an attribute with ``name``, unless ``name`` starts with
    an underscore."""

    if name.startswith("_"):  # (1)
        raise AttributeError(f"accessing private attribute '{name}' is
        prohibited")

    return getattr(self.env, name)
```

In the provided code, the __getattr__ method is overridden in the Wrapper class. It works by inspecting the attribute name.

1. If the attribute name starts with an underscore (_), it raises an AttributeError. This is used to enforce the private-like convention for the names starting with an underscore.

2. If the attribute name doesn't start with an underscore, it tries to access that attribute in the self.env object. It acts as a wrapper for accessing the self.env attributes.

The __getattr__ method can be used for

- Creating objects that implement a form of "lazy" behavior, where some attributes can be generated on demand

- Implementing a default behavior for unspecified properties or providing informative error messages for missing attributes

- Implementing patterns like Proxy or Wrapper (seen in the above example from OpenAI gym)

Dataclass

Dataclasses were introduced in Python 3.7 to simplify the creation of classes that are meant primarily for storing data. They will help reduce boilerplate code and auto-generate code for initialization, representation, and comparison (__init__, __repr__, and __eq__).

Why a Dataclass

A dataclass reduces the need for a lot of boilerplate code commonly used in classes, and it provides a more readable representation for classes that are primarily designed for storing data.

Below is the code for initializing a class using the conventional method and providing a __repr__ method:

```python
class Application:
    def __init__(self, name, requirements, constraints=None, path='',
    executable_links=None, executables_dir=()):
        self.name = name
        self.requirements = requirements
        self.constraints = {} if constraints is None else constraints
        self.path = path
        self.executable_links = [] if executable_links is None else
        executable_links
        self.executables_dir = executables_dir
        self.additional_items = []

def __repr__(self):
    return f'Application({self.name!r},{self.requirements!r},{self.
    constraints!r},{self.path!r},{self.executable_links!r},{self.
    executables_dir!r},{self.additional_items!r})'
```

This can be simplified using dataclasses, as seen below:

```python
@dataclass
class Application:
 name: str
 requirements: List[Requirement]
 constraints: Dict[str, str] = field(default_factory=dict)
 path: str = ''
 executable_links: List[str] = field(default_factory=list)
 executable_dir: Tuple[str] = ()
 additional_items: List[str] = field(init=False, default_factory=list)
```

The dataclass version is more declarative, has less code, supports typing, and includes auto-generated (__repr__ and __init__) methods.

Frozen Dataclass

The dataclass decorator has a frozen attribute. If set to true, fields cannot be modified after creating the dataclass instance.

The below code from the *OpenAI evals* library showcases the usage of frozen dataclasses:

```python
# File: openai/evals/elsuite/hr_ml_agent_bench/schema.py

@dataclass(frozen=True)
class ActionInfo:
    name: str
    description: str
    usage: dict
    return_value: str
    function: str
    is_primitive: bool = False

@dataclass(frozen=True)
class Action:
    name: str
    args: Union[dict[str, Any], str]

@dataclass(frozen=True)
class Step:
    action: Action
    observation: str  # What was returned
    timestamp: float  # When the action was taken
```

The dataclasses used here are meant to store benchmarking-related data, and they are set to be frozen to prevent accidental modifications once these have been instantiated.

Dataclass Field

Fields of the dataclass are defined as class attributes, and the behavior of these fields can be customized using the field() function. This can be used to specify default values, assign arbitrary metadata, etc.

The below snippet from the *homeassistant* library uses the dataclasses.field for specifying default values for attributes:

```
# File: homeassistant/components/zha/core/helpers.py

@dataclasses.dataclass(kw_only=True, slots=True)
class ZHAData:
    """ZHA component data stored in `hass.data`."""

    yaml_config: ConfigType = dataclasses.field(default_factory=dict)
    platforms: collections.defaultdict[Platform, list] = dataclasses.field(
        default_factory=lambda: collections.defaultdict(list)
    )
    gateway: ZHAGateway | None = dataclasses.field(default=None)
    device_trigger_cache: dict[str, tuple[str, dict]] = dataclasses.field(
        default_factory=dict
    )
    allow_polling: bool = dataclasses.field(default=False)
```

It can be seen that default values are assigned by specifying the default and default_factory arguments of the field().

Post Init

The __post_init__ method can be used to perform actions such as validation/modification once the dataclass has been initialized.

The snippet below showcases the usage of __post_init__ for performing validation:

```
# File: raiden/transfer/state_change.py

@dataclass(frozen=True)
class ContractReceiveNewTokenNetwork(ContractReceiveStateChange):
    """A new token was registered with the token network registry."""
```

```
token_network_registry_address: TokenNetworkRegistryAddress
token_network: TokenNetworkState

def __post_init__(self) -> None:
    super().__post_init__()
    typecheck(self.token_network, TokenNetworkState)
```

Here, __post_init__ is used to type-check the token_network field of the dataclass. The function will automatically be called once the dataclass is initialized with token_network_registry_address and token_network field values. It then calls a custom function typecheck to validate if the token_network attribute is provided with the correct type.

Inheritance

Inheritance is a concept in object-oriented programming that allows a class (called child class or subclass) to inherit attributes and methods from another class (called superclass or parent class).

Inheritance in Python

Python supports inheritance through a straightforward and flexible syntax. Python supports complex inheritance types such as multiple and multilevel inheritance.

Multiple Inheritance

Multiple inheritance occurs when a class inherits from more than one parent class. This allows the child class to access attributes and methods from multiple parent classes.

Django uses multiple inheritance to define its BaseDeleteView class. It is a base class that helps create Django views that support item deletions. It inherits from three classes: DeletionMixin, FormMixin, and BaseDetailView.

Parent class 1—DeletionMixin: Base for deleting objects.

```
# File: django/views/generic/edit.py

class DeletionMixin:
    """Provide the ability to delete objects."""

    success_url = None
```

```python
def delete(self, request, *args, **kwargs):
    """
    Call the delete() method on the fetched object and then
    redirect to the
    success URL.
    """
    self.object = self.get_object()
    success_url = self.get_success_url()
    self.object.delete()
    return HttpResponseRedirect(success_url)

# Add support for browsers which only accept GET and POST for now.
def post(self, request, *args, **kwargs):
    return self.delete(request, *args, **kwargs)

def get_success_url(self):
    if self.success_url:
        return self.success_url.format(**self.object.__dict__)
    else:
        raise ImproperlyConfigured("No URL to redirect to. Provide a
        success_url.")
```

Parent class 2—FormMixin: Base class that helps to show forms.

```python
# File: django/views/generic/edit.py

class FormMixin(ContextMixin):
    """Provide a way to show and handle a form in a request."""

    initial = {}
    form_class = None
    success_url = None
    prefix = None

    def get_initial(self):
        """Return the initial data to use for forms on this view."""
        return self.initial.copy()
```

```python
def get_prefix(self):
    """Return the prefix to use for forms."""
    return self.prefix

def get_form_class(self):
    """Return the form class to use."""
    return self.form_class

def get_form(self, form_class=None):
    """Return an instance of the form to be used in this view."""
    if form_class is None:
        form_class = self.get_form_class()
    return form_class(**self.get_form_kwargs())

def get_form_kwargs(self):
    """Return the keyword arguments for instantiating the form."""
    kwargs = {
        "initial": self.get_initial(),
        "prefix": self.get_prefix(),
    }

    if self.request.method in ("POST", "PUT"):
        kwargs.update(
            {
                "data": self.request.POST,
                "files": self.request.FILES,
            }
        )
    return kwargs

def get_success_url(self):
    """Return the URL to redirect to after processing a valid form."""
    if not self.success_url:
        raise ImproperlyConfigured("No URL to redirect to. Provide a
        success_url.")
    return str(self.success_url)  # success_url may be lazy

...
```

Parent class 3—BaseDetailView: A base class for displaying a single object. It inherits from two parent classes.

```python
# File: django/views/generic/detail.py

class BaseDetailView(SingleObjectMixin, View):
    """A base view for displaying a single object."""

    def get(self, request, *args, **kwargs):
        self.object = self.get_object()
        context = self.get_context_data(object=self.object)
        return self.render_to_response(context)
```

The class BaseDeleteView inherits from the three parent classes to fetch and display an object, get confirmation for its deletion, and perform the actual deletion operation from the database.

```python
# File: django/views/generic/edit.py

class BaseDeleteView(DeletionMixin, FormMixin, BaseDetailView):
    """
    Base view for deleting an object.

    Using this base class requires subclassing to provide a response mixin.
    """

    form_class = Form

    def post(self, request, *args, **kwargs):
        # Set self.object before the usual form processing flow.
        # Inlined because having DeletionMixin as the first base, for
        # get_success_url(), makes leveraging super() with ProcessFormView
        # overly complex.
        self.object = self.get_object()
        form = self.get_form()
        if form.is_valid():
            return self.form_valid(form)
        else:
            return self.form_invalid(form)
```

```python
def form_valid(self, form):
    success_url = self.get_success_url()
    self.object.delete()
    return HttpResponseRedirect(success_url)
```

Here, the child class composes functionality from multiple parent classes to implement the desired behavior.

Multilevel Inheritance

Multilevel inheritance occurs when a class is derived from a class, which is, in turn, derived from another class. This creates a chain of inheritance, with each level inheriting from the previous one.

The ORM library SQLAlchemy utilizes multilevel inheritance for defining generalized base classes and creating specialized subclasses for each database implementation it supports.

Dialect is the system SQLAlchemy uses to communicate with various database implementations. The snippets below show the usage of multiple inheritance to define the MariaDB dialect, which is used to connect with MariaDB databases using the library.

The Dialect acts as an interface that defines all the possible attributes and methods that should be implemented in subclasses:

```python
# File: lib/sqlalchemy/engine/interfaces.py

class Dialect(EventTarget):
    """Define the behavior of a specific database and DB-API combination.

    Any aspect of metadata definition, SQL query generation,
    execution, result-set handling, or anything else which varies
    between databases is defined under the general category of the
    Dialect.  The Dialect acts as a factory for other
    database-specific object implementations including
    ExecutionContext, Compiled, DefaultGenerator, and TypeEngine.

    .. note:: Third party dialects should not subclass :class:`.Dialect`
        directly.  Instead, subclass :class:`.default.DefaultDialect` or
        descendant class.

    """
```

```
CACHE_HIT = CacheStats.CACHE_HIT
CACHE_MISS = CacheStats.CACHE_MISS
CACHING_DISABLED = CacheStats.CACHING_DISABLED
NO_CACHE_KEY = CacheStats.NO_CACHE_KEY
NO_DIALECT_SUPPORT = CacheStats.NO_DIALECT_SUPPORT

dispatch: dispatcher[Dialect]

name: str
"""identifying name for the dialect from a DBAPI-neutral point of view
    (i.e. 'sqlite')
"""

driver: str
"""identifying name for the dialect's DBAPI"""

dialect_description: str

dbapi: Optional[ModuleType]
"""A reference to the DBAPI module object itself.
```

*SQLAlchemy dialects import DBAPI modules using the classmethod
:meth:`.Dialect.import_dbapi`. The rationale is so that any dialect
module can be imported and used to generate SQL statements without the
need for the actual DBAPI driver to be installed. Only when an
:class:`.Engine` is constructed using :func:`.create_engine` does the
DBAPI get imported; at that point, the creation process will assign
the DBAPI module to this attribute.*

*Dialects should therefore implement :meth:`.Dialect.import_dbapi`
which will import the necessary module and return it, and then refer
to ``self.dbapi`` in dialect code in order to refer to the DBAPI module
contents.*

*.. versionchanged:: The :attr:`.Dialect.dbapi` attribute is exclusively
    used as the per-:class:`.Dialect`-instance reference to the DBAPI
    module.   The previous not-fully-documented ``.Dialect.dbapi()``
    classmethod is deprecated and replaced by :meth:`.Dialect.
    import_dbapi`.*

```
"""

supports_alter: bool
""""``True`` if the database supports ``ALTER TABLE`` - used only for
generating foreign key constraints in certain circumstances
"""

max_identifier_length: int
"""The maximum length of identifier names."""

supports_server_side_cursors: bool
"""indicates if the dialect supports server side cursors"""

supports_default_values: bool
"""dialect supports INSERT... DEFAULT VALUES syntax"""

...

default_sequence_base: int
"""the default value that will be rendered as the "START WITH"
portion of a CREATE SEQUENCE DDL statement.

"""

...

def get_isolation_level(
    self, dbapi_connection: DBAPIConnection
) -> IsolationLevel:
    """Given a DBAPI connection, return its isolation level.

    When working with a :class:`_engine.Connection` object,
    the corresponding
    DBAPI connection may be procured using the
    :attr:`_engine.Connection.connection` accessor.

    Note that this is a dialect-level method which is used as part
    of the implementation of the :class:`_engine.Connection` and
    :class:`_engine.Engine` isolation level facilities;
    these APIs should be preferred for most typical use cases.
```

```
    .. seealso::

        :meth:`_engine.Connection.get_isolation_level`
        - view current level

        :attr:`_engine.Connection.default_isolation_level`
        - view default level

        :paramref:`.Connection.execution_options.isolation_level` -
        set per :class:`_engine.Connection` isolation level

        :paramref:`_sa.create_engine.isolation_level` -
        set per :class:`_engine.Engine` isolation level

    """

    raise NotImplementedError()

def get_default_isolation_level(
    self, dbapi_conn: DBAPIConnection
) -> IsolationLevel:
    """Given a DBAPI connection, return its isolation level, or
    a default isolation level if one cannot be retrieved.

    This method may only raise NotImplementedError and
    **must not raise any other exception**, as it is used
    implicitly upon first connect.

    The method **must return a value** for a dialect that supports
    isolation level settings, as this level is what will be reverted
    towards when a per-connection isolation level change is made.

    The method defaults to using the :meth:`.Dialect.get_isolation_
    level` method unless overridden by a dialect.

    .. versionadded:: 1.3.22

    """

    raise NotImplementedError()
```

By inheriting from this interface, a DefaultDialect class is created that consists of common default behaviors across a number of implementations:

```python
# File: lib/sqlalchemy/engine/default.py

class DefaultDialect(Dialect):
    """Default implementation of Dialect"""

    statement_compiler = compiler.SQLCompiler
    ddl_compiler = compiler.DDLCompiler
    type_compiler_cls = compiler.GenericTypeCompiler

    preparer = compiler.IdentifierPreparer
    supports_alter = True
    supports_comments = False

    ...

    connection_characteristics = util.immutabledict(
        {
            "isolation_level": characteristics.
            IsolationLevelCharacteristic(),
            "logging_token": characteristics.LoggingTokenCharacteristic(),
        }
    )

    engine_config_types: Mapping[str, Any] = util.immutabledict(
        {
            "pool_timeout": util.asint,
            "echo": util.bool_or_str("debug"),
            "echo_pool": util.bool_or_str("debug"),
            "pool_recycle": util.asint,
            "pool_size": util.asint,
            "max_overflow": util.asint,
            "future": util.asbool,
        }
    )
```

241

```
    # if the NUMERIC type
    # returns decimal.Decimal.
    # *not* the FLOAT type however.
    supports_native_decimal = False

    name = "default"

    # length at which to truncate
    # any identifier.
    max_identifier_length = 9999
    _user_defined_max_identifier_length: Optional[int] = None

    isolation_level: Optional[str] = None

    # sub-categories of max_identifier_length.
    # currently these accommodate for MySQL which allows alias names
    # of 255 but DDL names only of 64.
    max_index_name_length: Optional[int] = None
    max_constraint_name_length: Optional[int] = None

    supports_sane_rowcount = True
    supports_sane_multi_rowcount = True
    colspecs: MutableMapping[Type[TypeEngine[Any]],
    Type[TypeEngine[Any]]] = {}
    default_paramstyle = "named"

    supports_default_values = False
    """dialect supports INSERT... DEFAULT VALUES syntax"""

    ...

    def __init__(
        self,
        paramstyle: Optional[_ParamStyle] = None,
        isolation_level: Optional[IsolationLevel] = None,
        dbapi: Optional[ModuleType] = None,
        implicit_returning: Literal[True] = True,
        supports_native_boolean: Optional[bool] = None,
        max_identifier_length: Optional[int] = None,
```

```
    label_length: Optional[int] = None,
    insertmanyvalues_page_size: Union[_NoArg, int] = _NoArg.NO_ARG,
    use_insertmanyvalues: Optional[bool] = None,
    # util.deprecated_params decorator cannot render the
    # Linting.NO_LINTING constant
    compiler_linting: Linting = int(compiler.NO_LINTING),
    # type: ignore
    server_side_cursors: bool = False,
    **kwargs: Any,
):

    if server_side_cursors:
        if not self.supports_server_side_cursors:
            raise exc.ArgumentError(
                "Dialect %s does not support server side
                cursors" % self
            )
        else:
            self.server_side_cursors = True

    if getattr(self, "use_setinputsizes", False):
        util.warn_deprecated(
            "The dialect-level use_setinputsizes attribute is "
            "deprecated.  Please use "
            "bind_typing = BindTyping.SETINPUTSIZES",
            "2.0",
        )
        self.bind_typing = interfaces.BindTyping.SETINPUTSIZES

    self.positional = False
    self._ischema = None

    self.dbapi = dbapi

    ...
```

Specific dialects such as `MySQLDialect` inherit from the DefaultDialect, overriding the necessary attributes and methods:

```python
# File: lib/sqlalchemy/dialects/mysql/base.py

class MySQLDialect(default.DefaultDialect):
    """Details of the MySQL dialect.
    Not used directly in application code.
    """

    name = "mysql"
    supports_statement_cache = True

    supports_alter = True

    div_is_floordiv = False

    supports_native_enum = True

    returns_native_bytes = True

    supports_sequences = False  # default for MySQL ...
    # ... may be updated to True for MariaDB 10.3+ in initialize()

    sequences_optional = False

    supports_for_update_of = False  # default for MySQL ...
    # ... may be updated to True for MySQL 8+ in initialize()

    ...

    supports_comments = True
    inline_comments = True
    default_paramstyle = "format"
    colspecs = colspecs

    cte_follows_insert = True

    statement_compiler = MySQLCompiler
    ddl_compiler = MySQLDDLCompiler
    type_compiler_cls = MySQLTypeCompiler
```

```python
ischema_names = ischema_names
preparer = MySQLIdentifierPreparer

is_mariadb = False
_mariadb_normalized_version_info = None

...

def __init__(
    self,
    json_serializer=None,
    json_deserializer=None,
    is_mariadb=None,
    **kwargs,
):
    kwargs.pop("use_ansiquotes", None)  # legacy
    default.DefaultDialect.__init__(self, **kwargs)
    self._json_serializer = json_serializer
    self._json_deserializer = json_deserializer
    self._set_mariadb(is_mariadb, None)

def get_isolation_level_values(self, dbapi_conn):
    return (
        "SERIALIZABLE",
        "READ UNCOMMITTED",
        "READ COMMITTED",
        "REPEATABLE READ",
    )

def set_isolation_level(self, dbapi_connection, level):
    cursor = dbapi_connection.cursor()
    cursor.execute(f"SET SESSION TRANSACTION ISOLATION LEVEL {level}")
    cursor.execute("COMMIT")
    cursor.close()

...
```

The MariaDB database is a fork of MySQL, and hence, its dialect builds upon the MySQLDialect overriding the behavior as required:

```python
# File: lib/sqlalchemy/dialects/mysql/mariadb.py

class MariaDBDialect(MySQLDialect):
    is_mariadb = True
    supports_statement_cache = True
    supports_native_uuid = True

    _allows_uuid_binds = True

    name = "mariadb"
    preparer = MariaDBIdentifierPreparer

    colspecs = util.update_copy(MySQLDialect.colspecs, {Uuid: _MariaDBUUID})

    def initialize(self, connection):
        super().initialize(connection)

        self.supports_native_uuid = (
            self.server_version_info is not None
            and self.server_version_info >= (10, 7)
        )

def loader(driver):
    dialect_mod = __import__(
        "sqlalchemy.dialects.mysql.%s" % driver
    ).dialects.mysql
    ...
```

Only a few methods and attributes are overridden from MySQLDialect by MariaDBDialect since they share many common behaviors.

Method Resolution Order

The method resolution order (MRO) specifies the order in which the base classes are searched when executing a method or accessing an attribute. MRO of a class is an ordered list of classes (consisting of the child class and its superclasses) to be considered for method calls and attribute lookups in the child class objects.

The __mro__ attribute and mro method of a class can be used to fetch its method resolution order. The algorithm used for MRO calculation follows these rules:

1. A class always precedes its parents.

2. The order of parents is preserved (as they appear in the child class definition).

The snippet below showcases the MRO calculation in case of multiple inheritance:

```
class A:
    def method1(self):
        print("A")

    def method2(self):
        print("A")

    def method3(self):
        print("A")

class B(A):
    def method1(self):
        print("B")

class C(A):
    def method1(self):
        print("C")

    def method2(self):
        print("C")

class D(B, C):
    pass

d = D()

print(D.mro())
# Output: [<class '__main__.D'>, <class '__main__.B'>, <class '__
main__.C'>, <class '__main__.A'>, <class 'object'>]
# MRO is D -> B -> C -> A
```

```
d.method1()   # Output: B
d.method2()   # Output: C
d.method3()   # Output: A
```

The above example shows that methods are resolved in the order D -> B -> C -> A according to the MRO rules.

The **super** Built-In

The super built-in is used to call methods from a parent class. It is useful for accessing inherited methods that have been overridden in a class.

In the below example snippet from *Scrapy,* JsonLinesItemExporter uses super() to initialize the base class BaseItemExporter:

```
# File: scrapy/exporters.py

class BaseItemExporter:
    def __init__(self, *, dont_fail: bool = False, **kwargs: Any):
        self._kwargs: Dict[str, Any] = kwargs
        self._configure(kwargs, dont_fail=dont_fail)

    def _configure(self, options: Dict[str, Any], dont_fail: bool = False)
    -> None:
        """Configure the exporter by popping options from the
        ``options`` dict.
        If dont_fail is set, it won't raise an exception on
        unexpected options
        (useful for using with keyword arguments in subclasses ``__init__``
        methods)
        """
        self.encoding: Optional[str] = options.pop("encoding", None)
        self.fields_to_export: Union[Mapping[str, str], Iterable[str],
        None] = (
            options.pop("fields_to_export", None)
        )
        ...
```

```python
def export_item(self, item: Any) -> None:
    raise NotImplementedError

...

def serialize_field(
    self, field: Union[Mapping[str, Any], Field], name: str, value: Any
) -> Any:
    serializer: Callable[[Any], Any] = field.get("serializer",
    lambda x: x)
    return serializer(value)

def _get_serialized_fields(
    self, item: Any, default_value: Any = None, include_empty:
    Optional[bool] = None
) -> Iterable[Tuple[str, Any]]:
    """Return the fields to export as an iterable of tuples
    (name, serialized_value)
    """
    item = ItemAdapter(item)

    ...

    for field_name in field_iter:
        if isinstance(field_name, str):
            item_field, output_field = field_name, field_name
        else:
            item_field, output_field = field_name
        if item_field in item:
            field_meta = item.get_field_meta(item_field)
            value = self.serialize_field(field_meta, output_field,
            item[item_field])
        else:
            value = default_value

        yield output_field, value
```

```python
class JsonLinesItemExporter(BaseItemExporter):
    def __init__(self, file: BytesIO, **kwargs: Any):
        super().__init__(dont_fail=True, **kwargs)
        self.file: BytesIO = file
        self._kwargs.setdefault("ensure_ascii", not self.encoding)
        self.encoder: JSONEncoder = ScrapyJSONEncoder(**self._kwargs)

    def export_item(self, item: Any) -> None:
        itemdict = dict(self._get_serialized_fields(item))
        data = self.encoder.encode(itemdict) + "\n"
        self.file.write(to_bytes(data, self.encoding))
```

Here, the __init__ method of the JsonLinesItemExporter class also initializes its base class using super().__init__ so that it can utilize the methods inherited from the base class BaseItemExporter. This can also be done using the below call:

BaseItemExporter.__init__(self, dont_fail=True, **kwargs)

Using super with Multiple Inheritance

The super() can also be beneficial in multiple inheritance scenarios.

From Python docs, the signature of super is as follows:

> *class* super(*type, object_or_type=None*)
>
> Return a proxy object that delegates method calls to a parent or sibling class of *type*.
>
> The *object_or_type* determines the method resolution order to be searched. The search starts from the class right after the *type*.

The snippet below shows an example of multiple inheritance in which class C inherits from classes A and B:

```python
class A:
    def __init__(self):
        print("Initializing class A")
        self.a = "Class A"

    def display(self):
        print("Method call from class A")
```

```python
class B:
    def __init__(self):
        print("Initializing class B")
        self.b = "Class B"

    def display(self):
        print("Method call from class B")

class C(A, B):
    def __init__(self):
        super().__init__()  # Calls A's __init__ due to MRO
        super(A, self).__init__()  # Calls B's __init__ due to MRO after A
        print("Initializing class C")
        self.c = "Class C"

    def display(self):
        super().display()  # Calls A's display due to MRO
        super(A, self).display()  # Calls B's display due to MRO after A
        print("Method call from class C")

c_instance = C()
c_instance.display()

"""Output:
Initializing class A
Initializing class B
Initializing class C
Method call from class A
Method call from class B
Method call from class C
"""
```

As seen from the above example, the super() call without arguments will call class A's methods due to the method resolution order. To access class B's methods specifically, super(A, self) is used since B comes next to class A due to MRO.

The object Built-In

object is the base of all classes in Python. Methods on object can be called directly from within any class.

This behavior is identical in the case of other superclasses. Using the superclass name, its methods can be called from within a subclass like Superclass.method(self, *args, **kwargs).

Calls using object are normally made to override some behavior or restriction in the current class by calling the unmodified method definition found in the ultimate base class.

An example of such usage is in celery, a task queue:

```python
# celery/local.py

class Proxy:
    """Proxy to another object."""

    __slots__ = ('__local', '__args', '__kwargs', '__dict__')

    def __init__(self, local,
                 args=None, kwargs=None, name=None, __doc__=None):
        object.__setattr__(self, '_Proxy__local', local)
        object.__setattr__(self, '_Proxy__args', args or ())
        object.__setattr__(self, '_Proxy__kwargs', kwargs or {})
        if name is not None:
            object.__setattr__(self, '__custom_name__', name)
        if __doc__ is not None:
            object.__setattr__(self, '__doc__', __doc__)

    ...
```

The class Proxy is defined as a slotted class. In order to add some attributes that are not included in the class's slots, object.__setattr__ is used. Calling self.attribute or setattr(self, attribute_name) will lead to an error since the class is slotted. This is overridden by using the object base class call.

Alternatives to Inheritance

Sometimes, inheritance can lead to complexities such as

- *Tight coupling*: Strong dependency between the base class and its subclasses

- *Subclass explosion*: Increase in subclasses with growing requirements catering to minor behavioral variations

Depending on the situation, various other design approaches can also be adopted. Some of them are

1. *Composition*: Instead of creating subclasses, we can include instances of other classes as attributes.

2. *Using mixins*: These are specialized classes that are used to provide specialized functionality to subclasses.

3. *Delegation*: In delegation, one object handles a request by passing it to another (the delegatee).

Mixins

Mixins are classes used to supply commonly used functionality to other classes. These are not meant to be instantiated.

The concept of mixin classes isn't formally defined in the Python documentation; rather, it's a design pattern used to promote code reusability. This pattern is prevalent in open source projects and various CPython modules. They allow for the extension of class functionality through inheritance, offering a flexible way to reuse code.

Django provides mixins to enforce access control and permission checks. These are used by projects using Django to implement authorization:

```
# File: django/contrib/auth/mixins.py

class AccessMixin:
    """

    Abstract CBV mixin that gives access mixins the same customizable
    functionality.
    """
```

```python
login_url = None
permission_denied_message = ""
raise_exception = False
redirect_field_name = REDIRECT_FIELD_NAME

def get_login_url(self):
    """
    Override this method to override the login_url attribute.
    """
    login_url = self.login_url or settings.LOGIN_URL
    if not login_url:
        raise ImproperlyConfigured(
            f"{self.__class__.__name__} is missing the login_url "
            "attribute. Define "
            f"{self.__class__.__name__}.login_url, settings.LOGIN_URL, "
            "or override "
            f"{self.__class__.__name__}.get_login_url()."
        )
    return str(login_url)

def get_permission_denied_message(self):
    """
    Override this method to override the permission_denied_message
    attribute.
    """
    return self.permission_denied_message

def handle_no_permission(self):
    if self.raise_exception or self.request.user.is_authenticated:
        raise PermissionDenied(self.get_permission_denied_message())

    ...

    return redirect_to_login(
        path,
        resolved_login_url,
        self.get_redirect_field_name(),
    )
```

...

```python
class PermissionRequiredMixin(AccessMixin):
    """Verify that the current user has all specified permissions."""

    permission_required = None

    def get_permission_required(self):
        """
        Override this method to override the permission_required attribute.
        Must return an iterable.
        """
        if self.permission_required is None:
            raise ImproperlyConfigured(
                f"{self.__class__.__name__} is missing the "
                f"permission_required attribute. Define "
                f"{self.__class__.__name__}.permission_required, or "
                f"override "
                f"{self.__class__.__name__}.get_permission_required()."
            )
        if isinstance(self.permission_required, str):
            perms = (self.permission_required,)
        else:
            perms = self.permission_required
        return perms

    def has_permission(self):
        """
        Override this method to customize the way permissions are checked.
        """
        perms = self.get_permission_required()
        return self.request.user.has_perms(perms)

    def dispatch(self, request, *args, **kwargs):
        if not self.has_permission():
            return self.handle_no_permission()
        return super().dispatch(request, *args, **kwargs)
```

Django provides the following:

- AccessMixin to handle access controls based on the current user.

- PermissionRequiredMixin builds on AccessMixin to check if the user has all the required permissions (commonly used in role-based access control systems).

It can be seen that in PermissionRequiredMixin, the dispatch method is overridden and the parent dispatch is called only after the permission checks successfully complete. In Django, the dispatch method is responsible for processing HTTP requests from the frontend.

Pretalx, a popular event management system using Django, inherits the PermissionRequiredMixin from Django:

```python
# File: src/pretalx/common/mixins/views.py

class PermissionRequired(PermissionRequiredMixin):
    def __init__(self, *args, **kwargs):
        super().__init__(*args, **kwargs)
        if not hasattr(self, "get_permission_object"):
            for key in ("permission_object", "object"):
                if getattr(self, key, None):
                    self.get_permission_object = lambda self: getattr(self,
                    key)  # noqa

    def has_permission(self):
        result = super().has_permission()
        if not result:
            request = getattr(self, "request", None)
            if request and hasattr(request, "event"):
                key = f"pretalx_event_access_{request.event.pk}"
                if key in request.session:
                    sparent = SessionStore(request.session.get(key))
                    parentdata = []
                    with suppress(Exception):
                        parentdata = sparent.load()
                    return "event_access" in parentdata
        return result
```

```python
def get_login_url(self):
    """We do this to avoid leaking data about existing pages."""
    raise Http404()

def handle_no_permission(self):
    request = getattr(self, "request", None)
    if (
        request
        and hasattr(request, "event")
        and request.user.is_anonymous
        and "cfp" in request.resolver_match.namespaces
    ):
        params = "&" + request.GET.urlencode() if request.GET else ""
        return redirect(
            request.event.urls.login + f"?next={quote(request.path)}"
            + params
        )
    raise Http404()
```

Some of the methods are overridden in the implementation as per the application requirements.

This mixin is used to implement access control in the below Django view for displaying an event homepage:

```python
# File: src/pretalx/cfp/views/event.py

class EventPageMixin(PermissionRequired):
    permission_required = "cfp.view_event"

    def get_permission_object(self):
        return getattr(self.request, "event", None)

class EventStartPage(EventPageMixin, TemplateView):
    template_name = "cfp/event/index.html"

    @context
    def has_submissions(self):
        return (
            not self.request.user.is_anonymous
```

```
        and self.request.event.submissions.filter(
            speakers__in=[self.request.user]
        ).exists()
    )

@context
def has_featured(self):
    return self.request.event.submissions.filter(is_featured=True).
    exists()

@context
def submit_qs(self):
    params = [
        (key, self.request.GET.get(key))
        for key in ["track", "submission_type", "access_code"]
        if self.request.GET.get(key) is not None
    ]
    return f"?{urlencode(params)}" if params else ""
```

In the view file, an EventPageMixin class is created, and the permission to request the page is defined (cfp.view_event). The EventStartPage Django view inherits this mixin. Django calls the dispatch method of the view to respond to a user's requests to access pages, and hence, the dispatch method from PermissionRequiredMixin will get called whenever this view is accessed. After successfully checking for the cfp.view_event permission, the view will be rendered.

When Not to Use Classes

Classes will help us model real-world entities in our code utilizing object-oriented programming paradigms. Python is not purely object-oriented, and we can write Python code without utilizing classes.

Below are some of the scenarios where classes may not be the best choice:

1. *Short, simple scripts*: Short scripts with only one or very few associated methods can probably be modeled using functions instead of classes.

2. *Focus is on the data*: When the focus is on the data (and not on its operations), we should use appropriate data structures, namedtuples, or dataclasses to represent the data instead of opting for traditional classes.

3. *Performance is critical*: Classes add a bit of overhead compared with using functions. Using functions should be preferred when a script needs to weigh performance over readability or maintainability.

Conclusion

We have looked into various features of Python's classes, exploring techniques for improved code organization, data management, and flexibility.

The below concepts are related to classes and object-oriented programming but are not covered in this chapter. We will explore each one in their dedicated chapters:

- *Metaclasses (Chapter 10)*: Covers customizing the class creation process

- *Dunder methods (Chapter 8)*: Special methods that can override objects' behavior

- *Abstract base classes (Chapter 19)*: Contains abstract base classes for inheritance-based patterns

CHAPTER 8

Dunder Methods

In the previous chapter, we explored the concept of classes and object-oriented programming in Python. To customize the behavior of objects, Python provides special methods known as dunder methods. They get their name from the double underscores at the beginning and end of the name. These methods are called implicitly by Python to handle various operations. For example, the __init__ dunder method is called automatically when an object is created to initialize it.

From CPython docs:

> A class can implement certain operations that are invoked by special syntax (such as arithmetic operations or subscripting and slicing) by defining methods with special names. This is Python's approach to operator overloading, allowing classes to define their own behavior with respect to language operators. For instance, if a class defines a method named __getitem__() and x is an instance of this class, then x[i] is roughly equivalent to type(x).__getitem__(x, i).

We will explore some of Python's dunder methods and implement them in our classes to modify/extend the class functionality.

__str__ and __repr__ Dunder Methods

str and repr dunder methods allow us to define the behavior when the objects are converted to their string representations:

- __str__ is for creating a readable and user-friendly output. It is called by functions such as str() and print() to get a string representation of the object.

- __repr__ is for creating an unambiguous and developer-friendly output. It is used by the Python REPL to display the object.

© Adarsh Divakaran 2025
A. Divakaran, *Deep Dive Python*, https://doi.org/10.1007/979-8-8688-1261-3_8

If __repr__ is defined on an object and __str__ is missing, __repr__ will be called in place of the __str__.

The snippet below from PySpark showcases the usage of these methods:

```python
# File: python/pyspark/ml/param/__init__.py

class Param(Generic[T]):
    """
    A param with self-contained documentation.
    """

    def __init__(
        self,
        parent: Identifiable,
        name: str,
        doc: str,
        typeConverter: Optional[Callable[[Any], T]] = None,
    ):
        if not isinstance(parent, Identifiable):
            raise TypeError(
                "Parent must be an Identifiable but got type %s." %
                    type(parent)
            )
        self.parent = parent.uid
        self.name = str(name)
        self.doc = str(doc)
        self.typeConverter = (
            TypeConverters.identity if typeConverter is None else
            typeConverter
        )

    ...

    def __str__(self) -> str:
        return str(self.parent) + "__" + self.name
```

```python
def __repr__(self) -> str:
    return "Param(parent=%r, name=%r, doc=%r)" % (self.parent, self.
    name, self.doc)
```

    ...

In the snippet, the __str__ dunder is defined to return a string that contains the parent and name attributes of the object, whereas the __repr__ method returns a string that could be used to recreate the Param object (including parent, name, and doc attributes). The %r format specifier is used to get the __repr__ of the objects.

__add__ and __sub__ : Addition and Subtraction Operations

The __add__ method defines the addition operation (+) behavior for an object. Other dunder methods include __sub__ (subtraction), __mul__ (multiplication), __truediv__ (true division), __floordiv__ (floor division), __mod__ (modulus), and __pow__ (exponentiation), which can be customized to implement the behavior when these arithmetic operators are applied on objects.

The below snippet from CPython AddressList implementation shows the usage of __add__ and __sub__ dunders:

```python
# File: cpython/Lib/email/_parseaddr.py

class AddressList(AddrlistClass):
    """An AddressList encapsulates a list of parsed RFC 2822 addresses."""
    def __init__(self, field):
        AddrlistClass.__init__(self, field)
        if field:
            self.addresslist = self.getaddrlist()
        else:
            self.addresslist = []

    def __len__(self):
        return len(self.addresslist)
```

```python
def __add__(self, other):
    # Set union
    newaddr = AddressList(None)
    newaddr.addresslist = self.addresslist[:]
    for x in other.addresslist:
        if not x in self.addresslist:
            newaddr.addresslist.append(x)
    return newaddr

...

def __sub__(self, other):
    # Set difference
    newaddr = AddressList(None)
    for x in self.addresslist:
        if not x in other.addresslist:
            newaddr.addresslist.append(x)
    return newaddr
```

The __add__ method here combines the email addresses from two AddressList objects without any duplicates. It creates a new AddressList object, copies the addresses from the current object, and then appends any addresses from the other object not already in the list. The __sub__ method creates a new AddressList object that contains all the addresses from the current object that are not in the other object.

__eq__ and __lt__: Equality Check and Comparison

The __eq__ method defines the behavior of the equality comparison (==), whereas the __lt__ method defines the behavior of the less than comparison (<) between two objects.

__eq__ *example from the* requests *library*:

```python
# File: src/requests/auth.py

class HTTPBasicAuth(AuthBase):
    """Attaches HTTP Basic Authentication to the given Request object."""
```

```python
def __init__(self, username, password):
    self.username = username
    self.password = password

def __eq__(self, other):
    return all(
        [
            self.username == getattr(other, "username", None),
            self.password == getattr(other, "password", None),
        ]
    )

def __ne__(self, other):
    return not self == other
```

Here, the __eq__ dunder is defined to compare the class attributes (username and password) one by one and return True only if these are identical strings in both objects.

__lt__ *example from* ludwig:

```python
# File: ludwig/utils/version_transformation.py

class VersionTransformation:
    """Wrapper class for transformations to config dicts."""

    def __init__(
        self,
        transform: Callable[[Dict], Dict],
        version: str,
        prefixes: List[str] = None,
    ):
        """Constructor.

        Args:
            transform: A function or other callable from Dict -> Dict which
            returns a modified version of the config.
                    The callable may update the config in-place and
                    return it, or return a new dict.
            version: The Ludwig version, should be the first version which
            requires this transform.
```

   prefixes: A list of config prefixes this transform should apply
   to, i.e. ["hyperopt"]. If not specified, transform will be
   called with the entire config dictionary.
  """

```python
        self.transform = transform
        self.version = version
        self.pkg_version = pkg_version.parse(version)
        self.prefixes = prefixes if prefixes else []

    @property
    def max_prefix_length(self):
        """Returns the length of the longest prefix."""
        return (
            max(len(prefix.split(".")) for prefix in self.prefixes)
            if self.prefixes
            else 0
        )

    @property
    def longest_prefix(self):
        """Returns the longest prefix, or empty string if no prefixes
        specified."""
        prefixes = self.prefixes
        if not prefixes:
            return ""
        max_index = max(range(len(prefixes)), key=lambda i: prefixes[i])
        return prefixes[max_index]

    def __lt__(self, other):
        """Defines sort order of version transformations. Sorted by:
```

 - version (ascending)
 - max_prefix_length (ascending) Process outer config
  transformations before inner.
 *- longest_prefix (ascending) Order alphabetically by prefix if max_*
  prefix_length equal.

```
    """
    return (self.pkg_version, self.max_prefix_length, self.longest_
    prefix) < (
        other.pkg_version,
        other.max_prefix_length,
        other.longest_prefix,
    )
```

In the VersionTransformation class, the __lt__ method defines a custom sort order for instances of the class. When comparing two instances of VersionTransformation, they are sorted based on

1. pkg_version (ascending)

2. max_prefix_length (ascending), which is a property attribute

3. longest_prefix (ascending), also a property attribute

Python's built-in sorting functions, like sorted() and list.sort(), use comparison dunder methods (__lt__, __le__, __gt__, __ge__, __eq__, and __ne__) to determine the order of objects.

Instead of manually defining all six comparison dunder methods, we can use the functools.total_ordering decorator to automatically generate the missing methods based on the basic ones. For that we should apply the @functools.total_ordering decorator to the class and define at least the __eq__ method and one other comparison method (__lt__, __le__, __gt__, or __ge__) and the decorator will fill in the rest. The total_ordering decorator is covered in Chapter 6.

__int__ and __float__: Conversion to Numbers

The __int__ method defines how the object is converted to an integer (on calling the int() function). This is to be implemented in a class where the object representation can be meaningfully converted to an int. Similarly, __float__ is for conversion of an object to a floating-point number.

The below snippet from *hug* uses these dunders to convert the `Timer` object to int and float:

```python
# File: hug/directives.py

from timeit import default_timer as python_timer

@_built_in_directive
class Timer(object):
    """Keeps track of time surpassed since instantiation, outputted by
    doing float(instance)"""

    __slots__ = ("start", "round_to")

    def __init__(self, round_to=None, **kwargs):
        self.start = python_timer()
        self.round_to = round_to

    def __float__(self):
        time_taken = python_timer() - self.start
        return round(time_taken, self.round_to) if self.round_to else
        time_taken

    def __int__(self):
        return int(round(float(self)))
```

In the __float__ method, the time elapsed since the instance was created is calculated and returned as a float. If round_to is specified, the time is rounded to the specified number of decimal places. The __int__ dunder uses the float implementation and returns it by rounding and then converting to an integer.

__len__: Length Calculation

The __len__ dunder is used to return the length of an object. It is commonly used in collection-like objects to return the number of items it contains.

The below class from *localstack* acts as a wrapper over a list or sequence data:

```python
# File: localstack/utils/collections.py

class ImmutableDict(Mapping):
    """Wrapper class to create an immutable view of a given list or
    sequence."""

    def __init__(self, seq=None, **kwargs):
        self._dict = dict(seq, **kwargs)

    def __len__(self) -> int:
        return self._dict.__len__()

    def __iter__(self) -> Iterator:
        return self._dict.__iter__()

    ...
```

ImmutableDict uses a _dict attribute to store the sequence supplied to it. The __len__ dunder is implemented to proxy the call to the __len__ dunder of this dictionary attribute.

__call__: Callable Objects

The __call__ dunder can be defined on a class to give its objects function-like behavior. It allows an instance of a class to be called as if it were a function using the function call syntax (i.e., using parentheses ()).

The below snippet is of the Pythonic implementation of partial—it is used to create a new partial function with partial application of the given arguments:

```python
# File: cpython/Lib/functools.py

class partial:
    """New function with partial application of the given arguments
    and keywords.
    """

    __slots__ = "func", "args", "keywords", "__dict__", "__weakref__"
```

```
def __new__(cls, func, /, *args, **keywords):
    if not callable(func):
        raise TypeError("the first argument must be callable")

    ...

    self = super(partial, cls).__new__(cls)

    self.func = func
    self.args = args
    self.keywords = keywords
    return self

def __call__(self, /, *args, **keywords):
    keywords = {**self.keywords, **keywords}
    return self.func(*self.args, *args, **keywords)

...
```

In the snippet, the __new__ method in the partial class is used to store a callable (func), along with its arguments (args) and keyword arguments (keywords), in a newly created instance.

When an instance of the partial class is called as a function, the __call__ method is automatically invoked. This method combines the keywords provided at the time of the instance creation (self.keywords) and the keywords provided at the time of the call (keywords), with the latter having precedence in case of conflicts. Then, it calls the original function (self.func) with the combined arguments (self.args and args) and keywords. This allows for partial application of a function: you can create a partial instance with some arguments and keywords and then call this instance later with the remaining arguments and keywords.

__hash__: Hashability and Hash Calculation

This method provides a way to generate a hash value for an object. This hash value is used by hash-based collections such as sets and dictionaries to quickly compare keys and detect duplicates. The __hash__ dunder should be implemented if we want to use the class's instance as a dictionary key or members of a set.

The snippet below is from the Django Model class, which represents data in an SQL table when using the Django ORM:

```python
# File: django/db/models/base.py

class Model(AltersData, metaclass=ModelBase):
    def __init__(self, *args, **kwargs):
        # Alias some things as locals to avoid repeat global lookups
        cls = self.__class__
        opts = self._meta
        _setattr = setattr

        ...

    def __str__(self):
        return "%s object (%s)" % (self.__class__.__name__, self.pk)

    def __eq__(self, other):
        if not isinstance(other, Model):
            return NotImplemented
        if self._meta.concrete_model != other._meta.concrete_model:
            return False
        my_pk = self.pk
        if my_pk is None:
            return self is other
        return my_pk == other.pk

    def __hash__(self):
        if self.pk is None:
            raise TypeError("Model instances without primary key value are
                unhashable")
        return hash(self.pk)
```

In the Django Model class, the __hash__ method is used to compute a hash value for a model instance. A model instance stores a single row's data from an SQL table.

The hash value is computed based on the primary key (pk) of the model instance. If the model instance does not have a primary key, a TypeError is raised, indicating that model instances without a primary key value are unhashable. The usage of pk also ensures that each model instance has a unique hash value (since the primary key is unique across database rows).

__contains__, __getitem__, and __setitem__: Membership Checks and Item Access

The __contains__ method allows custom behavior for membership tests using the in keyword, enabling us to define the checks to see if an item is present in a container.

The __getitem__ method defines how to retrieve an item from a container using the indexing syntax (e.g., obj[key]), whereas the __setitem__ method allows us to define item setting behavior in a container using the indexing syntax. Here, the key can be an individual index or a slice.

Scrapy uses these dunders to modify the behavior of its CaselessDict, a custom dictionary subclass to make keys case insensitive:

```python
# File: scrapy/utils/datatypes.py

class CaselessDict(dict):
    __slots__ = ()

    def __new__(cls, *args, **kwargs):
        from scrapy.http.headers import Headers

        if issubclass(cls, CaselessDict) and not issubclass(cls, Headers):
            warnings.warn(
                "scrapy.utils.datatypes.CaselessDict is deprecated,"
                " please use scrapy.utils.datatypes.CaseInsensitiveDict"
                instead",
                category=ScrapyDeprecationWarning,
                stacklevel=2,
            )
        return super().__new__(cls, *args, **kwargs)

    def __init__(self, seq=None):
        super().__init__()
        if seq:
            self.update(seq)

    def __getitem__(self, key):
        return dict.__getitem__(self, self.normkey(key))

    def __setitem__(self, key, value):
        dict.__setitem__(self, self.normkey(key), self.normvalue(value))
```

```
def __delitem__(self, key):
    dict.__delitem__(self, self.normkey(key))

def __contains__(self, key):
    return dict.__contains__(self, self.normkey(key))

has_key = __contains__

def __copy__(self):
    return self.__class__(self)

copy = __copy__

def normkey(self, key):
    """Method to normalize dictionary key access"""
    return key.lower()

def normvalue(self, value):
    """Method to normalize values prior to be set"""
    return value

...
```

This dictionary subclass normalizes all its keys to lowercase. __setitem__, __getitem__, and __contains__ are defined in such a way that the keys are normalized to lowercase before performing the modification, access, or membership test.

__getattr__ and __getattribute__: Attribute Access

Python provides __getattribute__ and __getattr__ methods to control how a class's attributes are accessed:

1. __getattribute__:

    The __getattribute__ special method of a class is automatically called when an attribute of a class is accessed. It intercepts every attempt to access any attribute, regardless of whether it actually exists on the object or not. It can be overridden to implement custom behavior every time an attribute is accessed.

273

2. __getattr__:

Unlike __getattribute__, __getattr__ is called only when the attribute being accessed does not exist in the object. It acts as a fallback method to handle attribute lookups that would otherwise raise an AttributeError.

The below example illustrating __getattribute__ usage is from the *spacy* library:

```
# File: spacy/errors.py

class ErrorsWithCodes(type):
    def __getattribute__(self, code):
        msg = super().__getattribute__(code)
        if code.startswith("__"):  # python system attributes like
        __class__
            return msg
        else:
            return "[{code}] {msg}".format(code=code, msg=msg)
```

Here, ErrorsWithCodes is a metaclass. This can be used to create other classes with customized behavior. When an attribute (in this case, code) of such classes is accessed, the __getattribute__ method is called. It first calls the __getattribute__ method of the superclass (type) to get the actual value of the attribute (msg). If the attribute name does not start with "__", it returns a string that includes the attribute name and its value. This customization is done to include the attribute name along with each access for the attribute value.

The below snippet from *CPython* showcases the use of the __getattr__ dunder:

```
# File: Lib/idlelib/debugger_r.py

class FrameProxy:

    def __init__(self, conn, fid):
        self._conn = conn
        self._fid = fid
        self._oid = "idb_adapter"
        self._dictcache = {}
```

```python
def __getattr__(self, name):
    if name[:1] == "_":
        raise AttributeError(name)
    if name == "f_code":
        return self._get_f_code()
    if name == "f_globals":
        return self._get_f_globals()
    if name == "f_locals":
        return self._get_f_locals()
    return self._conn.remotecall(self._oid, "frame_attr",
                                 (self._fid, name), {})
```

The __getattr__ method is used here to return the value of the attribute requested dynamically. These attributes are not pre-set on the object but are to be calculated on the fly. Hence, __getattr__ is used to extend the attribute resolution mechanism when the required attribute is not found using the class's default access mechanism.

__setattr__: Setting Attributes

The __setattr__ method allows for the customization of attribute assignments. It is called every time when an attribute assignment is attempted.

The below snippet from *openpilot* uses the dunder to implement a check for attribute assignments:

```python
# File: openpilot/common/utils.py
...

class Freezable:
    _frozen: bool = False

    def freeze(self):
        if not self._frozen:
            self._frozen = True

    def __setattr__(self, *args, **kwargs):
        if self._frozen:
            raise Exception("cannot modify frozen object")
        super().__setattr__(*args, **kwargs)
```

In the snippet, __setattr__ is overridden in the Freezable class to prevent modification of the object once it has been "frozen." The method checks if the object is "frozen" before setting an attribute. If the object is "frozen," it raises an exception. If not, it calls the original __setattr__ method to set the attribute.

__missing__: Handle Missing Keys

The __missing__ method provides a way to handle missing keys in dictionaries and for handling invalid access to an enum.

In the code below, a class FormatDict is defined that inherits from Python's built-in dict class. The __missing__ method is overridden in this subclass:

```python
# File: bowtie/_component.py

class FormatDict(dict):
    """Dict to replace missing keys."""

    def __missing__(self, key: str) -> str:
        """Replace missing key with '{key}'."""
        return '{' + key + '}'
```

When we try to access a key that doesn't exist in the dictionary, instead of raising a KeyError, it returns a string in the format '{key}'. This can be useful in situations where we want to avoid exceptions when accessing non-existent keys and instead want to provide a dynamic default value.

The __missing__ method can also be used in enum classes to provide a default value when a non-existent member is accessed.

__copy__ and __deepcopy__: Copying Objects

These dunders are used for copying objects:

- The __copy__ method is used to create a shallow copy of an object. In a shallow copy, the new object is a separate instance, but its members/attributes are references to the same objects as those in the original.

- The __deepcopy__ method is used to create a deep copy of an object. In a deep copy, not only is the new object a separate instance, but all objects referenced by its attributes are also recursively copied, resulting in a fully independent clone.

The below snippet from *Pydantic* shows an implementation example of these dunders:

```python
# File: pydantic/root_model.py

object_setattr = object.__setattr__

class RootModel(BaseModel, typing.Generic[RootModelRootType],
metaclass=_RootModelMetaclass):
    """Usage docs: https://docs.pydantic.dev/2.7/concepts/
    models/#rootmodel-and-custom-root-types

    A Pydantic `BaseModel` for the root object of the model.

    Attributes:
        root: The root object of the model.
        __pydantic_root_model__: Whether the model is a RootModel.
        __pydantic_private__: Private fields in the model.
        __pydantic_extra__: Extra fields in the model.
    """

    __pydantic_root_model__ = True
    __pydantic_private__ = None
    __pydantic_extra__ = None

    root: RootModelRootType

    ...

    def __copy__(self: Model) -> Model:
        """Returns a shallow copy of the model."""
        cls = type(self)
        m = cls.__new__(cls)
        _object_setattr(m, '__dict__', copy(self.__dict__))
```

```
    _object_setattr(m, '__pydantic_fields_set__', copy(self.__pydantic_
    fields_set__))
    return m

def __deepcopy__(self: Model, memo: dict[int, Any] | None = None)
-> Model:
    """Returns a deep copy of the model."""
    cls = type(self)
    m = cls.__new__(cls)
    _object_setattr(m, '__dict__', deepcopy(self.__dict__, memo=memo))
    # This next line doesn't need a deepcopy because __pydantic_fields_
    set__ is a set[str],
    # and attempting a deepcopy would be marginally slower.
    _object_setattr(m, '__pydantic_fields_set__', copy(self.__pydantic_
    fields_set__))
    return m
```

In this code, the __copy__ method creates a new instance of the model's class and then copies the __dict__ and __pydantic_fields_set__ attributes from the original object to the new one. The __deepcopy__ method creates a new instance of the model's class and then deep copies the __dict__ attribute. The __pydantic_fields_set__ attribute is only shallow copied because it's a set of strings, and attempting a deep copy would be marginally slower and unnecessary as strings are immutable.

__instancecheck__ and __subclasscheck__: Instance and Subclass Checks

The __instancecheck__ method customizes the behavior of the isinstance() function, which checks if an object is an instance of a class or a tuple of classes.

The below example of __instancecheck__ is from *graphite,* a real-time graphing library:

```
# File: webapp/graphite/singleton.py

class Singleton(object):
    """

    The Singleton class decorator.
```

Like:

```
from singleton.singleton import Singleton

@Singleton
class IntSingleton(object):
    def __init__(self):
        pass
```
Use IntSingleton.instance() get the instance
`"""`

```
def __init__(self, cls):
    """

    :param cls: decorator class type
    """

    self.__cls = cls
    self.__instance = None

def initialize(self, *args, **kwargs):
    """

    Initialize singleton object if it has not been initialized
    :param args: class init parameters
    :param kwargs: class init parameters
    """

    if not self.is_initialized():
        self.__instance = self.__cls(*args, **kwargs)

def is_initialized(self):
    """

    :return: true if instance is initialized
    """

    return self.__instance is not None

def instance(self):
    """

    Get singleton instance
    :return: instance object
    """
```

```
    if not self.is_initialized():
        self.initialize()
    return self._instance

def __call__(self, *args, **kwargs):
    """

    Disable new instance of original class
    :raise TypeError:
    """

    raise TypeError("Singletons must be access by instance")

def __instancecheck__(self, inst):
    """

    Helper for isinstance check
    """

    return isinstance(inst, self.__cls)
```

Here, Singleton is used as a class decorator. It will restrict the instantiation of the classes it decorates and will only allow one instance per class.

In the Singleton class, the __instancecheck__ method is implemented to return True if the instance is of the class type that the Singleton is wrapping (self.__cls). This allows the Singleton to behave as if it is the class it is wrapping when using isinstance(), which can be useful when we need to check the type of the Singleton instance.

The __subclasscheck__ method customizes the behavior of the issubclass() function, which checks if a class is a subclass of another class or a tuple of classes.

The below snippet from *Amaranth* showcases __subclasscheck__ method usage:

```
# File: amaranth/lib/wiring.py

class MarkupMeta(StructMeta):
    def __new__(mcls, name, bases, dct, ns=None, **kwargs):
        cls = super().__new__(mcls, name, bases, dct, **kwargs)
        cls._markup_ns = ns

        ns_name = [name]
```

```
    for base in cls.__mro__:
        try:
            base_ns = base._markup_ns
        except AttributeError:
            pass
        else:
            if base_ns is not None:
                ns_name.append(base_ns)

    cls._markup_name = '.'.join(reversed(ns_name))
    cls._markup_name_safe = '_'.join(reversed(ns_name))

    return cls

def __init__(cls, name, bases, dct, ns=None, **kwargs):
    super().__init__(name, bases, dct, **kwargs)

def __instancecheck__(cls, inst):
    # We make OverflowBarier and SerializationError be instanceof
    # and subclassof any Markup class.  This avoids errors when
    # they are being added to various CheckedList & CheckedDict
    # collections.
    parent_check = type(RTStruct).__instancecheck__
    if parent_check(cls, inst):
        return True
    return type(inst) in (OverflowBarier, SerializationError)

def __subclasscheck__(cls, subcls):
    parent_check = type(RTStruct).__subclasscheck__
    if parent_check(cls, subcls):
        return True
    return subcls in (OverflowBarier, SerializationError)
```

Here, the __subclasscheck__ performs a standard issubclass check based on a parent class initially. If the standard check does not identify subcls as a subclass of cls, the method then checks if subcls is one of two specific classes: OverflowBarier and SerializationError. If subcls is either of these classes, the method returns

True; otherwise, it returns False. Here, the check is customized to allow the objects to behave as if they were subclasses of two classes (OverflowBarier and SerializationError) whenever a subclass check is performed.

Both of these methods (__subclasscheck__ and __instancecheck__) are commonly defined on metaclasses because they allow control over how instances of a class (or instances of classes inheriting from it) are checked.

Conclusion

In this chapter, we have seen the implementation examples of various dunder methods that can modify object behavior:

__str__ *and* __repr__: Provide meaningful string representations of objects

__add__: Enables custom behavior for the addition operation between objects

__eq__: Defines how equality is determined between two objects

__lt__: Customizes the behavior for "less than comparisons" between objects

__int__ *and* __float__: Convert an object to its numerical representations

__len__: Determines the length of an object, typically collections

__call__: Allows an instance to be called similar to a function

__hash__: Generates a unique hash value for an object

__contains__: Defines behavior for membership tests using the in keyword

__getattr__ *and* __getattribute__: Customize how attributes are accessed on objects

__setattr__: Controls the process of setting attribute values

__missing__: Handles cases where a dictionary key is missing or when an enum is accessed using an invalid value __copy__ *and* __deepcopy__: Facilitate shallow and deep copying of objects

__instancecheck__ *and* __subclasscheck__: Control the behavior of isinstance() and issubclass() checks

The below concepts use dunder methods to power their functionality and will be discussed in their dedicated chapters.

1. *Iterators*: Dunder methods __iter__ and __next__ are used to create iterators and will be covered in detail in Chapter 12.

2. *Context managers*: Dunder methods __enter__ and __exit__ are essential for context managers and will be explored in Chapter 18.

## CHAPTER 9

Decorators

In the previous chapter, we explored Python's dunder methods and saw how they enable us to define object behavior in a clean and expressive way.

In this chapter, we shift our focus to decorators—one of Python's most powerful and elegant features. Decorators are syntactic sugar that let us wrap functions with additional behavior without changing their internal logic. We'll learn how decorators work under the hood and how to write our own decorators and explore common usage patterns. We'll also look at examples from real-world codebases to understand how decorators can simplify and organize our code.

Closures

Closures are functions that remember the environment in which they were created. They can access variables from their enclosing scope even after that scope has finished execution. Python allows us to define nested functions—a function inside a function. A closure is a nested function that remembers the environment in which it was created.

The below example showcases a closure:

```python
def outer_function(msg):
    def inner_function():
        print(msg)

    return inner_function

closure = outer_function("Hello, World!")
closure()  # Output: Hello, World!
```

The `inner_function` is a closure that stores the `msg` attribute and retains the value even after execution of the `outer_function`.

The concept of closures is used when we define decorators.

© Adarsh Divakaran 2025
A. Divakaran, *Deep Dive Python*, https://doi.org/10.1007/979-8-8688-1261-3_9

Decorators: Syntactic Sugar

Decorators commonly utilize a closure that wraps the actual function, as seen below:

```python
def my_decorator(func):
    def wrapper():
        print("The function is about to be called.")
        func()
        print("The function was called.")

    return wrapper

def say_hello():
    print("Hello!")

say_hello = my_decorator(say_hello)
say_hello()

""" Output:
The function is about to be called.
Hello!
The function was called.
"""
```

Here, the say_hello function is wrapped with my_decorator to print something before and after it is called.

Python provides a more elegant and readable way to apply decorators using the @ symbol. It is Python's syntactic sugar for decorators:

```python
def my_decorator(func):
    def wrapper():
        print("The function is about to be called.")
        func()
        print("The function was called.")

    return wrapper
```

```
@my_decorator
def say_hello():
    print("Hello!")

say_hello()
```

In this version, we use the @my_decorator syntax directly above the say_hello function definition. This tells Python to apply my_decorator to say_hello automatically. The result is the same as the traditional approach, but the code is cleaner and more concise.

Usage of functools.wraps

When creating decorators, it's a good practice to use functools.wraps. This function helps preserve the original function's metadata, such as its name, docstring, and other attributes. Without functools.wraps, the decorated function might lose its identity, making debugging and introspection harder.

This can be seen from the below example where we define a decorator without using functools.wraps:

```
def my_decorator(func):
    def wrapper():
        print("The function is about to be called.")
        func()
        print("The function was called.")

    return wrapper

@my_decorator
def say_hello():
    "A function that says hello."
    print("Hello!")

def another_say_hello():
    "Another function that says hello."
    print("Hello!")
```

```
print(another_say_hello.__doc__)  # Output: Another function that
says hello.
print(another_say_hello.__name__)  # Output: another_say_hello

print(say_hello.__doc__)  # Output: None
print(say_hello.__name__)  # Output: wrapper
```

The decorated function loses its identity (name and docstring, in the example) and shows the identity of the wrapper.

The below example shows the decorator's definition using `wraps`:

```
import functools
def my_decorator(func):
    @functools.wraps(func)
    def wrapper():
        print("The function is about to be called.")
        func()
        print("The function was called.")

    return wrapper

@my_decorator
def say_hello():
    "A function that says hello."
    print("Hello!")

print(say_hello.__doc__)  # Output: A function that says hello.
print(say_hello.__name__)  # Output: say_hello
```

As seen from the snippet, the original identity of the decorator function is retained when we use `wraps`.

Practical Decorators

The simple decorators we have seen in the previous sections are not production-ready. They will not work on functions that take arguments and fail to return values emitted from the decorated functions.

Let's use a simple decorator like the ones we have seen earlier for a function taking arguments:

```python
import functools

def my_decorator(func):
    @functools.wraps(func)
    def wrapper():
        print("The function is about to be called.")
        func()
        print("The function was called.")

    return wrapper

@my_decorator
def say_hello(name):
    return f"Hello {name}"

print(say_hello("John"))
```

Running the snippet will raise an error, as seen below:

```
File "...", line 19, in <module>
    print(say_hello("John"))
          ^^^^^^^^^^^^^^^^^
TypcError: say_hello() takes 0 positional arguments but 1 was given
```

To fix the issue, we can modify the wrapper to accept arbitrary positional and keyword arguments:

```python
def my_decorator(func):
    @functools.wraps(func)
    def wrapper(*args, **kwargs):
        print("The function is about to be called.")
        func(*args, **kwargs)
        print("The function was called.")

    return wrapper
```

Using the decorator definition, the error will be fixed. But printing the decorated function's result using print(say_hello("John")) will print None. This is because we ignore the decorated function's return value from inside the wrapper.

To correct this behavior, we can use the decorator defined below:

```python
def my_decorator(func):
    @functools.wraps(func)
    def wrapper(*args, **kwargs):
        print("The function is about to be called.")
        result = func(*args, **kwargs)
        print("The function was called.")
        return result

    return wrapper
```

Now, print(say_hello("John")) will print Hello John as expected.

Nesting Decorators

We can apply multiple decorators to a function. In such a scenario, the body of the outermost decorator will be executed first, then the next outermost decorator, and so on, until the innermost decorator is executed. This means that the decorators are applied in a nested manner, with the innermost decorator being the last to be applied.

The below example illustrates this behavior:

```python
import functools

def decorator_1(func):
    @functools.wraps(func)
    def wrapper(*args, **kwargs):
        print("Decorator 1 - Before call")
        result = func(*args, **kwargs)
        print("Decorator 1 - After call")
        return result

    return wrapper
```

```python
def decorator_2(func):
    @functools.wraps(func)
    def wrapper(*args, **kwargs):
        print("Decorator 2 - Before call")
        result = func(*args, **kwargs)
        print("Decorator 2 - After call")
        return result

    return wrapper

@decorator_2
@decorator_1
def say_hello(name):
    print(f"Hello {name}")

say_hello("World")

""" Output:
Decorator 2 - Before call
Decorator 1 - Before call
Hello World
Decorator 1 - After call
Decorator 2 - After call
"""
```

Here is the breakdown of what happens:

1. decorator1 is applied to say_hello, creating a new function that includes the behavior of decorator1.

2. decorator2 is then applied to the result of the first decoration, creating a new function that includes the behavior of both decorator2 and decorator1.

3. When say_hello is called, the wrapper function inside decorator2 is executed first, which in turn calls the wrapper function inside decorator1, and finally, the original say_hello is executed.

The snippet below from *redash,* a data exploration and visualization framework, shows the usage of nested decorators:

```python
#  File: redash/handlers/embed.py

from flask import request
from flask_login import current_user, login_required
from redash.handlers import routes
from redash.handlers.base import (
    org_scoped_rule,
    record_event,
)
from redash.handlers.static import render_index
from redash.security import csp_allows_embeding

@routes.route(
    org_scoped_rule("/embed/query/<query_id>/
    visualization/<visualization_id>"),
    methods=["GET"],
)
@login_required
@csp_allows_embeding
def embed(query_id, visualization_id, org_slug=None):
    record_event(
        current_org,
        current_user._get_current_object(),
        {
            "action": "view",
            "object_id": visualization_id,
            "object_type": "visualization",
            "query_id": query_id,
            "embed": True,
            "referer": request.headers.get("Referer"),
        },
    )
    return render_index()
```

Here, multiple decorators are nested or chained over the embed function to extend its functionality. @routes.route assigns a *redash* route URL, @login_required enforces user login to access this route, and @csp_allows_embeding will set the content security policy for this path.

Decorators with Arguments

Decorators with arguments take additional parameters that can be used to customize the behavior of the decorator.

Below is an example from *Flask AppBuilder* where the decorator function itself takes arguments:

```python
# File: flask_appbuilder/api/__init__.py

def expose(url: str = "/", methods: Tuple[str] = ("GET",)) ->
Callable[..., Any]:
    """
    Use this decorator to expose API endpoints on your API classes.

    :param url:
        Relative URL for the endpoint
    :param methods:
        Allowed HTTP methods. By default only GET is allowed.
    """

    def wrap(f: Callable[..., Any]) -> Callable[..., Any]:
        if not hasattr(f, "_urls"):
            f._urls = []  # type: ignore
        f._urls.append((url, methods))  # type: ignore
        return f

    return wrap
```

The decorator takes the url and methods arguments, and the decorator will be used to expose decorated functions as API endpoints.

The below snippet from the same library shows the usage of the decorator defined above:

```python
# File: flask_appbuilder/views.py

class ModelView(RestCRUDView):
    """
    This is the CRUD generic view.
    If you want to automatically implement create, edit,
    delete, show, and list from your database tables,
    inherit your views from this class.

    """

    @expose("/list/")
    @has_access
    def list(self):
        self.update_redirect()
        try:
            widgets = self._list()
        except FABException as exc:
            flash(f"An error occurred: {exc}", "warning")
            return redirect(self.get_redirect())
        return self.render_template(
            self.list_template, title=self.list_title, widgets=widgets
        )

    @expose("/show/<pk>", methods=["GET"])
    @has_access
    def show(self, pk):
        pk = self._deserialize_pk_if_composite(pk)
        widgets = self._show(pk)
        return self.render_template(
            self.show_template,
            pk=pk,
            title=self.show_title,
            widgets=widgets,
            related_views=self._related_views,
        )
```

In the snippet, the expose decorator assigns the /list and /show/ paths to the methods defined in the ModelView class.

Usually, when we create a decorator with arguments, we need to add an extra layer of function calls. The outermost function takes the arguments for the decorator, and it returns a decorator function that takes the function to be decorated.

Below is a generic example of a decorator function that takes arguments used for permission checks:

```python
import functools

def require_permission(required_permission):
    def decorator(func):
        @functools.wraps(func)
        def wrapper(*args, **kwargs):
            user_permission = kwargs.get("user_permission", "guest")
            if user_permission != required_permission:
                raise PermissionError(
                    f"Permission denied: requires {required_permission}
                    permission"
                )
            return func(*args, **kwargs)

        return wrapper

    return decorator

@require_permission("user")
def view_dashboard(*args, **kwargs):
    pass

@require_permission("admin")
def delete_user(*args, **kwargs):
    return "User deleted"
```

In this example, the require_permission decorator takes an argument (required_permission) and uses an extra function to handle the decoration process. This extra function is necessary to capture the argument and apply the decorator logic correctly.

Let's break down the structure and the use of each function:

1. *Outer function (*require_permission*)*: This function takes the argument required_permission. It is responsible for capturing this argument and returning the actual decorator function. This is the first layer that allows the decorator to be parameterized.

2. *Decorator function (*decorator*)*: This function takes the function to be decorated (func) as its argument. It is responsible for defining the wrapper function that will add the permission-checking logic. This is the second layer that sets up the actual decoration process.

3. *Wrapper function (*wrapper*)*: This function contains the logic that will be executed when the decorated function is called. It checks if the user has the required permission and either raises a PermissionError or calls the original function. This is the third layer that implements the runtime behavior of the decorator.

Decorators with Optional Arguments Only

We have seen decorators that take arguments in the previous section. When a decorator function takes arguments, but all these arguments are optional, then this decorator can be used as @decorator (where we use all defaults) as well as @decorator(argument=value) (where we provide non-default argument values). In the first case, the decorator is not called when it decorates a function, whereas it is not the case when we provide an argument. This case should be handled by decorators that take all-optional arguments.

The below example from *Celery* shows an example of the shared_task decorator, which takes optional arguments only:

```
# File: celery/app/__init__.py

def shared_task(*args, **kwargs):
    """Create shared task (decorator).

    This can be used by library authors to create tasks that'll work
    for any app environment.
```

Returns:

~celery.local.Proxy: A proxy that always takes the task from the current apps task registry.

Example:

```
>>> from celery import Celery, shared_task
>>> @shared_task
... def add(x, y):
...     return x + y
...
>>> app1 = Celery(broker='amqp://')
>>> add.app is app1
True
>>> app2 = Celery(broker='redis://')
>>> add.app is app2
True
"""

def create_shared_task(**options):

    def __inner(fun):
        name = options.get('name')
        # Set as shared task so that unfinalized apps,
        # and future apps will register a copy of this task.
        _state.connect_on_app_finalize(
            lambda app: app._task_from_fun(fun, **options)
        )

        # Force all finalized apps to take this task as well.
        for app in _state._get_active_apps():
            if app.finalized:
                with app._finalize_mutex:
                    app._task_from_fun(fun, **options)

        # Return a proxy that always gets the task from the current
        # apps task registry.
```

```
        def task_by_cons():
            app = _state.get_current_app()
            return app.tasks[
                name or app.gen_task_name(fun.__name__, fun.__module__)
            ]
        return Proxy(task_by_cons)
    return __inner

if len(args) == 1 and callable(args[0]):
    return create_shared_task(**kwargs)(args[0])
return create_shared_task(*args, **kwargs)
```

The shared_task decorator can be used in two ways:

1. *Without any arguments*: @shared_task

2. *With optional arguments*: @shared_task(argument=value)

The decorator ensures that it behaves correctly in both scenarios by utilizing the conditional below, which is present at the end of the decorator function:

```
if len(args) == 1 and callable(args[0]):
    return create_shared_task(**kwargs)(args[0])
return create_shared_task(*args, **kwargs)
```

This conditional checks if the decorator is used without arguments:

- len(args) == 1 ensures there's only one positional argument.

- callable(args[0]) checks if this argument is a function.

If both conditions are true, it means the decorator is used without arguments. It directly calls create_shared_task with kwargs and applies it to the function (args[0]).

If the conditions are unmet, the decorator is used with arguments. In such a case, the function is called by usage such as shared_task(argument=value). So it returns the create_shared_task function, which will be called later with the actual function to be decorated (when the @ decorator syntax is encountered).

Decorating Classes

Apart from functions, classes can also be decorated. Similar to the usage with functions, decorators can enhance class behavior by providing additional functionality.

The below example is from CPython's @dataclass decorator, which is used to decorate Python classes as dataclasses, providing them with functionalities such as an automatically defined init dunder:

```
# File: cpython/Lib/dataclasses.py

def _process_class(
    cls,
    init,
    repr,
    eq,
    order,
    unsafe_hash,
    frozen,
    match_args,
    kw_only,
    slots,
    weakref_slot,
):
    ...

    setattr(
        cls,
        _PARAMS,
        _DataclassParams(
            init,
            repr,
            eq,
            order,
            unsafe_hash,
            frozen,
            match_args,
            kw_only,
```

299

```
            slots,
            weakref_slot,
        ),
    )

    # Annotations defined specifically in this class (not in base classes).
    cls_annotations = inspect.get_annotations(cls)

    # Now find fields in our class.  While doing so, validate some
    # things, and set the default values (as class attributes) where
    # we can.
    cls_fields = []
    # Get a reference to this module for the _is_kw_only() test.
    KW_ONLY_seen = False
    dataclasses = sys.modules[__name__]
    for name, type in cls_annotations.items():
        # See if this is a marker to change the value of kw_only.
        if _is_kw_only(type, dataclasses) or (
            isinstance(type, str)
            and _is_type(type, cls, dataclasses, dataclasses.KW_ONLY, _is_
            kw_only)
        ):
            # Switch the default to kw_only=True, and ignore this
            # annotation: it's not a real field.
            if KW_ONLY_seen:
                raise TypeError(
                    f"{name!r} is KW_ONLY, but KW_ONLY " "has already been
                    specified"
                )
            KW_ONLY_seen = True
            kw_only = True
        else:
            # Otherwise it's a field of some type.
            cls_fields.append(_get_field(cls, name, type, kw_only))
```

```
    # Do we have any Field members that don't also have annotations?
    for name, value in cls.__dict__.items():
        if isinstance(value, Field) and not name in cls_annotations:
            raise TypeError(f"{name!r} is a field but has no type
            annotation")

    # Get the fields as a list, and include only real fields.  This is
    # used in all of the following methods.
    field_list = [f for f in fields.values() if f._field_type is _FIELD]

    ...

    if frozen:
        _frozen_get_del_attr(cls, field_list, func_builder)

    ...

    return cls

def dataclass(
    cls=None,
    /,
    *,
    init=True,
    repr=True,
    eq=True,
    order=False,
    unsafe_hash=False,
    frozen=False,
    match_args=True,
    kw_only=False,
    slots=False,
    weakref_slot=False,
):
    """Add dunder methods based on the fields defined in the class.

    Examines PEP 526 __annotations__ to determine fields.
    """
```

```
def wrap(cls):
    return _process_class(
        cls,
        init,
        repr,
        eq,
        order,
        unsafe_hash,
        frozen,
        match_args,
        kw_only,
        slots,
        weakref_slot,
    )

# See if we're being called as @dataclass or @dataclass().
if cls is None:
    # We're called with parens.
    return wrap

# We're called as @dataclass without parens.
return wrap(cls)
```

The @dataclass decorator simplifies the creation of classes by automatically generating special methods like __init__, __repr__, __eq__, and others based on the class attributes. This decorator can be called with or without arguments. The _process_ class function handles the actual processing of the class, adding methods and attributes based on the provided parameters. It also performs validations, such as ensuring all fields have type annotations.

Using Classes as Decorators

We have seen various examples of decorators that are defined using functions. Apart from functions, classes can also act as decorators. In some cases, class-based decorators are better suited for use cases involving arguments, maintaining state, or when more complex behavior is required.

A class-based decorator typically involves defining a class with an __init__ method to accept arguments and a __call__ method to make the class instance callable. The __call__ method is where the decoration logic is implemented.

The below example from *rq* showcases a decorator job, which is defined as a class:

```python
# File: rq/decorators.py

from functools import wraps
from typing import TYPE_CHECKING, Any, Callable, Dict, List, Optional,
Type, Union

class job:  # noqa
    queue_class = Queue

    def __init__(
        self,
        queue: Union['Queue', str],
        connection: 'Redis',
        timeout: Optional[int] = None,
        result_ttl: int = DEFAULT_RESULT_TTL,
        ttl: Optional[int] = None,
        queue_class: Optional[Type['Queue']] = None,
        ...
    ):
        """A decorator that adds a ``enqueue`` method to the decorated
        function,
        which in turn creates a RQ job when called. Accepts a required
        ``queue`` argument that can be either a ``Queue`` instance or a
        string denoting the queue name.  For example::

        Args:
            queue (Union['Queue', str]): The queue to use, can be the Queue
            class itself, or the queue name (str)
            connection (Optional[Redis], optional): Redis Connection.
            Defaults to None.
            timeout (Optional[int], optional): Job timeout. Defaults
            to None.
```

```
            result_ttl (int, optional): Result time to live. Defaults to
            DEFAULT_RESULT_TTL.
            ttl (Optional[int], optional): Time to live. Defaults to None.
            ...
        """
        self.queue = queue
        self.queue_class = backend_class(self, 'queue_class',
        override=queue_class)
        self.connection = connection
        self.timeout = timeout
        self.result_ttl = result_ttl
        self.ttl = ttl

        ...

    def __call__(self, f):
        @wraps(f)
        def delay(*args, **kwargs):
            if isinstance(self.queue, str):
                queue = self.queue_class(name=self.queue, connection=self.
                connection)
            else:
                queue = self.queue

            depends_on = kwargs.pop('depends_on', None)
            job_id = kwargs.pop('job_id', None)
            at_front = kwargs.pop('at_front', False)

            if not depends_on:
                depends_on = self.depends_on

            if not at_front:
                at_front = self.at_front

            return queue.enqueue_call(
                f,
                args=args,
                kwargs=kwargs,
                timeout=self.timeout,
```

```
            result_ttl=self.result_ttl,
            ttl=self.ttl,
            depends_on=depends_on,
            job_id=job_id,
            at_front=at_front,
            ...
        )

    f.delay = delay  # TODO: Remove this in 3.0
    f.enqueue = delay
    return f
```

The job decorator defined above is a class-based decorator that adds an enqueue method to the decorated function. This method, when called, creates an RQ job and enqueues it. The decorator accepts several arguments to configure the job's behavior, such as the queue, connection, timeout, and TTL (time-to-live). The __init__ method initializes the decorator with the provided arguments, setting up the necessary attributes for the job configuration.

The __call__ method makes the class instance callable. It holds the actual decorator logic. In the snippet, the delay function is the wrapper function, which adds delay and enqueue attributes to the decorated function.

The below test cases from the RQ library show the usage examples of the decorator:

```
class TestDecorator(RQTestCase):
    def setUp(self):
        super().setUp()

        @job(queue='default', connection=self.connection)
        def decorated_job(x, y):
            return x + y

        self.decorated_job = decorated_job

    def test_decorator_preserves_functionality(self):
        """Ensure that a decorated function's functionality is still
        preserved."""
        self.assertEqual(self.decorated_job(1, 2), 3)
```

```python
    def test_decorator_adds_delay_attr(self):
        """"Ensure that decorator adds a delay attribute to function
        that returns
        a Job instance when called.
        """

        self.assertTrue(hasattr(self.decorated_job, 'delay'))
        job = self.decorated_job.enqueue(1, 2)
        self.assertTrue(isinstance(job, Job))

    def test_decorator_accepts_queue_name_as_argument(self):
        """"Ensure that passing in queue name to the decorator puts
        the job in
        the right queue.
        """

        @job(queue='queue_name', connection=self.connection)
        def hello():
            return 'Hi'

        result = hello.enqueue()
        self.assertEqual(result.origin, 'queue_name')
```

The decorator adds the enqueue attribute to the decorated function, and the function_name.enqueue() call is used for adding the job to the queue.

Decorators with Asyncio Support

So far, we have covered examples of decorators that support synchronous decorated functions. In the case of functions utilizing the asyncio patterns, the decorated function needs to be called using the await function_name() syntax.

The function_wrapper decorator defined below (defined in the *gradio* library) supports synchronous as well as asynchronous paradigms intelligently:

```python
# File: gradio/utils.py

def function_wrapper(
    f: Callable,
    before_fn: Callable | None = None,
```

```python
    before_args: Iterable | None = None,
    after_fn: Callable | None = None,
    after_args: Iterable | None = None,
):
    before_args = [] if before_args is None else before_args
    after_args = [] if after_args is None else after_args

    if inspect.isasyncgenfunction(f):

        ...

    elif asyncio.iscoroutinefunction(f):

        @functools.wraps(f)
        async def async_wrapper(*args, **kwargs):
            if before_fn:
                before_fn(*before_args)
            response = await f(*args, **kwargs)
            if after_fn:
                after_fn(*after_args)
            return response

        return async_wrapper

    elif inspect.isgeneratorfunction(f):

        @functools.wraps(f)
        def gen_wrapper(*args, **kwargs):
            iterator = f(*args, **kwargs)
            while True:
                if before_fn:
                    before_fn(*before_args)
                try:
                    response = next(iterator)
                except StopIteration:
                    if after_fn:
                        after_fn(*after_args)
                    break
```

```
        if after_fn:
            after_fn(*after_args)
        yield response

    return gen_wrapper

else:

    @functools.wraps(f)
    def wrapper(*args, **kwargs):
        if before_fn:
            before_fn(*before_args)
        response = f(*args, **kwargs)
        if after_fn:
            after_fn(*after_args)
        return response

    return wrapper
```

The function_wrapper decorator is designed to wrap a function f and optionally execute before_fn and after_fn functions before and after the main function f, respectively. The decorator is versatile and can handle different types of functions.

1. The block elif asyncio.iscoroutinefunction(f) checks if the decorated function is a coroutine function (defined using the async def syntax). The async_wrapper is an asynchronous function that ensures before_fn is called before the main function f and after_fn is called after f completes. Since f is a coroutine, it is invoked using await (await f(*args, **kwargs)).

2. Toward the end of the decorator, we can see the decorator supporting regular synchronous functions (in the else block). The wrapper, in this case, is similar to those we have seen previously.

Context Management Decorators

Context management decorators allow us to wrap a function call within a context. When we need a function to be always called inside a context manager block, instead of repeating the context manager usage every time the function is called, we can wrap the call inside a context manager using a decorator.

The following example from *Apache Superset* demonstrates how to implement such decorators to log events with additional context (such as the duration of the action and additional payload data):

```python
# File: superset/utils/log.py

@contextmanager
def log_context(
    self,
    action: str,
    object_ref: str | None = None,
    log_to_statsd: bool = True,
    **kwargs: Any,
) -> Iterator[Callable[..., None]]:
    """
    Log an event with additional information from the request context.
    :param action: a name to identify the event
    :param object_ref: reference to the Python object that triggered
    this action
    :param log_to_statsd: whether to update statsd counter for the action
    """
    payload_override = kwargs.copy()
    start = datetime.now()
    # yield a helper to add additional payload
    yield lambda **kwargs: payload_override.update(kwargs)
    duration = datetime.now() - start

     take the action from payload_override else take the function
    param action
    action_str = payload_override.pop("action", action)
```

```
    self.log_with_context(
        action_str, duration, object_ref, log_to_statsd, **payload_override
    )

def _wrapper(
    self,
    f: Callable[..., Any],
    action: str | Callable[..., str] | None = None,
    object_ref: str | Callable[..., str] | Literal[False] | None = None,
    allow_extra_payload: bool | None = False,
    **wrapper_kwargs: Any,
) -> Callable[..., Any]:
    @functools.wraps(f)
    def wrapper(*args: Any, **kwargs: Any) -> Any:
        action_str = (
            action(*args, **kwargs) if callable(action) else action
        ) or f.__name__
        object_ref_str = (
            object_ref(*args, **kwargs) if callable(object_ref) else
            object_ref
        ) or (f.__qualname__ if object_ref is not False else None)
        with self.log_context(
            action=action_str, object_ref=object_ref_str, **wrapper_kwargs
        ) as log:
            log(**kwargs)
            if allow_extra_payload:
                # add a payload updater to the decorated function
                value = f(*args, add_extra_log_payload=log, **kwargs)
            else:
                value = f(*args, **kwargs)
        return value

    return wrapper

def log_this(self, f: Callable[..., Any]) -> Callable[..., Any]:
    """Decorator that uses the function name as the action"""
    return self._wrapper(f)
```

In the snippet, `log_this` is the decorator, `_wrapper` is the wrapper function, and `log_context` is the context manager.

The `log_context` function logs an event with additional information from the request context. It takes parameters such as `action`, `object_ref`, etc. and yields a helper function to update the payload with additional data. Once the execution is finished, the context manager calculates the duration of the action and logs it along with the provided context.

The `_wrapper` function wraps a function f with the `log_context` context manager. It takes in parameters like `action`, `object_ref`, etc. It then uses the `log_context` context manager to log the action and its duration. If `allow_extra_payload` is True, an `add_extra_log_payload` argument is added to the function f when it's called, allowing the function to add extra payload to the log.

The decorator can be used as below:

```
@log_this
def some_function():
    # Function code here
    pass
```

When `some_function` is called, it will be logged with the function name as the action, and the duration of the function execution will also be logged.

Decorator Use Cases

In this section, we will explore some common use cases of decorators, including caching, validation, registration, etc.

Caching

Decorators can be used to cache the result of function calls. Based on the requirements, the cache key can be generated from the function's properties (name, arguments passed, etc.) or the cache decorator arguments.

The below snippet from CPython showcases _async_cache, a decorator to cache the results of asynchronous functions:

```python
# File: cpython/Tools/jit/_llvm.py

_P = typing.ParamSpec("_P")
_R = typing.TypeVar("_R")
_C = typing.Callable[_P, typing.Awaitable[_R]]

def _async_cache(f: _C[_P, _R]) -> _C[_P, _R]:
    cache = {}
    lock = asyncio.Lock()

    @functools.wraps(f)
    async def wrapper(
        *args: _P.args, **kwargs: _P.kwargs  # pylint: disable = no-member
    ) -> _R:
        async with lock:
            if args not in cache:
                cache[args] = await f(*args, **kwargs)
            return cache[args]

    return wrapper
```

In the code, the cache dictionary is used to store the result of function calls. The arguments tuple (args) acts as the cache key. On each invocation, the wrapper checks if the result is present in the cache before calling the decorator function.

Timing

Decorators are used for timing operations, and this can come in handy using debugging.

Given below is an example of a timing decorator from *PyTorch*:

```python
# File: pytorch/tools/nightly.py

@contextlib.contextmanager
def timer(logger: logging.Logger, prefix: str) -> Iterator[None]:
    """Timed context manager"""
    start_time = time.time()
```

```python
        yield
        logger.info("%s took %.3f [s]", prefix, time.time() - start_time)

F = TypeVar("F", bound=Callable[..., Any])

def timed(prefix: str) -> Callable[[F], F]:
    """Decorator for timing functions"""

    def dec(f: F) -> F:
        @functools.wraps(f)
        def wrapper(*args: Any, **kwargs: Any) -> Any:
            global LOGGER
            logger = cast(logging.Logger, LOGGER)
            logger.info(prefix)
            with timer(logger, prefix):
                return f(*args, **kwargs)

        return cast(F, wrapper)

    return dec
```

Here, the `timed` decorator in the provided code is designed to measure and log the execution time of functions. The context manager usage (`with timer(logger, prefix)`) handles the timing and logging of the function's execution time.

Registering

Decorators can be used for registration, i.e., for populating a registry of related functions so that these can be fetched from the registry and used at a later point. The registration happens immediately when the decoration syntax (`@decorator`) is encountered in the program so that the decorated function is added to the registry as soon as the module is imported or the script is executed. This allows for a centralized collection of functions that can be dynamically accessed and utilized based on specific criteria or events.

The `listens_for` decorator from SQLAlchemy is used for registering event listeners:

```python
# File: lib/sqlalchemy/event/api.py

from .registry import _EventKey

def _event_key(
    target: _ET, identifier: str, fn: _ListenerFnType
) -> _EventKey[_ET]:
    for evt_cls in _registrars[identifier]:
        tgt = evt_cls._accept_with(target, identifier)
        if tgt is not None:
            return _EventKey(target, identifier, fn, tgt)
    else:
        raise exc.InvalidRequestError(
            "No such event '%s' for target '%s'" % (identifier, target)
        )

def listen(
    target: Any, identifier: str, fn: Callable[..., Any], *args: Any,
    **kw: Any
) -> None:
    """Register a listener function for the given target.

    The :func:`.listen` function is part of the primary interface for the
    SQLAlchemy event system, documented at :ref:`event_toplevel`.
    """

    _event_key(target, identifier, fn).listen(*args, **kw)

def listens_for(
    target: Any, identifier: str, *args: Any, **kw: Any
) -> Callable[[Callable[..., Any]], Callable[..., Any]]:
    """Decorate a function as a listener for the given target + identifier.

    The :func:`.listens_for` decorator is part of the primary interface for
    the SQLAlchemy event system, documented at :ref:`event_toplevel`.
```

This function generally shares the same kwargs as :func:`.listen`.

e.g.::

```
from sqlalchemy import event
from sqlalchemy.schema import UniqueConstraint

@event.listens_for(UniqueConstraint, "after_parent_attach")
def unique_constraint_name(const, table):
    const.name = "uq_%s_%s" % (
        table.name,
        list(const.columns)[0].name
    )
```

"""

```
def decorate(fn: Callable[..., Any]) -> Callable[..., Any]:
    listen(target, identifier, fn, *args, **kw)
    return fn

return decorate
```

Below are the key components present in the above snippet:

1. _event_key *function*:

   This function generates an event key that uniquely identifies the event listener.

2. listen *function*:

   This function registers a listener function (fn) for a given target and identifier. It uses the _event_key function to get the event key and then calls the listen method on the event key to register the listener.

3. listens_for *decorator*:

   This is the decorator function that registers a function as an event listener.

The decorate function is the actual decorator that will be applied to the target function. Inside the decorate function, the listen function is called. This registers the function fn as a listener for the specified event.

Validation

Decorators can be used to enforce validation rules on functions, ensuring that certain conditions are met before the function is executed.

In the code snippet below from *Django*, the require_http_methods decorator is used to validate that a view function only accepts specific HTTP request methods:

```python
# File: django/views/decorators/http.py

def require_http_methods(request_method_list):
    """
    Decorator to make a view only accept particular request
    methods.  Usage::

        @require_http_methods(["GET", "POST"])
        def my_view(request):
            # I can assume now that only GET or POST requests make it
            this far
            # ...

    Note that request methods should be in uppercase.
    """

    def decorator(func):
        if iscoroutinefunction(func):

            @wraps(func)
            async def inner(request, *args, **kwargs):
                if request.method not in request_method_list:
                    response = HttpResponseNotAllowed(request_method_list)
                    log_response(
                        "Method Not Allowed (%s): %s",
                        request.method,
                        request.path,
```

```
                    response=response,
                    request=request,
                )
                return response
            return await func(request, *args, **kwargs)

    else:

        @wraps(func)
        def inner(request, *args, **kwargs):
            if request.method not in request_method_list:
                response = HttpResponseNotAllowed(request_method_list)
                log_response(
                    "Method Not Allowed (%s): %s",
                    request.method,
                    request.path,
                    response=response,
                    request=request,
                )
                return response
            return func(request, *args, **kwargs)

    return inner

return decorator

require_GET = require_http_methods(["GET"])
require_GET.__doc__ = "Decorator to require that a view only accepts the
GET method."

require_POST = require_http_methods(["POST"])
require_POST.__doc__ = "Decorator to require that a view only accepts the
POST method."

require_safe = require_http_methods(["GET", "HEAD"])
require_safe.__doc__ = (
    "Decorator to require that a view only accepts safe methods: GET
    and HEAD."
)
```

The decorator helps to ensure that only the allowed HTTP methods will execute the view functions for a Django web application. The decorator accepts the valid HTTP methods as the argument and will enforce these using the `inner()` that wraps the decorated function. The conditional `if request.method not in request_method_list` ensures that accessing the view using any other HTTP methods will return an error response.

Conditional Execution

Decorators can be used to control the execution of functions based on certain conditions.

The snippet below from *nova* showcases a decorator for conditional execution, ensuring that the decorated function is only called if specific conditions are met:

```
# File: nova/rpc.py

def if_notifications_enabled(f):
    """Calls decorated method only if versioned notifications are
    enabled."""
    @functools.wraps(f)
    def wrapped(*args, **kwargs):
        if (NOTIFIER.is_enabled() and
                CONF.notifications.notification_format in ('both',
                                                            'versioned')):
            return f(*args, **kwargs)
        else:
            return None
    return wrapped
```

The `wrapped` function defined above holds the logic for conditional execution. It checks if versioned notifications are enabled by evaluating two conditions:

- `NOTIFIER.is_enabled()`: This checks if the notifier is enabled.

- `CONF.notifications.notification_format in ('both', 'versioned')`: This checks if the notification format is either 'both' or 'versioned'.

If both conditions are met, the original function f is called with the provided arguments (*args and **kwargs). Otherwise, the function returns None, and the decorated function (f) is not executed.

Logging

Decorators can be used to add additional logging behavior to functions for purposes such as logging function execution details, handling exceptions, etc.

In the below code from *hydra*, the log_exceptions decorator is designed to log any uncaught exceptions that occur during the execution of the decorated function:

```
# File: hydra/utils.py

log = get_logger("utils")

def log_exceptions(func):
    """

    logs exceptions using logger, which includes host:port info
    """

    @functools.wraps(func)
    def wrapper(*args, **kwargs):
        if "stats" in kwargs:
            # stats could be a keyword arg
            stats = kwargs["stats"]
        elif len(args) > 0:
            # or the last positional arg
            stats = args[-1]
            if not hasattr(stats, "exceptions"):
                stats = None
        else:
            # or not...
            stats = None
```

```
    try:
        return func(*args, **kwargs)
    except SystemExit:
        # just exit, don't log / catch when we're trying to exit()
        raise
    except:
        log.exception("uncaught exception")
        # increment exception counter if one is available to us
        if stats:
            stats.exceptions += 1

    return wrapper
```

Here, the `log_exceptions` decorator adds additional logging for the decorated functions using a custom logger, when an exception occurs. For exceptions other than `SystemExit`, the except block logs the exception using `log.exception("uncaught exception")`. This added log information will be helpful in pinpointing and fixing application bugs and errors.

Exception Handling

We can delegate exception handling to decorators so that we can replicate this behavior across multiple functions.

The below example from *yt-dlp*, a YouTube video downloader library, shows a decorator (`_handle_extraction_exceptions`) that is used for handling exceptions:

```
# File: yt_dlp/YoutubeDL.py

def _handle_extraction_exceptions(func):
    @functools.wraps(func)
    def wrapper(self, *args, **kwargs):
        while True:
            try:
                return func(self, *args, **kwargs)
            except (DownloadCancelled, LazyList.IndexError, PagedList.
            IndexError):
                raise
```

```python
        except ReExtractInfo as e:
            if e.expected:
                self.to_screen(f'{e}; Re-extracting data')
            else:
                self.to_stderr('\r')
                self.report_warning(f'{e}; Re-extracting data')
            continue
        except GeoRestrictedError as e:
            msg = e.msg
            if e.countries:
                msg += '\nThis video is available in
                {}.'.format(', '.join(
                    map(ISO3166Utils.short2full, e.countries)))
            msg += '\nYou might want to use a VPN or a proxy server
            (with --proxy) to workaround.'
            self.report_error(msg)
        except ExtractorError as e:  # An error we somewhat expected
            self.report_error(str(e), e.format_traceback())
        except Exception as e:
            if self.params.get('ignoreerrors'):
                self.report_error(str(e), tb=encode_compat_
                str(traceback.format_exc()))
            else:
                raise
        break

return wrapper
```

The decorator here ensures that specific exceptions are caught and handled appropriately, such as re-extracting data on certain errors, reporting geo-restrictions, and logging unexpected errors. In this way, exception handling is centralized and can be reused across functions that are responsible for downloading and extracting the data.

Conclusion

Decorators are a powerful tool in Python. These are a form of Python's syntactic sugar that leverages closures to extend the behavior of functions or classes in a clean and readable way. They help us write cleaner, reusable code by separating extra tasks from our main logic. In this chapter, we explored various ways of defining decorators, including decorating classes, creating decorators that take arguments, applying decorators to asynchronous functions, and using classes as decorators. We also discussed practical use cases such as caching, validation, registration, and timing. By understanding and utilizing these techniques, we can significantly enhance the functionality and maintainability of our Python code.

CHAPTER 10

Metaclasses

In the previous chapter, we explored Python's decorators—functions that allow us to modify or enhance the behavior of other functions or classes in a clean and reusable way.

In this chapter, we shift our focus to metaprogramming—a powerful technique that lets us write code that can manipulate or generate other code. Python's dynamic nature and introspection features make metaprogramming especially accessible and expressive. At the core of this are *metaclasses*, which allow us to control how classes themselves are created and behave. While classes are blueprints for objects, metaclasses are the blueprints for classes.

We'll dive into how metaclasses work, when to use them, and how they can help us intercept class creation, enforce coding patterns, and dynamically modify behavior in advanced use cases.

Class Creation Process

When we define a class in Python, the class creation process follows a specific sequence of steps. These are as follows:

1. *MRO entries are resolved*: The method resolution order (MRO) is determined. This establishes the order in which Python will search for methods in the class hierarchy. We have seen about MRO in Chapter 7 on classes.

2. *The appropriate metaclass is determined*: In Python, each class has a metaclass associated with it. This step determines the appropriate metaclass for the class. We will be exploring this process in detail in the coming sections.

© Adarsh Divakaran 2025
A. Divakaran, *Deep Dive Python*, https://doi.org/10.1007/979-8-8688-1261-3_10

3. *The class namespace is prepared*: Classes have a namespace dictionary (see section "Namespace Dictionary" of Chapter 7) that stores class attributes and methods. This step allows for customization of how the namespace is initialized.

4. *The class body is executed*: The code inside the class definition is executed. This includes method definitions, class variables, and any other statements. These are added to the namespace created in the previous step.

5. *The class object is created*: In this step, the class is finally created by calling the appropriate metaclass methods.

We will explore the role of metaclasses in this process in detail in the coming sections.

type in Python

The type built-in can be called with either one or three arguments.

Calling with a Single Argument

When type is called with a single argument, it reveals the type of the object passed on as the argument. It is most commonly used for this purpose.

The below snippet illustrates this type of usage:

```
x = 42
print(type(x))  # <class 'int'>

y = 3.14
print(type(y))  # <class 'float'>

s = "Hello, World!"
print(type(s))  # <class 'str'>

my_list = [1, 2, 3]
print(type(my_list))  # <class 'list'>
```

```
def my_function():
    pass

print(type(my_function))  # <class 'function'>

class MyClass:
    pass

obj = MyClass()
print(type(obj))  # <class '__main__.MyClass'>
```

Calling with Three Arguments

The signature of type() when called with three arguments is

```
type(name, bases, dict)
```

It takes the below parameters:

1. name: A string that specifies the name of the class being created.

2. bases: A tuple of base classes from which the new class will inherit. If there are no base classes, an empty tuple can be used.

3. dict: A dictionary containing attribute names and their corresponding values. These will become the attributes and methods of the new class.

This three-argument form of type() allows us to dynamically create new classes at runtime. It's equivalent to using the class statement but allows for more programmatic control over class creation.

The snippet below exemplifies such a usage:

```
def initializer(self, val):
    self.attribute2 = val

class Parent:
    pass

C = type("C", (Parent,), {"__init__": initializer, "attribute1": 1})

print(f"{issubclass(C, Parent)=}")
```

```
obj = C(10)
print(f"{obj.attribute1=}")
print(f"{obj.attribute2=}")

"""Output:
issubclass(C, Parent)=True
obj.attribute1=1
obj.attribute2=10
"""
```

In the example, a class C is created using type(). The created class will be equivalent to the below definition:

```
class C(Parent):
    attribute1 = 1

    def __init__(self, val):
        self.attribute2 = val
```

Below is an open source example of dynamic class creation from Django:

```
# File: django/contrib/admin/options.py

class ModelAdmin(BaseModelAdmin):
    def get_form(self, request, obj=None, change=False, **kwargs):
        """
        Return a Form class for use in the admin add view. This is used by
        add_view and change_view.
        """

        ...

        # Remove declared form fields which are in readonly_fields.
        new_attrs = dict.fromkeys(
            f for f in readonly_fields if f in self.form.declared_fields
        )
        form = type(self.form.__name__, (self.form,), new_attrs)

        defaults = {
            "form": form,
            "fields": fields,
```

```
        "exclude": exclude,
        "formfield_callback": partial(self.formfield_for_dbfield,
        request=request),
        **kwargs,
    }
```

In this code, the three-argument form of type() is used to create a new form class dynamically. We do this to modify the existing form class (self.form) by removing certain fields that are in readonly_fields. This new form class is created by

1. Using the same name as the original form (self.form.__name__).

2. Inheriting from the original form class ((self.form,)).

3. Providing a dictionary of new attributes (new_attrs). The new_attrs dictionary contains keys for fields that are both in readonly_fields and self.form.declared_fields, with their values set to None.

By using type() in this way, we're able to create a modified version of the original form class on the fly without altering the original class itself.

Defining Metaclasses

In Python, we often say that everything is an object. Not only are the instances we create objects, but the classes themselves are also objects. To take this a step further, we can say that an object is an instance of a class and a class is an instance of a metaclass.

An object is an instance of a class, while a class itself is an instance of a metaclass. This hierarchy allows us to customize the behavior of class creation through metaclasses. Here's a simple example to illustrate:

```
class MyClass:
    pass

my_instance = MyClass()

print(type(my_instance))  # Output: <class '__main__.MyClass'>
print(type(MyClass))  # Output: <class 'type'>
```

In this example, my_instance is an instance of MyClass, and MyClass is an instance of the default metaclass type.

By default, Python uses type as the metaclass for all classes. This means that when we define a new class, it is automatically an instance of type, unless we specify otherwise.

Metamethods

When we work with metaclasses, it's important to understand the order in which their special methods (also called metamethods) are called. Let's explore the main metamethods and their invocation order:

1. __prepare__ *(Prepare)*: This method is called first. We use it to set up a custom namespace for the class being created. If we don't define this method, Python uses a regular dictionary by default.

2. __new__ *(New)*: After __prepare__, Python calls __new__. This method is responsible for creating and returning the new class object. We can use it to modify the class before it's created.

3. __init__ *(Initialize)*: Once the class is created by __new__, Python calls __init__ to initialize it. We use this method to make any final adjustments to the newly created class.

Let's look at a simple example to illustrate this order:

```python
class CustomMetaclass(type):
    def __prepare__(name, bases, **kwargs):
        print("1. Preparing...")
        return {"injected_attribute": "value"}

    def __new__(cls, name, bases, namespace, **kwargs):
        print("2. Creating...")
        print(f"{name=} {bases=} {namespace=}")
        return super().__new__(cls, name, bases, namespace)

    def __init__(self, name, bases, namespace, **kwargs):
        print("3. Initializing...")
        super().__init__(name, bases, namespace)
```

```
class Parent:
    pass

class Child(Parent, metaclass=CustomMetaclass):
    pass

print(f"{Child.injected_attribute=}")

obj = Child()
print(f"{obj.injected_attribute=}")
```

When we run this code, we'll see the following output:

```
1. Preparing...
2. Creating...
name='Child' bases=(<class '__main__.Parent'>,) namespace={'injected_
attribute': 'value', '__module__': '__main__', '__qualname__': 'Child'}
3. Initializing...
Child.injected_attribute='value'
obj.injected_attribute='value'
```

This output shows us the order in which these metamethods are invoked. We don't always need to implement all of these methods. We can choose which ones to define based on what we want to achieve with our metaclass. Understanding this invocation order helps us create more powerful and flexible metaclasses, allowing us to customize Python's class creation process to suit our needs.

Defining a Custom Metaclass

By defining a metaclass, we can intervene in the class creation process, automatically modify class attributes, enforce constraints, or register classes.

Steps to define a custom metaclass:

1. *Inherit from* type: A metaclass typically inherits from type, which is the base metaclass in Python.

2. *Override metaclass methods*: The most commonly overridden methods are __new__ and __init__. The __new__ method is used to customize the class creation, while __init__ can be used for additional initialization.

329

3. *Apply the metaclass*: Use the metaclass keyword when defining a class to specify that it should be created using the custom metaclass.

The below example shows the definition and usage of a custom metaclass:

```python
class LoggingMeta(type):
    def __new__(cls, name, bases, attrs):
        # Add a logging method to the class
        attrs["log"] = lambda self, msg: print(f"{name}: {msg}")

        # Log the class creation
        print(f"Creating class: {name}")

        # Call the original type.__new__ to create the class
        return super().__new__(cls, name, bases, attrs)

class MyClass(metaclass=LoggingMeta):
    def __init__(self, value):
        self.value = value

    def display(self):
        self.log(f"Displaying value: {self.value}")

# Usage
obj = MyClass(42)
obj.display()

"""Output:
Creating class: MyClass
MyClass: Displaying value: 42
"""
```

In this example

1. We define LoggingMeta as our custom metaclass, inheriting from type.

2. We override the __new__ method, which is called when creating a new class. This method receives the class name, its base classes, and a dictionary of attributes.

3. In __new__, we add a log method to the class and print a message about the class creation.

4. We use super().__new__() to call the original class creation method of type.

5. We apply our metaclass to MyClass using the metaclass keyword argument.

6. When we create an instance of MyClass and call its methods, we can see the effects of our metaclass:

   – The "Creating class: MyClass" message is printed when the class is defined.

   – The display method can use the log method that was added by the metaclass.

This example demonstrates how a metaclass can add functionality to a class and its instances, as well as perform actions during class creation.

Method Propagation

Methods defined in a metaclass can indeed propagate to classes that use it. This allows metaclasses to inject functionality into classes in a way that standard inheritance does not. For instance, consider the following example where we define a metaclass Meta with a custom method hello and an overridden __instancecheck__ method:

```
class Meta(type):
    def hello(cls):
        return "Hello from the metaclass!"

    def __instancecheck__(self, instance):
        return True

class MyClass(metaclass=Meta):
    pass

print(MyClass.hello())  # Output: Hello from the metaclass!

print(isinstance([1, 2, 3], MyClass))  # Output: True
```

In this example, `MyClass` inherits the `hello` method from its metaclass `Meta`, allowing us to call `MyClass.hello()` and receive the expected output. Furthermore, the overridden `__instancecheck__` method in `Meta` causes `isinstance([1, 2, 3], MyClass)` to return `True`, demonstrating how metaclasses can customize instance checks across the class hierarchy.

It is to be noted that the methods propagated in this manner are class methods and not instance methods.

Inheritance Behavior

Metaclasses can be a powerful tool for wrapping entire class hierarchies, allowing us to apply consistent behavior across multiple levels of inheritance. When a class is built using a custom metaclass, its child classes automatically inherit the metaclass of their parent unless explicitly specified otherwise. This means that the metaclass's influence extends throughout the hierarchy.

In the example provided below, we define a metaclass Meta with a **__new__** method that prints a message each time a class is created. It also includes a custom method custom_method and an overridden __len__ method. We then create a class hierarchy with Parent, Child, and GrandChild, where only Parent directly uses the Meta metaclass:

```python
class Meta(type):
    def __new__(cls, name, bases, dct):
        print(f"Creating class {name} with Meta")
        return super().__new__(cls, name, bases, dct)

    def custom_method(cls):
        return "This method is from the metaclass!"

    def __len__(self):
        return 42

class Parent(metaclass=Meta):
    pass

class Child(Parent):
    pass
```

```
class GrandChild(Child):
    pass

parent_instance = Parent()
child_instance = Child()
grandchild_instance = GrandChild()

print(f"Parent's metaclass: {type(Parent)}")
print(f"Child's metaclass: {type(Child)}")
print(f"GrandChild's metaclass: {type(GrandChild)}")

print(GrandChild.custom_method())
print(len(GrandChild))
```

The code produces the below output:

```
Creating class Parent with Meta
Creating class Child with Meta
Creating class GrandChild with Meta
Parent's metaclass: <class '__main__.Meta'>
Child's metaclass: <class '__main__.Meta'>
GrandChild's metaclass: <class '__main__.Meta'>
This method is from the metaclass!
42
```

Even though Child and GrandChild do not directly specify a metaclass, they are affected by Meta because they inherit from Parent, which does. As shown in the output, all three classes are created with Meta, and they all have access to custom_method and the overridden __len__ method.

Metaclass Determination Order

In Python, the language follows a specific order of precedence when determining which metaclass to use for a class. This process, known as metaclass resolution, occurs when a class is being created.

- First, Python checks if a metaclass is explicitly specified using the metaclass keyword argument in the class definition. If present, this metaclass is used.

- If no explicit metaclass is specified, Python then looks at the base classes of the class being defined. It examines each base class in the order they're listed and uses the first metaclass it finds. If a base class has a metaclass specified, that metaclass is used for the new class.

- If no metaclass is found in the base classes, Python defaults to using type as the metaclass. This is why type is referred to as the default metaclass in Python.

It's important to note that if multiple base classes have different metaclasses, Python will attempt to create a derived metaclass that inherits from all of them. If this isn't possible, a TypeError is raised.

Metaclass Usage Patterns

In this section, we will explore common patterns and examples of metaclass usage with open source library code examples.

Registration

Metaclasses can be used to implement automatic registration patterns. This can be employed in scenarios where we need to keep track of subclasses or instances for later use, such as in plugin systems, command handlers, or similar architectures.

The below example from Pandas illustrates such a usage:

```python
# File: pandas/tseries/holiday.py

holiday_calendars = {}

def register(cls) -> None:
    try:
        name = cls.name
    except AttributeError:
        name = cls.__name__
    holiday_calendars[name] = cls
```

```python
class HolidayCalendarMetaClass(type):
    def __new__(cls, clsname: str, bases, attrs):
        calendar_class = super().__new__(cls, clsname, bases, attrs)
        register(calendar_class)
        return calendar_class

class AbstractHolidayCalendar(metaclass=HolidayCalendarMetaClass):
    """

    Abstract interface to create holidays following certain rules.
    """

    rules: list[Holiday] = []
    start_date = Timestamp(datetime(1970, 1, 1))
    end_date = Timestamp(datetime(2200, 12, 31))
    _cache = None

    ...
```

In this code, a metaclass is used to automatically register holiday calendar classes as they're defined.

1. Initially, a HolidayCalendarMetaClass is defined that inherits from type. This is the custom metaclass.

2. In the __new__ method of this metaclass, the class is created as usual using super().__new__(), but then the register() function is called to add the newly created class to the holiday_calendars dictionary.

3. The AbstractHolidayCalendar class is defined with metaclass=HolidayCalendarMetaClass. This means that when Python creates this class (and any class that inherits from it), it will use the custom metaclass.

4. As a result, whenever a new calendar class is defined that inherits from AbstractHolidayCalendar, the HolidayCalendarMetaClass.__new__ method will be called, which will automatically register the new class.

5. The register function attempts to use the name attribute of the class if it exists. Otherwise, it falls back to using the class name itself. This name is then used as the key in the holiday_calendars dictionary.

This metaclass approach allows for automatic registration of calendar classes without requiring explicit registration calls in each subclass definition.

Validation or Enforcement

Metaclasses can be used for enforcing/validating constraints on classes such as

- Restricting instantiation

- Enforcing/validation/type checking of class attributes

- Restricting method or attribute definitions

The below snippet from Trio defines a metaclass that prevents normal instantiation:

```
# File: src/trio/_util.py

@final  # No subclassing of NoPublicConstructor itself.
class NoPublicConstructor(ABCMeta):
    """Metaclass that ensures a private constructor.

    If a class uses this metaclass like this::

        @final
        class SomeClass(metaclass=NoPublicConstructor):
            pass

    The metaclass will ensure that no instance can be initialized. This
    should always be used with @final.

    If you try to instantiate your class (SomeClass()), a TypeError will be
    thrown. Use _create() instead in the class's implementation.

    Raises
    ------
```

```
    - TypeError if an instance is created.
    """

    def __call__(cls, *args: object, **kwargs: object) -> None:
        raise TypeError(
            f"{cls.__module__}.{cls.__qualname__} has no public
            constructor"
        )

    def _create(cls: type[T], *args: object, **kwargs: object) -> T:
        return super().__call__(*args, **kwargs)  # type: ignore
```

The NoPublicConstructor metaclass prevents direct instantiation of classes by raising a TypeError if we try to create an instance normally. Instead, instances must be created using the _create method, which is intended for internal use.

Modifying Instance Creation

Metaclasses can be used to hook into the instance creation process of classes. In the below code, a metaclass is used to modify the instance creation process for certain data types in PySpark:

```
# File: python/pyspark/sql/types.py

class DataTypeSingleton(type):
    """Metaclass for DataType"""

    _instances: ClassVar[Dict[Type["DataTypeSingleton"],
    "DataTypeSingleton"]] = {}

    def __call__(cls: Type[T]) -> T:
        if cls not in cls._instances:  # type: ignore[attr-defined]
            cls._instances[cls] = super(  # type: ignore[misc,
            attr-defined]
                DataTypeSingleton, cls
            ).__call__()
        return cls._instances[cls]  # type: ignore[attr-defined]
```

```
class NullType(DataType, metaclass=DataTypeSingleton):
    """Null type.

    The data type representing None, used for the types that cannot be
    inferred.
    """

    @classmethod
    def typeName(cls) -> str:
        return "void"
```

Here, the DataTypeSingleton metaclass is defined to ensure that only one instance of each data type class is created, implementing a singleton pattern. When a class uses DataTypeSingleton as its metaclass, the __call__ method of the metaclass is invoked during instance creation. This method checks if an instance of the class already exists in the _instances dictionary. If it doesn't, a new instance is created using the superclass's __call__ method and stored in the dictionary. If an instance already exists, that instance is returned instead of creating a new one. The NullType class is an example of a data type that uses this singleton metaclass. By specifying metaclass=DataTypeSingleton in its class definition, NullType ensures that only one instance of itself will ever be created. This approach allows PySpark to maintain a single, consistent instance of each data type throughout the application.

Modifying Instance Features

Metaclasses can be used to modify the behavior of objects or to provide additional functionalities. In this code snippet from Django's ORM, a metaclass is used to modify the behavior of instance checks for a specific class:

```
# File: django/db/models/query.py

class InstanceCheckMeta(type):
    def __instancecheck__(self, instance):
        return isinstance(instance, QuerySet) and instance.query.is_empty()

class EmptyQuerySet(metaclass=InstanceCheckMeta):
    """
    Marker class to checking if a queryset is empty by .none():
```

```
    isinstance(qs.none(), EmptyQuerySet) -> True
"""

    def __init__(self, *args, **kwargs):
        raise TypeError("EmptyQuerySet can't be instantiated")
```

The code consists of a metaclass InstanceCheckMeta and the EmptyQuerySet, which is created using this metaclass.

*Metaclass definition (*InstanceCheckMeta*):*

- The InstanceCheckMeta class is a metaclass that overrides the __instancecheck__ method. This special method is invoked when isinstance() is called to determine if an object is an instance of a class.

- The custom implementation of __instancecheck__ in InstanceCheckMeta checks if the given instance both is a QuerySet and has an empty query (instance.query.is_empty()). This allows for a more nuanced instance check that goes beyond simple class inheritance.

*Class using the metaclass (*EmptyQuerySet*):*

- EmptyQuerySet is a class that uses InstanceCheckMeta as its metaclass. This means that any instance check against EmptyQuerySet will use the logic defined in InstanceCheckMeta.__instancecheck__.

- The class is designed as a marker to identify querysets that are empty, specifically those returned by the .none() method on a queryset.

- The __init__ method of EmptyQuerySet raises a TypeError, indicating that this class is not meant to be instantiated directly. Its purpose is solely for instance checking.

This setup allows developers to use isinstance(qs.none(), EmptyQuerySet) to determine if a queryset is effectively empty.

Usage in Enum

Metaclasses are used in the Python standard library in places such as the abc module and for defining enums. This snippet from the CPython source code demonstrates the use of metaclass EnumType to implement the Enum type in Python:

```python
# File: cpython/Lib/enum.py

class EnumType(type):
    """

    Metaclass for Enum
    """

    @classmethod
    def __prepare__(metacls, cls, bases, **kwds):
        # check that previous enum members do not exist
        metacls._check_for_existing_members_(cls, bases)
        # create the namespace dict
        enum_dict = EnumDict()
        enum_dict._cls_name = cls
        ...
        return enum_dict

    def __new__(
        metacls, cls, bases, classdict, *, boundary=None, _
        simple=False, **kwds
    ):
        # an Enum class is final once enumeration items have been
        defined; it
        # cannot be mixed with other types (int, float, etc.) if it has an
        # inherited __new__ unless a new __new__ is defined (or the
        resulting
        # class will fail).
        #
        if _simple:
            return super().__new__(metacls, cls, bases, classdict, **kwds)
```

```python
        #
        # remove any keys listed in _ignore_
        classdict.setdefault("_ignore_", []).append("_ignore_")
        ignore = classdict["_ignore_"]
        for key in ignore:
            classdict.pop(key, None)
        #
        # grab member names
        member_names = classdict._member_names
        #
        # check for illegal enum names (any others?)
        invalid_names = set(member_names) & {"mro", ""}
        if invalid_names:
            raise ValueError(
                "invalid enum member name(s) %s"
                % (",".join(repr(n) for n in invalid_names))
            )
        #

        # data type of member and the controlling Enum class
        member_type, first_enum = metacls._get_mixins_(cls, bases)
        __new__, save_new, use_args = metacls._find_new_(
            classdict,
            member_type,
            first_enum,
        )
        classdict["_new_member_"] = __new__
        classdict["_use_args_"] = use_args

        ...
        return enum_class

    def __bool__(cls):
        """

        classes/types should always be True.
        """

        return True
```

```python
def __call__(
    cls,
    value,
    names=_not_given,
    *values,
    module=None,
    qualname=None,
    type=None,
    start=1,
    boundary=None,
):
    """
    Either returns an existing member, or creates a new enum class.

    This method is used both when an enum class is given a value
    to match to an enumeration member (i.e. Color(3)) and for the
    functional API
    (i.e. Color = Enum('Color', names='RED GREEN BLUE')).
    """
    if cls._member_map_:
        # simple value lookup if members exist
        if names is not _not_given:
            value = (value, names) + values
        return cls.__new__(cls, value)
    # otherwise, functional API: we're creating a new Enum type
    if names is _not_given and type is None:
        # no body? no data-type? possibly wrong usage
        raise TypeError(
            f"{cls} has no members; specify `names=()` if you meant to
            create a new, empty, enum"
        )
    return cls._create_(
        class_name=value,
        names=None if names is _not_given else names,
        module=module,
        qualname=qualname,
```

```
            type=type,
            start=start,
            boundary=boundary,
        )

def __contains__(cls, value):
    """Return True if `value` is in `cls`.

    `value` is in `cls` if:
    1) `value` is a member of `cls`, or
    2) `value` is the value of one of the `cls`'s members.
    """

    if isinstance(value, cls):
        return True
    try:
        return value in cls._value2member_map_
    except TypeError:
        return value in cls._unhashable_values_

def __getitem__(cls, name):
    """
    Return the member matching `name`.
    """

    return cls._member_map_[name]

def __iter__(cls):
    """
    Return members in definition order.
    """

    return (cls._member_map_[name] for name in cls._member_names_)

def __len__(cls):
    """
    Return the number of members (no aliases)
    """

    return len(cls._member_names_)

...
```

In the definition, we can see the usage of

1. __prepare__ *method*:

   This method is called before class creation to set up the class namespace. It creates a special `EnumDict` for storing enum members and performs some initial checks.

2. __new__ *method*:

   This is where most of the enum creation logic happens. It processes the class definition, sets up the enum members, and creates the final class object. It handles things like

   – Removing ignored attributes

   – Validating enum member names

   – Setting up the enum's internal structures

3. The metaclass defines several special methods like __bool__, __call__, __contains__, __getitem__, etc. These methods define behavior for the enum class itself, not its instances.

4. __call__ *method*:

   The __call__ method in the metaclass allows for custom instance creation logic. This is used to either return existing enum members or create new enum classes (in the functional API). For example, the usage such as red = `Color('RED')` invokes `EnumType.__call__`.

Using the metaclass, the enum type is defined as below:

```
class Enum(metaclass=EnumType):
    """

    Create a collection of name/value pairs.
    """

    def __new__(cls, value):
        # all enum instances are actually created during class construction
        # without calling this method; this method is called by the
        metaclass'
```

```python
        # __call__ (i.e. Color(3) ), and by pickle
        if type(value) is cls:
            # For lookups like Color(Color.RED)
            return value
        # by-value search for a matching enum member
        # see if it's in the reverse mapping (for hashable values)
        try:
            return cls._value2member_map_[value]
        except KeyError:
            # Not found, no need to do long O(n) search
            pass
        except TypeError:
            # not there, now do long search -- O(n) behavior
            for name, values in cls._unhashable_values_map_.items():
                if value in values:
                    return cls[name]
        # still not found -- verify that members exist, in-case somebody
        got here mistakenly
        # (such as via super when trying to override __new__)
        if not cls._member_map_:
            if getattr(cls, "_%s__in_progress" % cls.__name__, False):
                raise TypeError(
                    "do not use `super().__new__; call the appropriate __
                    new__ directly"
                ) from None
            raise TypeError("%r has no members defined" % cls)
        #
        # still not found -- try _missing_ hook
        try:
            exc = None
            result = cls._missing_(value)
        except Exception as e:
            exc = e
            result = None
```

```
    try:
        if isinstance(result, cls):
            return result
        ...
    finally:
        # ensure all variables that could hold an exception are
        destroyed
        exc = None
        ve_exc = None

def __init__(self, *args, **kwds):
    pass

...

@classmethod
def _missing_(cls, value):
    return None

@property
def name(self):
    """The name of the Enum member."""
    return self._name_

@property
def value(self):
    """The value of the Enum member."""
    return self._value_
```

The Enum class uses EnumType as its metaclass. This means that every enum class defined with Enum inherits the behavior and constraints imposed by EnumType. The Enum class provides methods like __new__ and _missing_ to handle member creation and missing values. Other dunders are passed on from the metaclass to the enum class, such as the __len__, __getitem__, etc.

Metaclasses are used for defining Enum because

- Although Enum is defined as a class, it is not commonly instantiated by the user for defining enumerations; it is subclassed. So they need to be validated/registered whenever a class definition is encountered. Metaclasses provide the desired mechanism to control the class creation process.

- Metaclasses allow the enforcement of constraints that are specific to enums, such as ensuring that no duplicate names or values exist and that illegal names are not used. This helps maintain the integrity and reliability of enum classes.

Metaclass Alternatives

PEP 487

PEP 487 titled "Simpler customisation of class creation" proposed simple alternatives to customize class creation, which were previously possible only using metaclasses.

The PEP starts with the below introduction:

> Currently, customizing class creation requires the use of a custom metaclass. This custom metaclass then persists for the entire lifecycle of the class, creating the potential for spurious metaclass conflicts.

> This PEP proposes to instead support a wide range of customization scenarios through a new __init_subclass__ hook in the class body and a hook to initialize attributes.

> The new mechanism should be easier to understand and use than implementing a custom metaclass and thus should provide a gentler introduction to the full power of Python's metaclass machinery.

PEP 487 methods are generally simpler to implement and understand compared with metaclasses. We don't need to work with the intricacies of the class creation process directly. It was introduced in Python 3.6 and provides the __init_subclass__ method to modify subclass behavior at definition time and the __set_name__ method to customize descriptor naming.

The below snippet from Apache Superset shows a usage example of the __init_subclass__ dunder for registering classes:

```
# File: superset/reports/notifications/base.py

class BaseNotification:  # pylint: disable=too-few-public-methods
    """

    Serves has base for all notifications and creates a simple plugin
    system for extending future implementations.
    Child implementations get automatically registered and should identify
    the notification type
    """

    plugins: list[type["BaseNotification"]] = []
    type: Optional[ReportRecipientType] = None
    """

    Child classes set their notification type ex: `type = "email"` this
    string will be used by ReportRecipients.type to map to the correct
    implementation
    """

    def __init_subclass__(cls, *args: Any, **kwargs: Any) -> None:
        super().__init_subclass__(*args, **kwargs)
        cls.plugins.append(cls)
```

In this code, the __init_subclass__ method is used to implement a simple plugin system for notifications. It works as below:

1. The BaseNotification class defines a class variable plugins as an empty list.

2. The __init_subclass__ method is called automatically whenever a new subclass of BaseNotification is created.

3. Inside __init_subclass__, the new subclass (cls) is appended to the plugins list.

4. This allows the BaseNotification class to keep track of all its subclasses without requiring explicit registration.

This can be used in the code like below:

```python
class EmailNotification(BaseNotification):
    type = ReportRecipientType.EMAIL

    def send(self, recipient, message):
        # Implementation for sending email
        print(f"Sending email to {recipient}: {message}")

class SlackNotification(BaseNotification):
    type = ReportRecipientType.SLACK

    def send(self, recipient, message):
        # Implementation for sending Slack message
        print(f"Sending Slack message to {recipient}: {message}")
```

Now, BaseNotification.plugins will automatically contain [EmailNotification, SlackNotification].

Another example of the __init_subclass__ is given below from CPython:

```python
# File: cpython/Lib/typing.py

class _Final:
    """Mixin to prohibit subclassing."""

    __slots__ = ("__weakref__",)

    def __init_subclass__(cls, /, *args, **kwds):
        if "_root" not in kwds:
            raise TypeError("Cannot subclass special typing classes")
```

In this code snippet, the `__init_subclass__` method is used as a mechanism to prevent subclassing of certain special typing classes. Here's a breakdown of its usage:

1. The `_Final` class is defined as a mixin that can be used to prohibit subclassing.

2. The `__init_subclass__` method is overridden in this class. This method is automatically called whenever a subclass of `_Final` is created.

3. The method checks if the keyword argument `"_root"` is present in the `kwds` dictionary. This argument is used internally by the typing module to allow certain subclasses.

4. If `"_root"` is not present in `kwds`, the method raises a `TypeError` with the message "Cannot subclass special typing classes".

5. This effectively prevents any external code from subclassing classes that inherit from `_Final`, unless they somehow know about and provide the `_root` keyword argument.

The use of `__init_subclass__` here is a clean and straightforward way to enforce this subclassing restriction. It allows the typing module to create classes that are meant to be final (not subclassable) in a way that's more explicit and easier to manage than using metaclasses.

Class Decorators

Class decorators in Python provide a way to modify or enhance a class's behavior at the time of its definition. They are applied using the "@" symbol above the class declaration and can be used to add methods, alter attributes, or change the class's overall functionality. Unlike metaclasses, class decorators are more localized in their effect and don't automatically propagate changes to subclasses. They offer a simpler alternative to metaclasses for many use cases, allowing developers to hook into the object creation process of a specific class without affecting its entire hierarchy.

The snippet below shows a class decorator function in Django that modifies classes to make them compatible with Django's HTML escaping system:

```python
# File: django/utils/html.py

def html_safe(klass):
    """
    A decorator that defines the __html__ method. This helps non-Django
    templates to detect classes whose __str__ methods return SafeString.
    """
    if "__html__" in klass.__dict__:
        raise ValueError(
            "can't apply @html_safe to %s because it defines "
            "__html__()." % klass.__name__
        )
    if "__str__" not in klass.__dict__:
        raise ValueError(
            "can't apply @html_safe to %s because it doesn't "
            "define __str__()." % klass.__name__
        )
    klass_str = klass.__str__
    klass.__str__ = lambda self: mark_safe(klass_str(self))
    klass.__html__ = lambda self: str(self)
    return klass
```

The decorator does the following:

1. It checks if the class already has an __html__ method. If so, it raises a ValueError because the decorator can't be applied to classes that already define this method.

2. It checks if the class has a __str__ method. If not, it raises a ValueError because the decorator requires a __str__ method to function.

3. If both checks pass, it stores the original __str__ method of the class.

351

4. It then replaces the class's __str__ method with a new lambda function. This new function calls the original __str__ method and wraps its result with Django's mark_safe() function, which marks the string as safe for HTML rendering without escaping.

5. It adds a new __html__ method to the class, which simply returns the result of str(self).

6. Finally, it returns the modified class.

To apply this to classes, we need to decorate all the classes that are to be modified using the decorator below:

1. *Usage in* Media *class*

    ```python
    # File: django/forms/widgets.py

    @html_safe
    class Media:
        def __init__(self, media=None, css=None, js=None):
            if media is not None:
                css = getattr(media, "css", {})
                js = getattr(media, "js", [])
            else:
                ...

        def __repr__(self):
            return "Media(css=%r, js=%r)" % (self._css, self._js)

        def __str__(self):
            return self.render()

        ...
    ```

2. *Usage in* BoundWidget

    ```python
    # File: django/forms/boundfield.py

    @html_safe
    class BoundWidget:
        """
    ```

> *A container class used for iterating over widgets. This is*
> *useful for widgets that have choices.*
> *"""*

```
    def __init__(self, parent_widget, data, renderer):
        self.parent_widget = parent_widget
        self.data = data
        self.renderer = renderer

    def __str__(self):
        return self.tag(wrap_label=True)

    ...
```

The purpose of this decorator is to make it easier for non-Django templates to identify classes that return safe HTML strings. When a template system encounters an object with an **__html__** method, it knows it can safely render the object's string representation without additional escaping.

Conclusion

> *Metaclasses are deeper magic than 99% of users should ever worry about. If you wonder whether you need them, you don't (the people who actually need them know with certainty that they need them, and don't need an explanation about why).*

—Tim Peters

In our exploration of metaclasses, we've seen how they allow us to customize the class creation process, providing hooks that can modify behavior and attributes as classes are defined. Metaclasses propagate along class hierarchies, enabling us to apply consistent modifications across a series of related classes. This makes them a powerful tool for scenarios where we need to intervene in the class creation process itself.

However, metaclasses are inherently complex, and as Tim Peters famously noted, "Metaclasses are deeper magic than 99% of users should ever worry about." For many use cases, we now have simpler and more accessible alternatives. PEP 487 introduces features like __init_subclass__ and __set_name__, which allow us to achieve many of the same goals without the intricacies of metaclasses. Similarly, class decorators provide a flexible way to enhance class functionality in a clean and modular fashion. By leveraging these alternatives, we can often achieve the desired outcomes with greater simplicity and clarity. This allows us to focus on building maintainable and robust systems without getting bogged down in the complexities of metaclasses. For most developers, these tools provide a more approachable way to implement advanced class behaviors, ensuring that our code remains both powerful and understandable.

CHAPTER 11

Typing

In the previous chapter, we explored metaclasses and saw how they let us customize class creation and behavior at a deep level—effectively giving us control over Python's object model itself.

Python is a dynamically typed language. Types are assigned only at runtime; a variable can change its type while running. But there are cases where explicitly specifying types can be beneficial, similar to languages like C or Java.

Type annotations or type hints can be used to denote the types of variables, arguments, and return values of functions/methods. Type annotations are just hints for our understanding, and the Python interpreter won't check these.

Type annotations were introduced in Python 3.5 (PEP 483 and 484).

From PEP 484, which formalized type annotations:

> This PEP aims to provide a standard syntax for type annotations, opening up Python code to easier static analysis and refactoring, potential runtime type checking, and (perhaps, in some contexts) code generation utilizing type information.

As mentioned, typing can be useful for spotting errors early in the development process using static analysis, checking types during runtime, etc. In the following sections, we will see cases of type hints utilized for various purposes.

Type Checking

```
# File: script.py

number = input("What is your favourite number?")
print("It is", number + 1)
```

This code will result in an error because `input()` returns a string and trying to add a number to a string is not supported.

© Adarsh Divakaran 2025
A. Divakaran, *Deep Dive Python*, https://doi.org/10.1007/979-8-8688-1261-3_11

We can use a static type checker library like mypy to type-check this code. After installing mypy, running "mypy script.py" would generate the below error message:

```
error: Unsupported operand types for + ("str" and "int")
```

Since mypy is a static type checker, the code is not executed while running the above command. Mypy knows the return type of input (since it is a part of the Python standard library), and it analyzes the usage of its return value to point out the potential error. This way, we caught a bug that could have raised an error at runtime.

Annotating Variables

Here are some examples of type-annotating variables from mypy's cheatsheet:

```
# For most types, just use the name of the type in the annotation
# Note that mypy can usually infer the type of a variable from its value,
# so technically these annotations are redundant

x: int = 1
x: float = 1.0
x: bool = True
x: str = "test"

# For collections on Python 3.9+, the type of the collection item is in
brackets
x: list[int] = [1]
x: set[int] = {6, 7}

# For mappings, we need the types of both keys and values
x: dict[str, float] = {"field": 2.0}  # Python 3.9+

# For tuples of fixed size, we specify the types of all the elements
x: tuple[int, str, float] = (3, "yes", 7.5)  # Python 3.9+

# For tuples of variable size, we use one type and ellipsis
x: tuple[int, ...] = (1, 2, 3)  # Python 3.9+

# On Python 3.8 and earlier, the name of the collection type is
# capitalized, and the type is imported from the 'typing' module
```

```
from typing import List, Set, Dict, Tuple
x: List[int] = [1]
x: Set[int] = {6, 7}
x: Dict[str, float] = {"field": 2.0}
x: Tuple[int, str, float] = (3, "yes", 7.5)
x: Tuple[int, ...] = (1, 2, 3)

from typing import Union, Optional
# On Python 3.10+, use the I operator when something could be one of a
few types
x: list[int I str] = [3, 5, "test", "fun"]   # Python 3.10+

# On earlier versions, use Union
x: list[Union[int, str]] = [3, 5, "test", "fun"]

# Use Optional[X] for a value that could be None
# Optional[X] is the same as X I None or Union[X, None]
x: Optional[str] = "something" if some_condition() else None

if x is not None:
    # Mypy understands x won't be None here because of the if-statement
    print(x.upper())
```

Protocols

Protocols were introduced in Python 3.8 (PEP 544).

Protocols are classes defined for type annotation only, and they enable duck typing (structural subtyping) in Python programs. Protocols enable duck typing in Python by defining the required attributes and methods for objects, allowing type checking based on structural subtyping. Any object having these (attributes and methods) can pass type checking.

The code below is from the "Rich" library, which is used for text formatting in the terminal:

```
# File: rich/rich/_ratio.py
import sys
from typing import List, Optional, Sequence
```

```
if sys.version_info >= (3, 8):
    from typing import Protocol
else:
    from typing_extensions import Protocol  # pragma: no cover

class Edge(Protocol):  # <----
    """Any object that defines an edge (such as Layout)."""

    size: Optional[int] = None
    ratio: int = 1
    minimum_size: int = 1

def ratio_resolve(total: int, edges: Sequence[Edge]) -> List[int]:
    """Divide total space to satisfy size, ratio, and minimum_size,
    constraints."""

    ...

    # The edges argument of this function accepts a sequence of
    # objects that conform to the Edge protocol
```

Since Protocol was introduced in the typing module in Python 3.8, a check for the version can be seen in the code initially. The protocol class is imported from the typing_extensions library for lower versions, which should be installed separately via pip.

A protocol named Edge is defined, which has three attributes: *size, ratio*, and *minimum_size*. Any object with matching attributes will pass the type check for the Edge protocol.

It can be seen that the defined protocol class is used to annotate a function ratio_resolve, which accepts a sequence of Edge types. A sequence is a container, like a list or tuple, which allows access by integer index.

In the below test file of the library, we can see the ratio_resolve function being called:

```
# File: rich/test/test_ratio.py
import pytest
from typing import NamedTuple, Optional

from rich._ratio import ratio_reduce, ratio_resolve
```

```
class Edge(NamedTuple):
    size: Optional[int] = None
    ratio: int = 1
    minimum_size: int = 1

def test_ratio_resolve():
    ...
    assert ratio_resolve(100, [Edge(size=100), Edge(ratio=1)]) == [100, 1]
    assert ratio_resolve(100, [Edge(ratio=1), Edge(ratio=1)]) == [50, 50]
    # These will pass type check since the namedtuple Edge has -
    # all the protocol attributes defined
```

A list of namedtuple(Edge) objects is passed to the edges argument of the ratio_resolve function. Since this namedtuple has all the three required attributes of the Edge protocol, this usage will pass the type check.

In addition to defining attributes, protocols can also define functions as their members, and the presence of these member functions will also be verified by type checkers.

TypeVar

Type variables or typevars are used to denote generics while type-annotating. They can be of any type (int, str, etc.), but a type variable retains its type information once assigned.

Think of a function that returns inp * 3 considering inp as the argument to the function. This function can work with both integers and strings since both support the * operation. When we pass an int, its mathematical product is returned. On passing a string, it is repeated three times, and the resulting string is returned. In such scenarios, where a variable accepts generic arguments, TypeVar can be used. Note that in the above case, when an int is passed in as the argument, an int is returned, whereas a string input results in string output. Typevars can perfectly model such scenarios.

The below example is from urllib3, which uses TypeVar to define key and value types of a mapping:

```
# File: src/urllib3/_collections.py

# Key type
_KT = typing.TypeVar("_KT")
# Value type
_VT = typing.TypeVar("_VT")

...

class RecentlyUsedContainer(typing.Generic[_KT, _VT], typing.
MutableMapping[_KT, _VT]):
    _container: typing.OrderedDict[_KT, _VT]
    _maxsize: int

    ...

    def __getitem__(self, key: _KT) -> _VT:
        ...

    def __setitem__(self, key: _KT, value: _VT) -> None:
        evicted_item = None
        ...
```

Here, _KT and _VT are used to denote the key and value types, respectively. These are used multiple times in the annotations of the RecentlyUsedContainer class.

Since the __getitem__ and __setitem__ dunders of the class use the same typevars, the type checker can assume that if the key passed to __getitem__ of an object of this class is of integer type, then the __setitem__ of the object should also receive the same type.

Static Type Checking

Static type checks can be run over type-annotated code to catch bugs early on in the development cycle. The following section shows the bugs discovered when type checks were introduced to urllib3, a popular open source HTTP-client library.

urllib3

Example 1: **Incorrect default argument value**

Consider the below function, which was present in urllib3:

```
# File: src/urllib3/poolmanager.py
# Function signature before adding mypy

def connection_from_pool_key(self,
                             pool_key,
                             request_context=None):  # <-----
        """

    Get a :class:`urllib3.connectionpool.ConnectionPool` based on the
    provided pool key.
    ``pool_key`` should be a namedtuple that only contains immutable
    objects. At a minimum it must have the ``scheme``, ``host``, and
    ``port`` fields.
    """

    with self.pools.lock:
        # If the scheme, host, or port doesn't match existing open
        # connections, open a new ConnectionPool.

        pool = self.pools.get(pool_key)
        if pool:
            return pool

        # Make a fresh ConnectionPool of the desired type
        scheme = request_context["scheme"]  # <----
        host = request_context["host"]
        port = request_context["port"]

        ...
```

When the library started adopting typing and started type checking with mypy, they found out that there was a bug in this function.

The request_context argument was left optional in the code. But in reality, the argument was required (as it is used inside the function body without any checks for absence), which would have resulted in a runtime error.

On type checking using mypy, an error was reported due to this, and the bug was fixed as below:

```
# File: src/urllib3/poolmanager.py
# Function after adding mypy
```

```python
def connection_from_pool_key(
        self, pool_key: PoolKey, request_context: Dict[str, Any]
) -> HTTPConnectionPool:

    ...
    return pool
```

The function body remains unchanged between implementations. Since the request_context variable is directly used in the code (without any additional checks for it being None), mypy detected the error, and the issue was fixed by making this argument a required one.

Example 2: **Missing None checks**

The below increment function was used in the retry function of the urllib3:

```
# File: src/urllib3/util/retry.py
# Function increment before adding type annotations
```

```python
def increment(
        self,
        method=None,
        url=None,
        response=None,
        error=None,
        _pool=None,
        _stacktrace=None,
):
    """Return a new Retry object with incremented retry counters.
    :param response: A response object, or None, if the server did not
        return a response.
    :type response: :class:`~urllib3.response.HTTPResponse`
    :param Exception error: An error encountered during the request, or
        None if the response was received successfully.
```

```
    :return: A new ``Retry`` object.
    """

    ...

    elif error and self._is_read_error(error):
        # Read retry?
        if read is False or not self._is_method_retryable(method):
            raise reraise(type(error), error, _stacktrace)

        elif read is not None:
            read -= 1
```

It can be seen that the method argument is None by default.

The code calls _is_method_retryable by passing method as its argument. The definition of the function is as below:

```
# File: src/urllib3/util/retry.py

def _is_method_retryable(self, method):
    """ Checks if a given HTTP method should be retried upon, depending if
    it is included on the method whitelist.
    """

    if self.method_whitelist and method.upper() not in self.method_
    whitelist:
        return False

    return True
```

It can be seen that the method argument here expects a string (since method.upper() is called in the function body). Upon inspecting with mypy after adding type hints, this error was discovered, and a null check was added in the increment function as given below:

```
# File: src/urllib3/util/retry.py
# Function increment after type annotation

def increment(
        self,
        method: Optional[str] = None,
        url: Optional[str] = None,
```

```
        response: Optional["HTTPResponse"] = None,
        error: Optional[Exception] = None,
        _pool: Optional["ConnectionPool"] = None,
        _stacktrace: Optional[TracebackType] = None,
) -> "Retry":

    ...

    elif error and self._is_read_error(error):
        # Read retry?
        if read is False or method is None or not self._is_method_
        retryable(method):
            raise reraise(type(error), error, _stacktrace)
        elif read is not None:
            read -= 1
```

This way, _is_method_retryable won't be called when method is None.

Runtime Type Checking

Type hints can also be checked at runtime. But runtime type checking is less common or popular than static type checking.

The annotations of classes and functions can be obtained at runtime using the annotations dunder variable as given below:

```
def foo(bar: int) -> str:
    return "Hello"

print(foo.__annotations__)
# {'bar': <class 'int'>, 'return': <class 'str'>}

class Bar:
    attr: list[int] = []

    def method(self, foo: int) -> str:
        pass

print(Bar.__annotations__)
# {'attr': list[int]}
```

Beartype is a runtime type checker that provides a decorator that can be used to decorate functions or methods we need to type-check.

You may think that if wrong arguments are provided, they will lead to runtime errors anyway, so why use a runtime type checker? Taking the example of beartype, it will check if the decorated function receives the correct argument types when called. If not, it will raise an error, and the function body won't be run.

This can be employed when working with data/inputs that we do not trust, e.g., when writing a program that relies on external APIs for data or a library that accepts user data as input.

Let's start with an example:

```
import time

def scream(text: str):
    print('doing a sensitive operation\n')
    time.sleep(1)
    print(text.upper())

scream(10)

"""
doing a sensitive operation
Traceback (most recent call last):
  File "...", line 9, in <module>
    scream(10)
  File "...", line 7, in scream
    print(text.upper())
          ^^^^^^^^^^^
AttributeError: 'int' object has no attribute 'upper'
"""
```

The above function returns an error when the last line in the function body is run, which expects a string argument.

Now add beartype:

```
from beartype import beartype
import time

@beartype
```

```
def scream(text: str):

    print('doing a sensitive operation\n')
    time.sleep(1)
    print(text.upper())

scream(10)
"""
Traceback (most recent call last):
  File "...", line 11, in <module>
    scream(10)
  File "<@beartype(__main__.scream) at 0x19f69815580>", line 21, in scream
beartype.roar.BeartypeCallHintParamViolation: Function __main__.scream()
parameter text=10 violates type hint <class 'str'>, as int 10 not
instance of str.
"""
```

When beartype is added, no lines in the function body are run when the type check for the arguments fails.

Nebuly

Nebuly is a toolkit for making AI models better. Nebuly uses beartype for runtime type checking:

```
# File: nebuly/optimization/chatllama/chatllama/rlhf/config.py
class Config:
    "Store the config parameters for the whole pipeline"

    @beartype
    def __init__(
        self,
        path: str,
        device: Optional[torch.device] = None,
        debug: Optional[bool] = False,
    ) -> None:

        ...
```

The class `Config`'s init is decorated with the `beartype` decorator. When this class is initialized at runtime, beartype will type-check the passed arguments and will raise an error in case of a mismatch. Statements in the function body are executed only after passing this runtime type check.

Libraries Leveraging Type Hints

Since the type hints can be accessed dynamically, libraries can leverage this to implement certain functionalities like validation in a much more Pythonic way.

Both libraries mentioned in this section use the concept of metaclass to power their functionality. Refer to Chapter 10 on metaclasses for more details.

Pydantic

Pydantic is a data validation library. It leverages type annotations to define and validate Pydantic models, which can be considered a type-enforced version of Python's dataclasses.

Consider the below snippet:

```python
from pydantic import BaseModel

class Foo(BaseModel):
    bar: int

foo_obj = Foo(bar="hello")
```

This will raise an error as below:

```
Traceback (most recent call last):
  File "... foo.py", line 7, in <module>
    foo_obj = Foo(bar="hello")
              ^^^^^^^^^^^^^^^^^
```

```
File "... \venv\Lib\site-packages\pydantic\main.py", line 341, in
__init__
    raise validation_error

pydantic.error_wrappers.ValidationError: 1 validation error for Foo
bar
  value is not a valid integer (type=type_error.integer)
```

Pydantic uses the type annotation for the field (bar: int) to validate the creation of foo_obj. Let's look at how this is implemented under the hood.

Pydantic models are normally defined by inheriting from the Pydantic BaseModel class:

```python
# Pydantic BaseModel class
# File: pydantic/v1/main.py

class BaseModel(Representation, metaclass=ModelMetaclass):
    ...
    def __init__(__pydantic_self__, **data: Any) -> None:
        """
        Create a new model by parsing and validating input data from
        keyword arguments.
        Raises ValidationError if the input data cannot be parsed to form a
        valid model.
        """

        # Uses something other than `self` the first arg to allow "self" as
        a settable attribute
        values, fields_set, validation_error = validate_model(__pydantic_
        self__.__class__, data)

        if validation_error:
            raise validation_error

        ...
```

As seen from the above snippet, when creating a new object, the `validate_model` function is called:

```python
# Function validate_model
# File: pydantic/main.py

def validate_model(  # noqa: C901 (ignore complexity)
    model: Type[BaseModel], input_data: 'DictStrAny', cls:
    'ModelOrDc' = None
) -> Tuple['DictStrAny', 'SetStr', Optional[ValidationError]]:
    """
    validate data against a model.
    """

    values = {}
    errors = []

    # input_data names, possibly alias
    names_used = set()

    # field names, never aliases
    fields_set = set()
    ...

    for name, field in model.__fields__.items():
        value = input_data.get(field.alias, _missing)
        ...

        v_, errors_ = field.validate(value, values, loc=field.alias,
        cls=cls_)  # <----

        if isinstance(errors_, ErrorWrapper):
            errors.append(errors_)
        elif isinstance(errors_, list):
            errors.extend(errors_)
        else:
            values[name] = v_

    ...
```

369

```
    if errors:
        return values, fields_set, ValidationError(errors, cls_)
    else:
        return values, fields_set, None
```

The function iterates over each field(attribute) defined in the model and calls the validate function for that field (in our case, the field bar was the one that caused the error).

Each field in a Pydantic model is an instance of the ModelField class, and the code of the validate method used above can be seen in its definition:

```
# File: pydantic/fields.py
# class ModelField - Every field defined in the BaseModel is stored
# as an instance of this class

class ModelField(Representation):
    ...

    def __init__(
        self,
        *,
        name: str,
        type_: Type[Any],
        class_validators: Optional[Dict[str, Validator]],
        model_config: Type['BaseConfig'],
        default: Any = None,
        default_factory: Optional[NoArgAnyCallable] = None,
        required: 'BoolUndefined' = Undefined,
        final: bool = False,
        alias: Optional[str] = None,
        field_info: Optional[FieldInfo] = None,
    ) -> None:

        self.name: str = name
        self.has_alias: bool = alias is not None
        self.alias: str = alias if alias is not None else name
        self.annotation = type_
        ...
```

```python
        self.allow_none: bool = False
        self.validate_always: bool = False
        ...

        self.validators: 'ValidatorsList' = []
        self.pre_validators: Optional['ValidatorsList'] = None
        self.post_validators: Optional['ValidatorsList'] = None
        ...

        self.shape: int = SHAPE_SINGLETON
        ...

        self.prepare()
        ...

def validate(
        self, v: Any, values: Dict[str, Any], *, loc: 'LocStr', cls:
        Optional['ModelOrDc'] = None
    ) -> 'ValidateReturn':

        ...

        if self.shape == SHAPE_SINGLETON:  # <----
            v, errors = self._validate_singleton(v, values, loc, cls)
        elif self.shape in MAPPING_LIKE_SHAPES:
            v, errors = self._validate_mapping_like(v, values,
            loc, cls)
        elif self.shape == SHAPE_TUPLE:
            v, errors = self._validate_tuple(v, values, loc, cls)
        elif self.shape == SHAPE_ITERABLE:
            v, errors = self._validate_iterable(v, values, loc, cls)
        elif self.shape == SHAPE_GENERIC:
            v, errors = self._apply_validators(v, values, loc, cls,
            self.validators)
        else:
            #  sequence, list, set, generator, tuple with ellipsis,
            frozen set
```

```
        v, errors = self._validate_sequence_like(v, values,
            loc, cls)

    if not errors and self.post_validators:
        v, errors = self._apply_validators(v, values, loc, cls,
            self.post_validators)

    return v, errors
```

Each field has a shape attribute and its own set of validators. Since the field bar we defined is an integer, its shape is SHAPE_SINGLETON, and int_validator is added as the validator in self.validators. The error we saw was created by this validator executing on the bar attribute.

> Operations like parsing of annotations defined in the "BaseModel" and population of validators happen when the "BaseModel" subclass's definition is encountered by the interpreter (in our case, when the class "Foo" is seen by the interpreter). The mechanism behind this subclass registration is explained in detail in Chapter 10.

SQLModel

SQLModel is an ORM library powered by type hints. Under the hood, it uses Pydantic (for validation) and SQLAlchemy, another highly powerful and customizable ORM. It can be thought of as a wrapper over the SQLAlchemy ORM. It allows us to define SQL column types using type hints.

Here's an example definition of a table using SQLAlchemy ORM:

```
from sqlalchemy import Column, Integer, String

class Hero(Base):
    id = Column(Integer, primary_key=True, nullable=True)
    name = Column(String(255))
    secret_name = Column(String(255))
    age = Column(Integer, nullable=True, default=None)
```

Integer and String classes defined in sqlalchemy are used in this case to define the column types.

The same can be defined using SQLModel leveraging type annotations:

```python
from typing import Optional
from sqlmodel import Field, SQLModel

class Hero(SQLModel, table=True):
    id: Optional[int] = Field(default=None, primary_key=True)
    name: str
    secret_name: str
    age: Optional[int] = None
```

The model definition now looks much cleaner.

Under the hood, SQLModel converts all its child classes to SQLAlchemy classes:

```python
# File: sqlmodel/main.py
# class SQLModelMetaclass, the metaclass of SQLModel

@__dataclass_transform__(kw_only_default=True, field_descriptors=(Field,
FieldInfo))
class SQLModelMetaclass(ModelMetaclass, DeclarativeMeta):

    ...

    # From Pydantic
    def __new__(
        cls,
        name: str,
        bases: Tuple[Type[Any], ...],
        class_dict: Dict[str, Any],
        **kwargs: Any,
    ) -> Any:

        ...

        config_table = get_config("table")
        if config_table is True:
            # If it was passed by kwargs, ensure it's also set in config
            new_cls.__config__.table = config_table
```

```
        for k, v in new_cls.__fields__.items():
            col = get_column_from_field(v) # <-----
            setattr(new_cls, k, col)

    ...

    return new_cls
```

The above code runs when model definitions are encountered, and it converts the columns defined to SQLAlchemy style. See the pointed line in the code. The function get_column_from_field gets invoked for each column defined.

```
# File: sqlmodel/main.py

from sqlalchemy import Column

def get_column_from_field(field: ModelField) -> Column:  # type: ignore
    sa_column = getattr(field.field_info, "sa_column", Undefined)
    if isinstance(sa_column, Column):  # Check if it is an SQLAlchemy
    column already
        return sa_column

    sa_type = get_sqlachemy_type(field)  # <----

    primary_key = getattr(field.field_info, "primary_key", False)
    index = getattr(field.field_info, "index", Undefined)

    ...

    return Column(sa_type, *args, **kwargs)  # type: ignore
```

The above function calls the get_sqlalchemy_type function, which converts the column to corresponding sqlalchemy types, if not already converted.

```
# File: sqlmodel/main.py
# Function get_sqlachemy_type: maps python types to sqlalchemy -
# column types

from sqlalchemy import Float, Integer, Numeric
from sqlalchemy import Boolean, Column, Date, DateTime
from datetime import datetime, date
from decimal import Decimal
```

```python
def get_sqlachemy_type(field: ModelField) -> Any:
    ...

    if issubclass(field.type_, float):
        return Float

    if issubclass(field.type_, bool):
        return Boolean

    if issubclass(field.type_, int):
        return Integer

    if issubclass(field.type_, datetime):
        return DateTime

    if issubclass(field.type_, date):
        return Date

    ...

    if issubclass(field.type_, Decimal):
        return Numeric(
            precision=getattr(field.type_, "max_digits", None),
            scale=getattr(field.type_, "decimal_places", None),
        )

    ...

    raise ValueError(f"The field {field.name} has no matching
    SQLAlchemy type")
```

This function is used to map Python type definitions to SQLAlchemy types. The type_ attribute is provided by Pydantic and returns the root Python type. For example, the type_ attribute of a field annotated with Optional[int] will be int (this parsing is done by Pydantic), which helps with the issubclass checks. This way, a column annotated with Optional[int] will get converted to sqlalchemy.Integer type.

Type Stubs

What if our program relies heavily on other open source libraries, whose source we have no control over? It will be better to have those libraries type-annotated so that we can check if we are passing the correct arguments to the interfaces provided by these libraries. Type stubs can be useful in such scenarios.

Type stubs can be used to provide type information for untyped packages/modules. They are stored with a .pyi file extension.

The code below is from the CPython source code:

```python
# file: cpython/Lib/logging/config.py
class ConvertingDict(dict, ConvertingMixin):
    """"A converting dictionary wrapper."""

    def __getitem__(self, key):
        value = dict.__getitem__(self, key)
        return self.convert_with_key(key, value)

    def get(self, key, default=None):
        value = dict.get(self, key, default)
        return self.convert_with_key(key, value)

    def pop(self, key, default=None):
        value = dict.pop(self, key, default)
        return self.convert_with_key(key, value, replace=False)
```

Below is the type stub from the Python typeshed library, holding the type information of the above:

```python
# File: stdlib/logging/config.pyi

class ConvertingMixin:   # undocumented

    def convert_with_key(self, key: Any, value: Any, replace: bool = True) -> Any: ...

    def convert(self, value: Any) -> Any: ...
```

```
class ConvertingDict(dict[Hashable, Any], ConvertingMixin):  # undocumented

    def __getitem__(self, key: Hashable) -> Any: ...

    def get(self, key: Hashable, default: Any = None) -> Any: ...

    def pop(self, key: Hashable, default: Any = None) -> Any: ...
```

As you can see, stubs just hold type information, and definitions of the functions can be omitted in the pyi stub file.

We can add stub files for libraries and point type checkers such as mypy to read the annotations from the type stub's path.

Adopting Type Annotations in Your Project

Type annotations will allow us to spot errors early on in the development cycle and will help the code be easier to understand for other developers. After it was introduced, type annotations were widely adopted by Python programmers. While type annotations offer many benefits, there are some costs to consider before adopting them. First, type hints introduce additional code that must be maintained as the code evolves. In rapidly evolving codebases, keeping annotations up to date can demand significant effort, especially in scenarios where the types are complex or frequently changing. Also, type hints can make code seem more rigid and verbose to some Python developers who value dynamism and brevity.

In practice, most find the benefits outweigh the costs in the context of large and complex codebases. Their utility and popularity are evident because several major technology companies have developed their own type-checking tools. Notably, Meta has created "Pyre," and Microsoft has developed "Pyright," both of which are open-sourced.

When adding type annotations to an existing project, you can do so incrementally, initially starting with a few files and maintaining this list of files to check for your type checker. Once you are fully ready, you may add this type check to your Continuous Integration/Continuous Deployment (CI/CD) workflow and as a pre-commit hook.

Conclusion

Type hints are no longer just a "nice to have"—they've become a practical necessity in large Python codebases. As projects grow, so does the need for clarity, maintainability, and early error detection. Type annotations bring all of that and more, bridging the gap between Python's dynamic nature and the safety nets of static typing. Whether we're writing libraries, working in teams, or just aiming for cleaner code, type hints give us a way to express intent and catch mistakes before they become bugs.

In this chapter, we explored the core concepts and building blocks of typing in Python. We started with the basics of annotations and moved on to advanced features like `Protocol` and `TypeVar`. We saw how to do both static and runtime type checking using tools like `mypy` and `Nebuly` and how libraries like `Pydantic` and `SQLModel` use type hints to enhance developer experience.

## CHAPTER 12

Generators and Iterators

In the previous chapter, we looked at Python's type system and how using type hints can make our code more predictable, maintainable, and self-documenting.

In the world of programming, we often work with collections of data. Whether it's a list of numbers, a set of names, or a sequence of events, we need efficient ways to process and manipulate these collections. This is where the concept of iteration comes into play. Iteration allows us to traverse through elements of a collection one by one, processing each item in turn.

To fully grasp these ideas, we need to differentiate between iterables and iterators. An iterable is any Python object capable of returning its members one at a time, allowing it to be looped over in a for loop. However, iterables are not the ones performing the iteration; that's where iterators come in. An iterator is an object that performs the actual iteration over an iterable, consuming its elements as needed.

One of the key advantages of iteration is lazy evaluation. With lazy evaluation, we don't need to generate all the elements of a sequence up front. Instead, we can produce them on demand, as we need them. This approach can lead to significant performance improvements, especially when dealing with large datasets or infinite sequences.

In this chapter, we'll also explore the two powerful tools that build upon the concept of iteration: generators and iterators.

Iterators

Iterators, as we'll see, offer a standardized way to traverse sequences, whether finite or infinite.

379

© Adarsh Divakaran 2025
A. Divakaran, *Deep Dive Python*, https://doi.org/10.1007/979-8-8688-1261-3_12

The Iterator Protocol

The iterator protocol is a fundamental concept in Python that defines how we can traverse through a collection of items. It's a set of rules that objects must follow to be considered iterators.

The iterator protocol is a set of methods that an object must implement to be iterable. Specifically, it involves two key methods: __iter__() and __next__().

- __iter__(): This method should return the iterator object itself. It is called once by the iter() function to get the iterator object.

- __next__(): This method should return the next item in the sequence. When there are no more items to return, it should raise a StopIteration exception.

By implementing these two methods, we create objects that can be used in for loops, list comprehensions, and other constructs that expect iterables. The beauty of the iterator protocol is that it provides a uniform interface for iteration, regardless of the underlying data structure.

This protocol allows for lazy evaluation, meaning items are generated one at a time only when needed. This can lead to significant memory savings when working with large datasets or infinite sequences.

Here is a simple example of a custom iterator:

```python
class CountDown:
    def __init__(self, start):
        self.current = start

    def __iter__(self):
        return self

    def __next__(self):
        if self.current <= 0:
            raise StopIteration
        else:
            self.current -= 1
            return self.current
```

```
countdown = CountDown(5)
for number in countdown:
    print(number)
```

In this example, CountDown is a simple iterator that counts down from a given number. The __iter__() method returns the iterator object itself, and the __next__() method decrements the current value until it reaches zero, at which point it raises a StopIteration exception.

In the snippet below from PaddleNLP, the BaseDocumentStore class implements the iterator protocol to allow iteration over its documents:

```
# File: PaddleNLP/legacy/pipelines/pipelines/document_stores/base.py

class BaseDocumentStore(BaseComponent):
    """

    Base class for implementing Document Stores.
    """

    index: Optional[str]
    label_index: Optional[str]
    similarity: Optional[str]
    duplicate_documents_options: tuple = ("skip", "overwrite", "fail")
    ids_iterator = None

    def __iter__(self):
        if not self.ids_iterator:
            self.ids_iterator = [x.id for x in self.get_all_documents()]
        return self

    def __next__(self):
        if len(self.ids_iterator) == 0:
            raise StopIteration
        curr_id = self.ids_iterator[0]
        ret = self.get_document_by_id(curr_id)
        self.ids_iterator = self.ids_iterator[1:]
        return ret
```

In this code, __iter__() checks if ids_iterator is None. If it is, it initializes the ids_iterator attribute with a list of document IDs obtained from the get_all_documents() method. The __next__() method first checks if ids_iterator is empty. If it is, it raises StopIteration to signal that iteration is complete. If there are still IDs left in ids_iterator, it retrieves the first ID (curr_id), uses it to get the corresponding document using get_document_by_id(curr_id), and then removes this ID from ids_iterator.

This definition allows the BaseDocumentStore to be used in a loop to iterate over all documents, fetching each document by its ID one at a time. This is useful for processing or accessing documents sequentially without needing to load them all into memory at once.

The "ids_iterator" can be further improved. It currently performs a slice operation on every iteration, which can be inefficient for longer lists or large-scale operations. For an improved implementation, we can construct "ids_iterator" using a generator expression, which avoids both slicing and the need to create a new list each time.

next() and __iter__ Methods

In Python, the next() and iter() functions, along with their corresponding dunder methods __next__() and __iter__(), are the backbone of the iterator protocol. Let's explore each of these in detail and see how they work together to create and use iterators.

The iter() Function and __iter__() Dunder Method

The iter() function is used to obtain an iterator from an iterable object. When we call iter() on an object, Python looks for the object's __iter__() method. This method should return an iterator object.

The __iter__() method serves two main purposes:

1. For iterable objects, it returns an iterator.

2. For iterator objects, it returns the iterator itself (usually just return self).

This design allows us to use the same object as both an iterable and an iterator, which is a common pattern in Python.

The **next()** Function and **__next__()** Dunder Method

Once we have an iterator, we use the next() function to retrieve the next item in the sequence. The next() function calls the iterator's __next__() method, which is responsible for

1. Returning the next item in the sequence

2. Keeping track of the current state of iteration

3. Raising a StopIteration exception when there are no more items

The StopIteration exception is a crucial part of the iterator protocol. It signals that the iteration is complete, allowing loops and other constructs to know when to stop.

Here's how these methods work together in practice:

1. When we start an iteration (e.g., in a for loop), Python calls iter() on the object, which invokes __iter__() to get an iterator.

2. Python then repeatedly calls next() on this iterator, which invokes __next__() to get each item.

3. This continues until __next__() raises a StopIteration exception, signaling the end of the sequence.

This mechanism allows Python to work with various types of sequences and even infinite generators in a uniform way. It's what enables the clean, consistent syntax we use in for loops, list comprehensions, and other iterable contexts.

Here is an example illustrating these concepts:

```python
class Range:
    def __init__(self, start, end):
        self.current = start
        self.end = end

    def __iter__(self):
        return self

    def __next__(self):
        if self.current >= self.end:
            raise StopIteration
```

```python
        current = self.current
        self.current += 1
        return current

my_range = Range(1, 4)
iterator = iter(my_range)

print(next(iterator))   # Output: 1
print(next(iterator))   # Output: 2
print(next(iterator))   # Output: 3
next(iterator)   # Raise the below exception
"""
Traceback (most recent call last):
  File "...\iterator.py", line 23, in <module>
    next(iterator)
  File "...\iterator.py", line 11, in __next__
    raise StopIteration
StopIteration
"""
```

In this example, Range is an iterator that mimics a simple range function. The iter() function is used to obtain an iterator from my_range, and next() is used to fetch each subsequent value until a StopIteration exception is raised.

Here is an example of iter() and next() usage from the *pgcli* library:

```python
# File: pgcli/main.py

def format_status(cur, status):
    ...

    formatted = formatter.format_output(cur, headers, **output_kwargs)

    if isinstance(formatted, str):
        formatted = iter(formatted.splitlines())
    first_line = next(formatted)

    formatted = itertools.chain([first_line], formatted)
```

In this code

- The iter() function is employed to transform the string output into an iterator of lines. When formatted is detected to be a string, it's first split into lines using splitlines(), and then iter() converts this list of lines into an iterator. This conversion ensures that the output can be processed uniformly, regardless of whether it started as a string or was already in an iterable format.

- Following the creation of the iterator, the next() function is utilized to extract and store the first line from this iterator. By calling next(formatted), the code retrieves the first item (in this case, the first line) from the iterator, simultaneously removing it from the sequence. This operation allows for separate handling or processing of the first line.

Converting Functions to Iterators Using **iter()**

While commonly used with iterable objects like lists or strings, iter() can also be used with functions to create custom iterators.

When used with functions, iter() takes two arguments:

1. A function that returns the next value in the sequence

2. A sentinel value that, when returned by the function, signals the end of the iteration

Below is an example of its usage:

```python
def get_number():
    return input("Enter a number (or 'stop' to end): ")

number_iterator = iter(get_number, "stop")

total_sum = 0

for value in number_iterator:
    number = float(value)
    total_sum += number

print(f"The total sum of the numbers entered is: {total_sum}")
```

In this example

- The get_number() function prompts the user to enter a number or "stop" to end the input.

- The iter() function creates an iterator that stops when "stop" is returned from the get_number().

- The for loop iterates over each value returned by the iterator, converting it to a float and adding it to total_sum.

- Finally, the total sum of all entered numbers is printed once the iterator gets exhausted due to the input of "stop".

Async Iterators

Async iterators are similar to regular iterators, but they're designed to work with asynchronous code. They allow us to iterate over data that may not be immediately available, such as items coming from a network stream or a database cursor. The key difference is that async iterators use coroutines to fetch the next item, potentially yielding control while waiting for data.

The Async Iterator Protocol

Just as regular iterators follow the iterator protocol, async iterators adhere to the async iterator protocol. This protocol involves two main methods:

1. __aiter__(): This method returns the async iterator object itself. It's not a coroutine and works similarly to the regular __iter__() method.

2. __anext__(): This is a coroutine method that returns the next item in the sequence. When the sequence is exhausted, it raises a StopAsyncIteration exception.

These methods allow async iterators to integrate seamlessly with Python's asynchronous features.

Async iterators shine in scenarios where we're dealing with asynchronous data sources. Some common use cases include

- Streaming data from a web API

- Reading large files line by line without blocking

- Processing items from a message queue

- Iterating over results from an asynchronous database query

In these situations, async iterators allow us to process data as it becomes available without holding up the entire application.

The below snippet from *aiohttp* defines an async iterator class:

```python
# File: aiohttp/streams.py

class AsyncStreamIterator(Generic[_T]):
    __slots__ = ("read_func",)

    def __init__(self, read_func: Callable[[], Awaitable[_T]]) -> None:
        self.read_func = read_func

    def __aiter__(self) -> "AsyncStreamIterator[_T]":
        return self

    async def __anext__(self) -> _T:
        try:
            rv = await self.read_func()
        except EofStream:
            raise StopAsyncIteration
        if rv == b"":
            raise StopAsyncIteration
        return rv
```

This code defines an asynchronous iterator class `AsyncStreamIterator` designed to work with asynchronous streams. Here's how it is used:

- *Initialization*: The class is initialized with a `read_func`, which is a callable that returns an awaitable. This function is expected to perform some asynchronous operation to read data from a stream.

- *Iteration*: The `__aiter__` method returns the iterator object itself, which is a standard pattern for iterators.

- *Fetching the next item*: The __anext__ method is where the asynchronous iteration logic is implemented. It uses await to call the read_func, which should return the next chunk of data from the stream.

- *Handling the end of stream*: If the read_func raises an EofStream exception or returns an empty byte string (b""), the iteration stops by raising StopAsyncIteration. This signals that there are no more items to iterate over.

Python provides the async for loop to work with async iterators. This special loop can be used inside an asynchronous context (like an async function) to iterate over an async iterator. Below is the basic structure:

```
async for item in async_iterable:
    # Process item
```

The async for loop automatically handles the awaiting of the __anext__() method and the StopAsyncIteration exception, making it easy to work with async iterators.

Generators

Generators provide a concise way to create iterators, allowing us to define sequences using functions.

Generator vs. Iterators

Iterators, as we've discussed, are objects that implement the iterator protocol with __iter__() and __next__() methods. They allow us to iterate over a sequence of items, but they require us to maintain the state of iteration explicitly.

Generators, on the other hand, are a special type of iterator that is defined using functions. The key features of generators are

1. *Simplicity*: Generators are created using functions with the yield keyword. This makes them much easier to write than full iterator classes.

2. *State management*: Generators automatically manage their state. When a generator function is called, it returns a generator object that remembers where it left off between calls.

3. *Lazy evaluation*: Like iterators, generators produce values on demand, which is memory-efficient for large or infinite sequences.

4. *Readability*: Generator functions often lead to more readable and maintainable code compared with complex iterator classes.

5. *Bidirectional communication*: Generators allow for bidirectional communication through the send() method, which we'll discuss later.

Here's a simple comparison:

Iterator (as a class):

```
class CountUp:
    def __init__(self, start, end):
        self.current = start
        self.end = end

    def __iter__(self):
        return self

    def __next__(self):
        if self.current > self.end:
            raise StopIteration
        else:
            self.current += 1
            return self.current - 1
```

Generator (as a function):

```
def count_up(start, end):
    current = start
    while current <= end:
        yield current
        current += 1
```

As we can see, the generator version is more concise and easier to understand at a glance. It achieves the same result with less code and without explicitly managing the iteration state.

Generators shine in scenarios where we need to work with sequences of data, especially when those sequences are large or even infinite. They provide a clean, efficient way to produce data on demand, making them a valuable tool in a Python programmer's toolkit.

Yield and Yield From

The `yield` keyword and its extension `yield from` are fundamental to working with generators in Python. They provide powerful mechanisms for creating generators and for delegating to sub-generators.

Yield

The `yield` keyword is what turns a regular function into a generator function. When a function contains `yield`, it becomes a generator function that returns a generator object when called.

Key points about `yield`:

1. *State preservation*: When a generator function yields a value, it pauses its execution, preserving its state. When called again, it resumes from where it left off.

2. *Lazy evaluation*: Values are generated one at a time, only when requested, which is memory-efficient for large sequences.

3. `yield` allows for the creation of infinite sequences, as values are produced on demand.

Below is an example of `yield` usage in a generator:

```python
def number_generator(upto):
    print(f"Starting generator with {upto=}")
    for i in range(upto):
        print(f"Yielding {i}")
        yield i
        print(f"Continuing after Yielding {i}")
```

```
gen = number_generator(10)
```

```
print(f"First yielded value: {next(gen)}")
print(f"Second yielded value: {next(gen)}")
print(f"Third yielded value: {next(gen)}")
```

In this generator, each call to next() will yield the next number up to the argument provided.

This produces an output as below:

```
Starting generator with upto=10
Yielding 0
First yielded value: 0
Continuing after Yielding 0
Yielding 1
Second yielded value: 1
Continuing after Yielding 1
Yielding 2
Third yielded value: 2
```

We can see that the execution resumes from the yield statement in the code when next() is called.

Continuing after Yielding 3 is missing in the output since the statement that prints the message is below the yield usage and will only get executed in the subsequent next() call.

Yield From

yield from is an extension to yield that allows a generator to delegate part of its operations to another generator. It's useful for creating composite generators and for flattening nested structures.

Key points about yield from:

1. *Delegation*: It delegates the generation of values to another generator or iterable.

2. *Simplification*: It simplifies the process of yielding all values from a sub-generator.

3. *Bidirectional communication*: It allows for bidirectional communication between the caller and the sub-generator.

Here's an example of yield from:

```python
def chain(*iterables):
    for it in iterables:
        yield from it
```

This generator chains multiple iterables together. The yield from statement takes care of iterating over each iterable and yielding its values.

Another common use case is flattening nested structures:

```python
def flatten(nested_list):
    for item in nested_list:
        if isinstance(item, list):
            yield from flatten(item)
        else:
            yield item
```

This generator recursively flattens a nested list structure, using yield from to delegate to recursive calls for nested lists.

The below snippet shows an example of using yield and yield from to define the __iter__ dunder of the _BatchLoader class as a generator function:

```python
# File: src/deepsparse/transformers/loaders.py

class _BatchLoader(ABC):
    # Base class for all BatchLoaders
    def __init__(self, data_file: str, batch_size: int = 1):
        self.data_file = data_file
        self.batch_size = batch_size
        self.header = None

    @abstractmethod
    def _get_reader(self, filename) -> List[Dict[str, str]]:
        raise NotImplementedError

    def add_to_batch(
        self,
```

```python
        input_sample: Dict[str, Any],
        batch: Optional[Dict[str, List[Any]]],
    ) -> Dict[str, List[Any]]:
        """
        Add dict type input to batch
        """

        if not batch:
            self.header = list(input_sample.keys())
            batch = {key: [input_sample[key]] for key in self.header}
        else:
            for key in self.header:
                batch[key].append(input_sample[key])
        return batch

    def pad_last_batch(self, batch):
        """
        Pads the batch with last added value
        """

        if self.header and 0 < len(batch[self.header[0]]) < self.
        batch_size:
            for key in self.header:
                repeat_element = batch[key][-1]
                copies_needed = self.batch_size - len(batch[key])
                extra_elements = [repeat_element] * copies_needed
                batch[key].extend(extra_elements)

            yield batch

    def __iter__(self) -> Optional[Dict[str, Any]]:
        # Note: json file should contain one json object per line
        batch = None
        with open(self.data_file) as _input_file:
            for _input in self._get_reader(_input_file):
                batch = self.add_to_batch(_input, batch)
                if len(batch[self.header[0]]) == self.batch_size:
                    yield batch
                    batch = {key: [] for key in batch}
        yield from self.pad_last_batch(batch)
```

In this code, the __iter__ method turns the _BatchLoader class into an iterable. It's implemented as a generator function.

The __iter__ method does the following:

- The method reads inputs one by one using self._get_reader(_ input_file).

- It accumulates inputs into a batch using self.add_to_batch().

- When a batch reaches the specified size, it's yielded to the caller, and a new empty batch is started.

The yield from *statement*:

yield from self.pad_last_batch(batch)

- This is used at the end of __iter__ to handle the last, potentially incomplete batch.

- pad_last_batch is itself a generator that yields the padded last batch if necessary.

- yield from delegates the yielding to pad_last_batch, integrating its output into the main generator's stream.

Async Generators

Async generators combine the concepts of generators and asynchronous programming. They allow us to create asynchronous code that can produce a series of values over time, making them ideal for working with asynchronous streams of data. Async generators are defined using the async def syntax along with the yield keyword. They allow for asynchronous iteration, meaning we can use them in async for loops. They were introduced in Python 3.6 by PEP 525.

- Like regular generators, async generators produce values on demand but in an asynchronous context.

- Async generators implement the async iterator protocol automatically.

Here's a simple example of an async generator:

```python
import asyncio

async def countdown(n):
    while n > 0:
        yield n
        n -= 1
        await asyncio.sleep(1)  # Simulate an asynchronous operation

async def main():
    async for value in countdown(5):
        print(value)

asyncio.run(main())
```

In this example, countdown is an async generator that yields numbers from n down to 1, with a one-second delay between each yield.

The relationship between async generators and async iterators is similar to that between regular generators and iterators. Async generators automatically implement the async iterator protocol, making them a convenient way to create async iterators without having to manually implement the __aiter__() and __anext__() methods.

For consuming async generators, we can use async for loops, as we have seen with async iterators. Here's a basic example of how to use an async for loop:

```python
async def process_data():
    async for item in async_generator():
        await process_item(item)
```

In this example, async_generator() could be an async generator or any object that implements the async iterator protocol. The loop will wait for each item to be produced asynchronously before processing it.

Async for loops can also be used with async comprehensions, providing a concise way to create lists, sets, or dictionaries from asynchronous data sources:

```python
results = [result async for result in async_generator() if await is_
valid(result)]
```

Generator Methods: **send()**, **throw()**, and **close()**

Generators in Python are not just for producing values; they also support advanced control flow through methods like send(), throw(), and close(). These methods allow for bidirectional communication with generators and provide ways to influence their execution.

send()

The send() method allows us to send a value into the generator, which becomes the result of the current yield expression. The first call to send() should generally be send(None) to start the generator.

Example:

```python
def echo_generator():
    while True:
        received = yield
        print(f"Received: {received}")

gen = echo_generator()
next(gen)  # Prime the generator
gen.send("Hello")  # Output: Received: Hello
gen.send("World")  # Output: Received: World
```

The snippet below from *pyglossary* showcases an example of a generator that can accept send() calls:

```python
# File: pyglossary/plugins/sql.py

class Writer:
    def write(self) -> "Generator[None, EntryType, None]":
        newline = self._newline

        fileObj = self._file

        def fixStr(word: str) -> str:
            return word.replace("'", "''").replace("\r", "").replace("\n",
            newline)
```

```
_id = 1
while True:
    entry = yield
    if entry is None:
        break
    if entry.isData():
        # FIXME
        continue

    words = entry.l_word
    word = fixStr(words[0])
    defi = fixStr(entry.defi)
    fileObj.write(
        f"INSERT INTO word VALUES({_id}, '{word}', '{defi}');\n",
    )
    ...

if self._transaction:
    fileObj.write("END TRANSACTION;\n")
```

The write method is defined as a generator function, as indicated by the yield statement and the return type hint Generator[None, EntryType, None]. This means it yields None, receives EntryType objects, and returns None.

- When this generator is first called (e.g., writer = Writer(). write()), it runs until it hits the first yield statement.

- At this point, it's ready to receive the first entry.

- The caller can use send() to pass entries into the generator:

  writer.send(some_entry)

- Each call to send() resumes the generator from where it last yielded, with the sent value replacing the yield expression.

- Inside the while True loop, entry = yield receives the entry sent from outside.

- The generator processes this entry and writes it in the SQL file. After processing, it yields again (when it re-enters the loop body), ready for the next entry.

- To signal the end of entries, the caller sends None.

throw()

The throw() method allows us to inject an exception into the generator at the point where it's paused.

Key points about throw():

1. It raises an exception at the point where the generator was paused.

2. The generator can catch and handle the exception or let it propagate.

Example:

```python
def number_generator():
    try:
        yield 1
        yield 2
        yield 3
    except ValueError:
        yield 'Error occurred'

gen = number_generator()
print(next(gen))  # Prints: 1
print(gen.throw(ValueError("Custom error")))  # Output: Error occurred
```

close()

The close() method is used to terminate the generator.

Key points about close():

1. Once close() is called, the generator should perform any cleanup operations and then raise GeneratorExit or return.

2. After close(), further calls to next() or send() will raise StopIteration.

Example:

```python
def cleanup_generator():
    try:
        yield 1
        yield 2
        yield 3
    finally:
        print("Generator is being closed")

gen = cleanup_generator()
print(next(gen))  # Output: 1
gen.close()  # Output: Generator is being closed
```

The below code from CPython showcases the use of close and throw in the definition of _GeneratorContextManager:

```python
# File: CPython/Lib/contextlib.py

class _GeneratorContextManager(
    _GeneratorContextManagerBase,
    AbstractContextManager,
    ContextDecorator,
):
    """Helper for @contextmanager decorator."""

    ...

    def __exit__(self, typ, value, traceback):
        if typ is None:
            try:
                next(self.gen)
            except StopIteration:
                return False
            else:
                try:
                    raise RuntimeError("generator didn't stop")
                finally:
                    self.gen.close()
```

```
    else:
        if value is None:
            # Need to force instantiation so we can reliably
            # tell if we get the same exception back
            value = typ()
        try:
            self.gen.throw(value)
        except StopIteration as exc:
            # Suppress StopIteration *unless* it's the same
            exception that
            # was passed to throw().  This prevents a StopIteration
            # raised inside the "with" statement from being suppressed.
            return exc is not value

        ...
        try:
            raise RuntimeError("generator didn't stop after throw()")
        finally:
            self.gen.close()
```

In the _GeneratorContextManager class, the __exit__ method manages the behavior of a generator when exiting a context (i.e., when the block of code under a with statement is done). The typ, value, and traceback will contain the exception type, value, and traceback if the context manager was exited due to an exception.

1. *Usage of* throw():

    The throw() method is used to inject an exception into the generator at the point where it was paused (i.e., at the last yield statement).

    – When an exception (typ, value, traceback) is raised in the with block, the throw() method is called with the exception value.

    – This allows the generator to catch the exception and decide how to handle it internally.

    – If the generator handles the exception and raises a StopIteration, this can be used to suppress the exception from propagating outside the context manager.

2. *Usage of* close():

The close() method is used to finalize the generator. It raises a GeneratorExit exception inside the generator to allow it to perform any necessary cleanup. In this code, close() is called in two scenarios:

1. If the generator is expected to stop after a next() call but doesn't, indicating a logical error, close() ensures the generator is properly finalized (usage inside the if block in the code).

2. If an exception is thrown into the generator and it does not handle it correctly (i.e., it doesn't stop), close() is used to ensure the generator exits cleanly (usage inside the else block).

Generator Comprehension

Generator comprehensions are a concise way to create generators in Python. They are similar to list comprehensions but produce a generator object instead of a list. This makes them memory-efficient for large datasets or when we don't need all the values at once.

Key points about generator comprehension:

1. *Syntax*: They use parentheses () instead of square brackets [] used in list comprehensions.

2. *Lazy evaluation*: They generate values on demand, not all at once.

3. *Memory efficiency*: They're ideal for working with large datasets as they don't store all values in memory.

4. *One-time use*: Unlike lists, generator comprehensions can only be iterated over once.

The basic syntax of a generator comprehension is given below:

```
(expression for item in iterable if condition)
```

Here's a simple example comparing a list comprehension with a generator comprehension:

```
# List comprehension
squares_list = [x**2 for x in range(10)]
```

```
# Generator comprehension
squares_gen = (x**2 for x in range(10))
```

The squares_list immediately creates and stores all squared values in memory, while squares_gen creates a generator object that will produce squared values on demand.

Generator comprehensions are useful in scenarios where

1. We are working with large datasets and want to conserve memory.

2. We only need to iterate over the sequence once.

3. We are passing the result to a function that will iterate over it.

We should keep in mind that generators get exhausted once they are iterated over:

```
squares_gen = (x**2 for x in range(3))

for sqr in squares_gen:
    print(sqr)
```

```
# This won't print anything
for sqr in squares_gen:
    print(sqr)
```

The snippet above will print 0, 1, and 4 once, and the body of the second for loop won't get executed since the generator is exhausted.

Generator comprehensions can also be used in function calls directly:

```
sum(x**2 for x in range(1000000))
```

This calculates the sum of squares without creating an intermediate list of all squared values.

The below code from the *ml-agents* library uses generator comprehension to create sample batches:

```python
# File: ml-agents/mlagents/trainers/buffer.py

class AgentBuffer(MutableMapping):
    def sample_mini_batch(
        self, batch_size: int, sequence_length: int = 1
    ) -> "AgentBuffer":
        """
        Creates a mini-batch from a random start and end.
        :param batch_size: number of elements to withdraw.
        :param sequence_length: Length of sequences to sample.
            Number of sequences to sample will be batch_size/
            sequence_length.
        """
        num_seq_to_sample = batch_size // sequence_length
        mini_batch = AgentBuffer()
        buff_len = self.num_experiences
        num_sequences_in_buffer = buff_len // sequence_length
        start_idxes = (
            np.random.randint(num_sequences_in_buffer, size=num_seq_
            to_sample)
            * sequence_length
        )  # Sample random sequence starts
        for key in self:
            buffer_field = self[key]
            mb_list = (buffer_field[i : i + sequence_length] for i in
            start_idxes)
            # See comparison of ways to make a list from a list of
            lists here:
            # https://stackoverflow.com/questions/952914/how-to-make-a-
            flat-list-out-of-list-of-lists
            mini_batch[key].set(list(itertools.chain.from_
            iterable(mb_list)))
        return mini_batch
```

In the code, `sample_mini_batch` method of the `AgentBuffer` class uses generator comprehension as below:

```
mb_list = (buffer_field[i : i + sequence_length] for i in start_idxes)
```

The generator comprehension is used to create an iterable sequence of slices from `buffer_field`. Each slice corresponds to a sequence of experiences starting at an index specified in `start_idxes` and extending for `sequence_length` elements.

- `buffer_field[i : i + sequence_length]` extracts a sublist from `buffer_field` starting at index i and continuing for `sequence_length` elements.

- `for i in start_idxes` iterates over each starting index in the `start_idxes` array, which contains randomly chosen starting points for sequences in the buffer.

The generator comprehension is used directly as an argument to `itertools.chain.from_iterable`. This combination allows for efficient flattening of the sequences without materializing the entire list of sequences in memory.

Conclusion

In this chapter, we've explored the world of iteration in Python. We learned about iterators, generators, and their async versions. These tools help us work with data more efficiently, especially when dealing with large amounts of information. We saw how generators make it easy to create iterators and how async iterators help us handle data that comes in asynchronously. We also looked at some advanced features like `yield from` and generator methods, which give us more control over how our code runs.

When choosing between these iteration tools, consider the following guidelines:

1. Use generators when you need to create a sequence of values on the fly without storing them all in memory. They're ideal for large datasets or infinite sequences.

2. Opt for iterators when you need more control over the iteration process or when implementing custom iterable objects.

3. Choose generator comprehensions for simple, one-line generator expressions. They're more memory-efficient than list comprehensions for large datasets. Use list comprehensions when you need to create and store a complete list in memory, especially for smaller datasets or when you need to use the result multiple times.

4. Implement async generators when dealing with asynchronous data sources or when you need to yield values that are produced asynchronously.

By choosing the right tool for each situation, we can write more efficient, readable, and maintainable code. Generators and iterators allow us to work with data in a lazy, memory-efficient manner, while their async counterparts enable us to handle asynchronous data flows elegantly.

CHAPTER 13

Itertools

In the previous chapter, we explored generators and iterators and understood how they help us write lazy, memory-efficient code.

The `itertools` module in Python is a collection of fast, memory-efficient tools that are useful for handling iterators. This module helps in creating iterators for efficient looping and offers a standard library of tools for working with iterators. In this chapter, we will explore the various functions provided by `itertools`, understand their use cases, and see examples of how they can be applied in real-world scenarios.

count

`itertools.count` is used to create infinite iterators. It produces consecutive integers, by default, starting from zero. It accepts `start` and `step` parameters as well to control the resulting behavior. Since it generates an infinite iterator, the control flow should be manually broken out.

The below code from `youtube-dl` uses `count()` to generate an infinite iterator:

```
# File: youtube_dl/extractor/googlesearch.py

def _get_n_results(self, query, n):
    """Get a specified number of results for a query"""

    entries = []
    res = {
        '_type': 'playlist',
        'id': query,
        'title': query,
    }
```

© Adarsh Divakaran 2025
A. Divakaran, *Deep Dive Python*, https://doi.org/10.1007/979-8-8688-1261-3_13

```python
for pagenum in itertools.count():
    webpage = self._download_webpage(
        'http://www.google.com/search',
        'gvsearch:' + query,
        note='Downloading result page %s' % (pagenum + 1),
        query={
            'tbm': 'vid',
            'q': query,
            'start': pagenum * 10,
            'hl': 'en',
        })

    ...

    if (len(entries) >= n) or not re.search(r'id="pnnext"', webpage):
        res['entries'] = entries[:n]
        return res
```

In the snippet, `itertools.count()` is used in a for loop to generate page numbers for the Google search query. A new web page is downloaded per iteration, starting from the first page (pagenum + 1). The loop continues indefinitely until the desired number of results (n) is reached or there are no more pages to be fetched (determined by the absence of "pnnext" in the scraped web page content). When this happens, the loop is broken, and the function returns the results.

cycle

The `cycle()` function in the `itertools` module returns an iterator that produces elements from the iterable we provide to it as the argument in an endless cycle. When the iterable is exhausted, `cycle()` starts over from the beginning.

The below example from *twisted* uses cycle to assign alternative classes to a table's contents:

```python
# File: src/twisted/web/static.py

class DirectoryLister(resource.Resource):
    ...
```

```python
def _buildTableContent(self, elements):
    """

    Build a table content using C{self.linePattern} and giving elements
    odd and even classes.
    """
    tableContent = []
    rowClasses = itertools.cycle(["odd", "even"])
    for element, rowClass in zip(elements, rowClasses):
        element["class"] = rowClass
        tableContent.append(self.linePattern % element)
    return tableContent

def render(self, request):
    """

    Render a listing of the content of C{self.path}.
    """
    request.setHeader(b"content-type", b"text/html; charset=utf-8")
    ...

    dirs, files = self._getFilesAndDirectories(directory)

    tableContent = "".join(self._buildTableContent(dirs + files))

    ...

    done = self.template % {"header": header, "tableContent":
    tableContent}
    done = done.encode("utf8")

    return done
```

In the code, the cycle() function is given an iterable of two elements, ["odd", "even"]. It will return an iterator that produces "odd", "even", "odd", "even", etc., indefinitely. This is used to style the rows of a table with alternating classes. The zip() function is then used to pair each element in elements with a class from rowClasses. This will result in alternating "odd" and "even" classes for each element.

repeat

The `itertools.repeat()` function is used to create an iterator that produces the same value each time it is accessed. It accepts two arguments:

1. The `object` that needs to be repeated.

2. An optional argument that represents the number of times the object should be repeated. It keeps returning the object indefinitely unless this optional argument is provided.

The snippet below from *label studio* uses repeat to generate string placeholders to use in an SQL query:

```python
# File: label_studio/core/bulk_update_utils.py

def bulk_update(
    objs,
    meta=None,
    update_fields=None,
    exclude_fields=None,
    using="default",
    batch_size=None,
    pk_field="pk",
):
    ...

    if pk_field == "pk":
        pk_field = meta.get_field(meta.pk.name)
    else:
        pk_field = meta.get_field(pk_field)

    connection = connections[using]
    query = UpdateQuery(meta.model)
    compiler = query.get_compiler(connection=connection)

    ...
```

```python
lenpks = 0
for objs_batch in grouper(objs, batch_size):
    pks = []
    parameters = defaultdict(list)
    placeholders = defaultdict(list)

    for obj in objs_batch:
        pk_value, _ = _as_sql(obj, pk_field, query, compiler,
        connection)
        pks.append(pk_value)

    ...

    parameters = flatten(parameters.values(), types=list)
    parameters.extend(pks)

    n_pks = len(pks)
    del pks

    ...

    in_clause = '"{pk_column}" in ({pks})'.format(
        pk_column=pk_field.column,
        pks=", ".join(itertools.repeat("%s", n_pks)),
    )  # --> (1) Using repeat()

    sql = "UPDATE {dbtable} SET {values} WHERE {in_clause}".
    format(  # nosec
        dbtable=dbtable,
        values=values,
        in_clause=in_clause,
    )
    del values

    lenpks += n_pks

    connection.cursor().execute(sql, parameters)

return lenpks
```

As seen in the comment (1), the `itertools.repeat()` function is used in this code to generate a sequence of placeholders for SQL query parameters. Here, `itertools.repeat("%s", n_pks)` is used to create a string of placeholders (%s) repeated n_pks times. This string is then used in the `in_clause` of the SQL query to match the primary keys (pks) of the objects to be updated.

Here is a simplified example of how `itertools.repeat()` is used in this context:

```python
import itertools

# Suppose we have 3 primary keys

n_pks = 3

# Create a string of placeholders repeated n_pks times

placeholders = ", ".join(itertools.repeat("%s", n_pks))

print(placeholders) # Output: %s, %s, %s
```

In the SQL query, this would be used as follows:

```sql
UPDATE table SET values WHERE pk_column IN (%s, %s, %s)
```

Each %s would then be replaced with the actual primary key values when the query is executed.

From the itertools module, `count`, `cycle`, and `repeat` are the functions that can be used to create infinite iterators.

product

The `product(*iterables, repeat=1)` function returns the Cartesian product of input iterables. It is equivalent to nested for loops. For example, `product(A, B)` returns the same as `((x,y) for x in A for y in B)`.

The below code snippet from Apache Airflow uses product to create filename variations:

```
# File:  airflow/dev/check_files.py

def expand_name_variations(files):
    return sorted(base + suffix for base, suffix in itertools.
    product(files, ["", ".asc", ".sha512"]))

def check_upgrade_check(files: list[str], version: str):
    print(f"Checking upgrade_check for version {version}:\n")
    version = strip_rc_suffix(version)

    expected_files = expand_name_variations(
        [
            f"apache-airflow-upgrade-check-{version}-bin.tar.gz",
            f"apache-airflow-upgrade-check-{version}-source.tar.gz",
            f"apache_airflow_upgrade_check-{version}-py2.py3-none-any.whl",
        ]
    )
    return check_all_files(expected_files=expected_files, actual_
    files=files)
```

In this case, it is used to generate all possible combinations of the filenames and the suffixes. The `itertools.product(files, ["", ".asc", ".sha512"])` will generate a list of tuples where the first element of each tuple is a filename from the `files` list and the second element is a suffix from the list `["", ".asc", ".sha512"]`. This is then used in a comprehension to create a new list of filenames with each possible suffix. This results in filename variations like

- `filename`
- `filename.asc`
- `filename.sha512`

The `.asc` and `.sha512` files are signature files that can be used to verify the integrity of the original file.

It should be kept in mind that the `product` completely consumes the input iterables, keeping pools of values in memory to generate the products. Due to this, it is only useful with finite inputs.

permutations

The permutations(iterable, r=None) function returns successive r length permutations of elements in the iterable. Permutations are emitted in lexicographic sort order. So, if the input iterable is sorted, the permutation tuples will be produced in a sorted order.

```python
# File: google-research/summae/model.py

def create_perm_label_table(num_s_per_p):
    """Create a table for permutation-label lookup.

    For example, if num_s_per_p is 3, will create a table where keys are
    strings of all possible permutations: {'012', '021', '102', '120',
    '201', '210'} and the values are unique IDs of each permutation: {0, 1,
    2, 3, 4, 5}.

    Args:
      num_s_per_p: number of sentences per paragraph, should be an int

    Returns:
      A lookup table that returns an unique class ID given a permutation.
    """
    assert isinstance(num_s_per_p, int), type(num_s_per_p)
    perms = list(itertools.permutations(list(range(num_s_per_p))))
    # For example, when num_s_per_p = 3, perms is as follows:
    # [(0, 1, 2), (0, 2, 1), (1, 0, 2), (1, 2, 0), (2, 0, 1), (2, 1, 0)].
    perms_as_str = []
    for perm in perms:
        perms_as_str.append("".join(str(n) for n in perm))
    # perms_as_str = ['012', '021', '102', '120', '201', '210'].
    num_s_per_p_factorial = math.factorial(num_s_per_p)  # 6
    # This table will map each string in perms_as_str to a unique ID 0 ~ 5.
    return tf.lookup.StaticHashTable(
```

```
        tf.lookup.KeyValueTensorInitializer(
            tf.convert_to_tensor(perms_as_str), tf.range(num_s_per_p_
            factorial)
        ),
        -1,
    )
```

The `itertools.permutations` function is used in this code to generate all possible permutations of a list of integers from 0 to `num_s_per_p - 1`.

Here, it is used as seen below:

```
perms = list(itertools.permutations(list(range(num_s_per_p)))):
```

This line generates all possible permutations of the list of integers from 0 to `num_s_per_p - 1`. For example, if `num_s_per_p` is 3, it generates the list $[(0, 1, 2),$ $(0, 2, 1), (1, 0, 2), (1, 2, 0), (2, 0, 1), (2, 1, 0)]$. Creating a full list of all permutations using `list()` can quickly exhaust memory, especially for large input sizes, so it's safer to iterate over the generator lazily instead.

combinations

The `combinations(iterable, r)` function returns r length subsequences of elements from the input iterable. Combinations are emitted in lexicographic sort order. So, if the input iterable is sorted, the combination tuples will be produced in a sorted order.

The below snippet from *salt* exemplifies the usage of `combinations`:

```
# File: salt/utils/schedule.py

class Schedule:
    def eval(self, now=None):
        """

        Evaluate and execute the schedule
        """

        ...

        for job, data in schedule.items():
            ...
```

```
# Used for quick lookups when detecting invalid option
# combinations.
schedule_keys = set(data.keys())

time_elements = ("seconds", "minutes", "hours", "days")
scheduling_elements = ("when", "cron", "once")

invalid_sched_combos = [
    set(i) for i in itertools.combinations(scheduling_
    elements, 2)
]

if any(i <= schedule_keys for i in invalid_sched_combos):
    log.error(
        'Unable to use "%s" options together. Ignoring.',
        '", "'.join(scheduling_elements),
    )
    continue
    ...
...
```

Here the invalid_sched_combos will have the value [{'when', 'cron'}, {'when', 'once'}, {'cron', 'once'}]. These combinations are used to check if any invalid combinations of scheduling options are present in the schedule_keys set. If any invalid combination is found (i.e., if any member of invalid combinations is a subset of schedule_keys), an error message is logged, and the loop continues to the next job.

itertools also contains the function combinations_with_replacement(iterable, r) that behaves similarly to combinations with the exception that it allows individual elements to be repeated more than once.

The functions product, permutations, combinations, and combinations_with_replacement can be used to create combinatoric iterators.

The itertools functions we are going to visit, starting from the next section, are those that produce iterators that terminate on the shortest input sequence.

accumulate

The `itertools.accumulate` creates an iterator that returns accumulated results. By default, it returns accumulated sums. It can also accumulate results using other binary functions.

The function signature is given below:

```
def itertools.accumulate(iterable[, function=operator.add, *,
initial=None])
```

The `function` argument can be provided for customizing the accumulation behavior. For example, it can be set to `max()` to get the running maximum.

If the `initial` argument is provided, the accumulation process starts with that value.

The below example from *aiohttp* showcases the usage of `accumulate()`:

```python
# File: aiohttp/cookiejar.py

class CookieJar(AbstractCookieJar):
    def filter_cookies(self, request_url: URL = URL()) ->
    "BaseCookie[str]":
        """Returns this jar's cookies filtered by their attributes."""
        ...

        if is_ip_address(hostname):
            if not self._unsafe:
                return filtered
            domains: Iterable[str] = (hostname,)
        else:
            # Get all the subdomains that might match a cookie (e.g. "foo.
            bar.com", "bar.com", "com")
            domains = itertools.accumulate(
                reversed(hostname.split(".")), lambda x, y: f"{y}.{x}"
            )  # --> (1)

        # Get all the path prefixes that might match a cookie (e.g. "", "/
        foo", "/foo/bar")
        paths = itertools.accumulate(
            request_url.path.split("/"), lambda x, y: f"{x}/{y}"
        )  # --> (2)
```

```
# Create every combination of (domain, path) pairs.
pairs = itertools.product(domains, paths)

# Point 2: https://www.rfc-editor.org/rfc/rfc6265.html#section-5.4
cookies = itertools.chain.from_iterable(
    self._cookies[p].values() for p in pairs
)
path_len = len(request_url.path)

for cookie in cookies:
    name = cookie.key
    domain = cookie["domain"]

    if (domain, name) in self._host_only_cookies:
        if domain != hostname:
            continue

    # Skip edge case when the cookie has a trailing slash but
    # request doesn't.
    if len(cookie["path"]) > path_len:
        continue

    if is_not_secure and cookie["secure"]:
        continue

    # It's critical we use the Morsel so the coded_value
    # (based on cookie version) is preserved
    mrsl_val = cast("Morsel[str]", cookie.get(cookie.key,
    Morsel()))
    mrsl_val.set(cookie.key, cookie.value, cookie.coded_value)
    filtered[name] = mrsl_val

return filtered
```

In this code (comments (1) and (2)), itertools.accumulate is used to generate all possible subdomains and path prefixes that might match a cookie.

In the case of domains, itertools.accumulate is used with the reversed hostname split by "." and a lambda function that concatenates the elements with a "." in between. This generates all the subdomains that might match a cookie. For example, if the hostname is "foo.bar.com", the function will generate "com", "bar.com", and "foo.bar.com".

Similarly, for paths, `itertools.accumulate` is used with the request URL path split by "/" and a lambda function that concatenates the elements with a "/" in between. This generates all the path prefixes that might match a cookie. For example, if the path is "/foo/bar", the function will generate "/foo" and "/foo/bar".

These accumulated results are then used to create every combination of (domain, path) pairs, which are used to filter the cookies.

batched

The `batched` function in `itertools` is used to group items from an iterable into fixed-size batches or chunks. The function consumes the input iterable lazily, and the result is yielded as soon as the current batch is full or when the iterable gets exhausted.

The below example from *CPython's* `concurrent.futures` module uses the `batched` function:

```
# File: Lib/concurrent/futures/process.py

class ProcessPoolExecutor(_base.Executor):
    def map(self, fn, *iterables, timeout=None, chunksize=1):
        """Returns an iterator equivalent to map(fn, iter)."""
        if chunksize < 1:
            raise ValueError("chunksize must be >= 1.")

        results = super().map(partial(_process_chunk, fn),
                              itertools.batched(zip(*iterables), chunksize),
                              timeout=timeout)
        return _chain_from_iterable_of_lists(results)
```

Here, `zip(*iterables)` is used to combine the input iterables into one iterable, where each item is a tuple containing one item from each of the input iterables.

The `batched` function then takes this combined iterable and the `chunksize` as inputs and returns an iterator that yields the items from the combined iterable in chunks of size `chunksize`. These chunks are then passed to the `map` function of the parent class (`_base.Executor`) along with the function `fn` to be applied to each chunk.

This usage of `batched` allows for efficient parallel processing of large iterables, as the data can be divided into manageable chunks that can be processed independently.

chain

The chain function in the itertools module is used to concatenate multiple iterables into a single iterable. It effectively creates a single sequence from multiple input sequences, allowing us to iterate over them as if they were one.

The below snippet from *bridgy* exemplifies the use of chain:

```python
# File: bridgy/cron.py

@app.route("/cron/replace_poll_tasks")
def replace_poll_tasks():
    """Finds sources missing their poll tasks and adds new ones."""
    queries = [
        cls.query(
            Source.features == "listen",
            Source.status == "enabled",
            Source.last_poll_attempt < util.now() - timedelta(days=2),
        )
        for cls in models.sources.values()
        if cls.AUTO_POLL
    ]
    for source in itertools.chain(*queries):
        age = util.now() - source.last_poll_attempt
        logger.info(
            f"{source.bridgy_url()} last polled {age} ago. Adding new
            poll task."
        )
        util.add_poll_task(source)

    return ""
```

In the provided code, itertools.chain(*queries) is used to iterate over all the queries in the queries list. The queries list is created by iterating over all the values in models.sources. For each source class (cls) that has AUTO_POLL set to True, a query is created. This query looks for sources that have the feature "listen", are enabled, and have not attempted to poll in the last two days. The result is a list of queries, each potentially returning multiple source objects that meet these criteria. The * operator is used to unpack this list of queries when passed to chain.

Itertools also provide a `chain.from_iterable()` that is an alternate constructor for `chain()`. While `chain` takes multiple iterables as separate arguments, `chain.from_iterable` takes a single iterable of iterables. This difference allows `chain.from_iterable` to handle a dynamic list of iterables.

compress

The `compress` function selectively filters elements from an iterable. It takes two iterables as arguments:

1.   The data to be filtered

2.   A `selector` iterable of booleans

Only the elements in the data iterable for which the corresponding selector is `True` are included in the output. This can be used for selective filtering of elements or for applying masks.

The example below from *alphamissense* shows an example usage of compress:

```python
# File: alphamissense/data/parsers.py

def remove_empty_columns_from_stockholm_msa(stockholm_msa: str) -> str:
    """Removes empty columns (dashes-only) from a Stockholm MSA."""
    processed_lines = {}
    unprocessed_lines = {}
    for i, line in enumerate(stockholm_msa.splitlines()):
        if line.startswith("#=GC RF"):
            ...
            mask = []

            for j in range(len(first_alignment)):
                for _, unprocessed_line in unprocessed_lines.items():
                    prefix, _, alignment = unprocessed_line.rpartition(" ")
                    if alignment[j] != "-":
                        mask.append(True)
                        break
```

```
        else:  # Every row contained a hyphen - empty column.
            mask.append(False)

    # Add reference annotation for processing with mask.
    unprocessed_lines[reference_annotation_i] = reference_
    annotation_line

    if not any(mask):  # All columns were empty. Output empty lines
    for chunk.
        for line_index in unprocessed_lines:
            processed_lines[line_index] = ""
    else:
        for line_index, unprocessed_line in unprocessed_lines.
        items():
            prefix, _, alignment = unprocessed_line.rpartition(" ")
            masked_alignment = "".join(
                itertools.compress(alignment, mask)
            )  # (1)
            processed_lines[line_index] = f"{prefix} {masked_
            alignment}"

    ...
```

In the code, `itertools.compress` is used to remove empty columns from a table of sequences in a specific text format. The `mask` list is a boolean mask where each position corresponds to a column in the alignment. If a column is not empty (i.e., it contains at least one non-hyphen character), the corresponding position in the `mask` list is True; otherwise, it's False.

The line with `itertools.compress` (marked as (1)) uses this `mask` to filter the alignment string. It keeps only the characters in positions where the `mask` is True, effectively removing the empty columns.

dropwhile

The `dropwhile` function from `itertools` takes two arguments: a `predicate` and an `iterable`. It drops elements from the beginning of the `iterable` as long as a specified `predicate` is true. Once the predicate becomes false, the rest of the elements are returned without further checking the predicate.

The below snippet from the library *skorch* illustrates the usage of dropwhile:

```python
# File: skorch/_version.py

def _cmpkey(epoch, release, pre, post, dev, local):
    # When we compare a release version, we want to compare it with all of
    # the trailing zeros removed. So we'll use a reverse the list, drop all
    # the now leading zeros until we come to something non-zero, then take
    # the rest, re-reverse it back into the correct order, and make it a
    # tuple and use that for our sorting key.
    release = tuple(
        reversed(
            list(
                itertools.dropwhile(
                    lambda x: x == 0,
                    reversed(release),
                )
            )
        )
    )
    ...
```

In the code, `itertools.dropwhile` is used to drop leading zeros from a reversed list of release version numbers. The lambda function `lambda x: x == 0` is the predicate that checks if an element is zero. The `itertools.dropwhile` function drops elements from the reversed list as long as they are zero. Once it encounters a non-zero element, it stops dropping and returns every element afterward. The list is then reversed back into the correct order and converted to a tuple to get the correct version number for comparison.

filterfalse

The `filterfalse` function is the inverse of the built-in `filter` function. Similar to `dropwhile`, it takes two arguments, a `predicate` and `iterable`. It returns elements from the iterable for which the specified `predicate` is false. This is useful for excluding elements that meet a certain condition.

The below snippet from CPython shows a usage example of `filterfalse`:

```
# File: cpython/Lib/importlib/resources/_common.py

def _infer_caller():
    """

    Walk the stack and find the frame of the first caller not in
    this module.
    """

    def is_this_file(frame_info):
        return frame_info.filename == __file__

    def is_wrapper(frame_info):
        return frame_info.function == "wrapper"

    not_this_file = itertools.filterfalse(is_this_file, inspect.stack())
    # also exclude 'wrapper' due to singledispatch in the call stack
    callers = itertools.filterfalse(is_wrapper, not_this_file)
    return next(callers).frame
```

In the code snippet, `filterfalse` is used twice.

The first usage of `filterfalse` is in the line

```
not_this_file = itertools.filterfalse(is_this_file, inspect.stack())
```

Here, `filterfalse` is used to filter out the frames from the call stack that are not from the current file. The `is_this_file` function checks if the filename of the frame is the same as the filename of the current file (`__file__`). If it is, `filterfalse` filters it out because it returns `True` for these frames, and `filterfalse` only keeps the elements for which the function returns `False`.

The second usage of `filterfalse` is used to filter out the frames from the previous result (`not_this_file`) that are not from the function named "wrapper". The final result, `callers`, is an iterator over the frames of the call stack that are neither from the current file nor from the function "wrapper". The `next(callers).frame` line then returns the frame of the first such caller.

groupby

The `itertools.groupby` function groups elements from an iterable that have the same key value. It returns keys and groups of elements, making it useful for categorizing or aggregating data based on a common property. It accepts two arguments: the `iterable` and the key. The key argument is optional. If it is not specified or None, an identity function is used.

```
# File: plugincompat/web.py

def get_latest_versions(names_and_versions):
    """

    Returns an iterator of (name, version) from the given list of (name,
    version), but returning only the latest version of the package.
    """

    names_and_versions = sorted((name, parse(version)) for (name, version)
    in names_and_versions)
    for name, grouped_versions in itertools.groupby(names_and_versions,
    key=lambda x: x[0]):
        name, loose_version = list(grouped_versions)[-1]
        yield name, str(loose_version)
```

In this code, the key function provided is `lambda x: x[0]`, which means the elements are grouped by the first element of each tuple (the package name).

The code works as follows:

1. The `names_and_versions` list is sorted. The `parse` function is applied to the version part of each tuple, which converts the version string into a format that can be correctly sorted.

2. The sorted list is then grouped by package name using `itertools.groupby`. This results in an iterator of tuples, where the first element is the package name and the second element is an iterator of all the (name, version) tuples for that package.

3. For each group, `list(grouped_versions)[-1]` is used to get the last (name, version) tuple in the group. Because the list was sorted before grouping, this will be the tuple with the highest version number.

425

4. The function then yields the package name and the string representation of the version. This means the function is a generator, and it will return a new (name, version) tuple each time it's iterated over until it has returned the latest version of every package in the original list.

islice

The `islice` function allows the slicing of an iterable. It is similar to the built-in `slice` (which works on sequences) but for iterables. It returns selected elements from the iterable, specified by a range of indices (start, stop, and step). This is useful for working with iterables that do not support direct indexing or slicing, such as generators or iterators, enabling efficient access to specific portions of the data.

Its signature is similar to `slice`, as seen below:

```
def islice(iterable, stop)
def islice(iterable, start, stop[, step])
```

It can be either called with an iterable and

1. A stop value

2. `start` and `stop` with an optional `step`

The arguments are used as below:

- Elements from the iterable are skipped until *start* is reached.

- If *stop* is specified as None, iteration continues until the iterator is exhausted. Otherwise, it stops at the specified position.

- If *step* is None, the step defaults to one. Using a *step* higher than one results in items being skipped.

The below code from Apache Spark uses `islice` to generate element batches from an iterator:

```
# File: python/pyspark/shuffle.py

class ExternalSorter:
    def __init__(self, memory_limit, serializer=None):
```

```
        self.memory_limit = memory_limit
        self.local_dirs = _get_local_dirs("sort")
        self.serializer = _compressed_serializer(serializer)

    ...

    def sorted(self, iterator, key=None, reverse=False):
        """

        Sort the elements in iterator, do external sort when the memory
        goes above the limit.
        """

        global MemoryBytesSpilled, DiskBytesSpilled
        batch, limit = 100, self._next_limit()
        chunks, current_chunk = [], []
        iterator = iter(iterator)
        while True:
            # pick elements in batch
            chunk = list(itertools.islice(iterator, batch))
            current_chunk.extend(chunk)
            if len(chunk) < batch:
                break

            used_memory = get_used_memory()
            ...
```

In this code, islice(iterator, batch) is used to get the next batch number of items from iterator. This is done in a loop until there are fewer than batch number of items left in the iterator, at which point the loop breaks.

pairwise

itertools.pairwise generates consecutive pairs of elements from an iterable. For example, list(pairwise([1, 2, 3, 4])) will generate [(1, 2), (2, 3), (3, 4)].

The below example from *cloudnetpy* illustrates pairwise use:

```
# File: cloudnetpy/instruments/vaisala.py

def split_string(string: str, indices: list) -> list:
```

> """*Splits string between indices.*
>
> *Notes*
> > *It is possible to skip characters from the beginning and end of the*
> > *string but not from the middle.*
>
> *Examples*
> > *>>> s = 'abcde'*
> > *>>> indices = [1, 2, 4]*
> > *>>> split_string(s, indices)*
> > *['b', 'cd']*
>
> *"""*

```
    return [string[n:m] for n, m in itertools.pairwise(indices)]
```

In the above split_string function, if the string argument is 'abcde' and the indices argument is [1, 2, 4], itertools.pairwise(indices) will produce pairs (1, 2) and (2, 4). The string is then sliced between these pairs of indices, producing the substrings 'b' and 'cd'.

starmap

starmap applies a function to arguments unpacked from tuples in an iterable. It is somewhat similar to the built-in map. The map function is suitable for functions taking a single argument, whereas starmap applies the function to arguments unpacked from tuples in an iterable.

For example, list(starmap(math.pow, [(2, 3), (3, 2), (10, 3)])) will produce the output [8.0, 9.0, 1000.0].

The code snippet below illustrates the use of starmap:

```
# File: pyomo/core/base/piecewise.py

def _characterize_function(name, tol, f_rule, model, points, *index):
    """

    Generates a list of range values and checks
    for convexity/concavity. Assumes domain points
    are sorted in increasing order.
    """
```

```
points = [value(_p) for _p in points]

...

values = [value(_p) for _p in values]

step = False
try:
    slopes = [
        (values[i] - values[i - 1]) / (points[i] - points[i - 1])
        for i in range(1, len(points))
    ]
except ZeroDivisionError:
    # we have a step function
    step = True
    slopes = [
        (
            (None)
            if (points[i] == points[i - 1])
            else ((values[i] - values[i - 1]) / (points[i] -
            points[i - 1]))
        )
        for i in range(1, len(points))
    ]

# TODO: Warn when the slopes of two consecutive line
#       segments are nearly equal since this is likely
#       due to a user mistake and may cause issue with
#       the solver.
#       *** This is already done below but there
#           is probably a more correct way
#           to send this warning through Pyomo
if not all(
    itertools.starmap(
        lambda x1, x2: (
            (True) if ((x1 is None) or (x2 is None)) else
            (abs(x1 - x2) > tol)
```

```
            ),
            zip(slopes, itertools.islice(slopes, 1, None)),
        )
    ):
        msg = (
            "**WARNING: Piecewise component '%s[%s]' has detected slopes of
            consecutive piecewise "
            "segments to be within "
            + str(tol)
            + " of one another. Refer to the Piecewise help "
            "documentation for information on how to disable this warning."
        )
        if index == ():
            index = None
        print(msg % (name, flatten_tuple(index)))

    ...
```

In the above code, `itertools.starmap` is used to apply a lambda function to every pair of consecutive slopes. The lambda function checks if either of the slopes is None or if the absolute difference between the slopes is greater than a tolerance value `tol`.

The `zip(slopes, itertools.islice(slopes, 1, None))` generates pairs of consecutive slopes. `itertools.islice(slopes, 1, None)` is used to create a new iterable that starts from the second element of `slopes`, effectively shifting the original `slopes` iterable by one position.

The `all` function checks if all elements of the iterable returned by `itertools.starmap` are True. If any pair of slopes does not satisfy the condition, `all` will return False and a warning message will be printed.

takewhile

`itertools.takewhile` creates an iterable that returns elements from another iterable as long as a condition is true.

For example, `list(takewhile(lambda x: x < 5, [1, 2, 3, 5, 1, 2]))` will give `[1, 2, 3]`.

The below code snippet from the *ibis* library exemplifies the usage of takewhile:

```python
# File: ibis/util.py

def append_admonition(
    func: Callable, *, msg: str, body: str = "", kind: str = "warning"
) -> str:
    """Append a `kind` admonition with `msg` to `func`'s docstring."""
    if docstr := func.__doc__:
        preamble, *rest = docstr.split("\n\n", maxsplit=1)

        # count leading spaces and add them to the deprecation warning so #
        # the docstring parses correctly
        leading_spaces = " " * sum(
            1 for _ in itertools.takewhile(str.isspace, rest[0] if rest
            else [])
        )

        lines = [f"::: {{.callout-{kind}}}", f"## {msg}", ":::"]
        admonition_doc = textwrap.indent("\n".join(lines), leading_spaces)

        if body:
            rest = [indent(body, spaces=len(leading_spaces) + 4), *rest]

        docstr = "\n\n".join([preamble, admonition_doc, *rest])

    ...
    return docstr
```

In this case, the callable predicate is str.isspace, which checks if a string consists of whitespace. The iterable is rest[0] if rest else [], which is the first paragraph of the rest of the docstring if it exists, otherwise an empty list. itertools.takewhile(str. isspace, rest[0] if rest else []) will return an iterator that yields the leading spaces of the first paragraph of the rest of the docstring.

The sum(1 for _ in ...) part then counts the number of elements in this iterator, which is the number of leading spaces. This count is used to create a string of spaces (" " * count) that is used to indent the admonition in the docstring so that it aligns correctly with the rest of the docstring.

tee

itertools.tee splits a single iterable into multiple independent iterators. It is commonly used when we need multiple passes over the same iterable without reevaluating it.

Its signature is as follows:

```
itertools.tee(iterable, n=2)
```

n is the number of independent iterators generated from the iterable.

For example, a, b = tee([1, 2, 3]); list(a), list(b) will return ([1, 2, 3], [1, 2, 3]) in the console.

Below is an example of tee usage from the *oppia* library:

```python
# File: oppia/core/utils.py

def partition(
    iterable: Iterable[T],
    predicate: Callable[..., bool] = bool,
    enumerated: bool = False
) -> Tuple[
        Iterable[Union[T, Tuple[int, T]]],
        Iterable[Union[T, Tuple[int, T]]]]:
    """Returns two generators which split the iterable based on the
    predicate.

    NOTE: The predicate is called AT MOST ONCE per item.

    Example:
        is_even = lambda n: (n % 2) == 0
        evens, odds = partition([10, 8, 1, 5, 6, 4, 3, 7], is_even)
        assert list(evens) == [10, 8, 6, 4]
        assert list(odds) == [1, 5, 3, 7]

    Args:
        iterable: iterable. Any kind of iterable object.
        predicate: callable. A function which accepts an item and returns
        True or False. enumerated: bool. Whether the partitions should
        include their original indices.
```

Returns:

   tuple(iterable, iterable). Two distinct generators. The first
   generator will hold values which passed the predicate. The second
   will hold the values which did not. If enumerated is True, then
   the generators will yield (index, item) pairs. Otherwise, the
   generators will yield items by themselves.
   """

```
if enumerated:
    new_iterable: Iterable[Union[T, Tuple[int, T]]] = enumerate(
        iterable)
    old_predicate = predicate
    predicate = lambda pair: old_predicate(pair[1])
else:
    new_iterable = iterable

# Creates two distinct generators over the same iterable. Memory-
efficient.
true_part, false_part = itertools.tee(
    (i, predicate(i)) for i in new_iterable)
return (
    (i for i, predicate_is_true in true_part if predicate_is_true),
    (i for i, predicate_is_true in false_part if not predicate_
    is_true))
```

In the partition() function, the tee() function is used to split the iterable into two parts based on the predicate function. The true_part iterator will hold values for which the predicate function returns True, and the false_part iterator will hold values for which the predicate function returns False. This is achieved by using generator expressions that filter the true_part and false_part iterators based on the result of the predicate function.

zip_longest

zip_longest is used to combine elements from multiple iterables, filling in missing values with a specified fill value. zip_longest is similar to the zip function in that it combines elements from multiple iterables into tuples. But it continues until the longest iterable is exhausted, filling shorter iterables with a specified fill value.

For example, `list(zip_longest('AB', '1234', fillvalue='-'))` will output
`[('A', '1'), ('B', '2'), ('-', '3'), ('-', '4')]`.

The below example from *salt* showcases the use of `itertools.zip_longest`:

```python
# File: salt/key.py

class KeyCLI:
    """

    Manage key CLI operations
    """

    def __init__(self, opts):
        self.opts = opts
        self.client = salt.wheel.WheelClient(opts)
        self.key = Key
        # instantiate the key object for masterless mode
        if not opts.get("eauth"):
            self.key = self.key(opts)
        self.auth = None

    ...

    def _get_args_kwargs(self, fun, args=None):
        argspec = salt.utils.args.get_function_argspec(fun)
        if args is None:
            args = []
            if argspec.args:
                # Iterate in reverse order to ensure we get the
                correct default
                # value for the positional argument.
                for arg, default in itertools.zip_longest(
                    reversed(argspec.args), reversed(argspec.
                    defaults or ())
                ):
                    args.append(self.opts.get(arg, default))
            # Reverse the args so that they are in the correct order
            args = args[::-1]
```

```
    if argspec.keywords is None:
        kwargs = {}
    else:
        args, kwargs = salt.minion.load_args_and_kwargs(fun, args)
    return args, kwargs
```

In this code, zip_longest is used to iterate over argspec.args and argspec.defaults in reverse order. argspec.args is a list of argument names that the function fun takes, and argspec.defaults is a list of default values for those arguments.

The zip_longest function pairs each argument name with its corresponding default value. If the function has more argument names than default values (which is common, as not all function arguments have default values), zip_longest will pair the extra argument names with None.

Conclusion

The itertools module provides a wide range of tools for working with iterators. It will help us optimize our code with fast, memory-efficient tools for creating and manipulating iterators. Throughout this chapter, we have explored a variety of itertools functions, each designed to handle specific tasks and enhance the capabilities of looping and data processing. By utilizing functions like count(), cycle(), and repeat(), we can generate infinite sequences. Tools such as chain(), compress(), and filterfalse() allow us to combine and filter iterables with ease, while product(), permutations(), and combinations() enable us to perform combinatoric operations. Additionally, advanced functions like accumulate(), groupby(), and tee() offer powerful ways to aggregate, group, and duplicate iterators, to handle complex data transformations.

CHAPTER 14

Multithreading

In the previous chapter, we explored the `itertools` module and learned how to write cleaner and more memory-efficient loops using powerful iterator tools.

In computer science, concurrency denotes the ability of a program to execute multiple computations simultaneously. In Python, the threading module provides a framework for implementing concurrency through the concept of threads—lightweight subprocesses within a single process. Currently, Python's threads can be used to speed up programs that are I/O blocked. This can come in handy in programs that are limited by I/O operations, such as a program that might require multiple network calls to fetch data or a script that requires reading multiple files.

Threads can speed up the program by running parts of code concurrently, but they come with additional overhead (for the creation and management of the threads) and require extra care not to run into race conditions. We will look into race conditions that may occur when using threading and learn to use synchronization primitives to avoid them.

Thread Class for Creating Threads

From the Python docs:

> The Thread class represents an activity that is run in a separate thread of control. You can specify the activity by passing a callable object to the constructor or by overriding the run() method in a subclass.

The `Thread` class from the threading module can be used to create one-off threads. The `start` method of the thread object can be used to start the thread's execution, and the join method blocks waiting for the task to be executed.

© Adarsh Divakaran 2025
A. Divakaran, *Deep Dive Python*, https://doi.org/10.1007/979-8-8688-1261-3_14

The below example uses multiple threads to perform multiple network requests concurrently:

```python
import threading
import time
import requests

def perform_get(url):
    print(f"Task {threading.current_thread().ident} starting.")
    requests.get(url)
    print(f"Task {threading.current_thread().ident} completed")

if __name__ == "__main__":
    start = time.perf_counter()
    for path_ in range(1, 4):
        perform_get(f"http://example.org/{path_}")

    end = time.perf_counter()
    print(f"Time of non-threaded calls: {end-start} \n")

    start = time.perf_counter()

    task1 = threading.Thread(target=perform_get, args=("http://example.org/1",))
    task2 = threading.Thread(target=perform_get, args=("http://example.org/2",))
    task3 = threading.Thread(target=perform_get, args=("http://example.org/3",))

    task1.start()
    task2.start()
    task3.start()

    task1.join()
    task2.join()
    task3.join()
```

```
    end = time.perf_counter()
    print(f"Time of threaded calls: {end-start}")

# Output
"""

Task 12372 starting.
Task 12372 completed
Task 12372 starting.
Task 12372 completed
Task 12372 starting.
Task 12372 completed
Time of non-threaded calls: 1.4105191999988165

Task 14696 starting.
Task 13040 starting.
Task 13464 starting.
Task 14696 completed
Task 13464 completed
Task 13040 completed
Time of threaded calls: 0.512633399994229
"""
```

It can be seen that using multiple threads has significantly improved the execution time of the program.

Implications of the GIL on Threading

The Global Interpreter Lock (GIL) is a mutex that protects access to Python objects, preventing multiple threads from executing Python bytecodes simultaneously. A GIL allows only one thread to execute at a single point in time. This can lead to performance penalties if we try to use multithreading in CPU-bound programs.

Concurrency refers to the ability to manage multiple tasks simultaneously.

Parallelism deals with the simultaneous execution of multiple tasks. It is about executing two or more tasks all at once, leveraging multiple processing units (CPU cores).

A GIL limits parallelism but allows for concurrency by allowing multiple threads to run concurrently.

> A GIL-free alternative version of Python will be available starting with Python 3.13. The default Python interpreter will have the GIL, but it can be disabled based on a build-time flag.

The example below shows the execution time of a CPU-bound task running on multiple threads vs. its single-thread execution time:

```python
import threading
import time

def cpu_blocked_task(number):
    print(f"Task {threading.current_thread().ident} starting.")
    _ = number**number
    print(f"Task {threading.current_thread().ident} completed")

if __name__ == "__main__":
    start = time.perf_counter()
    for number in range(10000, 10003):
        cpu_blocked_task(number=number)

    end = time.perf_counter()
    print(f"Time of single-threaded calls: {end-start} \n")

    start = time.perf_counter()

    task1 = threading.Thread(target=cpu_blocked_task, args=(10000,))
    task2 = threading.Thread(target=cpu_blocked_task, args=(10001,))
    task3 = threading.Thread(target=cpu_blocked_task, args=(10002,))

    task1.start()
    task2.start()
    task3.start()

    task1.join()
    task2.join()
    task3.join()
```

```
    end = time.perf_counter()
    print(f"Time of multi-threaded calls: {end-start}")

# Output:

"""
Task 16200 starting.
Task 16200 completed
Task 16200 starting.
Task 16200 completed
Task 16200 starting.
Task 16200 completed
Time of single-threaded calls: 0.0038736999995307997

Task 21916 starting.
Task 21916 completed
Task 22228 starting.
Task 22228 completed
Task 19184 starting.
Task 19184 completed
Time of multi-threaded calls: 0.0046670000010657
"""
```

In the above snippet, a CPU-blocked task is executed using multiple threads. The performance is degraded compared with the simple-threaded performance in this case. This is because of the added overhead of managing the threads. This is partially due to the switch interval. The switch interval in Python specifies how long the Python interpreter will allow a Python thread to run, after which it is forced for a context switch. Since only one thread runs at a time due to a GIL, the interpreter tries to switch threads after this interval. If the threads are waiting (e.g., for I/O operations), this switching allows for a parallel execution–like effect. If threads are running any CPU-bound operations, this context switch causes a performance penalty. The methods sys. getswitchinterval and sys.setswitchinterval can be used to retrieve and set the switch interval. However, changing the switch interval is rarely needed and can lead to subtle bugs or performance issues if misused.

Daemon Threads

A thread can be marked as a daemon thread by passing the daemon keyword argument of the Thread constructor. If the argument is not passed, the daemonic property is inherited from the creator thread.

From Python docs:

> The significance of this flag is that the entire Python program exits when only daemon threads are left. The initial value is inherited from the creating thread. The flag can be set through the daemon property or the daemon constructor argument.

The program exits when all the non-daemonic threads have finished their execution. Due to this, daemon threads can be abruptly shut down.

We can mark a thread as a daemon if it does not have an independent lifecycle apart from the main thread.

The below example from httpie-cli, a CLI tool, uses daemon threads to ensure that creation of a new sub-thread does not block program exit, once the user exits the main thread:

```
# File: cli/httpie/uploads.py

def observe_stdin_for_data_thread(
    env: Environment, file: IO, read_event: threading.Event
) -> None:
    ...

    def worker(event: threading.Event) -> None:
        if not event.wait(timeout=READ_THRESHOLD):
            env.stderr.write(
                f"> warning: no stdin data read in {READ_THRESHOLD}s "
                f"(perhaps you want to --ignore-stdin)\n"
                f"> See: https://httpie.io/docs/cli/best-practices\n"
            )

    # Making it a daemon ensures that if the user exits from the main
    # program # (e.g., either regularly or with Ctrl-C), the thread will not
    # block them.
```

```
thread = threading.Thread(target=worker, args=(read_event,),
daemon=True)  # <-- (1)
thread.start()
```

The function creates a thread that waits for stdin data. Since this is a CLI tool and this thread just supports the main thread's functionality, it doesn't make sense to keep it running when the main process exits. So this thread is initialized with daemon=True, as seen in comment # <-- (1).

Thread-Local Data

Threads share the memory space of their parent process. This will allow us to seamlessly access and share variables, data structures, etc. across threads. But this comes with its own challenges. There may be scenarios where we need to isolate variables and might need to store data specific to each thread. Thread-local data can be leveraged in this case.

```
import threading
import time

# Create a thread-local storage object (1)
thread_local = threading.local()

def init_data(number):
    thread_local.number = number * 100

def show_data():
    print(f"Thread {threading.current_thread().name} has number {thread_
    local.number}")

def worker(number):
    init_data(number)

    for _ in range(3):
        time.sleep(1)
        show_data()

thread1 = threading.Thread(target=worker, name="A", kwargs={"number": 1})
thread2 = threading.Thread(target=worker, name="B", kwargs={"number": 2})
```

```
thread1.start()
thread2.start()

thread1.join()
thread2.join()

""" Output:
Thread A has number 100
Thread B has number 200
Thread A has number 100
Thread B has number 200
Thread A has number 100
Thread B has number 200
"""
```

As seen in (1), a thread-local storage object was created and assigned to the variable thread_local. Arbitrary attributes can be assigned to this variable, which are specific to the thread that performs the assignment and is isolated from others.

In the example, each thread stores its own number attribute in the thread_local object and accesses the thread-specific value during their concurrent execution.

Pewee, a Python ORM, utilizes thread-local data in its ThreadSafeDatabaseMetadata to support dynamic database switches at runtime in multithreaded applications:

```
# File: peewee/playhouse/shortcuts.py

class ThreadSafeDatabaseMetadata(Metadata):
    """

    Metadata class to allow swapping database at run-time in a
    multi-threaded
    application. To use:

    class Base(Model):
        class Meta:
            model_metadata_class = ThreadSafeDatabaseMetadata
    """

    def __init__(self, *args, **kwargs):
        # The database attribute is stored in a thread-local.
        self._database = None
```

```
        self._local = threading.local()
        super(ThreadSafeDatabaseMetadata, self).__init__(*args, **kwargs)

    def _get_db(self):
        return getattr(self._local, "database", self._database)

    def _set_db(self, db):
        if self._database is None:
            self._database = db
        self._local.database = db

    database = property(_get_db, _set_db)
```

In multithreaded applications using peewee ORM, database switching at runtime without using ThreadSafeDatabaseMetadata can lead to errors. If multiple threads work in parallel, this can lead to errors such as writing to the wrong DB, inconsistent writes (in case of non-atomic DB operations), etc.

ThreadSafeDatabaseMetadata solves this by keeping the database attributes in a thread-local object (self._local). In this way, dynamic changes to the database will only affect the thread that made the change. Other threads will keep working with their existing databases.

threading.Timer

The Timer class in the threading module is a subclass of the Thread class. It performs an action after a certain amount of time has passed.

Its signature is as follows:

```
class threading.Timer(interval, function, args=None, kwargs=None)
```

The timer object will wait interval seconds before running the function in a new thread. Since Timer is a subclass of Thread, its objects should be started similarly using the start method.

The below example from Apache Airflow uses a timer object to handle an operation timeout:

```python
# File: airflow/utils/timeout.py

from threading import Timer

_timeout = ContextManager[None]

class TimeoutWindows(_timeout, LoggingMixin):
    """Windows timeout version: To be used in a ``with`` block and timeout
    its content."""

    def __init__(self, seconds=1, error_message="Timeout"):
        super().__init__()
        self._timer: Timer | None = None
        self.seconds = seconds
        self.error_message = error_message + ", PID: " + str(os.getpid())

    def handle_timeout(self, *args):
        """Log information and raises AirflowTaskTimeout."""
        self.log.error("Process timed out, PID: %s", str(os.getpid()))
        raise AirflowTaskTimeout(self.error_message)

    def __enter__(self):
        if self._timer:
            self._timer.cancel()
        self._timer = Timer(self.seconds, self.handle_timeout) # <-- (1)
        self._timer.start()

    def __exit__(self, type_, value, traceback):
        if self._timer:
            self._timer.cancel()
            self._timer = None

if IS_WINDOWS:
    timeout: type[TimeoutWindows | TimeoutPosix] = TimeoutWindows
```

The above code creates a context manager that handles operation timeouts. It can be seen in comment # <-- (1) that on entering the context manager, the timer object is created and then started. If the execution remains inside the context manager even after the timeout (self.seconds), the handle_timeout function will get called, leading to an exception.

This is used in Airflow code, as seen below:

```
dagbag_import_timeout = settings.get_dagbag_import_timeout(filepath)
...
with timeout(dagbag_import_timeout, error_message=timeout_msg):
    return parse(mod_name, filepath)
```

Here, the parse operation should be completed within the dagbag_import_timeout, or else an AirflowTaskTimeout exception will be raised.

ThreadPoolExecutor

ThreadPoolExecutor belongs to the `concurrent.futures` module, which was introduced in the standard library in Python 3.2. It provides a simpler and more efficient way to utilize a pool of threads for concurrent execution. It automatically manages a pool of worker threads, taking away the complexity of managing the thread lifecycle from the user. Tasks (the callables that are to be run concurrently) are submitted to the ThreadPoolExecutor as callable objects. Upon submission, a `Future` object is returned, representing the eventual completion of the callable's execution and its result.

Key methods of ThreadPoolExecutor objects:

- `submit(fn, *args, **kwargs)`: Submits a callable to be executed with the given arguments and keyword arguments. It returns a `Future` object.

- `map(func, *iterables, timeout=None, chunksize=1)`: This is similar to the built-in `map` function. It applies the given function (`func`) to each iterable in parallel.

The signature of the ThreadPoolExecutor class is as below:

```
class concurrent.futures.ThreadPoolExecutor(
    max_workers=None,
    thread_name_prefix='',
    initializer=None,
    initargs=()
)
```

The ThreadPoolExecutor uses a pool of, at most, *max_workers* threads to execute calls asynchronously. The max_workers value should be chosen carefully not to overload the system. The initializer argument accepts a callable, which will be called at the start of each worker thread. initargs can be used to provide arguments to the initializer callable.

Below is an example of performing multiple network requests concurrently using the ThreadPoolExecutor:

```python
import concurrent.futures
import threading

import requests

def perform_request(url):
    with threading.Lock():
        print(f"Thread {threading.current_thread().native_id}
        requesting {url}")
    result = requests.get(url)
    with threading.Lock():
        print(f"Thread {threading.current_thread().ident} completed the
        request: {url}")
    return result

with concurrent.futures.ThreadPoolExecutor(max_workers=2) as executor:
    futures = []
    for path in range(5):
        future = executor.submit(perform_request, url=f"https://example.
        org/{path+1}")
        futures.append(future)

    for future in concurrent.futures.as_completed(futures):
        print(f"Got result from the `Future`: {future.result().url}")
```

Output:

```
Thread 23512 requesting https://example.org/1
Thread 19984 requesting https://example.org/2
Thread 19984 completed the request: https://example.org/2
Thread 19984 requesting https://example.org/3
```

```
Got result from the `Future`: https://example.org/2
Thread 23512 completed the request: https://example.org/1
Thread 23512 requesting https://example.org/4
Got result from the `Future`: https://example.org/1
Thread 19984 completed the request: https://example.org/3
Thread 19984 requesting https://example.org/5
Got result from the `Future`: https://example.org/3
Thread 23512 completed the request: https://example.org/4
Got result from the `Future`: https://example.org/4
Thread 19984 completed the request: https://example.org/5
Got result from the `Future`: https://example.org/5
```

We have used the as_completed function from the concurrent.futures module. It takes an iterable of future objects as the first argument and returns an iterator that yields future objects (from the futures provided as its argument) as and when they complete.

Calling the result method of a Future object directly is similar to calling the join method of a thread. The current thread blocks till the thread execution is complete.

The below example from the library ray uses ThreadPoolExecutor to fetch data from remote notes and add it to an archive:

```python
# File: ray/python/ray/autoscaler/_private/cluster_dump.py

def create_archive_for_remote_nodes(
    archive: Archive, remote_nodes: Sequence[Node], parameters:
GetParameters
):
    """Create an archive combining data from the remote nodes.

    This will parallelize calls to get data from remote nodes.

    """
    if not archive.is_open:
        archive.open()

    with ThreadPoolExecutor(max_workers=MAX_PARALLEL_SSH_WORKERS) as
    executor:
        for remote_node in remote_nodes:
            executor.submit(
                create_and_add_remote_data_to_local_archive,
```

```
        archive=archive,
        remote_node=remote_node,
        parameters=parameters,
    )

return archive
```

The program flow exits out of the ThreadPoolExecutor's context manager only after the completion of all the submitted tasks. If we are not concerned with the return of the functions (or the exceptions raised by them) that are executed inside the thread, we can ignore the future objects, as in the above example.

ThreadPoolExecutors are commonly used in situations like this, where we have to perform I/O-related tasks with a limit on the number of parallel tasks under execution.

ThreadPoolExecutor also has a map method, which is similar to the built-in map function in the structure. It takes a function and an iterable as its arguments and returns an iterator. The function is individually called on each iterable member concurrently.

The below example from black utilizes the executor's map method to load top Python packages from PyPI:

```
# File: black/gallery/gallery.py

def download_and_extract_top_packages(
    directory: Path,
    workers: int = 8,
    limit: slice = DEFAULT_SLICE,
) -> Generator[Path, None, None]:
    with ThreadPoolExecutor(max_workers=workers) as executor:
        bound_downloader = partial(get_package, version=None,
        directory=directory)
        for package in executor.map(bound_downloader, get_top_packages()
        [limit]):
            if package is not None:
                yield package
```

The generator function above uses the executor's map method to apply the bound_ downloader function to the top packages list. When we used the submit method to run functions in threads, we needed to track the futures and get their results so as to obtain the return values from the threaded functions (or to fetch exceptions raised in them). When using map, we do not need to create the list of futures and track them separately. An iterator of result of the map operation is directly returned by the map method.

Handling Exceptions in Threads

When using the Thread class to handle multiple threads, exceptions raised in child threads won't interrupt the main thread execution. They just get logged into the standard error stream.

```python
import threading

def delegated_function():
    raise Exception("An error occurred")

t = threading.Thread(target=delegated_function)

t.start()
t.join()

print("Execution completed")
```

The above snippet will produce the following output when run.

```
Execution completed
Exception in thread Thread-1 (delegated_function):
Traceback (most recent call last):
  File "...\Lib\threading.py", line 1045, in _bootstrap_inner
    self.run()
  File "...\Lib\threading.py", line 982, in run
    self._target(*self._args, **self._kwargs)
  File "...exc.py", line 5, in delegated_function
    raise Exception("An error occurred")
Exception: An error occurred
```

The main thread execution is uninterrupted even though the exception was raised in the sub-thread.

In the case of ThreadPoolExecutor, errors won't get logged by default.

```
import concurrent.futures

def delegated_function():
    raise Exception("An error occurred")

with concurrent.futures.ThreadPoolExecutor() as executor:
    executor.submit(delegated_function)

print("Threadpool finished")
```

This will give the below output:

```
Threadpool finished
```

Future objects that are returned once a task is submitted to the executor will allow us to get the result of the tasks as well as the exceptions that occurred in them.

```
import concurrent.futures

def delegated_function():
    raise Exception("An error occurred")

with concurrent.futures.ThreadPoolExecutor() as executor:
    future = executor.submit(delegated_function)

future.result()

print("Threadpool finished")
```

Calling future.result() will lead to raising the exception in the main thread, stopping the program execution.

```
Traceback (most recent call last):
  File "...", line 11, in <module>
    future.result()
  File "...\Lib\concurrent\futures\_base.py", line 449, in result
    return self.__get_result()
           ^^^^^^^^^^^^^^^^^^^^
  File "...\Lib\concurrent\futures\_base.py", line 401, in __get_result
    raise self._exception
```

```
File "...\Lib\concurrent\futures\thread.py", line 58, in run
    result = self.fn(*self.args, **self.kwargs)
             ^^^^^^^^^^^^^^^^^^^^^^^^^^^^^^^^^^^
File "...", line 5, in delegated_function
    raise Exception("An error occurred")
Exception: An error occurred
```

Note that the line print("Threadpool finished") is not executed in this case due to the exception being raised in the previous line. The future.exception() method can be used to fetch the exception object raised inside the threaded function.

Custom Thread Classes

We can create custom thread classes by inheriting the Thread class and by overriding the run method. When the start method of the child object of this custom class is invoked, the run method will be invoked in a separate thread control.

The below example from Luigi, a batch job pipeline management library from Spotify, inherits the Thread class in the implementation of the KeepAliveThread class:

```
# File: luigi/worker.py

class KeepAliveThread(threading.Thread):
    """
    Periodically tell the scheduler that the worker still lives.
    """

    def __init__(self, scheduler, worker_id, ping_interval, rpc_message_
    callback):
        super(KeepAliveThread, self).__init__()
        self._should_stop = threading.Event()
        self._scheduler = scheduler
        self._worker_id = worker_id
        self._ping_interval = ping_interval
        self._rpc_message_callback = rpc_message_callback

    def stop(self):
        self._should_stop.set()
```

```python
    def run(self):
        while True:
            self._should_stop.wait(self._ping_interval)
            if self._should_stop.is_set():
                logger.info("Worker %s was stopped. Shutting down Keep-
                Alive thread" % self._worker_id)
                break
            with fork_lock:
                response = None
                try:
                    response = self._scheduler.ping(worker=self._worker_id)
                except BaseException:  # httplib.BadStatusLine:
                    logger.warning('Failed pinging scheduler')

                # handle rpc messages
                if response:
                    for message in response["rpc_messages"]:
                        self._rpc_message_callback(message)

def rpc_message_callback(fn):
    fn.is_rpc_message_callback = True
    return fn

class Worker:
    """

    Worker object communicates with a scheduler.

    Simple class that talks to a scheduler and:

    * tells the scheduler what it has to do + its dependencies
    * asks for stuff to do (pulls it in a loop and runs it)
    """

    def __init__(self, scheduler=None, worker_id=None, worker_processes=1,
    assistant=False, **kwargs):
        if scheduler is None:
            scheduler = Scheduler()

        ...
```

```python
def __enter__(self):
    """

    Start the KeepAliveThread.
    """

    self._keep_alive_thread = KeepAliveThread(self._scheduler,
                                              self._id,
                                              self._config.ping_
                                              interval,
                                              self._handle_rpc_message)
    self._keep_alive_thread.daemon = True
    self._keep_alive_thread.start()
    return self

def __exit__(self, type, value, traceback):
    """

    Stop the KeepAliveThread and kill still running tasks.
    """

    self._keep_alive_thread.stop()
    self._keep_alive_thread.join()
    for task in self._running_tasks.values():
        if task.is_alive():
            task.terminate()
    self._task_result_queue.close()
    return False  # Don't suppress exception
```

The custom KeepAliveThread class is used to periodically send a ping message to the scheduler to inform it that the worker is still alive. It extends the threading.Thread class and overrides the run method to define the behavior of the thread.

The run method of the KeepAliveThread class is executed in a loop. It waits for the specified ping_interval and then sends a ping message to the scheduler using the ping method of the scheduler object. If a response is received, the method iterates over the RPC messages in the response and calls the rpc_message_callback function for each message.

The Worker class uses the KeepAliveThread class in its __enter__ method to start the keep-alive thread. It creates an instance of KeepAliveThread with the necessary parameters and starts the thread. The __exit__ method is used to stop the keep-alive thread and terminate any still-running tasks.

Thread Safety

Thread safety refers to the property of an algorithm or program being able to function correctly during simultaneous execution by multiple threads. We must keep in mind that threads do not have independent memory, and bugs can occur when multiple threads are trying to manipulate shared mutable data. As previously seen, to store data specific to individual threads, we can use thread-local storage. But if mutable data is needed to be shared across threads, we might need to use thread-safe data structures (such as queue.Queue) or synchronization primitives to enforce thread safety.

Race Conditions

A race condition occurs when the outcome of a program depends on the sequence or timing of uncontrollable events like thread execution order. If two threads simultaneously read and write to a shared variable without adequate synchronization, they can interfere with each other, leading to incorrect results and behaviors.

The below example shows a thread-unsafe code that can produce unexpected results:

```
import threading
import time

# Account balance
balance = 2000

def withdraw(amount):
    global balance

    if balance >= amount:
        new_balance = balance - amount
        time.sleep(
            0.1
        )  # A sleep to simulate any I/O operation. E.g: Database reads,
        network calls, etc.
        balance = new_balance
    else:
        raise Exception("Insufficient balance")
```

```
thread1 = threading.Thread(target=withdraw, args=(500,))
thread2 = threading.Thread(target=withdraw, args=(700,))

thread1.start()
thread2.start()

thread1.join()
thread2.join()

print(f"Final account balance: {balance}")
```

The output of the script alternates between 1500 and 1300 when run multiple times rather than the desired value of 800. This is an example of a race condition caused by improper synchronization between threads when accessing and modifying shared data (in this case, the balance variable).

In the snippet, both thread1 and thread2 attempt to withdraw money from the same account balance almost simultaneously. The key issue here is that there is no locking mechanism around the check and update of the balance. Both threads operate based on the global state they read upon entering the withdraw function, which might no longer be valid after the sleep delay. Suppose thread1 reads the balance as 2000 and then gets preempted (temporarily paused) just after calculating new_balance as 1500 but before it can update the global balance. In that pause, thread2 runs, reads the balance as still 2000, and proceeds to deduct 700, setting the balance to 1300. When thread1 resumes, it sets the balance to its previously computed new_balance of 1500, unaware that thread2 has already modified the balance to 1300. Thus, the last write to balance (by thread1) sets it to 1500, overwriting thread2's update. The value alternates between 1500 and 1300 based on which thread completes its execution at the latest.

In the coming sections, we will take a look into various synchronization primitives that will help us enforce thread safety and coordination between threads.

Locks: Mutual Exclusion

A lock can be used for exclusive access to a resource. Once a thread acquires a lock, no other threads can acquire it (and proceed further) unless the lock is released.

Lock

We can use locks to wrap a statement or group of statements that should be executed atomically.

Below is an example snippet using locks to enforce thread safety to the problematic script discussed above:

```python
import threading
import time

# Account balance
balance = 2000
# Lock for synchronizing threads
lock = threading.Lock()

def withdraw(amount):
    global balance

    lock.acquire() # (1) Acquiring the lock
    if balance >= amount:
        new_balance = balance - amount
        time.sleep(0.1)  # Simulate I/O operation
        balance = new_balance
    else:
        raise Exception("Insufficient balance")
    lock.release()

thread1 = threading.Thread(target=withdraw, args=(500,))
thread2 = threading.Thread(target=withdraw, args=(700,))

thread1.start()
thread2.start()

thread1.join()
thread2.join()

print(f"Final account balance: {balance}")

# Output: Final account balance: 800
```

In the script, as seen in comment #(1), we have acquired the lock before entering the critical section of our code. Read and modify operations on the balance variable will now be running concurrently, and only one thread will execute this critical section between acquire and release method calls of the lock. Instead of calling the acquire and release methods separately, we can use the lock variable as a context manager enclosing the critical section of the code inside the with statement.

The below example from the cachecontrol library uses threading.Lock to make DictCache write operations thread-safe:

```python
# File: cachecontrol/cache.py

from threading import Lock

class DictCache(BaseCache):
    def __init__(self, init_dict: MutableMapping[str, bytes] | None = None)
    -> None:
        self.lock = Lock()
        self.data = init_dict or {}

    def get(self, key: str) -> bytes | None:
        return self.data.get(key, None)

    def set(
        self, key: str, value: bytes, expires: int | datetime | None = None
    ) -> None:
        with self.lock:
            self.data.update({key: value})

    def delete(self, key: str) -> None:
        with self.lock:
            if key in self.data:
                self.data.pop(key)
```

DictCache stores cache data inside its data attribute, which is a dictionary. Dictionary operations are not thread-safe by default. If modification is done without using locks by concurrent threads, it may lead to data inconsistencies. This issue is mitigated here by acquiring a lock by using the lock object (self.lock) for modification operations (set and delete methods).

Deadlock

If a lock is not released properly due to an error or oversight in the code, it can lead to a deadlock where other threads wait indefinitely for the lock to be released. The reasons for deadlock include

Nested lock acquisition:

Deadlocks can occur if a thread attempts to acquire a lock it already holds. In conventional locks, trying to acquire the same lock multiple times within the same thread leads to the thread blocking itself, a situation that does not resolve without external intervention.

Multiple lock acquisition:

Deadlocks are particularly likely when multiple locks are used and threads acquire them in inconsistent orders. If two threads each hold one lock and wait for the other, neither thread can proceed, resulting in a deadlock.

RLock

RLock is a re-entrant lock. It does not block when a holding thread requests the lock again. In other words, an RLock allows a thread to acquire the lock multiple times before it releases the lock. This is useful in recursive functions or in situations where a thread needs to re-enter a locked resource that it has already locked.

The Calibre ebook manager uses RLock in its UserManager class:

```
# File: src/calibre/srv/users.py

class UserManager:
    lock = RLock()

    @property
    def conn(self):
        with self.lock:
            if self._conn is None:
                self._conn = connect(self.path)
                with self._conn:
                    c = self._conn.cursor()
                    ...
                    c.close()
```

```python
        return self._conn

    def __init__(self, path=None):
        self.path = (
            os.path.join(config_dir, "server-users.sqlite") if path is None
            else path
        )
        self._conn = None

    def get_session_data(self, username):
        with self.lock:
            for (data,) in self.conn.cursor().execute(
                "SELECT session_data FROM users WHERE name=?", (username,)
            ):
                return load_json(data)
        return {}

    def set_session_data(self, username, data):
        with self.lock:
            conn = self.conn
            c = conn.cursor()
            data = as_json(data)
            if isinstance(data, bytes):
                data = data.decode("utf-8")
            c.execute("UPDATE users SET session_data=? WHERE name=?",
            (data, username))
```

The UserManager class uses a lock (self.lock) to lock database access and allow only one thread to perform DB operations concurrently. RLock is required in this case because a single method, such as set_session_data, requires multiple lock acquisitions. set_session_data initially acquires the lock and then accesses the conn property, which will call the conn method. Since the conn method also requires acquiring the lock, this might have led to a deadlock in the case of the simple Lock class.

Semaphores: Limiting Access

A semaphore is useful when the number of resources is limited and a number of threads try to access these limited resources. It uses a counter to limit access to a critical section by multiple threads. Like locks, a semaphore has `acquire` and `release` methods and can be used as a context manager. Each `acquire` call reduces a semaphore's counter by 1, and further acquire calls are blocked when the counter reaches zero. In the case of usage as a context manager, entering the context manager block happens after a successful (automatic) `acquire` call, and once the control exits the `with` block, the `release` method is automatically called.

The below snippet from `numpy` uses a semaphore to limit the maximum number of concurrent build jobs:

```python
# File: numpy/distutils/ccompiler.py

def CCompiler_compile(self, sources, output_dir=None, macros=None,
                      include_dirs=None, debug=0, extra_preargs=None,
                      extra_postargs=None, depends=None):
    """
    Compile one or more source files.

    """

    global _job_semaphore

    jobs = get_num_build_jobs()

    # setup semaphore to not exceed number of compile jobs when
    parallelized at
    # extension level (python >= 3.5)
    with _global_lock:
        if _job_semaphore is None:
            _job_semaphore = threading.Semaphore(jobs)

    ...

    def single_compile(args):
        obj, (src, ext) = args

        ...
```

```
    try:
        # retrieve slot from our #job semaphore and build
        with _job_semaphore:
            self._compile(obj, src, ext, cc_args, extra_postargs,
            pp_opts)
    finally:
        # register being done processing
        with _global_lock:
            _processing_files.remove(obj)
...
```

The semaphore _job_semaphore is initialized with a counter value equaling the maximum number of build jobs allowed to run in parallel. Inside the single_compile closure, the semaphore's acquire() method is called while entering the with _job_ semaphore statement, and it blocks until the number of currently executing jobs is less than the allowed number of parallelized build jobs. When the context manager exits, the release() method is automatically called, incrementing the counter.

Events: Signaling

Events are used for signaling. They allow a thread to notify one or more threads that some action has occurred. An event maintains an internal flag that can be set to true with the set() method and reset to false with the clear() method. Threads can wait for the flag to become true using the wait() method.

The below snippet from IPython uses Event to synchronize the execution of the HistorySavingThread thread with the parent thread:

 # File: IPython/core/history.py

```
class HistoryManager(HistoryAccessor):
    """A class to organize all history-related functionality in one
    place."""

    save_thread = Instance("IPython.core.history.HistorySavingThread",
    allow_none=True)

    ...
```

```
def __init__(self, shell=None, config=None, **traits):
    Create a new history manager associated with a shell instance."""
    ...
    self.save_flag = threading.Event()  # (1)
    self.db_input_cache_lock = threading.Lock()
    ...

    if self.enabled and self.hist_file != ":memory:":
        self.save_thread = HistorySavingThread(self)
        self.save_thread.start()

def store_output(self, line_num):
    """If database output logging is enabled, this saves all the
    outputs from the indicated prompt number to the database. It's
    called by run_cell after code has been executed.

    Parameters
    ----------
    line_num : int
        The line number from which to save outputs
    """
    if (not self.db_log_output) or (line_num not in self.output_
    hist_reprs):
        return
    output = self.output_hist_reprs[line_num]

    with self.db_output_cache_lock:
        self.db_output_cache.append((line_num, output))
    if self.db_cache_size <= 1:  # (2)
        self.save_flag.set()

class HistorySavingThread(threading.Thread):
    """This thread takes care of writing history to the database, so that
    the UI isn't held up while that happens.

    It waits for the HistoryManager's save_flag to be set, then writes out
    the history cache. The main thread is responsible for setting the flag
    when the cache size reaches a defined threshold."""
```

```python
    daemon = True
    stop_now = False
    enabled = True

    def __init__(self, history_manager):
        super(HistorySavingThread, self).__init__(name="IPythonHistorySavi
        ngThread")
        self.history_manager = history_manager

    @only_when_enabled
    def run(self):
        atexit.register(self.stop)
        # We need a separate db connection per thread:
        try:
            self.db = sqlite3.connect(
                str(self.history_manager.hist_file),
                **self.history_manager.connection_options,
            )
            while True:
                self.history_manager.save_flag.wait()  # (3)
                if self.stop_now:
                    self.db.close()
                    return
                self.history_manager.save_flag.clear()  # (4)
                self.history_manager.writeout_cache(self.db)
        except Exception as e:
            print(
                (
                    "The history saving thread hit an unexpected "
                    "error (%s)."
                    "History will not be written to the database."
                )
                % repr(e)
            )
        finally:
            atexit.unregister(self.stop)
```

```
def stop(self):
    """This can be called from the main thread to safely stop this
    thread."""
    self.stop_now = True
    self.history_manager.save_flag.set()
    self.join()
```

In the HistoryManager class, an instance of Event is created and assigned to the save_flag attribute (comment # (1)). In the store_output method of the HistoryManager class, the save_flag is set using the set() method (comment # (2)).

In the HistorySavingThread class, the thread waits for the save_flag to be set using the wait() method (comment # (3)). Since the HistoryManager class starts HistorySavingThread when initialized, the thread will be blocked, waiting for this flag to be set. When the save_flag is set (happens when the db_cache_size becomes desirably low), the thread writes out the history cache and then clears the save_flag using the clear() method (comment # (4)). The process happens in the loop, and the thread waits for the next set of history logs to write.

The Event class allows the parent/main thread to signal the HistorySavingThread thread to perform a specific action, in this case writing out the history cache.

Conditions: Conditional Waiting

A condition object is built on top of a Lock or RLock object and supports additional methods that allow threads to wait for certain conditions to be met and to signal other threads that those conditions have changed.

Condition objects are always associated with a lock. The lock argument used in the Condition's constructor accepts a Lock or RLock object. If this argument is omitted, a new RLock object is created and used as the underlying lock. Condition is commonly used in producer–consumer scenarios.

Various methods associated with Condition are

1. *acquire()*

   This method is used to acquire the underlying lock associated with the condition. It must be called before a thread can wait on or signal a condition.

2. *release()*

   This method releases the underlying lock.

3. *wait(timeout=None)*

   wait() is used to block the thread until it is notified or until a specified timeout occurs. The method releases the lock before blocking and reacquires it upon notification or when the timeout expires. It is used when a thread needs to wait for a specific condition to be true before proceeding.

4. *notify(n=1)*

   This method wakes up one of the threads waiting for the condition, if any are waiting. If multiple threads are waiting, the method selects one to notify at random.

5. *notify_all()*

   This method wakes up all threads waiting for the condition. It is the broadest way to handle notification, ensuring that all waiting threads are notified. It is useful when a change affects all waiting threads or when all threads need to recheck the condition they wait upon.

The below example from Horovod, a deep learning training framework, uses Condition to create a Pipe class that can be written and read concurrently in a thread-safe manner:

```python
# File: horovod/runner/util/streams.py

import threading

class Pipe:
    """
    
    A pipe that can be written and read concurrently.
    Works with strings and bytes. Buffers the last written string/
    bytes only.
    """
```

```python
    def __init__(self):
        self._buf = None
        self._offs = None
        self._wait_cond = threading.Condition()  # (1)
        self._closed = False

    def write(self, buf):
        self._wait_cond.acquire()  # (2)
        try:
            while self._buf is not None and not self._closed:
                self._wait_cond.wait()  # (3)

            if self._closed:
                raise RuntimeError("Pipe is closed")

            self._buf = buf
            self._offs = 0
        finally:
            self._wait_cond.notify_all()  # (4)
            self._wait_cond.release()

    def read(self, length=-1):
        self._wait_cond.acquire()
        try:
            while self._buf is None and not self._closed:
                self._wait_cond.wait()

            if self._buf is None:
                return None

            if 0 < length < len(self._buf) - self._offs:
                end = self._offs + length
                buf = self._buf[self._offs : end]
                self._offs = end
            else:
                buf = self._buf[self._offs :]
                self._buf = None

            return buf
```

```
    finally:
        self._wait_cond.notify_all()
        self._wait_cond.release()

...
```

In the Pipe constructor, a Condition object is created and assigned to the _wait_cond attribute. Inside the write method, as seen in the comment # (2), the lock is acquired. Then the thread waits until the buffer is empty (self._buf is None) before it writes new data into the buffer. self._wait_cond.wait() releases the lock and blocks the thread until it is awakened by a notify() or notify_all() call for the same condition variable. Once awakened, it reacquires the lock and continues. After the data is written to the buffer, the notify_all() call (in comment # (4)) wakes up all threads waiting on this condition. Note that this does not release the lock; the threads that are awakened will not run until the lock is released.

In the read method, the thread waits until the buffer is not empty (self._buf is not None) before it reads data from the buffer. This ensures that the write and read operations do not interfere with each other, even when they are called from different threads.

Conclusion

Threading will help us to speed up I/O-bound tasks. This is bound to change in coming Python versions, where GIL-less Python emerges. In such a case, multithreading will be capable of speeding up both CPU-bound and I/O-bound tasks.

Multithreading comes with its own set of challenges. One of the primary sources of errors in threaded programs is shared mutable data. If multiple threads modify mutable data concurrently without proper synchronization, it can lead to race conditions and data inconsistencies. External library code should not be blindly trusted as thread-safe, as not all external libraries are designed to be thread-safe. Extra care should be taken to confirm whether they are safe to use in a multithreaded environment.

In the upcoming chapters, we will examine other concurrency frameworks in Python, including multiprocessing and asyncio, and discuss choosing between one of them based on the application and environment.

## CHAPTER 15

Multiprocessing

In the previous chapter, we explored multithreading in Python and discussed how threads enable concurrent execution within a single process.

While multithreading is suitable for I/O-bound tasks, it doesn't fully utilize multiple CPU cores due to Python's Global Interpreter Lock (with non-free threaded versions, which is the default as of Python 3.13). That's where multiprocessing comes in. Multiprocessing is a technique that allows us to achieve true parallelism by using multiple processor cores to run separate processes simultaneously. Each process runs independently with its own memory space, bypassing the limitations of the GIL and making this approach well-suited for CPU-bound tasks.

In this chapter, we'll dive into Python's `multiprocessing` module, understand how processes differ from threads, and learn how to create, manage, and communicate between processes. We'll also explore practical use cases and discuss the trade-offs of using multiprocessing in real-world applications.

Processes vs. Threads

Let's quickly recap the differences between processes and threads:

- *Memory space*: Processes have their own separate memory space. Each process has its own private memory area, and variables in one process are not directly accessible to another process. Threads, on the other hand, share the memory space of the process they belong to. Shared memory in threads allows easier data sharing but also introduces complexities like race conditions if not managed properly.

- *Overhead*: Creating and managing processes is generally more resource-intensive than threads. Processes are considered "heavyweight" because they require more system resources

471

© Adarsh Divakaran 2025
A. Divakaran, *Deep Dive Python*, https://doi.org/10.1007/979-8-8688-1261-3_15

(memory, OS overhead) to create and manage. Threads are "lightweight" as they exist within a process and share resources, leading to lower overhead in terms of creation and context switching.

- *Isolation*: Because processes have separate memory spaces, they provide better isolation. A crash or misbehavior in one process is less likely to corrupt the memory of another. In contrast, threads share memory, so a misbehaving thread can potentially corrupt shared data and affect the entire process.

- *Communication*: Communication between processes (Inter-process Communication, or IPC) is more complex than communication between threads. Since processes do not share memory by default, they typically use mechanisms like pipes, queues, or shared memory segments to exchange data, which often involves serialization (converting Python objects into bytes). Threads can communicate more directly through shared variables in the same memory space (though that requires synchronization to avoid conflicts).

In short, threads are easier to create and share data with but come with risks of shared-state bugs, whereas processes are safer in terms of isolation at the cost of more overhead in communication and creation.

Bypassing the Global Interpreter Lock (GIL)

One of the main reasons to use multiprocessing in Python, especially for CPU-bound tasks, is to overcome the limitations of the Global Interpreter Lock (GIL). As seen in Chapter 14, the GIL in standard CPython only allows one thread to execute Python bytecode at a time within a single process. This means that for CPU-intensive tasks, multithreading in Python might not achieve true parallelism on multi-core processors; threads could end up running one after the other (concurrently but not in parallel) because of the GIL.

Multiprocessing, however, bypasses the GIL because each process has its own Python interpreter and memory space. Separate processes can truly execute in parallel on different CPU cores. For CPU-bound tasks that can be partitioned, multiprocessing can offer significant performance improvements over multithreading in CPython by utilizing multiple cores.

To illustrate, if there is a CPU-heavy calculation (say, computing large prime numbers or heavy mathematical transformations), using threads won't speed it up much due to the GIL. But using multiple processes can divide the work across cores. Each process runs on its own core simultaneously, potentially reducing overall execution time nearly proportionally to the number of cores (minus some overhead for managing processes). In other words, multiprocessing allows Python to achieve parallelism for CPU-bound workloads, whereas threads in CPython would be limited to concurrency (interleaved execution) but not parallel execution for such workloads.

When to Use Multiprocessing

Multiprocessing is well-suited for

- *CPU-bound tasks*: Tasks that heavily utilize the CPU, such as complex calculations, data processing, scientific computations, or image/video processing. If the program spends most of its time doing computations rather than waiting for I/O, multiprocessing can help us leverage multiple CPU cores to speed up execution.

- *Parallel computations*: When a program needs to perform the same operation on multiple independent sets of data, or run independent tasks concurrently, multiprocessing allows us to distribute these tasks across multiple processes for true parallelism. This fan-out of work across processes and fan-in of results can greatly reduce execution time for large workloads.

- *Tasks that benefit from isolation*: If an application needs to run tasks that might crash or have memory leaks, using separate processes provides isolation. If one process fails or misbehaves, it generally won't bring down other processes or the entire application. This can improve the robustness of long-running programs.

- *Utilizing multi-core processors*: Modern machines have many cores. Multiprocessing is the way to effectively utilize all cores in Python for CPU-intensive workloads. Threads on CPython cannot use multiple cores for CPU-heavy work due to the GIL (with non-free threaded versions, which is the default as of Python 3.13), but processes can, so we get true parallel execution and can significantly reduce overall processing time by spreading work across cores.

On the other hand, multiprocessing is not always the best choice for every scenario. For I/O-bound tasks (network calls, disk I/O, etc.), threads or async may be more lightweight. Also, spawning processes has more overhead, so for very short-lived tasks or a huge number of tiny tasks, the cost of managing processes might outweigh the gains. We'll discuss later how to choose between threading, multiprocessing, and other concurrency models.

Creating and Managing Processes

To use multiprocessing in Python, we first need to understand how to create and run processes. Python's `multiprocessing` module gives us a `Process` class, which we can use to start new processes. This class has an interface similar to the `threading` module, which makes it easier to switch from threads to processes when needed.

The `multiprocessing.Process` Class

We can use the `Process` class to create and manage individual processes. To do this, we create a `Process` object, give it a function to run, and then start it.

When creating a `Process`, we usually provide

- `target`: The function that the new process should run

- `args`: A tuple of values to pass to that function

- `kwargs`: A dictionary of keyword arguments to pass to the function

- `name` *(optional)*: A name for the process (useful in logs)

- `daemon` *(optional)*: A boolean that tells if this should be a daemon process

Just like threads, processes don't run until we call the `start()` method.

Here's a basic example:

```
import multiprocessing

def worker(name):
    print(f"Hello from {name}!")

process = multiprocessing.Process(target=worker, args=("Process-1",))
print("Created process:", process)
```

At this point, the process is only created, not running yet.

Starting Processes with `start()`

After creating the `Process` object, we use the `start()` method to begin running the function in a separate process. The operating system starts a new process and runs the function in it.

Let's continue the earlier example:

```
if __name__ == "__main__":
    process = multiprocessing.Process(target=worker, args=("Process-1",))
    process.start()
    print("Process started!")
```

Here's an example output:

```
Process started!
Hello from Process-1!
```

The child process and the main process run at the same time, so the output order may vary.

We use `if __name__ == "__main__":` to make sure the process creation code doesn't run again inside the child.

Waiting for Processes to Finish with `join()`

Once a process is started, the main process continues to run. If we want to wait for the child process to finish before moving on, we use `join()`.

Example:

```
process = multiprocessing.Process(target=worker, args=("Process-1",))
process.start()
print("Waiting for process to finish...")
process.join()
print("Process finished. Exit code:", process.exitcode)
```

join() blocks the main process until the child finishes. This is useful when we want to make sure all work is done before exiting or continuing.

Here's a usual pattern:

1. Create Process objects.

2. Start them with start().

3. Optionally do other work.

4. Use join() to wait for each one.

5. Collect results if needed.

Custom Processes with a Class

In some cases, we might want to organize process logic inside a class. We can do this by creating a class that inherits from multiprocessing.Process and overrides the run() method.

Example:

```
import multiprocessing

class SquareProcess(multiprocessing.Process):
    def __init__(self, number):
        super().__init__()
        self.number = number

    def run(self):
        result = self.number * self.number
        print(f"Square of {self.number} is {result}")
```

```
if __name__ == "__main__":
    p = SquareProcess(7)
    p.start()
    p.join()
```

This lets us store data in the process object and keep related logic together.

Daemon Processes

A daemon process runs in the background and will be stopped automatically when the main process ends. It will not finish cleanly—it will be stopped immediately.

To mark a process as a daemon, set daemon=True before starting it.

Example:

```
import time

def background_task():
    while True:
        print("Background task is running...")
        time.sleep(1)

if __name__ == "__main__":
    p = multiprocessing.Process(target=background_task)
    p.daemon = True
    p.start()
    time.sleep(3)
    print("Main process exiting...")
```

Here, the background task runs for three seconds and then is stopped. Daemon processes are useful for tasks like logging or cleanup, where we don't need to wait for them to finish.

Daemon processes cannot be joined. They are stopped immediately when the main process exits.

Checking Process Information

We can also inspect running processes using these functions from the `multiprocessing` module:

- `current_process()`: Gives details about the current process

- `parent_process()`: Tells which process started this one

- `active_children()`: Lists child processes that are still running

Example:

```python
def info_task():
    current = multiprocessing.current_process()
    parent = multiprocessing.parent_process()
    print(f"Process {current.name} (PID {current.pid}) started by {parent.
    name if parent else 'None'} (PID {parent.pid if parent else 'N/A'})")

if __name__ == "__main__":
    p = multiprocessing.Process(target=info_task, name="InfoProcess")
    p.start()
    p.join()
```

This helps in debugging and logging when working with multiple processes.

Inter-process Communication (IPC) and Data Sharing

A key difference between multiprocessing and multithreading is how memory is handled. Threads share a common memory space; processes do not. Each process in Python has its own memory, which means that, by default, processes cannot access each other's variables or data directly. This separation is useful—it avoids many kinds of bugs and makes programs more reliable—but it also means that coordination between processes requires some extra tools.

When there's a need to coordinate tasks or exchange data between processes, we rely on Inter-process Communication (IPC) mechanisms. Python's `multiprocessing` module includes several ways to share data and synchronize behavior across process boundaries.

Why Processes Don't Share Memory

Unlike threads, which live inside the same process and share the same memory space, processes are isolated. Each one is given its own memory area by the operating system.

This isolation has several effects:

- *Isolation and stability*: Since processes do not share memory, a crash in one process is unlikely to affect another. This keeps the program more stable and secure, as one process cannot read or overwrite another's memory.

- *No shared variables*: Any variable created in one process exists only in that process. If a process sets a global variable, that change is not visible to its parent or sibling processes. This is different from threads, where global variables are shared across all threads in the same process.

- *Need for explicit communication*: Because memory isn't shared, coordination between processes requires deliberate communication. This is done using mechanisms like pipes, queues, and shared memory constructs. While this may seem like more work, it prevents many types of bugs caused by unintended memory access or modification.

In short, memory isolation means giving up the convenience of shared memory in return for increased safety and control. When sharing is needed, Python gives us several well-defined tools to make it happen.

Shared Memory with `multiprocessing.Value` and `multiprocessing.Array`

Sometimes there's a need to share simple values, like a single integer or a small list of numbers, between processes. For this, `multiprocessing` provides shared memory objects: `Value` and `Array`.

- **Value** is used to share a single piece of data—such as an integer or float—between processes. Internally, this allocates a chunk of shared memory and wraps it in a synchronized object that uses a lock by default to make access safe.

479

- **Array** is used to share a sequence of data—like a list of numbers—between processes. Like Value, it stores data in a shared block of memory that multiple processes can access and modify.

Both are backed by ctypes under the hood and are restricted to primitive types (such as signed integers or floats).

Example: Using **Value** to Share a Counter

```python
from multiprocessing import Value, Process

# create a shared integer, initial value 0
counter = Value('i', 0)

def increment(shared_counter):
    with shared_counter.get_lock():     # acquire lock for safe update
        shared_counter.value += 1

if __name__ == "__main__":
    # Spawn multiple processes to increment the counter
    processes = [Process(target=increment, args=(counter,)) for _ in range(5)]
    for p in processes: p.start()
    for p in processes: p.join()
    print("Final counter value:", counter.value)
```

In this example, five processes each increase a shared counter. The lock that comes with the Value ensures that updates do not happen at the same time, which would cause incorrect results. Without the lock, it's possible for processes to overwrite each other's updates due to race conditions.

Example: Using **Array** to Share a List of Numbers

```python
from multiprocessing import Array, Process

# create a shared array of 5 integers, initially all zeros
shared_arr = Array('i', 5)

def fill_array(arr):
    for i in range(len(arr)):
        arr[i] = i * 2
```

```
if __name__ == "__main__":
    p = Process(target=fill_array, args=(shared_arr,))
    p.start()
    p.join()
    print("Shared array contents:", shared_arr[:])
```

In this case, the child process fills the array with values. After the child process finishes, the parent process prints the updated values. Just like Value, Array also has a built-in lock for safe access when used by multiple processes.

These shared memory objects are efficient and lightweight. However, they are only suited for simple data types. For more complex data (like dictionaries or lists of arbitrary Python objects), we use different tools, like managers.

Message Passing with Pipes (`multiprocessing.Pipe`)

Another way for processes to exchange information is through message passing. A **pipe** is a simple communication channel that connects two processes. One process writes data into one end, and the other reads it from the other end.

Calling Pipe() returns two connection objects, one for each end of the pipe. By default, both ends can send and receive. Python uses pickling to send Python objects through the pipe, so the data must be picklable.

Example: Sending a Message from Child to Parent

```
from multiprocessing import Process, Pipe

def worker(pipe_conn):
    msg = "Hello from child"
    pipe_conn.send(msg)
    pipe_conn.close()

if __name__ == "__main__":
    parent_conn, child_conn = Pipe()
    p = Process(target=worker, args=(child_conn,))
    p.start()
    received = parent_conn.recv()
    print("Parent received:", received)
    p.join()
```

In this example, the child process sends a string to the parent. The parent receives the message through its end of the pipe. The pipe is a good choice when two processes need to communicate directly. However, for more complex communication patterns, such as many-to-one or one-to-many, a queue is more flexible.

Message Passing with Queues (`multiprocessing.Queue` and `multiprocessing.SimpleQueue`)

A **queue** is a first-in-first-out (FIFO) data structure that can be safely shared between multiple processes. The `multiprocessing.Queue` is similar to `queue.Queue` from the `threading` module, but it is designed for Inter-process Communication.

Queues support multiple producers and consumers. Objects placed into the queue are pickled and sent to the other processes safely.

Example: Multiple Processes Sending Results to a Shared Queue

```python
from multiprocessing import Process, Queue

def worker(number, output_queue):
    output_queue.put(number * 2)

if __name__ == "__main__":
    numbers = [1, 2, 3, 4, 5]
    queue = Queue()
    processes = []

    for n in numbers:
        p = Process(target=worker, args=(n, queue))
        processes.append(p)
        p.start()

    results = []
    for _ in numbers:
        result = queue.get()
        results.append(result)
```

```
for p in processes:
    p.join()

results.sort()
print("Results:", results)
```

In this code, each worker process puts its result into the queue. The main process collects the results. Since the queue is shared, processes can safely communicate this way, and the program avoids direct memory sharing.

There is also a `multiprocessing.SimpleQueue`, which offers a simpler, lighter-weight version of the queue. It does not support task tracking, but can be slightly faster in cases where extra features are not needed.

One caution with queues: If a process ends before its queued data is fully sent, the data may be lost. It is good practice to join all processes and, if needed, call `queue.close()` and `queue.join_thread()` to ensure everything is properly flushed.

In general

- Use pipes for two-way or one-on-one communication.

- Use queues for multiple senders or receivers.

Managers for Shared Objects

When we need to share more complex data structures like dictionaries, lists, or custom Python objects across processes, `multiprocessing.Manager` provides a higher-level solution.

A manager starts a server process that holds the actual shared objects. Other processes can access and modify these objects through proxies. This makes it easy to share data across processes without needing to manage communication or synchronization manually.

Example: Using a Manager to Share a Dictionary

```
from multiprocessing import Manager, Process

def worker(shared_dict, key, value):
    shared_dict[key] = value
```

```python
if __name__ == "__main__":
    manager = Manager()
    shared_dict = manager.dict()
    procs = []

    for i in range(3):
        p = Process(target=worker, args=(shared_dict, f"proc{i}", i*100))
        procs.append(p)
        p.start()

    for p in procs:
        p.join()

    print("Shared dict final state:", dict(shared_dict))
```

In this example, three worker processes each add an item to the shared dictionary. The manager makes it appear as though all processes are working with the same object, even though they are in separate memory spaces.

Managers can also create shared lists, Value and Lock objects, and more. These are particularly useful when processes need to coordinate using high-level Python objects.

Manager-based shared objects are convenient and make code easier to write, especially for prototyping or small-scale use. However, they can be slower than using raw shared memory or queues because all operations involve proxy communication and serialization.

Managers are often used in real-world projects. For example, the pytest-xdist plugin uses them to share state between test workers.

Process Pools for Task Distribution

When we have many independent tasks to run, starting a separate process for each one can be inefficient and hard to manage. For example, if there's a need to apply the same function to thousands of items, creating thousands of Process objects is wasteful and slow. This is where **process pools** come in.

A process pool is a group of worker processes that are started once and reused to run multiple tasks. The idea is similar to thread pools: instead of launching a new process every time, we keep a fixed number of worker processes running and hand off tasks to them as needed.

Python provides two main ways to use process pools:

- `multiprocessing.Pool`

- `concurrent.futures.ProcessPoolExecutor`

Both allow tasks to run in parallel using multiple processes, but they differ slightly in syntax and behavior. We'll explore both.

Introduction to `multiprocessing.Pool`

The `multiprocessing.Pool` class gives us a convenient way to manage a group of worker processes and distribute tasks among them. Instead of managing each `Process` manually, we can hand off tasks to the pool, and it will assign them to available workers.

Here are some of the benefits of using a pool:

- We define how many worker processes to use.

- The pool automatically distributes tasks across the available workers.

- It provides methods like `map()`, `apply()`, and their asynchronous versions.

- It supports context management (using `with`), which helps shut down the pool cleanly.

Example: Using `pool.map()` to Compute Squares in Parallel

```
from multiprocessing import Pool

def square(x):
    return x * x

if __name__ == "__main__":
    data = [1, 2, 3, 4, 5]
    with Pool(processes=3) as pool:
        results = pool.map(square, data)
    print("Squares:", results)
```

Output:

```
Squares: [1, 4, 9, 16, 25]
```

Here, we create a pool with three worker processes. The map() function takes care of splitting the data across workers. Each process runs square(x) on a portion of the data, and the final list contains the results, in the same order as the input.

Internally, Pool uses queues to send tasks to workers and collect results. All communication is handled for us. The only requirement is that data and functions passed to the pool must be picklable.

Submitting Tasks to the Pool: apply_async() and map_async()

The methods map() and apply() are **blocking**—they wait for results before moving forward. If we want to continue doing other work while the pool processes tasks, we can use their asynchronous versions: apply_async() and map_async().

These return an AsyncResult object that acts like a placeholder for the result. We can later call .get() on it to retrieve the result once it's ready. Optional callback functions can be used to handle results when they arrive.

apply_async(func, args=(), kwds={}, callback=None, error_callback=None)

This submits a single task to the pool. It returns immediately with an AsyncResult object. When the result is ready, we can fetch it using .get(). A callback can be provided to handle the result, and an error callback can handle exceptions raised in the worker.

map_async(func, iterable, chunksize=None, callback=None, error_callback=None)

This submits a batch of tasks, like map(), but returns immediately. The results will be available through the returned AsyncResult.

Example: Using apply_async() and map_async()

```python
from multiprocessing import Pool
import time

def heavy_computation(x):
    time.sleep(1)
    return x * x
```

```
if __name__ == "__main__":
    pool = Pool(processes=2)

    result1 = pool.apply_async(heavy_computation, args=(10,))
    result2 = pool.apply_async(heavy_computation, args=(5,))

    print("Doing other work in main process...")

    output1 = result1.get()
    output2 = result2.get()
    print("Results:", output1, output2)

    async_res = pool.map_async(heavy_computation, range(4))
    results = async_res.get()
    print("Map results:", results)

    pool.close()
    pool.join()
```

Output:

```
Doing other work in main process...
Results: 100 25
Map results: [0, 1, 4, 9]
```

The pool runs tasks in the background. The main process can continue doing other work while the pool is busy.

To avoid problems, it's important to call close() to stop accepting new tasks and join() to wait for running tasks to finish before exiting.

concurrent.futures.ProcessPoolExecutor: A Modern Alternative

The concurrent.futures module provides a high-level API for asynchronous execution. It includes both ThreadPoolExecutor and ProcessPoolExecutor, which have the same interface. This makes it easy to switch between threads and processes by changing one line of code.

Here are advantages of ProcessPoolExecutor:

- It uses submit() and map() just like ThreadPoolExecutor.

- It returns Future objects instead of AsyncResult. These have methods like .result() and .exception().

- It can be used as a context manager to ensure proper cleanup.

Example: Using **ProcessPoolExecutor** to Compute Squares

```
from concurrent.futures import ProcessPoolExecutor, as_completed

def f(x):
    return x * x

if __name__ == "__main__":
    data = [3, 5, 7, 9]
    with ProcessPoolExecutor(max_workers=3) as executor:
        futures = [executor.submit(f, num) for num in data]

        for fut in as_completed(futures):
            result = fut.result()
            print("Got result:", result)

        results_in_order = [fut.result() for fut in futures]
        print("Results in order:", results_in_order)
```

Output (order may vary for the first loop):

```
Got result: 9
Got result: 25
Got result: 49
Got result: 81
Results in order: [9, 25, 49, 81]
```

This example shows two ways to collect results: as they complete or in the original order of submission. as_completed() is useful when results arrive at different times.

We can also use executor.map() to simplify things:

```
with ProcessPoolExecutor(max_workers=3) as executor:
    results = list(executor.map(f, data))
    print("Results:", results)
```

This works like pool.map()—it returns results in the same order as the input.

In many modern Python projects, ProcessPoolExecutor is the preferred approach for multiprocessing because its interface is clean, consistent, and easy to use.

Handling Results and Exceptions in Pools

When tasks raise exceptions, we need to handle them properly. Each API provides ways to catch or inspect errors:

- With multiprocessing.Pool, calling .get() on an AsyncResult will re-raise the exception. The apply_async() method can take an error_callback to handle errors in a separate function.

- With ProcessPoolExecutor, calling .result() on a Future will raise any exceptions that occurred in the worker. We can also call .exception() to check for errors without raising them.

Example: Handling Exceptions from Worker Functions

```
def worker(x):
    if x == 5:
        raise ValueError("Bad value!")
    return x * 2

if __name__ == "__main__":
    with ProcessPoolExecutor(max_workers=2) as executor:
        futures = [executor.submit(worker, i) for i in [3, 5, 7]]
        for fut in futures:
            try:
                res = fut.result()
```

```
        except Exception as e:
            print("A task raised an exception:", e)
        else:
            print("Result:", res)
```

Here's the output:

```
Result: 6
A task raised an exception: Bad value!
Result: 14
```

This ensures the program doesn't crash if one task fails.

Comparing Pool and Executor with Threads

The ProcessPoolExecutor API is nearly identical to ThreadPoolExecutor. This is by design. It allows developers to switch from threads to processes when performance needs change.

The key difference is in memory:

- Threads share memory. They can read and write shared data easily, but that also brings risks.

- Processes do not share memory. Any shared state must be passed explicitly using queues, pipes, or managers.

This difference means that switching from threads to processes may require changes to how shared data is handled. For example, if a thread-based version updates a global variable, the process-based version will not see those updates unless a shared object is used.

Some real-world systems combine threads and processes. For instance, a system might use processes to spread CPU-heavy tasks across cores and use threads for handling I/O or internal coordination. However, managing both at once adds complexity and is usually done only when the benefits are clear.

Process Start Methods: Choosing the Right Approach

When a new process is created using Python's `multiprocessing` module, the operating system can use different ways to start that process. These ways are called **start methods**, and each one has different behavior and trade-offs.

Python supports three start methods:

- spawn

- fork

- forkserver

The default method depends on the operating system. For example, Windows always uses spawn. On Linux, the default is fork. On macOS, Python used to default to fork, but changed to spawn in Python 3.8 and later.

Understanding how these start methods work helps us write code that behaves correctly and runs consistently across platforms.

Explanation of Start Methods: **spawn, fork, forkserver**

Let's take a closer look at each method.

spawn

- *What it does*: Starts a completely new Python interpreter process. The new process doesn't inherit anything except what is passed explicitly.

- *How it works*: The child process imports the main module and runs the target function.

- *Platform availability*: Works on all platforms. It is the default on Windows and macOS (from Python 3.8 onward).

- *Advantages*:

  - More predictable because the child starts from scratch

  - Safer when the parent process has already created threads or used system resources

- *Disadvantages*:

  - Slower to start because it imports everything again

  - Requires all code that creates processes to be inside an `if __name__ == "__main__"` block

fork

- *What it does*: Makes an exact copy of the parent process

- *How it works*: Uses the `fork()` system call available on Unix-based systems

- *Platform availability*: Available only on Unix (Linux, older macOS)

- *Advantages*:

  - Very fast to start.

  - The child process gets access to the parent's memory, which is useful if we want to share read-only data (like large datasets).

- *Disadvantages*:

  - Unsafe if the parent has threads. Thread-related locks and states get copied, which can lead to deadlocks or unpredictable behavior.

  - Apple now restricts what can be done in a forked child without an `exec()` call, which is why Python changed the default on macOS to `spawn`.

forkserver

- *What it does*: Starts a special server process when the program first sets the start method. Later, this server forks new processes on demand.

- *How it works*: The first time it's needed, a single-threaded fork server starts. When new processes are requested, they're created by the server (not the main program).

- *Platform availability*: Unix only.

- *Advantages*:

  – Avoids the thread safety problems of fork

  – Slightly faster than spawn for many processes because the server is already running

- *Disadvantages*:

  – Slightly more complex and has a bit more overhead than fork

  – Not available on Windows

Here's a summary:

Method	Available On	Inherits Memory	Starts Fresh	Thread-Safe	Default On
spawn	All	No	Yes	Yes	Windows, macOS
fork	Unix	Yes	No	No	Linux
forkserver	Unix	No	Yes	Yes	None (opt-in)

When to Use Each Start Method and Platform Dependencies

Each platform has its own default behavior:

- *Windows*: Only spawn is available. All processes start from scratch.

- *Linux*: Defaults to fork, which is fast and works well for many cases. But care is needed when using threads or libraries that aren't safe after forking.

- *macOS*: Python switched the default to spawn in version 3.8, due to system-level restrictions that make fork unreliable for GUI applications and other system calls.

When to Choose `spawn`

- If writing code that needs to run on Windows

- If the program uses threads before starting child processes

- If unexpected behavior is happening with `fork`, such as crashes or deadlocks

- If using libraries that don't work well after a `fork` (e.g., GUI frameworks, logging, or libraries that use C extensions with threads)

The downside is that `spawn` is slower and requires every object and function passed to child processes to be picklable.

When to Choose `fork`

- When running on Unix and performance is critical

- When the program is simple and doesn't use threads or other complex state before forking

- When the goal is to share large read-only data with child processes to save memory

Be careful not to use `fork` if the main program starts threads before forking or uses libraries that expect a clean state.

When to Choose `forkserver`

- When thread safety is important and speed matters more than with `spawn`

- When there's a need to start many short-lived processes quickly on Unix

- When wanting the benefits of `spawn` (clean state) without its full startup cost

This is a good choice when the program needs to avoid `fork`'s problems but still gain some performance benefits over `spawn`.

Setting the Start Method in Code

We can explicitly set the start method at the beginning of a program. This gives full control and makes the code consistent across platforms:

```
import multiprocessing

if __name__ == "__main__":
    multiprocessing.set_start_method('spawn')
```

The method must be set before any child processes are created. It only works once per program run, so it should be placed at the top of the script and inside the __main__ block.

Here's how to check which method is currently in use:

```
import multiprocessing
print(multiprocessing.get_start_method())
```

Here's how to change it even if it was already set:

```
multiprocessing.set_start_method('fork', force=True)
```

Instead of changing the global setting, it's also possible to create a context with a specific start method:

```
ctx = multiprocessing.get_context('forkserver')
p = ctx.Process(target=some_function)
p.start()
p.join()
```

This lets us choose the start method only for certain parts of the program.

When using concurrent.futures.ProcessPoolExecutor, we can also pass a start method context:

```
from concurrent.futures import ProcessPoolExecutor
import multiprocessing

if __name__ == "__main__":
    ctx = multiprocessing.get_context('spawn')
    with ProcessPoolExecutor(max_workers=4, mp_context=ctx) as executor:
        ...
```

This makes the program's behavior more predictable and helps avoid bugs that are hard to trace.

Synchronization Between Processes

Even though processes run in separate memory spaces, there are situations where coordination is still needed. For example, if multiple processes write to the same file or update shared data (like a counter or a queue), we want to avoid interference. That's where **synchronization** comes in.

Python's `multiprocessing` module provides several synchronization tools. These work across processes, just like the tools in the `threading` module work across threads. The key difference is that these are designed to operate across isolated processes, often using operating system resources under the hood.

The available tools include

- Lock

- RLock

- Semaphore

- Event

- Condition

- Barrier

Each one is useful for a different type of coordination problem.

Need for Synchronization Primitives in Multiprocessing

Here are the main reasons we use synchronization in multiprocessing:

- *To control access to shared resources*: If multiple processes write to the same file, database, or shared memory, we need to make sure they don't do it at the same time.

- *To coordinate process execution*: Some processes might need to wait for others to finish part of their work before moving on. For example, a process may wait until another one has created a file or finished processing data.

- *To manage dependencies*: In a pipeline of processes, one process may need to wait until others reach a certain stage before continuing.

Although processes don't share memory by default, synchronization objects themselves are designed to be shared. For example, a Lock can be passed to multiple processes so that they all use the same lock object.

Overview and Usage of Synchronization Primitives

Let's walk through each of the synchronization tools provided by multiprocessing.

Locks and RLocks (multiprocessing.Lock, multiprocessing.RLock)

- *Purpose*: Allow only one process at a time to run a certain section of code.

- *Behavior*: When one process acquires the lock, other processes trying to acquire it will wait until it's released.

- *RLock*: A re-entrant lock that can be acquired multiple times by the same process.

Example: Protecting a Shared Counter

```
lock = multiprocessing.Lock()
shared_val = multiprocessing.Value('i', 0)

def safe_increment(val, lock):
    with lock:
        val.value += 1
```

Here, the lock makes sure that only one process updates the counter at a time. This prevents race conditions where two processes could read and update the value at the same time.

Important   Always release the lock after use. Using `with lock:` is the safest way, since it automatically releases the lock even if an error occurs.

Semaphores (`multiprocessing.Semaphore`, `multiprocessing.BoundedSemaphore`)

- *Purpose*: Limit how many processes can access a resource at the same time.

- *Behavior*: A semaphore has a counter. Each call to `acquire()` decreases the counter, and `release()` increases it.

For example, if only three processes are allowed to access a database, the semaphore is initialized with the value 3. If all three are in use, the next `acquire()` will block until another process releases one.

BoundedSemaphore is similar, but it raises an error if the count goes above the initial value. This helps detect programming errors where `release()` is called too many times.

Events (`multiprocessing.Event`)

- *Purpose*: Let one process signal other processes to proceed.

- *Behavior*: An event starts in the "unset" state. Other processes can call `wait()` to pause until it's set. One process calls `set()` to trigger the event and unblock others.

Example: Starting All Workers at the Same Time

```python
event = multiprocessing.Event()

def worker(event):
    print("Worker waiting...")
    event.wait()
    print("Worker started!")

if __name__ == "__main__":
    processes = [multiprocessing.Process(target=worker, args=(event,)) for
 _ in range(3)]
    for p in processes: p.start()
    time.sleep(2)
```

```
print("Starting all workers...")
event.set()
for p in processes: p.join()
```

Here, all workers wait for the event to be set before doing their job. This is a simple way to coordinate a simultaneous start.

Note   Events are binary—they are either set or not. They do not carry any data.

Conditions (`multiprocessing.Condition`)

- *Purpose*: Wait for more complex situations than just "go" or "stop."
- *Behavior*: A condition is associated with a lock. Processes can wait for some condition to be true, and others can notify them when it's time to continue.

Conditions allow finer control than events, especially when we want to wait until a certain state is true before proceeding.

Example: Signaling a Consumer When a Queue Is Non-empty

```
from multiprocessing import Condition, Value

condition = Condition()
shared_data_ready = Value('b', False)

def producer(cond, flag):
    time.sleep(1)
    with cond:
        flag.value = True
        cond.notify()

def consumer(cond, flag):
    with cond:
        cond.wait_for(lambda: flag.value)
        print("Consumer received signal")
```

```
if __name__ == "__main__":
    p1 = multiprocessing.Process(target=producer, args=(condition, shared_
    data_ready))
    p2 = multiprocessing.Process(target=consumer, args=(condition, shared_
    data_ready))
    p1.start()
    p2.start()
    p1.join()
    p2.join()
```

Here, the consumer waits for a condition to be true (a flag set by the producer) and is only unblocked when that happens.

Important   Always use the `with` statement to safely acquire and release the lock when using `Condition`.

Barrier (`multiprocessing.Barrier`)

- *Purpose*: Makes a group of processes wait until all of them have reached the same point.

- *Behavior*: A barrier is initialized with a count. Each process calls `wait()` on it. When the last process arrives, all of them are released.

Example: Synchronizing Three Processes

```
from multiprocessing import Barrier

barrier = Barrier(3)

def wait_at_barrier(b):
    print("Waiting at barrier")
    b.wait()
    print("Passed the barrier")
```

```
if __name__ == "__main__":
    procs = [multiprocessing.Process(target=wait_at_barrier,
    args=(barrier,)) for _ in range(3)]
    for p in procs: p.start()
    for p in procs: p.join()
```

Once all three processes reach the barrier, they are released together.

Caution   If one process crashes or times out while waiting at the barrier, the others will raise a `BrokenBarrierError`.

Real-World Use: Shared Locks with Managers

Sometimes, we create locks and other synchronization objects using a manager so they can be shared between processes even if not created through `fork()`.

Example: Locking Access to a Shared Dictionary

```
manager = multiprocessing.Manager()
shared_dict = manager.dict()
shared_lock = manager.Lock()

def update_dict(lock, d, key, value):
    with lock:
        d[key] = value
```

This approach is used in tools like `pytest-xdist` to safely coordinate shared state between worker processes running tests in parallel.

Using Synchronization Primitives with Context Managers

All synchronization primitives in `multiprocessing` can be used as context managers. This is the recommended way to use them because it ensures they are always released, even if an exception occurs.

Examples:

```
with lock:
    # critical section
    ...

with semaphore:
    # limited-access section
    ...

with condition:
    # check and wait
    ...
```

Using `with` makes the code easier to read and safer.

Shared State vs. Message Passing

When using multiprocessing, it's often better to avoid shared state altogether. Instead, passing messages (e.g., using queues or pipes) is easier to reason about and leads to fewer bugs.

Still, in some cases, shared state is useful or necessary. Examples include

- A shared counter or flag

- A read-only data structure that should be shared for performance reasons

- A shared log or dictionary that multiple processes update

In those cases, the synchronization tools above help us manage access safely.

Conclusion

Python's `multiprocessing` module gives us a way to run code in true parallel across multiple CPU cores. Unlike threads, which are limited by the Global Interpreter Lock (GIL), each process runs in its own Python interpreter and memory space. This allows us to make full use of multi-core systems for CPU-heavy tasks like data processing, computations, or simulations. Multiprocessing is especially useful when tasks are independent and can be split across cores for faster execution.

In this chapter, we covered the basics of creating and managing processes using the Process class. We explored how to share data using shared memory (Value, Array), pipes, queues, and manager objects. We looked at synchronization tools like Lock, Semaphore, Event, Condition, and Barrier and when to use each. We also examined how process pools (Pool, ProcessPoolExecutor) help distribute tasks across workers efficiently and how to handle results and exceptions. Finally, we discussed different process start methods—spawn, fork, and forkserver—and how to choose the right one based on the platform and the program's needs.

Multiprocessing works best for CPU-bound work. For I/O-bound tasks, threads or async code is often better suited. In some projects, combining different concurrency models makes sense—e.g., using processes to parallelize CPU tasks and threads to handle networking or file I/O. The right choice depends on the task at hand. In the next chapter, we'll explore asyncio, Python's library for asynchronous programming, and see how it compares to multiprocessing and threading in different scenarios.

CHAPTER 16

Asyncio

In the previous chapter, we explored multiprocessing as a way to achieve true parallelism by running tasks across multiple CPU cores. While multiprocessing is great for CPU-bound tasks, it comes with the overhead of creating and managing separate processes.

In this chapter, we shift our focus to asynchronous programming, a technique that enables a single thread to handle multiple tasks efficiently. Instead of executing each task sequentially, we can pause a task while it's waiting for something—like a network response or file read—and switch to another task in the meantime. This non-blocking approach is particularly useful for I/O-bound operations, allowing us to write code that is both fast and responsive, even when dealing with many concurrent tasks. We'll dive into Python's `asyncio` module, understand how the event loop works, and learn how to write and structure async code effectively.

What Is Asynchronous Programming?

With synchronous programming, any function that waits (like reading a file or making a web request) stops everything else from running until it finishes. In contrast, asynchronous programming allows us to kick off an operation and continue doing other things while waiting. When the operation is done, we get notified and can resume where we left off. In Python's `asyncio`, this notification system is handled by the event loop.

Event Loop and Cooperative Multitasking

The event loop is the engine that drives asynchronous programs. When we launch an async operation, we register it with the event loop. The loop keeps checking to see if the operation is complete and resumes it when it's ready.

© Adarsh Divakaran 2025
A. Divakaran, *Deep Dive Python*, https://doi.org/10.1007/979-8-8688-1261-3_16

Asyncio relies on cooperative multitasking. This means tasks must voluntarily yield control by using `await`. Unlike threads or processes, where the operating system can interrupt them at any time, async tasks won't stop unless they explicitly choose to. This predictability makes debugging easier, since a coroutine will run uninterrupted until it hits an `await`.

`async` and `await` Keywords

Python introduced `async` and `await` to make asynchronous programming easier to read and write.

- `async def`: Marks a function as a coroutine, which can pause and resume execution

- `await`: Pauses the coroutine until another coroutine or awaitable is done

Calling an `async def` function returns a coroutine object. This object doesn't run until we await it or schedule it on the event loop.

When to Use Asyncio (I/O Bound vs. CPU Bound)

Asyncio works best for I/O-bound tasks. These include

- Making network requests

- Reading/writing files or sockets

- Querying databases or remote services

In these situations, while one task is waiting, others can run. This makes efficient use of a single thread.

Asyncio is not ideal for CPU-bound tasks. These keep the processor busy with heavy calculations. Since asyncio runs everything on one thread, CPU-bound tasks block others unless we explicitly offload them to separate threads or processes. For such cases, it's better to use `multiprocessing` or similar options.

Benefits of Asyncio

Here's why asyncio can be a good choice:

- Handles many tasks with one thread, reducing memory usage.

- Task switching happens only at `await` points, making behavior easier to predict.

- I/O waits don't freeze the program; other tasks can proceed.

- Offers both high-level APIs and low-level control for flexibility.

Context Switching in Asyncio

Asyncio's concurrency relies on cooperative context switching. Every `await` marks a place where the event loop can pause one task and run another. This ensures tasks share execution time efficiently.

Unlike threads, where switching can happen anytime, async tasks switch only at `await`. This avoids many of the problems with shared data and race conditions.

However, this also means we must place `await` in the right spots. A long-running loop with no `await` will block other tasks. We should insert `await` (even something like `asyncio.sleep(0)`) in such loops to keep the program responsive.

Creating and Running Asyncio Programs

To begin writing asyncio programs, we define asynchronous functions (coroutines) and run them using the asyncio event loop.

`async def` for Coroutines

Coroutines are the building blocks of asyncio programs. We define a coroutine using `async def`. When such a function is called, it does not execute immediately. Instead, it returns a coroutine object. This object represents a pending task that must be either awaited or scheduled to run.

```python
async def my_coroutine():
    print("Hello")
    await asyncio.sleep(1)
    print("World")
```

In this example, calling my_coroutine() simply creates a coroutine object. To actually run it, we must await it from another coroutine or schedule it with a task.

asyncio.run() to Start the Event Loop

The simplest way to execute an asyncio program is to use asyncio.run(). This function takes a coroutine, starts a new event loop, runs the coroutine to completion, and then closes the loop. It hides the boilerplate involved in managing the event loop manually.

```python
async def main():
    print("Starting main")
    await asyncio.sleep(1)
    print("Finishing main")

if __name__ == "__main__":
    asyncio.run(main())
```

Here, asyncio.run(main()) creates an event loop, executes the main coroutine, and cleans up when done. This is the preferred method since Python 3.7. In older versions, we had to manually get the loop and use loop.run_until_complete(main()).

This function should be called once in the main entry point of the program. Inside coroutines, we should use await or schedule new tasks. Calling asyncio.run() from within an existing event loop will raise an error.

Basic Example: Concurrent Network Requests

To see the benefits of asyncio, let's look at a basic example of making multiple HTTP requests concurrently. We'll use the aiohttp library to fetch several web pages in parallel.

```python
import asyncio
import aiohttp
import time
```

```python
async def fetch_url(session, url):
    print(f"Fetching {url}")
    async with session.get(url) as response:
        data = await response.text()
        return data[:50]  # return first 50 characters of response

async def main():
    urls = [
        "http://example.com",
        "http://httpbin.org/delay/1",
        "http://example.org"
    ]
    start_time = time.time()
    async with aiohttp.ClientSession() as session:
        coros = [fetch_url(session, url) for url in urls]
        results = await asyncio.gather(*coros)
    duration = time.time() - start_time

    for url, result in zip(urls, results):
        print(f"{url}: {result}...")
    print(f"Fetched {len(urls)} URLs in {duration:.2f} seconds")

if __name__ == "__main__":
    asyncio.run(main())
```

In this example

- A single aiohttp.ClientSession is used to manage HTTP connections efficiently.

- We build a list of coroutine objects using fetch_url. These are not running yet.

- asyncio.gather(*coros) schedules all of them to run concurrently. The event loop handles them in parallel, switching between them at await points.

- The slowest request determines the total time. Because the event loop overlaps the waiting times, the program completes much faster than making each request sequentially.

- The results are printed alongside the time taken. This shows how we can gain efficiency by not waiting for one task to finish before starting the next.

This fan-out/fan-in pattern—starting many tasks at once and waiting for them to complete together—is a powerful tool for I/O-bound applications. It's a pattern we'll use frequently when dealing with multiple network or file operations.

Working with Tasks

In asyncio, a task is an object that wraps a coroutine and schedules it to run on the event loop. When we create a task, we're telling the event loop: run this coroutine in the background and let us continue. The event loop handles the scheduling and runs the task whenever it reaches an `await` point.

If we `await` a coroutine directly, the program waits for it to finish before continuing. But if we want other code to run while the coroutine is executing, we need to convert it into a task.

Creating Tasks with `asyncio.create_task()`

The most common way to schedule a coroutine is with `asyncio.create_task()`. This wraps the coroutine in a task and registers it with the event loop. The function returns immediately with a task object.

```python
import asyncio

async def work(task_id):
    print(f"Task {task_id}: starting")
    await asyncio.sleep(2)
    print(f"Task {task_id}: finished")
    return f"result{task_id}"

async def main():
    task1 = asyncio.create_task(work(1))
    task2 = asyncio.create_task(work(2))
    print("Tasks created, now waiting for results...")
```

```
    results = await asyncio.gather(task1, task2)
    print("Both tasks done, results:", results)
asyncio.run(main())
```

In this example

- Two coroutines are wrapped as tasks using create_task().

- As soon as they are created, the event loop can begin executing them.

- The call to gather waits for both to complete and collects their results.

This pattern is useful when we want to start tasks immediately but wait for them later. If we never await the tasks, they will still run, but any exception inside them will be printed as an unhandled error.

Task Cancellation

We may need to cancel a task before it finishes. This is done using the .cancel() method. When we cancel a task, a CancelledError is raised inside the coroutine at its next await.

```
import asyncio

async def long_task():
    try:
        print("long_task: started")
        await asyncio.sleep(5)
        print("long_task: completed")
    except asyncio.CancelledError:
        print("long_task: cancelled!")
        raise

async def main():
    task = asyncio.create_task(long_task())
    await asyncio.sleep(1)
    print("main: cancelling long_task")
    task.cancel()
```

```
    try:
        await task
    except asyncio.CancelledError:
        print("main: long_task was cancelled")

asyncio.run(main())
```

In this example

- `long_task` is cancelled after running for one second.

- When it reaches its `await`, the event loop injects a `CancelledError`.

- The task handles the error and exits. The main coroutine catches the same error after awaiting the task.

Task cancellation is cooperative: the task must reach an `await` point to be cancelled. Long-running coroutines without `await` can block cancellation. To keep the event loop responsive, coroutines should include regular `await` calls even if the wait is short.

If a cancelled task is not awaited, the event loop will warn that the exception was never retrieved. It's good practice to track tasks and handle their completion or failure properly.

Synchronization Primitives

When multiple coroutines run concurrently, there are times when we need to coordinate their behavior or protect shared data. Asyncio provides asynchronous versions of common synchronization primitives: `Lock`, `Semaphore`, `Event`, and `Condition`. These are designed to work without blocking the thread, unlike their `threading` counterparts.

Asyncio Lock

An `asyncio.Lock` is a mutual exclusion primitive. It ensures that only one coroutine can enter a protected section at a time. Any coroutine that tries to acquire the lock while it's already held will pause until the lock is released.

This is useful when we want to safely update shared state without race conditions.

Here's a simplified example that illustrates how an asyncio lock can protect shared state:

```python
import asyncio

lock = asyncio.Lock()
shared_state = 0

async def critical_task(name):
    global shared_state
    async with lock:
        current = shared_state
        print(f"{name}: read shared_state = {current}")
        await asyncio.sleep(0.1)
        shared_state = current + 1
        print(f"{name}: updated shared_state to {shared_state}")

async def main():
    await asyncio.gather(*(critical_task(f"Task{i}") for i in range(5)))

asyncio.run(main())
```

The lock ensures that only one task modifies shared_state at a time. Without the lock, tasks could interleave in a way that causes inconsistent updates.

Under the hood, asyncio.Lock suspends the coroutine when it cannot acquire the lock and resumes it when the lock becomes available. Using async with lock: is the recommended pattern for clarity and safety.

This type of locking mechanism is commonly used in libraries such as aiobotocore, which ensures that only one coroutine at a time creates or tears down shared AWS client sessions.

Asyncio Semaphore

A Semaphore is a more flexible synchronization primitive than a lock. It allows a fixed number of coroutines to access a shared section at once. For example, a Semaphore(3) permits three concurrent accesses.

Semaphores are useful when we want to limit concurrency, such as restricting the number of concurrent HTTP requests or database queries.

Here's a real-world example using the aiohttp library (a popular asynchronous HTTP client):

```python
import asyncio
import aiohttp

URL = "https://httpbin.org/delay/2"
sem = asyncio.Semaphore(3)

async def fetch_with_limit(session, idx):
    async with sem:
        print(f"Task {idx}: starting request")
        async with session.get(URL) as response:
            data = await response.text()
            print(f"Task {idx}: got response (length {len(data)})")

async def main():
    async with aiohttp.ClientSession() as session:
        tasks = [asyncio.create_task(fetch_with_limit(session, i)) for i in
        range(1, 7)]
        await asyncio.gather(*tasks)

asyncio.run(main())
```

In this setup, we launch six fetch tasks but limit the concurrency to three at a time. This technique is useful in real projects like web scrapers, API clients, or bots that need to respect rate limits or avoid overloading services.

Asyncio Event

An Event acts as a simple flag shared between coroutines. Initially, it is unset. Coroutines can wait for it to be set using `await event.wait()`. Another coroutine can call `event.set()` to signal all waiting coroutines to proceed.

Events are commonly used in setup or configuration scenarios. For example, a service may need to finish initializing before other components can begin:

```python
import asyncio

config_loaded = asyncio.Event()

async def worker(name):
    print(f"{name}: waiting for config...")
```

```
    await config_loaded.wait()
    print(f"{name}: config is loaded! Working...")

async def main():
    w1 = asyncio.create_task(worker("Worker1"))
    w2 = asyncio.create_task(worker("Worker2"))
    print("Main: loading config (sleeping 2s)...")
    await asyncio.sleep(2)
    print("Main: setting event now.")
    config_loaded.set()
    await asyncio.sleep(1)

asyncio.run(main())
```

In this example, both workers start and wait for the configuration to load. When config_loaded.set() is called, both resume immediately. This kind of signaling is common in applications with startup phases, like background workers that wait for initialization steps to complete.

Asyncio Condition

A Condition combines a lock with the ability to notify waiting coroutines. Coroutines can wait for a condition to be true using await condition.wait(), and other coroutines can use condition.notify() or condition.notify_all() to wake them.

This pattern is useful for coordination where shared state changes over time and multiple consumers wait for certain conditions to proceed.

Here's an example that simulates a producer–consumer pattern using asyncio. Condition. This pattern is also used in open source projects such as Home Assistant for coordinating entity state updates:

```
import asyncio
import random

buffer = []
condition = asyncio.Condition()
```

```python
async def consumer(name):
    while True:
        async with condition:
            while not buffer:
                await condition.wait()
            item = buffer.pop(0)
        print(f"{name} consumed {item}")
        await asyncio.sleep(random.uniform(0.5, 1.0))

async def producer(count):
    for i in range(1, count + 1):
        await asyncio.sleep(random.uniform(0.1, 0.5))
        async with condition:
            buffer.append(i)
            print(f"Producer added item {i}")
            condition.notify(1)
    async with condition:
        buffer.append(None)
        condition.notify_all()

async def main():
    consumers = [asyncio.create_task(consumer(f"Consumer{n}")) for n
    in (1, 2)]
    prod = asyncio.create_task(producer(5))
    await prod
    await asyncio.gather(*consumers)

asyncio.run(main())
```

The producer creates items and adds them to a shared buffer. The consumers wait for items to appear and then process them. Once all items are produced, a sentinel value (None) is added to signal termination.

This kind of condition-based coordination is powerful for controlling interactions between multiple tasks that depend on shared state changes. It's particularly useful when designing internal event systems, custom task queues, or buffering mechanisms.

Context Variables

When dealing with concurrency, especially in asynchronous applications, it's often necessary to carry context-specific information—like a request ID or user identity—through multiple layers of function calls. In threaded programs, this is commonly handled using thread-local storage. But in asyncio, where tasks are multiplexed on a single thread, this approach does not work. That's where Python's `contextvars` module comes in.

Context variables provide task-local storage. Each coroutine can have its own version of a variable, even if all tasks share the same thread. This makes it possible to manage context cleanly in asynchronous code.

The Need for Context Variables in Asyncio

In threaded applications, it's common to use thread-local variables to store request-specific data without passing it explicitly through every function. However, this approach fails with asyncio because all coroutines run on a single thread. Any global or thread-local state would be shared across tasks, leading to incorrect or unsafe behavior.

Context variables solve this by giving each task its own isolated copy of a variable. These variables propagate automatically across `await` boundaries and are isolated from other tasks.

A common real-world scenario involves web frameworks like FastAPI or Starlette. These frameworks use context variables to hold data like the current request or database session. Middleware can set these variables at the start of a request, and deep layers of the codebase can access them without needing to explicitly pass them down the stack.

Creating and Using Context Variables

We create a context variable using the `ContextVar` class from the `contextvars` module. We can set and retrieve its value using `.set()` and `.get()`.

```python
from contextvars import ContextVar

current_request = ContextVar("current_request", default=None)
current_db = ContextVar("current_db_session", default=None)
```

```python
async def request_handler(request):
    token_req = current_request.set(request)
    db_session = object()  # placeholder for DB session
    token_db = current_db.set(db_session)
    try:
        print("Handling request, current_request:", current_request.get())
        await process_request()
    finally:
        current_db.reset(token_db)
        current_request.reset(token_req)

async def process_request():
    db = current_db.get()
    req = current_request.get()
    print("Processing request:", req, "using db session:", db)
```

In this snippet, request_handler sets up context variables for a request and a database session. These can then be accessed deep within the stack—such as in process_request()—without being passed explicitly. This is useful for things like logging, error handling, or transaction management.

FastAPI uses a similar pattern to associate objects like the request or authentication context with the currently executing task.

Context Variables and Task Hierarchies

When a task is created, it inherits a copy of the current context. That means if a variable is set before a task is created, that task will see the same initial value. Any changes the task makes to the variable remain local to that task.

Here's an example:

```python
from contextvars import ContextVar
import asyncio

var = ContextVar("var", default="initial")

async def subtask():
    print("Subtask sees var =", var.get())
    var.set("subtask-val")
```

```
    print("Subtask changed var to", var.get())

async def main():
    var.set("main-val")
    print("Main set var to", var.get())
    t = asyncio.create_task(subtask())
    await t
    print("Back in main, var =", var.get())

asyncio.run(main())
```

Here's the output:

```
Main set var to main-val
Subtask sees var = main-val
Subtask changed var to subtask-val
Back in main, var = main-val
```

This shows that `subtask` inherits the value of `var` from the main task, but changes inside `subtask` don't affect the main task's view.

Default Values and Token Management

When we call `.set()` on a context variable, it returns a token object. This token stores the previous value (or indicates that no value was set). We can later pass this token to `.reset()` to restore the variable to its earlier state. This is useful in nested contexts to avoid leaking values across coroutine boundaries.

If we try to call `.get()` on a context variable that has no value set and no default, it raises an error. So providing a default value at creation time is often a good idea.

Managing tokens properly ensures that context variables do not interfere with each other, especially when multiple tasks or requests are involved.

Concurrency Patterns in Asyncio

Asyncio offers flexible tools for building concurrent applications. Over time, some concurrency patterns tend to appear frequently in real-world use cases. By understanding these patterns, we can design systems that are easier to reason about and perform better under load.

Fan-Out/Fan-In

Fan-out/fan-in is a pattern where one coroutine triggers multiple concurrent tasks (fan-out), waits for them to complete, and collects their results (fan-in).

This pattern is especially useful when we need to run several independent I/O-bound operations concurrently, such as fetching from multiple APIs or loading multiple files.

```python
import asyncio
import aiohttp

async def fetch(session, url):
    async with session.get(url) as response:
        data = await response.text()
        print(f"Fetched {url}")
        return data

async def main():
    urls = [
        "https://api.github.com",
        "https://httpbin.org/delay/2",
        "https://www.python.org"
    ]
    async with aiohttp.ClientSession() as session:
        tasks = [asyncio.create_task(fetch(session, url)) for url in urls]
        print("Launched fetch tasks, now waiting for results...")
        results = await asyncio.gather(*tasks)
    print("Got all results. Sizes:", [len(r) for r in results])

asyncio.run(main())
```

This example demonstrates

- Kicking off several fetch operations at once (fan-out)

- Using `asyncio.gather()` to wait for them all (fan-in)

The pattern is often used in web applications when collecting data from multiple services to construct a response. Python 3.11 introduced `asyncio.TaskGroup` for structured task management, which formalizes this pattern.

Producer–Consumer

In this pattern, one or more producer tasks create data and place it in a queue. One or more consumer tasks retrieve and process that data. Asyncio makes this easy with asyncio.Queue, which handles synchronization under the hood.

This is useful when producers and consumers operate at different speeds or when we want to decouple the generation of data from its processing.

```python
import asyncio
import random

async def producer(queue, count):
    for i in range(1, count + 1):
        await asyncio.sleep(random.uniform(0.1, 0.5))
        item = f"item-{i}"
        await queue.put(item)
        print(f"Produced {item}")
    for _ in range(num_consumers):
        await queue.put(None)

async def consumer(queue, name):
    while True:
        item = await queue.get()
        if item is None:
            print(f"{name}: No more items. Exiting.")
            queue.task_done()
            break
        print(f"{name}: got {item}")
        await asyncio.sleep(random.uniform(0.2, 0.5))
        print(f"{name}: finished processing {item}")
        queue.task_done()

num_consumers = 2

async def main():
    queue = asyncio.Queue()
    consumers = [asyncio.create_task(consumer(queue, f"Consumer{i}")) for i
    in range(1, num_consumers + 1)]
```

```
    await producer(queue, count=5)
    await queue.join()
    for c in consumers:
        if not c.done():
            c.cancel()

asyncio.run(main())
```

This model is useful in event-driven systems, data pipelines, or anywhere that work needs to be buffered and handled by multiple workers.

Worker Pool

A worker pool is a specific form of the producer–consumer pattern. Here, we have a fixed number of consumer tasks (workers) and a stream of work items pushed into a queue. This limits concurrency while still allowing all tasks to be processed eventually.

This approach is widely used in web scraping, batch processing, and systems that require rate limiting or resource pooling.

```
import asyncio
import aiohttp
import random

async def worker(name, session, queue):
    while True:
        url = await queue.get()
        if url is None:
            queue.task_done()
            print(f"{name}: exiting")
            break
        try:
            print(f"{name}: fetching {url}")
            async with session.get(url) as response:
                data = await response.text()
                print(f"{name}: fetched {url} (size {len(data)})")
        finally:
            queue.task_done()
```

```python
async def main():
    urls = [f"https://httpbin.org/delay/{random.randint(1,3)}" for _ in
    range(10)]
    queue = asyncio.Queue()
    async with aiohttp.ClientSession() as session:
        workers = [asyncio.create_task(worker(f"Worker{i}", session,
        queue)) for i in range(1, 4)]
        for url in urls:
            await queue.put(url)
        for _ in workers:
            await queue.put(None)
        await queue.join()
        for w in workers:
            await w

asyncio.run(main())
```

In this example, only three workers are running at a time, even though there are ten URLs to fetch. This reduces memory usage and avoids overwhelming the remote server.

This pattern is often used in open source libraries that implement crawlers, job dispatchers, or background processors. It gives a good balance between parallelism and control.

Error Handling in Asyncio

Handling errors in asyncio code comes with unique considerations. Because tasks may run independently and exceptions may not immediately propagate, we need deliberate strategies for capturing and responding to failures. In this section, we explore common patterns and best practices for managing errors in asynchronous applications.

Try–Except Blocks in Coroutines

Inside a coroutine, error handling works the same way as in synchronous code: we use try/except blocks. For example, when performing I/O operations like HTTP requests or database calls, it's important to catch exceptions that are expected in real-world conditions.

```python
import asyncio
import aiohttp

async def fetch_data(session, url):
    try:
        async with session.get(url, timeout=5) as resp:
            return await resp.text()
    except asyncio.TimeoutError:
        print(f"Timeout fetching {url}")
        return None
    except aiohttp.ClientError as e:
        print(f"Network error fetching {url}: {e}")
        return None

async def main():
    async with aiohttp.ClientSession() as session:
        content = await fetch_data(session, "http://example.com/delay/10")
        if content is None:
            ...  # handle failure

asyncio.run(main())
```

In this example, we handle timeout and general network errors explicitly. This ensures our application can respond gracefully to transient failures.

This pattern is used extensively in open source libraries such as redis-py, which wraps low-level socket timeouts or I/O errors in application-specific exceptions, ensuring that higher-level logic is insulated from network flakiness.

Exceptions in Tasks

When tasks are scheduled using asyncio.create_task() and not awaited immediately, any exception they raise may go unnoticed unless we handle it explicitly. This can result in warning messages like "Task exception was never retrieved."

To prevent this, we must either

- Await the task later.

- Use task.add_done_callback() to inspect the result.

- Wrap multiple tasks using asyncio.gather().

Here's an example using gather with exception capturing:

```python
async def failing_task():
    raise RuntimeError("Something went wrong")

async def main():
    results = await asyncio.gather(
        failing_task(),
        return_exceptions=True
    )
    for result in results:
        if isinstance(result, Exception):
            print("Caught exception:", result)

asyncio.run(main())
```

This ensures that exceptions are caught and processed, even if the tasks are launched and managed in parallel.

Handling `asyncio.CancelledError`

Task cancellation is a core part of asyncio's cooperative concurrency. When a task is cancelled using .cancel(), the event loop raises asyncio.CancelledError inside the coroutine at the next await point. This exception inherits from BaseException (not Exception), so it won't be caught by except Exception:.

It's important to either allow this exception to propagate or catch it and re-raise it after performing any necessary cleanup.

```python
async def upload_file(session, file):
    try:
        await session.upload(file)
    finally:
        await session.close()
```

In this example, even if the task is cancelled during upload(), the finally block will run, ensuring resources are cleaned up.

If we catch `CancelledError`, we should usually re-raise it:

```
async def handler():
    try:
        await some_long_task()
    except asyncio.CancelledError:
        log("Task was cancelled")
        raise  # re-raise so the task is properly cancelled
```

If we forget to re-raise, the cancellation will be swallowed, and the program may behave as if the task finished normally.

Best Practices

- Always use try/except blocks around known failure points, especially I/O.

- Use `finally` to ensure resources like connections or locks are released.

- If creating background tasks, track them or attach callbacks to handle failures.

- Let `CancelledError` propagate unless we're doing cleanup—and re-raise it when caught.

Real-world asyncio applications—especially web servers, scraping tools, and messaging systems—must be resilient to partial failures. Solid error handling ensures our code doesn't silently fail or hang due to unexpected issues and that cleanup and recovery happen in predictable ways.

Multithreading vs. Multiprocessing vs. Asyncio

Choosing the right concurrency model depends on the nature of the workload. Python offers three main approaches to achieving concurrency: multithreading, multiprocessing, and asyncio. Each has trade-offs and is suitable for different scenarios.

Multithreading

Python's `threading` module allows multiple threads to run concurrently. However, due to the Global Interpreter Lock (GIL), only one thread executes Python bytecode at a time. This makes multithreading suitable primarily for I/O-bound tasks rather than CPU-bound workloads.

Use multithreading when

- We need to perform blocking I/O (file operations, network calls) and want to overlap them.

- We're working with libraries that release the GIL (like many C extensions).

- We need to integrate with legacy code or APIs that are thread-based.

Limitations: Threads share memory and state, so care must be taken with locking to prevent race conditions. Debugging threaded programs can be complex due to preemptive context switches.

Multiprocessing

Python's `multiprocessing` module spawns separate processes that run in parallel and bypass the GIL. Each process has its own memory space. This makes multiprocessing well-suited for CPU-bound workloads.

Use multiprocessing when

- We need to perform CPU-intensive computations (image processing, scientific calculations).

- We want to leverage multiple cores for true parallelism.

Limitations: Inter-process Communication is slower than threads due to serialization (e.g., `pickle`) and the lack of shared memory by default. Startup cost of new processes can also be high.

Asyncio

Asyncio enables cooperative multitasking using coroutines and an event loop. It's designed for high-throughput I/O-bound applications, where tasks spend a lot of time waiting.

Use asyncio when

- The program is I/O-bound: making HTTP requests, talking to databases, or handling user input.

- We want to manage thousands of concurrent operations in a single thread efficiently.

- We need fine-grained control over task scheduling and cancellation.

Limitations: Asyncio does not make use of multiple CPU cores. For CPU-bound tasks, it must be combined with threads or processes. Learning the async/await model and debugging asynchronous flows may require a mindset shift.

Summary Table

Model	Best for	GIL Impact	Parallelism	Memory Sharing	Suitable for
Multithreading	I/O bound	GIL limits	No	Yes	Web scraping, file/network I/O
Multiprocessing	CPU bound	No GIL	Yes	No (by default)	Data analysis, ML training
Asyncio	I/O bound, high concurrency	GIL applies	No	N/A	Network servers, event loops

In many real-world systems, a hybrid approach works best: asyncio for managing I/O concurrency, with background tasks offloaded to a thread or process pool. Libraries like `concurrent.futures`, `asyncio.to_thread()`, or external tools like `Celery` help bridge these paradigms.

Conclusion

Asyncio provides a powerful model for writing concurrent I/O-bound programs in Python. With its event loop, coroutine-based design, and cooperative multitasking, it gives us the tools to handle thousands of concurrent operations efficiently without the overhead of threads.

We explored how the event loop orchestrates asynchronous tasks, how `async` and `await` enable readable async code, and how constructs like tasks, locks, semaphores, and context variables allow us to write robust concurrent systems. We also looked at real-world patterns like fan-out/fan-in, worker pools, and producer–consumer queues—all essential for building scalable applications.

Understanding how to structure asynchronous code, manage cancellation, and handle errors is essential for building reliable asyncio applications. With practice, we can design systems that are both performant and maintainable. Asyncio isn't a drop-in replacement for threads or multiprocessing—it excels in specific scenarios, particularly where concurrency is I/O bound and coordination is critical.

CHAPTER 17

Data Serialization and Persistence

In the previous chapter, we explored asynchronous programming with `asyncio`, learning how to handle multiple I/O-bound operations efficiently within a single thread.

Now, we turn our attention to data serialization and persistence—two key concepts when it comes to storing, transmitting, and recovering data. Serialization refers to converting a data structure or object state into a format that can be stored or sent over a network and later reconstructed. Persistence, on the other hand, means that data remains available even after the program that created it has ended.

These techniques are essential when we want to save application state, share data between systems, or cache objects for later use. In this chapter, we'll dive into several built-in tools Python provides for these tasks:

- *JSON*: A lightweight, text-based format that is both human-readable and machine-parsable

- *Pickle*: A Python-specific binary format capable of serializing complex Python objects

- *Shelve*: A module offering a dictionary-like API to persist Python objects in files

- *Marshal*: A lower-level format used internally by Python, primarily for serializing code objects

- *CSV*: A simple text format for working with tabular data, compatible with many tools

- *XML*: A structured, extensible markup format often used in data exchange and configuration files

531

© Adarsh Divakaran 2025
A. Divakaran, *Deep Dive Python*, https://doi.org/10.1007/979-8-8688-1261-3_17

By the end of this chapter, we'll understand when and how to use each of these tools effectively depending on the use case and data portability needs.

JSON

The json module in Python provides a simple and efficient way to work with JSON (JavaScript Object Notation) data. JSON is a lightweight data interchange format that is easy for humans to read and write and easy for machines to parse and generate. It is widely used for data exchange in APIs, web applications, configuration files, and data storage.

The json module offers methods to serialize Python objects into JSON-formatted strings and deserialize JSON strings back into Python objects. In the coming sections, we will explore various functions and classes provided by the module.

json.dumps()

The json.dumps() method serializes a Python object into a JSON-formatted string.

The signature of the function is as follows:

```
json.dumps(obj, *, skipkeys=False, ensure_ascii=True, check_circular=True,
allow_nan=True, cls=None, indent=None, separators=None, default=None, sort_
keys=False)
```

Parameters:

- obj: The Python object to be serialized.

- skipkeys *(default:* False*)*: If True, dictionary keys that are not of a basic type (str, int, float, bool, None) will be skipped instead of raising a TypeError.

- ensure_ascii *(default:* True*)*: If True, the output will be ASCII-only, with non-ASCII characters escaped. If False, the output can contain non-ASCII characters.

- check_circular *(default:* True*)*: If True, the function will check for circular references and raise a ValueError if any are found. If False, circular references will result in an OverflowError or worse.

- allow_nan (*default:* True): If True, NaN, Infinity, and -Infinity will be serialized as such. If False, a ValueError will be raised if these values are encountered.

- cls (*default:* None): A custom JSONEncoder subclass that will be used to serialize the object. If not provided, the default JSONEncoder is used.

- indent (*default:* None): If a non-negative integer or string is provided, it will be used to pretty-print the JSON output with that level of indentation. If None, the most compact representation is used.

- separators (*default:* None): A tuple specifying how to separate items in the JSON output. The default is (',', ': '). For the most compact representation, we can use (',', ':').

- default (*default:* None): A function that gets called for objects that cannot be serialized by default. It should return a serializable version of the object or raise a TypeError.

- sort_keys (*default:* False): If True, the output will have dictionary keys sorted.

Below are some examples of json.dumps() usage in open source projects:

```
# File: libs/core/langchain_core/load/dump.py

def dumps(obj: Any, *, pretty: bool = False, **kwargs: Any) -> str:
    """Return a json string representation of an object.

    Args:
        obj: The object to dump.
        pretty: Whether to pretty print the json. If true, the json will be
            indented with 2 spaces (if no indent is provided as part of
            kwargs).
            Default is False.
        kwargs: Additional arguments to pass to json.dumps

    Returns:
        A json string representation of the object.
```

```
    Raises:
        ValueError: If `default` is passed as a kwarg.
    """
    if "default" in kwargs:
        raise ValueError("`default` should not be passed to dumps")
    try:
        if pretty:
            indent = kwargs.pop("indent", 2)
            return json.dumps(obj, default=default, indent=indent,
            **kwargs)
        else:
            return json.dumps(obj, default=default, **kwargs)
    except TypeError:
        if pretty:
            indent = kwargs.pop("indent", 2)
            return json.dumps(to_json_not_implemented(obj), indent=indent,
            **kwargs)
        else:
            return json.dumps(to_json_not_implemented(obj), **kwargs)
```

Here, if pretty is True, the custom dumps() function sets the indent parameter to 2 (or a custom value from kwargs) and calls json.dumps to produce a more readable JSON string. If pretty is False, the function calls json.dumps with the provided object and any additional keyword arguments.

In the below example, the js() serializes various class attributes to JSON using the dumps():

```
# File: modules/processing.py

class Processed:
    ...

    def js(self):
        obj = {
            "prompt": self.all_prompts[0],
            "all_prompts": self.all_prompts,
            "negative_prompt": self.all_negative_prompts[0],
```

```
            "all_negative_prompts": self.all_negative_prompts,
            "seed": self.seed,
            "all_seeds": self.all_seeds,
            "subseed": self.subseed,
            "all_subseeds": self.all_subseeds,
            "subseed_strength": self.subseed_strength,
            "width": self.width,
            "height": self.height,
            "sampler_name": self.sampler_name,
            "cfg_scale": self.cfg_scale,
            "steps": self.steps,
            "batch_size": self.batch_size,
            "restore_faces": self.restore_faces,
            "face_restoration_model": self.face_restoration_model,
            "sd_model_name": self.sd_model_name,
            "sd_model_hash": self.sd_model_hash,
            "sd_vae_name": self.sd_vae_name,
            "sd_vae_hash": self.sd_vae_hash,
            "seed_resize_from_w": self.seed_resize_from_w,
            "seed_resize_from_h": self.seed_resize_from_h,
            "denoising_strength": self.denoising_strength,
            "extra_generation_params": self.extra_generation_params,
            "index_of_first_image": self.index_of_first_image,
            "infotexts": self.infotexts,
            "styles": self.styles,
            "job_timestamp": self.job_timestamp,
            "clip_skip": self.clip_skip,
            "is_using_inpainting_conditioning": self.is_using_inpainting_
            conditioning,
            "version": self.version,
        }
    return json.dumps(obj, default=lambda o: None)
```

When json.dumps encounters an object that it cannot serialize, it will call the default function with that object as the argument. In this case, the default function is lambda o: None, which means it will return None for any non-serializable object.

json.loads()

The json.loads() method deserializes a JSON-formatted string into a Python object.
Its signature is as follows:

```
json.loads(s, *, cls=None, object_hook=None, parse_float=None, parse_
int=None, parse_constant=None, object_pairs_hook=None)
```

Parameters:

- s: The JSON-formatted string to be deserialized.

- cls *(default:* None*)*: A custom JSONDecoder subclass that will be
  used to deserialize the JSON string. If not provided, the default
  JSONDecoder is used.

- object_hook *(default:* None*)*: A function that will be called with the
  result of any object literal decoded (a dict). The return value of
  object_hook will be used instead of the dict.

- parse_float *(default:* None*)*: A function that will be called with the
  string of every JSON float to be decoded. By default, this is equivalent
  to float(num_str).

- parse_int *(default:* None*)*: A function that will be called with the
  string of every JSON int to be decoded. By default, this is equivalent
  to int(num_str).

- parse_constant *(default:* None*)*: A function that will be called with
  the string of every JSON constant (-Infinity, Infinity, NaN) to be
  decoded.

- object_pairs_hook *(default:* None*)*: A function that will be called
  with the result of any object literal decoded with an ordered list of
  pairs. The return value of object_pairs_hook will be used instead of
  the dict.

We will explore some usage examples of loads() below:

Example 1: **Posthog**

```python
# File: posthog/utils.py
import json

def decompress(data: Any, compression: str):
    ...

    try:
        # Use custom parse_constant to handle NaN, Infinity, etc.
        data = json.loads(data, parse_constant=lambda x: None)
    except (json.JSONDecodeError, UnicodeDecodeError) as error_main:
        if compression == "":
            ...
```

When json.loads encounters NaN, Infinity, or -Infinity in the JSON string, it will call the parse_constant function. In this case, the parse_constant is a lambda function that replaces these special constants with None.

Example 2: **Cobalt**

```python
# File: v8/tools/v8_presubmit.py
def _CheckStatusFileForDuplicateKeys(filepath):
    comma_space_bracket = re.compile(", *]")
    lines = []
    with open(filepath) as f:
        for line in f.readlines():
            # Skip all-comment lines.
            if line.lstrip().startswith("#"):
                continue
            ...

    contents = "\n".join(lines)

    ...

    status = {"success": True}

    def check_pairs(pairs):
        keys = {}
        for key, value in pairs:
```

```
        if key in keys:
            print("%s: Error: duplicate key %s" % (filepath, key))
            status["success"] = False
        keys[key] = True

    json.loads(contents, object_pairs_hook=check_pairs)
    return status["success"]
```

In this snippet, a function check_pairs that checks for duplicate keys in the JSON content is defined. If a duplicate key is found, it prints an error message and sets the status to False. The JSON content is loaded using json.loads with the object_pairs_ hook parameter set to check_pairs, which allows it to check for duplicate keys during the loading process.

Example 3: **Apache Superset**

```
# File: superset/commands/dashboard/importers/v0.py

def decode_dashboards(o: dict[str, Any]) -> Any:
    """

    Function to be passed into json.loads obj_hook parameter
    Recreates the dashboard object from a json representation.
    """

    if "__Dashboard__" in o:
        return Dashboard(**o["__Dashboard__"])
    if "__Slice__" in o:
        return Slice(**o["__Slice__"])
    if "__TableColumn__" in o:
        return TableColumn(**o["__TableColumn__"])
    if "__SqlaTable__" in o:
        return SqlaTable(**o["__SqlaTable__"])
    if "__SqlMetric__" in o:
        return SqlMetric(**o["__SqlMetric__"])
    if "__datetime__" in o:
        return datetime.strptime(o["__datetime__"], "%Y-%m-%dT%H:%M:%S")

    return o
```

```
def import_dashboards(
    content: str,
    database_id: Optional[int] = None,
    import_time: Optional[int] = None,
) -> None:
    """Imports dashboards from a stream to databases"""
    current_tt = int(time.time())
    import_time = current_tt if import_time is None else import_time
    data = json.loads(content, object_hook=decode_dashboards)
```

The object_hook parameter allows us to specify a custom function that will be called with the result of any JSON object literal decoded (a dictionary). The return value of this function will be used instead of the dictionary. In this case, the decode_dashboards is the custom function that processes the dictionary and reconstructs specific objects based on special keys.

When json.loads encounters a JSON object, it calls the decode_dashboards function with the dictionary representation of that object. The decode_dashboards function checks for specific keys (e.g., "__Dashboard__", "__Slice__", etc.) and reconstructs the corresponding Python objects (e.g., Dashboard, Slice, TableColumn, SqlaTable, SqlMetric, datetime). If none of the special keys are found, the original dictionary is returned.

json.dump() and json.load()

The json.dump() and json.load() methods have a similar signature to json.dumps() and json.loads(), but they work with file-like objects instead of strings.

- json.dump(obj, fp, ...): Serializes obj to a JSON-formatted stream to fp (a .write()-supporting file-like object)

- json.load(fp, ...): Deserializes a JSON-formatted stream from fp (a .read()-supporting file-like object) to a Python object

JSONEncoder Class

The JSONEncoder class is used to convert a Python object into a JSON-formatted string. By subclassing JSONEncoder, we can customize the serialization process.

- *Custom serialization*: By subclassing JSONEncoder and overriding the default method, we can define how complex or non-standard Python objects should be serialized into JSON.

- *Integration with* json.dumps: We can pass the custom JSONEncoder subclass to the cls parameter of the json.dumps function to use our custom serialization logic.

The class has the following signature:

```
class json.JSONEncoder(skipkeys=False, ensure_ascii=True, check_
circular=True, allow_nan=True, sort_keys=False, indent=None,
separators=None, default=None)
```

The arguments are similar to those seen in the dumps() function.

Below are some examples of using custom JSONEncoder classes:

Example 1: **Node**

```python
# File: node/deps/v8/tools/locs.py

class LocsEncoder(json.JSONEncoder):
  def default(self, o):
    if isinstance(o, File):
      return {"file": o.file, "target": o.target, "loc": o.loc, "in_bytes":
      o.in_bytes,
              "expanded": o.expanded, "expanded_bytes": o.expanded_bytes}
    if isinstance(o, Group):
      return {"name": o.name, "loc": o.loc, "in_bytes": o.in_bytes,
              "expanded": o.expanded, "expanded_bytes": o.expanded_bytes}
    if isinstance(o, Results):
      return {"groups": o.groups, "units": o.units,
              "source_dependencies": o.source_dependencies,
              "header_dependents": o.header_dependents}
    return json.JSONEncoder.default(self, o)
```

The LocsEncoder class in the provided code is a custom JSON encoder that extends the json.JSONEncoder class to handle the serialization of specific custom objects (File, Group, and Results). By overriding the default method, it checks the type of the object being serialized and returns a dictionary representation of the object's attributes if it matches one of the specified types. For File objects, it includes attributes like file, target, loc, in_bytes, expanded, and expanded_bytes. For Group objects, it includes name, loc, in_bytes, expanded, and expanded_bytes. For Results objects, it includes groups, units, source_dependencies, and header_dependents. If the object does not match any of these types, it falls back to the default serialization method provided by json.JSONEncoder.

This is used in the repository like

```
def Main():
  out = sys.stdout
  if ARGS['json']:
    out = sys.stderr

  ...

  with tempfile.TemporaryDirectory(dir='/tmp/', prefix="locs.") as temp:
    ...
    if ARGS['json']:
      print(json.dumps(result, ensure_ascii=False, cls=LocsEncoder))

  ...
```

Here, dumps is called with the custom encoder we defined.

Example 2: **homeassistant**

```
# File: homeassistant/helpers/json.py

import json

class JSONEncoder(json.JSONEncoder):
    """JSONEncoder that supports Home Assistant objects."""

    def default(self, o: Any) -> Any:
        """Convert Home Assistant objects.

        Hand other objects to the original method.
```

```
    """

    if isinstance(o, datetime.datetime):
        return o.isoformat()
    if isinstance(o, set):
        return list(o)
    if hasattr(o, "as_dict"):
        return o.as_dict()

    return json.JSONEncoder.default(self, o)

class ExtendedJSONEncoder(JSONEncoder):
    """JSONEncoder that supports Home Assistant objects and falls back to
    repr(o)."""

    def default(self, o: Any) -> Any:
        """Convert certain objects.

        Fall back to repr(o).
        """
        if isinstance(o, datetime.timedelta):
            return {"__type": str(type(o)), "total_seconds": o.total_
            seconds()}
        if isinstance(o, datetime.datetime):
            return o.isoformat()
        if isinstance(o, (datetime.date, datetime.time)):
            return {"__type": str(type(o)), "isoformat": o.isoformat()}
        try:
            return super().default(o)
        except TypeError:
            return {"__type": str(type(o)), "repr": repr(o)}
```

In this code, a custom JSONEncoder class is defined. This class is designed to support the serialization of Home Assistant objects. It overrides the default method to provide custom serialization logic for certain types of objects:

- datetime.datetime: Converts datetime objects to their ISO 8601 string representation using isoformat().

- set: Converts sets to lists, as JSON does not support sets.

- *Objects with the* as_dict *method*: If an object has an as_dict method, it calls this method to get a dictionary representation of the object.

The ExtendedJSONEncoder class builds on JSONEncoder and adds support for additional types of objects, with a fallback to the repr function for unsupported types.

These custom classes are used in the library and are supplied as arguments to the cls attribute of json.dumps() when custom encoding behavior is desired.

JSONDecoder Class

The JSONDecoder class is used to convert a JSON-formatted string into a Python object. By subclassing JSONDecoder, we can customize the deserialization process.

- By subclassing JSONDecoder and providing custom hooks (such as object_hook), we can define how JSON objects should be converted into complex or non-standard Python objects.

- *Integration with* json.loads: We can pass the custom JSONDecoder subclass to the cls parameter of the json.loads function to use the custom deserialization logic.

It has the signature below with attributes resembling those of the json.loads():

```
class json.JSONDecoder(object_hook=None, parse_float=None, parse_int=None,
parse_constant=None, strict=True, object_pairs_hook=None)
```

Parameters:

- object_hook *(default:* None*)*: A function that will be called with the result of any object literal decoded (a dict). The return value of object_hook will be used instead of the dict.

- parse_float *(default:* None*)*: A function that will be called with the string of every JSON float to be decoded. By default, this is equivalent to float(num_str).

- parse_int *(default:* None*)*: A function that will be called with the string of every JSON int to be decoded. By default, this is equivalent to int(num_str).

- parse_constant (*default:* None): A function that will be called with
  the string of every JSON constant (-Infinity, Infinity, NaN) to be
  decoded.

- strict (*default:* True): If False, control characters will be allowed
  inside strings.

- object_pairs_hook (*default:* None): A function that will be called
  with the result of any object literal decoded with an ordered list of
  pairs. The return value of object_pairs_hook will be used instead of
  the dict.

Below is an example of a custom decoder class used in Django:

```python
# File: django/contrib/messages/storage/cookie.py

class MessageDecoder(json.JSONDecoder):
    """
    Decode JSON that includes serialized ``Message`` instances.
    """

    def process_messages(self, obj):
        if isinstance(obj, list) and obj:
            if obj[0] == MessageEncoder.message_key:
                if obj[1]:
                    obj[3] = mark_safe(obj[3])
                return Message(*obj[2:])
            return [self.process_messages(item) for item in obj]
        if isinstance(obj, dict):
            return {key: self.process_messages(value) for key, value in
                obj.items()}
        return obj

    def decode(self, s, **kwargs):
        decoded = super().decode(s, **kwargs)
        return self.process_messages(decoded)
```

The MessageDecoder class in the code is a custom JSON decoder that extends
Python's built-in json.JSONDecoder to handle the deserialization of JSON data that
includes serialized Message instances. It overrides the decode method to first decode

the JSON string into a Python object using the standard JSON decoding process. Then, it processes the decoded object through the process_messages method, which recursively traverses the object structure. If it encounters a list that starts with a specific message_ key (indicating a serialized Message), it reconstructs the Message object, optionally marking its content as safe if required. For lists and dictionaries, it recursively processes each element or key–value pair to ensure all nested Message instances are properly decoded.

Python docs on the json module warn us of an issue that might arise when parsing data obtained from untrusted sources:

> Be cautious when parsing JSON data from untrusted sources.
> A malicious JSON string may cause the decoder to consume
> considerable CPU and memory resources. Limiting the size of
> data to be parsed is recommended.

Limiting the size of the received untrusted data is recommended to prevent server resource exhaustion.

Pickle

The pickle module in Python is a powerful tool for serializing and deserializing Python object structures, also known as "pickling" and "unpickling." This process allows complex data types such as lists, dictionaries, and custom objects to be converted into a byte stream, which can then be stored in a file or transmitted over a network. Later, this byte stream can be reconstructed back into the original object. The pickle module is particularly useful for saving program state, caching data, or transferring data between different Python programs. It supports a wide range of Python data types and is designed to be easy to use while providing robust functionality for object serialization.

While using this module, we should be aware of potential security issues we can run into. Python docs warn us of the following:

> The pickle module **is not secure**. Only unpickle data you trust.

> It is possible to construct malicious pickle data that will **execute
> arbitrary code during unpickling**. Never unpickle data that could
> have come from an untrusted source or that could have been
> tampered with.

Consider signing data with hmac if you need to ensure that it has not been tampered with.

Safer serialization formats such as json may be more appropriate if you are processing untrusted data.

This means that unpickling untrusted or user-provided data is risky. An attacker can craft a pickle dump, which can execute arbitrary code on the server when unpickled. Extra checks should, therefore, be enforced when working with untrusted data.

Pickle Module Functions

The pickle module functions are similar to those in the json module, providing a straightforward way to serialize and deserialize Python objects. The key functions in the pickle module include pickle.dumps for serializing an object into a byte stream, pickle.loads for deserializing a byte stream back into an object, pickle.dump for writing a serialized object to a file-like object, and pickle.load for reading and deserializing an object from a file-like object.

pickle.dump

The signature of the function is as follows:

```
pickle.dump(obj, protocol=None, *, fix_imports=True, buffer_callback=None)
```

Arguments:

- obj: The Python object to be serialized

- protocol: An optional integer that specifies the pickling protocol to use. If not specified, the default protocol is used

- fix_imports: A boolean flag that, when set to True, attempts to map the new Python 3 names to the old module names used in Python 2, ensuring compatibility

- buffer_callback: An optional callable that can be used to handle out-of-band buffers

pickle.load

The load() function has the below signature:

pickle.load(obj, *, fix_imports=True, encoding="ASCII", errors="strict", buffers=None)

Arguments:

- obj: The Python object to be deserialized.

- fix_imports: A boolean flag that, when set to True, attempts to map the old Python 2 names to the new module names used in Python 3, ensuring compatibility.

- encoding: The encoding to use for decoding str objects. The default is "ASCII".

- errors: The error handling scheme to use for decoding errors. The default is "strict".

- buffers: An optional list of out-of-band buffers.

We will see examples of these functions from open source projects below:

Example 1: **Scrapy**

```python
# File: scrapy/extensions/httpcache.py

class FilesystemCacheStorage:

    def store_response(
        self, spider: Spider, request: Request, response: Response
    ) -> None:
        """Store the given response in the cache."""
        rpath = Path(self._get_request_path(spider, request))
        if not rpath.exists():
            rpath.mkdir(parents=True)
        metadata = {
            "url": request.url,
            "method": request.method,
            "status": response.status,
```

```
            "response_url": response.url,
            "timestamp": time(),
        }
        with self._open(rpath / "meta", "wb") as f:
            f.write(to_bytes(repr(metadata)))
        with self._open(rpath / "pickled_meta", "wb") as f:
            pickle.dump(metadata, f, protocol=4)
        with self._open(rpath / "response_headers", "wb") as f:
            f.write(headers_dict_to_raw(response.headers))
        with self._open(rpath / "response_body", "wb") as f:
            f.write(response.body)
        with self._open(rpath / "request_headers", "wb") as f:
            f.write(headers_dict_to_raw(request.headers))
        with self._open(rpath / "request_body", "wb") as f:
            f.write(request.body)

    def _read_meta(self, spider: Spider, request: Request) ->
Optional[Dict[str, Any]]:
        rpath = Path(self._get_request_path(spider, request))
        metapath = rpath / "pickled_meta"
        if not metapath.exists():
            return None  # not found
        mtime = metapath.stat().st_mtime
        if 0 < self.expiration_secs < time() - mtime:
            return None  # expired
        with self._open(metapath, "rb") as f:
            return cast(Dict[str, Any], pickle.load(f))  # nosec
```

The pickle and unpickle operations in the code are as follows:

pickle.dump *usage in the* store_response *method*:

- It serializes the metadata dictionary and writes it to a file.

- The metadata is stored in a file named pickled_meta within the request-specific directory.

- The code here specifies `protocol=4` for serialization, which is a more efficient binary format introduced in Python 3.4.

`pickle.load` *usage in the* `_read_meta` *method*:

- It deserializes the metadata from the file back into a dictionary.

- It reads from the `pickled_meta` file within the request-specific directory, which was stored as a part of the `dump` operation.

Example 2: **Lichess/Lila**

```
# File: lila/bin/deploy

@contextlib.contextmanager
def workflow_run_db(repo):
    with open(os.path.join(repo.common_dir, "workflow_runs.pickle"),
    "ab+") as f:
        try:
            f.seek(0)
            db = pickle.load(f)
        except EOFError:
            print("Created workflow run database.")
            db = {}

        yield db

        f.seek(0)
        f.truncate()
        pickle.dump(db, f)
        print("Saved workflow run database.")
```

In this snippet, `pickle.load` in `workflow_run_db` deserializes the workflow run database from the workflow_runs pickle file. Initially, the script opens the `workflow_runs.pickle` file in append-binary-plus mode (`"ab+"`), which allows reading and writing and uses `f.seek(0)` to move the file pointer to the beginning of the file. It then attempts to load the database using `pickle.load(f)`. If the file is empty (causing an `EOFError`), it initializes an empty dictionary (`db = {}`) and prints a message indicating that a new database has been created.

The `workflow_run_db` function is used as a context manager here. When the context manager exits, the file contents are cleared, and the updated db dict is written using `pickle.dump()`.

pickle.loads() and pickle.dumps()

The `pickle.loads()` and `pickle.dumps()` functions are similar to `pickle.load()` and `pickle.dump()`, respectively, but they operate on byte streams directly rather than file-like objects. This allows for in-memory serialization and deserialization of Python objects.

Pickler and Unpickler Classes

The `Pickler` and `Unpickler` classes in Python are part of the `pickle` module, which is used for serializing and deserializing Python object structures. Serialization, also known as pickling, is the process of converting a Python object into a byte stream, while deserialization, or unpickling, is the reverse process of converting a byte stream back into a Python object.

The `Pickler` class is responsible for writing the serialized byte stream to a file or a file-like object, and the `Unpickler` class reads the byte stream and reconstructs the original object. These classes provide more control over the pickling and unpickling processes compared with the higher-level `pickle.dump` and `pickle.load` functions.

The arguments for `Pickler` and `Unpickler` are similar to those used in the `pickle.dump` and `pickle.load` functions, respectively. When we need to define custom pickling behavior, these classes can be subclassed.

The below snippet illustrates the usage of a custom `Pickler` class to modify the pickling behavior:

```python
import pickle
import copyreg
import datetime

class CustomPickler(pickle.Pickler):
    def __init__(self, file, protocol=None):
        super().__init__(file, protocol)
        self.dispatch_table = copyreg.dispatch_table.copy()
```

```
        # Add custom pickling function for datetime objects
        self.dispatch_table[datetime.datetime] = self.pickle_datetime

    def pickle_datetime(self, obj):
        return type(obj), (obj.isoformat(),)

    def save(self, obj):
        t = type(obj)
        f = self.dispatch_table.get(t)
        if f:
            f(self, obj)  # Call custom pickler
        else:
            super().save(obj)  # Fall back to default pickling

data = {"name": "John Doe", "timestamp": datetime.datetime.now()}

with open("data.pickle", "wb") as file:
    CustomPickler(file).dump(data)
```

In this example

1. We define a CustomPickler class that inherits from pickle.
   Pickler.

2. In the __init__ method, we create a copy of the default dispatch
   table and add our custom pickling function for datetime objects.

3. We define a custom pickling function, pickle_datetime, that
   converts a datetime object to its ISO format string.

4. We override the save method to use our custom dispatch table. If
   a custom pickler is found for the object type, it's used; otherwise, it
   falls back to the default pickling behavior.

To deserialize this data, we can use a custom unpickler as defined below:

```
import pickle
import datetime

class CustomUnpickler(pickle.Unpickler):
    def find_class(self, module, name):
        if module == "datetime" and name == "datetime":
```

```
        return self.unpickle_datetime
    return super().find_class(module, name)

def unpickle_datetime(self, iso_string):
    return datetime.datetime.fromisoformat(iso_string)
```

The Unpickler class is overridden here to define custom unpickling behavior. The pickle.Unpickler class reads a pickled representation of an object from a binary file or a byte stream and reconstructs the original object. This class provides a more granular control over the unpickling process compared with the high-level pickle.load() function. By using Unpickler, we can customize the deserialization process, handle custom object types, and manage the security aspects of unpickling untrusted data.

In the CustomUnpickler class defined above

- We override the find_class method. This method is called when the unpickler encounters a class it needs to reconstruct.

- In find_class, we check if the module and name correspond to datetime.datetime. If so, we return our custom unpickle_datetime method.

- The unpickle_datetime method takes the ISO format string (which was how we pickled the datetime in the CustomPickler) and uses datetime.fromisoformat() to reconstruct the datetime object.

- For all other classes, we fall back to the default behavior by calling the superclass's find_class method.

Below is an open source usage example of the Unpickler class:

```
# File: dill/_dill.py

from pickle import Unpickler as StockUnpickler

class Unpickler(StockUnpickler):
    """python's Unpickler extended to interpreter sessions and more
    types"""

    from .settings import settings

    _session = False
```

```
def find_class(self, module, name):
    if (module, name) == ("__builtin__", "__main__"):
        return self._main.__dict__   # XXX: above set w/save_module_dict
    elif (module, name) == ("__builtin__", "NoneType"):
        return type(None)   # XXX: special case: NoneType missing
    if module == "dill.dill":
        module = "dill._dill"
    return StockUnpickler.find_class(self, module, name)

def __init__(self, *args, **kwds):
    settings = Pickler.settings
    _ignore = kwds.pop("ignore", None)
    StockUnpickler.__init__(self, *args, **kwds)
    self._main = _main_module
    self._ignore = settings["ignore"] if _ignore is None else _ignore

def load(self):   # NOTE: if settings change, need to update attributes
    obj = StockUnpickler.load(self)
    if type(obj).__module__ == getattr(_main_module, "__name__", "__main__"):
        if not self._ignore:
            # point obj class to main
            try:
                obj.__class__ = getattr(self._main, type(obj).__name__)
            except (AttributeError, TypeError):
                pass   # defined in a file
    # _main_module.__dict__.update(obj.__dict__) #XXX: should update globals ?
    return obj

load.__doc__ = StockUnpickler.load.__doc__
pass
```

In this example, the custom unpickler class inherits from the standard Unpickler class from the pickle module and adds several enhancements and customizations.

In this code, the `find_class` and `__init__` methods are overridden.

- The `__init__` method initializes the custom `Unpickler` with additional settings:

  - It retrieves settings from the `Pickler` class.

  - It includes an `ignore` keyword argument to control whether certain objects should be ignored during unpickling.

- `find_class` *method*

  The `find_class` method is responsible for locating and returning the class object for a given module and name during unpickling. The custom implementation includes special handling for certain cases:

  - If the module and name are (`"__builtin__"`, `"__main__"`), it returns the main module's dictionary.

  - If the module and name are (`"__builtin__"`, `"NoneType"`), it returns the `NoneType`.

  - If the module is `dill.dill`, it adjusts the module name to `dill._dill` for compatibility.

- The `load` method is responsible for reading and reconstructing the next object from the pickle data stream. The custom implementation includes additional handling for objects defined in the main module:

  - It calls the standard `StockUnpickler.load` method to load the object.

  - If the object's type is defined in the main module and the `_ignore` setting is not enabled, it attempts to point the object's class to the main module's class definition.

Picklability

Below is a list of Python types that can be pickled:

- *Built-in constants*: None, True, False, Ellipsis, and NotImplemented

- *Numbers*: Integers, floating-point numbers, and complex numbers

- *Sequences and collections*: Strings, bytes, bytearrays, tuples, lists, sets, and dictionaries containing only picklable objects

- *Functions*: Both built-in and user-defined functions that are accessible from the top level of a module (defined using def, not lambda)

- *Classes*: Classes that are accessible from the top level of a module

- *Class instances*: Instances of such classes whose result of calling __getstate__() is picklable

Attempts to pickle unpicklable objects will raise the PicklingError exception. Here are a couple of examples to illustrate what can be pickled:

Example 1: **Pickling basic data types**

```python
import pickle

data = {
    "integer": 42,
    "float": 3.14,
    "string": "hello",
    "list": [1, 2, 3],
    "dict": {"key": "value"},
}

# Serialize the data
with open("data.pkl", "wb") as f:
    pickle.dump(data, f)

# Deserialize the data
with open("data.pkl", "rb") as f:
    loaded_data = pickle.load(f)

print(loaded_data)
"""
{
    "integer": 42,
    "float": 3.14,
    "string": "hello",
```

```
    "list": [1, 2, 3],
    "dict": {"key": "value"},
}
"""
```

Example 2: **Pickling a user-defined class object**

```python
import pickle

class MyClass:
    def __init__(self, value):
        self.value = value

obj = MyClass(10)

# Serialize the object
with open("object.pkl", "wb") as f:
    pickle.dump(obj, f)

# Deserialize the object
with open("object.pkl", "rb") as f:
    loaded_obj = pickle.load(f)

print(loaded_obj.value)  # Output: 10
```

In these examples, we demonstrate how to pickle and unpickle basic data types and a user-defined class.

Pickling Limitations

Pickling Class Restrictions

Classes are pickled by their fully qualified name, meaning that only the class name and the module it belongs to are stored. The actual code and data of the class are not pickled. This implies that the defining module must be importable in the unpickling environment and the module must contain the named class. If these conditions are not met, an exception will be raised.

```python
# File: dir/pickling_example_1.py

import pickle

class MyClass:
    attr = "class attribute"

    def __init__(self, value):
        self.value = value

obj = MyClass(10)

# Serialize the object
with open("class.pkl", "wb") as f:
    pickle.dump(obj, f)
```

The above snippet pickles and stores the object in the "class.pkl" file. We can try to unpickle the same from another file.

```python
# File: dir/pickling_example_2.py

import pickle

class MyClass:
    def __init__(self, value):
        self.value = value

# Deserialize the object
with open("class.pkl", "rb") as f:
    loaded_obj = pickle.load(f)

print(loaded_obj.value)  # Output: 10
print(hasattr(loaded_obj, "attr"))  # Output: False
```

In this example, the class MyClass is pickled and unpickled. Note that the class attribute attr is not restored from the pickle file. The attribute seems to be missing after unpickling. This is expected because the MyClass defined in the second file where the unpickling occurs does not hold the attribute. Also, if we try to omit the definition of MyClass entirely where the object is unpickled, this will lead to an error.

We can see that pickling and unpickling can perform unexpectedly for class objects if the definition of the class changes across pickling and unpickling operations.

Class Constructor Behavior

When a class instance is unpickled, its __init__() method is usually not invoked. Instead, an uninitialized instance is created, and the saved attributes are restored.

```python
# File: dir/init_1.py
import pickle

class MyClass:
    def __init__(self, value):
        self.value = value
        print("Initialized with value:", value)

obj = MyClass(10)

# Serialize the object
with open("class_instance.pkl", "wb") as f:
    pickle.dump(obj, f)

"""Output:
Initialized with value: 10
"""
```

In the above code, the obj instance is pickled and stored. This object can be unpickled like in the below snippet:

```python
# File: dir/init_2.py
import pickle

class MyClass:
    def __init__(self, value):
        self.value = value
        print("Initialized with value:", value)

# Deserialize the object
with open("class_instance.pkl", "rb") as f:
    loaded_obj = pickle.load(f)
```

```
print(loaded_obj.value)
"""Output:
10
"""
```

In the above code, the stored object is loaded from the pickle, and the `.value` attribute is printed. Note that the __init__ constructor was not run. The instance is created in an uninitialized state, and then its attributes are restored from the pickle file.

Pickling Function Restrictions

Functions, both built-in and user-defined, are also pickled by their fully qualified name. This means that only the function name, along with the name of the containing module and classes, is stored. The function's code and any of its attributes are not pickled. Therefore, the defining module must be importable in the unpickling environment, and the module must contain the named function.

```
import pickle

def my_function(x):
    return x * x

# Serialize the function
with open("function.pkl", "wb") as f:
    pickle.dump(my_function, f)

def my_function(x):
    return x + x

# Deserialize the function
with open("function.pkl", "rb") as f:
    loaded_function = pickle.load(f)

print(loaded_function(5))  # Output: 10
```

In this example, the function my_function is pickled and unpickled. The function's code is not stored in the pickle file; only its name and the module it belongs to are stored. The module must be importable in the unpickling environment for the function to be restored correctly. In this case, before unpickling, the function is redefined, and the latest definition is being used when it is run.

Pickling Stateful Objects

When working with stateful objects in Python, the __setstate__() and __getstate__() methods allow us to define how an object's state is saved and restored, which is useful when pickling and unpickling these.

The __getstate__() Method

The __getstate__() method is called when an object is being pickled. It should return a dictionary representing the object's state. This dictionary can include any attributes that need to be saved.

The __setstate__() Method

The __setstate__() method is called when an object is being unpickled. It is used to define the operations to recreate the saved object from the pickle.

Below is an example demonstrating how to use these methods:

```python
import pickle

class MyClass:
    def __init__(self, name, age):
        self.name = name
        self.age = age
        self._secret = "This is a secret attribute"

    def __getstate__(self):
        # Return a dictionary representing the object's state
        state = self.__dict__.copy()
        # Remove the _secret attribute from the state
        del state["_secret"]
        return state

    def __setstate__(self, state):
        # Restore the object's state
        self.__dict__.update(state)
        # Restore the _secret attribute
        self._secret = "This is a secret attribute"
```

```
# Create an instance of MyClass
obj = MyClass("Alice", 30)

# Serialize the object
serialized_obj = pickle.dumps(obj)

# Deserialize the object
deserialized_obj = pickle.loads(serialized_obj)

print(deserialized_obj.name)  # Output: Alice
print(deserialized_obj.age)  # Output: 30
print(deserialized_obj._secret)  # Output: This is a secret attribute
```

In this example, the __getstate__() method removes the _secret attribute from the state dictionary before serialization. The __setstate__() method restores the _secret attribute after deserialization.

Pickle vs. JSON

When deciding between JSON and pickle for data serialization, it's important to consider various factors such as human readability, interoperability, type support, and security.

Human Readability

- *JSON*: JSON is easy to read and understand by humans, making it suitable for configuration files, data interchange, and debugging.

- *Pickle*: Pickle is not designed to be human-readable, which can make it difficult to inspect or modify serialized data manually.

Interoperability

- *JSON*: JSON is widely used across different programming languages and systems, making it a versatile choice for data interchange between diverse platforms.

- *Pickle*: Pickle is specific to Python and not intended for use outside the Python ecosystem, limiting its interoperability with other languages.

Type Support

- *JSON*: By default, JSON can only represent a subset of Python built-in types (e.g., dictionaries, lists, strings, numbers) and does not support custom classes.

- *Pickle*: Pickle can represent a large number of Python types, including custom classes, often automatically, making it suitable for complex data structures.

Security

- *JSON*: Deserializing untrusted JSON does not pose a risk of arbitrary code execution, making it safer for handling data from untrusted sources. Resource exhaustion attacks are still possible when parsing JSON.

- *Pickle*: Deserializing untrusted pickle data can create an arbitrary code execution vulnerability, so it should only be used with trusted data sources.

Performance

- *JSON*: Serialization and deserialization are slower due to its text-based nature and the need for converting Python types to string representations and back. It's not optimized for speed or binary data.

- *Pickle*: Typically much faster for both serialization and deserialization. It works directly with Python's memory structures and uses a compact binary format, especially with higher protocol versions (e.g., protocol 4 or 5).

Based on the above factors, here are some guidelines on when to use JSON and when to use pickle.

We should use JSON when

- We need a human-readable format.

- We require interoperability with other programming languages or systems.

- We are working with simple data structures (e.g., dictionaries, lists, strings, numbers).

- Security is a concern, and we need to deserialize data from untrusted sources.

We must use pickle when

- We are working within the Python ecosystem.

- We need to serialize and deserialize complex Python objects, including custom classes.

- Human readability is not a priority.

- We can ensure the data being deserialized is from a trusted source to avoid security risks.

Shelve

The shelve module in Python is a part of the standard library that provides a simple yet effective way to persistently store Python objects. It is essentially a dictionary-like object that allows us to store and retrieve data using keys, similar to how we would with a regular dictionary. However, unlike a regular dictionary, the data is stored in a file on disk, making it persistent across program executions.

Key features:

1. *Persistence*: The primary advantage of using shelve is its ability to store data persistently. This means that the data remains available even after the program that created it has terminated.

2. *Dictionary-like interface*: shelve provides a familiar dictionary-like interface, making it easy to use for those already comfortable with Python dictionaries. We can use standard dictionary operations such as getting, setting, and deleting items.

3. *Automatic serialization*: The module automatically handles the serialization and deserialization of objects using the `pickle` module. This means we can store complex Python objects, not just basic data types.

4. *File-based storage*: Data is stored in a file on disk, which can be specified when opening the shelf. This file can be shared between different programs or instances of the same program.

5. *Cross-platform*: The `shelve` module is cross-platform. It works on different operating systems without requiring any modifications to the code.

While `shelve` supports concurrent read access, it does not support concurrent write access. This means that if multiple processes need to write to the same shelf, we will need to implement our own locking mechanism to prevent data corruption.

Key Methods

A shelf file can be opened using the `open()` method. The function has the below signature:

`shelve.open(filename, flag='c', protocol=None, writeback=False)`

It opens a shelf file and returns a dictionary-like object.
Parameters:

- `filename`: The name of the file where the shelf will be stored.

- `flag`: The mode in which to open the file. Options include

  - `'r'`: Open existing database for reading only.

  - `'w'`: Open existing database for reading and writing.

  - `'c'`: Open database for reading and writing, creating it if it doesn't exist (default).

  - `'n'`: Always create a new, empty database open for reading and writing.

- protocol: The pickling protocol to use. If None, the default protocol is used.

- writeback: If True, all accessed entries are cached in memory and written back on sync or close. This can be useful for mutable entries but can consume more memory.

Shelf Object Methods

The open() returns a dict-like Shelf object which supports all common dict operations. The additional methods of the Shelf object are

1. sync():

   - Writes any cached data to the disk. This is useful when writeback=True is used, as it ensures that all changes are saved.

2. close():

   - Closes the shelf file. It is important to call this method to ensure that all data is properly written to disk and resources are released.

A Shelf object can also be used as a context manager, in which case it will be automatically closed when the with block ends.

Below is an example of shelve in action:

```python
import shelve

# Open a shelve file
with shelve.open("my_shelve.db") as db:
    # Store data
    db["key1"] = "value1"
    db["key2"] = [1, 2, 3, 4, 5]
    db["key3"] = {"nested_key": "nested_value"}

# Reopen the shelve file to retrieve data
with shelve.open("my_shelve.db") as db:
    print(db["key3"])  # Output: {'nested_key': 'nested_value'}
    print(db["key1"])  # Output: value1
```

The shelve module simplifies the serialization process by taking care of file handling, pickling of the key objects, and storing them. The shelve module allows storing multiple objects by keys, and once stored, it allows for arbitrary access by keys.

For an open source example, the snippet below from the histogram library illustrates the use of shelve:

```
# File: histogram/benchmark/run_benchmarks.py
"""

This script runs the benchmarks on previous versions of this library to
track changes in performance.
"""
import subprocess as subp
import shelve
import json
import argparse

def get_commits():
    commits = []
    comments = {}
    for line in (
        subp.check_output(("git", "log", "--oneline")).decode("ascii").
        split("\n")
    ):
        if line:
            ispace = line.index(" ")
            hash = line[:ispace]
            commits.append(hash)
            comments[hash] = line[ispace + 1 :]
    commits = commits[::-1]
    return commits, comments

def run(results, comments, hash, update):
    if not update and hash in results:
        return
    ...
    print(hash, "run")
```

```python
    s = subp.check_output(
        ("./histogram_filling", "--benchmark_format=json", "--benchmark_
        filter=normal")
    )
    d = json.loads(s)
    if update and hash in results and results[hash] is not None:
        d2 = results[hash]
        for i, (b, b2) in enumerate(zip(d["benchmarks"],
        d2["benchmarks"])):
            d["benchmarks"][i] = b if b["cpu_time"] < b2["cpu_
time"] else b2
    results[hash] = d
    for benchmark in d["benchmarks"]:
        print(benchmark["name"], min(benchmark["real_time"],
        benchmark["cpu_time"]))


def main():
    commits, comments = get_commits()

    parser = argparse.ArgumentParser(
        description=__doc__, formatter_class=argparse.
        RawDescriptionHelpFormatter
    )
    parser.add_argument(
        "first",
        type=str,
        default="begin",
        help="first commit in range, special value `begin` is allowed",
    )
    parser.add_argument(
        "last",
        type=str,
        default="end",
        help="last commit in range, special value `end` is allowed",
    )
```

```
    parser.add_argument("-f", action="store_true", help="override previous
    results")

    args = parser.parse_args()

    if args.first == "begin":
        args.first = commits[0]
    if args.last == "end":
        args.last = commits[-1]

    with shelve.open("benchmark_results") as results:
        a = commits.index(args.first)
        b = commits.index(args.last)
        if args.f:
            for hash in commits[a : b + 1]:
                del results[hash]
        run(results, comments, args.first, False)
        run(results, comments, args.last, False)
        ...

if __name__ == "__main__":
    main()
```

From the code, it can be seen that

- The script opens a shelf file named "benchmark_results" using
  shelve.open("benchmark_results"). This file acts as a persistent
  storage for the benchmark results.

- The with statement ensures that the shelf is properly closed after the
  operations are completed, which is important for data integrity and
  resource management.

- In the run function, the results are stored in the shelf:

```
results[hash] = d
```

Here, hash is the commit hash, and d is the dictionary containing the benchmark
results. This line stores the results in the shelf with the commit hash as the key.

- When the script runs, it first checks if the results for a given commit hash already exist on the shelf. If they do and the -f flag (force update) is not set, it skips running the benchmarks for that commit.

- This helps avoid redundant benchmark runs and speeds up the process by reusing previously stored results.

- If the -f flag is set, the script deletes the existing results for the specified range of commits. This ensures that the benchmarks are rerun and the results are updated.

Shelve vs. Pickle

The shelve and pickle modules in Python both provide mechanisms for serializing and deserializing Python objects, but they serve different purposes and have distinct advantages and differences. shelve uses pickle under the hood to handle the serialization of objects.

Here are some key advantages of using shelve over pickle:

1. *Dictionary-like interface*:

    - *Shelve*: Acts like a dictionary, allowing easy storage and retrieval of objects using keys

    - *Pickle*: Serializes entire objects or collections, requiring full data load for access

2. *Persistent storage*:

    - *Shelve*: Automatically handles file storage, enabling efficient access and modification of individual entries

    - *Pickle*: Requires manual file handling for serialization and deserialization

3. *Ease of use*:

    - *Shelve*: Simplifies object management with a familiar dictionary API, reducing boilerplate code

    - *Pickle*: Needs more code for file operations and does not support direct access to individual objects

4. *Selective access*:

- *Shelve*: Allows retrieval, update, or deletion of specific entries without affecting others

- *Pickle*: Requires loading the entire dataset to access or modify any part

Differences Between `shelve` and `pickle`

Despite their similarities, `shelve` and `pickle` have some important differences:

1. *Data access*:

- *Shelve*: Supports random access to individual objects using keys

- *Pickle*: Provides sequential access, needing full data load

2. *Storage format*:

- *Shelve*: Uses a key–value format for storage

- *Pickle*: Serializes objects into a byte stream

3. *Use cases*:

- *Shelve*: Ideal for persistent storage with frequent access to individual objects (e.g., configuration, caching)

- *Pickle*: Best for serializing entire objects or collections, especially for network transmission or complex data structures

Marshal

The `marshal` module in Python is used for serializing and deserializing Python objects. It is primarily intended for writing and reading the "pseudo-compiled" code for Python modules, which is used by the Python interpreter to store compiled bytecode. The `marshal` module is much faster than other serialization modules like `pickle`, but it comes with significant limitations and risks.

Here are functions in the `marshal` module:

- `marshal.dump(value, file)`: Writes the serialized representation of value to the open file object `file`

- `marshal.load(file)`: Reads the serialized representation of an object from the open file object `file` and reconstructs the object

- `marshal.dumps(value)`: Returns the serialized representation of value as a bytes object

- `marshal.loads(bytes)`: Deserializes the bytes object and reconstructs the original object

The `marshal` is not intended to be a general-purpose serialization module. It is not recommended for normal data serialization or persistence use cases because of the following:

1. *Limited object support*: The `marshal` module supports only a subset of Python's built-in types. It does not handle user-defined classes or more complex data structures, making it less versatile than other serialization modules like `pickle` or `json`.

2. *Lack of backward compatibility*: The serialized format used by `marshal` is not guaranteed to be stable across different Python versions. This means that data serialized with one version of Python may not be deserializable with another version, leading to potential compatibility issues.

3. The primary use case for `marshal` is internal to the Python interpreter, specifically for reading and writing compiled bytecode. It is not intended for general-purpose serialization tasks, and using it for such purposes can lead to unexpected behavior and maintenance challenges.

CSV

The csv module in Python provides functionality to both read from and write to CSV (comma-separated values) files, which are commonly used for storing tabular data in a plain-text format. Each line in a CSV file corresponds to a row in the table, and each field in the row is separated by a comma or another delimiter.

The **reader()** and **writer()** Functions

The csv.reader function is used to read data from a CSV file. It takes an iterable (usually a file object) and returns an object that iterates over lines in the given CSV file. Each line is returned as a list of strings.

The csv.writer function is used to write data to a CSV file. It takes a file object and returns a writer object that converts the user's data into delimited strings on the given file-like object. The writerow method writes a single row at a time, while the writerows method can write multiple rows at once.

The below example shows the usage of these methods to write to and read from a CSV file:

```python
import csv

data = [
    ["Name", "Age", "City"],
    ["Alice", "30", "New York"],
    ["Bob", "25", "Los Angeles"],
    ["Charlie", "35", "Chicago"],
]

# Writing to a CSV file
with open("example.csv", "w", newline="") as file:
    writer = csv.writer(file)
    writer.writerows(data)

print("Data written to example.csv")

with open("example.csv", "r") as file:
    print(file.read())
```

```
"""Output:
Data written to example.csv
Name,Age,City
Alice,30,New York
Bob,25,Los Angeles
Charlie,35,Chicago
"""

# Reading from CSV file
with open("example.csv", "r") as file:
    reader = csv.reader(file)
    for row in reader:
        print(row)

"""Output:
['Name', 'Age', 'City']
['Alice', '30', 'New York']
['Bob', '25', 'Los Angeles']
['Charlie', '35', 'Chicago']
"""
```

In the snippet, we have written a CSV from the data list to a file and have used the reader() function to fetch the data from the file.

The DictReader() and DictWriter() Classes

The csv.DictReader class reads CSV files into a dictionary format. Each row in the CSV file is read as a dict (or OrderedDict, in Python versions prior to 3.8), where the keys are taken from the first row of the CSV file (the header). This makes it easy to access data by column name rather than by index, which can improve code readability and reduce errors.

The csv.DictWriter class writes data to a CSV file from a dictionary format. It takes a list of field names (keys) and writes each dictionary in the list as a row in the CSV file. This is particularly useful when we have data stored in dictionaries and want to write it out to a CSV file in a structured manner.

The snippet below from localstack illustrates the usage of dict reader and writer objects:

```python
# File: localstack/scripts/capture_notimplemented_responses.py

def run_script(services: list[str], path: None):
    """send requests against all APIs"""
    print(
        f"writing results to '{path}implementation_coverage_full.csv' and "
        '{path}implementation_coverage_aggregated.csv'..."
    )
    with (
        open(f"{path}implementation_coverage_full.csv", "w") as csvfile,
        open(f"{path}implementation_coverage_aggregated.csv", "w") as
        aggregatefile,
    ):
        full_w = csv.DictWriter(
            csvfile,
            fieldnames=[
                "service",
                "operation",
                "status_code",
                "error_code",
                "error_message",
                "is_implemented",
            ],
        )
        aggregated_w = csv.DictWriter(
            aggregatefile,
            fieldnames=["service", "implemented_count", "full_count",
            "percentage"],
        )

        full_w.writeheader()
        aggregated_w.writeheader()

        total_count = 0
```

```python
for service_name in services:
    service = service_models.get(service_name)
    for op_name in service.operation_names:
        if op_name in PHANTOM_OPERATIONS.get(service_name, []):
            continue
        total_count += 1

time_start = time.perf_counter_ns()
counter = 0
responses = {}
for service_name in services:
    c.print(f"\n=====  {service_name} =====")
    service = service_models.get(service_name)
    for op_name in service.operation_names:
        if op_name in PHANTOM_OPERATIONS.get(service_name, []):
            continue
        counter += 1
        c.print(
            f"{100 * counter/total_count:3.1f}% | Calling endpoint "
            {counter:4.0f}/{total_count}: {service_name}.{op_name}"
        )

        # here's the important part (the actual service call!)
        response = simulate_call(service_name, op_name)

        responses.setdefault(service_name, {})[op_name] = response
        is_implemented = str(not map_to_notimplemented(response))
        full_w.writerow(response | {"is_implemented": is_implemented})

    # calculate aggregate for service
    all_count = len(responses[service_name].values())
    implemented_count = len(
        [
            r
            for r in responses[service_name].values()
            if not map_to_notimplemented(r)
        ]
    )
```

```python
        implemented_percentage = implemented_count / all_count

        aggregated_w.writerow(
            {
                "service": response["service"],
                "implemented_count": implemented_count,
                "full_count": all_count,
                "percentage": f"{implemented_percentage * 100:.1f}",
            }
        )
    time_end = time.perf_counter_ns()
    delta = timedelta(microseconds=(time_end - time_start) / 1000.0)
    c.print(f"\n\nDone.\nTotal time to completion: {delta}")

def calculate_percentages():
    aggregate = {}

    implemented_aggregate = {}
    aggregate_list = []

    with open("./output-notimplemented.csv", "r") as fd:
        reader = csv.DictReader(fd, fieldnames=["service", "operation",
        "implemented"])
        for line in reader:
            if line["implemented"] == "implemented":
                continue
            aggregate.setdefault(line["service"], {}).setdefault(
                line["operation"], line
            )

        for service in aggregate.keys():
            vals = aggregate[service].values()
            all_count = len(vals)
            implemented_count = len([v for v in vals if v["implemented"] ==
            "True"])
            implemented_aggregate[service] = implemented_count / all_count
```

```
        aggregate_list.append(
            {
                "service": service,
                "count": all_count,
                "implemented": implemented_count,
                "percentage": implemented_count / all_count,
            }
        )

aggregate_list.sort(key=lambda k: k["percentage"])

with open("implementation_coverage_aggregated.csv", "w") as csv_fd:
    writer = csv.DictWriter(
        csv_fd, fieldnames=["service", "percentage", "implemented",
        "count"]
    )
    writer.writeheader()

    for agg in aggregate_list:
        agg["percentage"] = f"{agg['percentage'] * 100:.1f}"
        writer.writerow(agg)
```

`csv.DictWriter` *usage*:

1. *Opening files for writing*:

   - The code opens two CSV files for writing: one for detailed information (`implementation_coverage_full.csv`) and one for aggregated information (`implementation_coverage_aggregated.csv`).

2. *Creating* `DictWriter` *objects*:

   - `csv.DictWriter` is used to create writer objects (`full_w` and `aggregated_w`) for each file. These objects are initialized with the file object and a list of field names that define the structure of the CSV.

3. *Writing headers*:

- The writeheader method is called on both writer objects to write the header row to each CSV file. This ensures that the first row of the CSV contains the column names.

4. *Writing rows*:

- The writerow method is used to write individual rows to the CSV files. For full_w, it writes detailed information about each service operation, including whether it is implemented. For aggregated_w, it writes aggregated statistics for each service, such as the count of implemented operations and the percentage of implementation.

csv.DictReader *usage*:

1. *Opening a file for reading*:

- The code opens a CSV file (output-notimplemented.csv) for reading.

2. *Creating a* DictReader *object*:

- csv.DictReader is used to create a reader object (reader) that reads the CSV file into dictionaries. Each row in the CSV file is interpreted as a dictionary with keys specified by the fieldnames parameter.

3. *Reading rows*:

- The code iterates over each row in the CSV file using a for loop. Each row is processed and stored in the aggregate dictionary. The loop checks if the "implemented" field is set to "implemented" and skips such rows. For other rows, it organizes the data by service and operation.

CSV Dialects and Sniffer

CSV dialects are variants of the CSV format that define specific formatting parameters such as the delimiter, quote character, and line terminator. The csv module supports different CSV dialects, which are predefined sets of these parameters. The module comes with a few built-in dialects, and we can also define our own custom dialects using the csv.register_dialect function. This flexibility allows us to handle various CSV formats without manually specifying all the parameters each time.

The csv.Sniffer class is used to automatically detect the format of a CSV file. It can deduce the delimiter, quote character, and other formatting details by examining a sample of the file. The Sniffer class also provides a method to determine if a given file has a header row. This can be particularly useful when dealing with CSV files of unknown or inconsistent formats, as it allows us to programmatically adapt to different CSV structures.

The below snippet shows the usage of Sniffer to detect a CSV dialect:

```python
# File: pandas/io/parsers/python_parser.py

class PythonParser(ParserBase):
    def _make_reader(self, f: IO[str] | ReadCsvBuffer[str]) ->
Iterator[list[str]]:
        sep = self.delimiter

        if sep is None or len(sep) == 1:
            if self.lineterminator:
                raise ValueError(
                    "Custom line terminators not supported in python
                    parser (yet)"
                )

            class MyDialect(csv.Dialect):
                delimiter = self.delimiter
                quotechar = self.quotechar
                escapechar = self.escapechar
                doublequote = self.doublequote
                skipinitialspace = self.skipinitialspace
                quoting = self.quoting
                lineterminator = "\n"

            dia = MyDialect

            if sep is not None:
                dia.delimiter = sep
```

```python
    else:
        # attempt to sniff the delimiter from the first valid line,
        # i.e. no comment line and not in skiprows
        line = f.readline()
        lines = self._check_comments([[line]])[0]
        while self.skipfunc(self.pos) or not lines:
            self.pos += 1
            line = f.readline()
            lines = self._check_comments([[line]])[0]
        lines_str = cast(list[str], lines)

        # since `line` was a string, lines will be a list containing
        # only a single string
        line = lines_str[0]

    self.pos += 1
    self.line_pos += 1
    sniffed = csv.Sniffer().sniff(line)
    dia.delimiter = sniffed.delimiter

    # Note: encoding is irrelevant here
    line_rdr = csv.reader(StringIO(line), dialect=dia)
    self.buf.extend(list(line_rdr))
```

In the snippet, if the delimiter (sep) is not provided (sep is None), the code attempts to determine the delimiter by reading the first valid line of the file. The code reads the first line of the file that is not a comment and not in the rows to be skipped.

The csv.Sniffer().sniff(line) method is called on this line. The sniff method analyzes the line and returns a csv.Dialect object that contains the detected delimiter.

The Sniffer class can also be used to detect the presence of a header row in a CSV file:

```python
# File: airflow/providers/google/marketing_platform/operators/analytics.py

class GoogleAnalyticsModifyFileHeadersDataImportOperator(BaseOperator):
    def _modify_column_headers(
        self, tmp_file_location: str, custom_dimension_header_mapping:
        dict[str, str]
```

```
) -> None:
    # Check headers
    self.log.info("Checking if file contains headers")
    with open(tmp_file_location) as check_header_file:
        has_header = csv.Sniffer().has_header(check_header_file.
        read(1024))
        if not has_header:
            raise NameError(
                "CSV does not contain headers, please add them "
                "to use the modify column headers functionality"
            )
    ...
```

In this code, the csv.Sniffer().has_header(check_header_file.read(1024))
method is called to read the first 1,024 bytes of the file and determine if the file has
a header row. The has_header method returns True if it detects a header and False
otherwise. If the file does not contain headers (has_header is False), the method raises
a NameError with a message indicating that headers are required for the functionality
to work.

XML

Python provides several built-in modules for working with XML data, each offering
different levels of abstraction and functionality for parsing, creating, and manipulating
XML documents.

xml.etree.ElementTree (etree)

xml.etree.ElementTree (often referred to as etree) is a lightweight and efficient
module for parsing and creating XML data. The module represents XML documents as a
tree structure, which is intuitive for many XML-related tasks. It is designed to be easy to
use and efficient in both memory usage and performance.

xml.dom

The `xml.dom` module provides a Document Object Model (DOM) API for working with XML data. The DOM API represents an XML document as a tree of nodes, allowing for detailed and fine-grained manipulation of the document's structure and content. This module is more complex and powerful than `etree`, offering greater control over the XML document but at the cost of increased complexity and memory usage.

xml.sax

The `xml.sax` module provides a Simple API for XML (SAX) for parsing XML documents. SAX is an event-driven, stream-based API that reads XML documents sequentially and triggers events (such as the start and end of elements) as it encounters them. This approach is highly efficient for processing large XML files, as it does not require loading the entire document into memory. However, it can be more challenging to use compared with tree-based approaches like `etree` and `xml.dom`.

Parsing untrusted XML can pose significant security risks, including XML External Entity (XXE) attacks, which can lead to data breaches, denial of service, and other vulnerabilities. When dealing with XML data from untrusted sources, it is crucial to use secure parsing techniques to mitigate these risks. One effective way to enhance security is by using the `defusedxml` library, which provides a safer alternative to the standard XML libraries in Python. `defusedxml` disables potentially dangerous features and ensures that the XML parsing process is secure by default, protecting our application from common XML-related attacks.

In the coming section, we will explore the usage of the etree module for parsing XML.

The `etree` Module

The `xml.etree.ElementTree` module, often referred to as `etree`, is a part of Python's standard library that provides a lightweight and efficient way to parse, create, and manipulate XML data. It offers a simple and Pythonic API. The module represents XML documents as a tree structure, which is intuitive for many XML-related tasks.

Here is a basic example of how to use `xml.etree.ElementTree` to parse an XML string with two different types of tags and access their elements:

```python
import xml.etree.ElementTree as ET

xml_data = """
<root>
  <child name="child1">Text1</child>
  <child name="child2">Text2</child>
  <sibling name="sibling1">Text3</sibling>
  <sibling name="sibling2">Text4</sibling>
</root>
"""

# Parse the XML data
root = ET.fromstring(xml_data)

for element in root:
    print(f"Tag: {element.tag}, Attribute: {element.attrib}, Text:
    {element.text}")

"""Output:
Tag: child, Attribute: {'name': 'child1'}, Text: Text1
Tag: child, Attribute: {'name': 'child2'}, Text: Text2
Tag: sibling, Attribute: {'name': 'sibling1'}, Text: Text3
Tag: sibling, Attribute: {'name': 'sibling2'}, Text: Text4
"""
```

In this example, we parse a simple XML string that includes two different types of tags: `<child>` and `<sibling>`. We then iterate over all elements in the root, printing their tags, attributes, and text content.

The below open source examples illustrate the usage of the etree module to work with XML:

```python
# File: servo/etc/patch-trace-template.py

...

plist = ElementTree.ElementTree(ElementTree.fromstring(xml))
```

583

```
elems = iter(plist.findall("./dict/*"))
for elem in elems:
    if elem.tag != "key" or elem.text != "$objects":
        continue
    array = elems.next()
    break

elems = iter(array.findall("./*"))
for elem in elems:
    if elem.tag != "string" or elem.text != "kdebugIntervalRule":
        continue
    dictionary = elems.next()
    break

elems = iter(dictionary.findall("./*"))
for elem in elems:
    if elem.tag != "key" or elem.text != "NS.objects":
        continue
    objects_array = elems.next()
    break

child_count = sum(1 for _ in iter(array.findall("./*")))

...
```

In the provided code snippet, the ElementTree module from Python's xml.etree package is used to parse and manipulate an XML document. The snippet uses the below element tree methods:

1. ElementTree.fromstring(xml):

   Parses an XML string and returns the root element of the parsed XML tree.

2. ElementTree.ElementTree:

   Creates an ElementTree object from the root element, allowing for further manipulation and traversal of the XML tree.

3. findall(xpath):

   Finds all elements that match the specified XPath expression. It returns a list of matching elements.

4. iter:

   Creates an iterator over a sequence (in this case, the list of elements returned by findall).

These are used in the code as below:

- The ElementTree.fromstring(xml) method parses the XML string and returns the root element of the parsed XML tree.

- ElementTree.ElementTree is then used to create an ElementTree object from the root element.

- The findall method is used to find all elements that match the specified XPath expression. In this case, it finds all child elements of the <dict> element.

- The iter function is used to create an iterator over the found elements.

- The code iterates over the elements and performs conditional checks based on the tag and text of each element. If a specific condition is met, it proceeds to the next element using the iterator.

The below snippet from the pattern library showcases the usage of the etree module for writing XML files:

```python
# File: pattern/graph/__init__.py

class GraphMLRenderer(GraphRenderer):

    ...

    def export(self, path, directed=False, encoding="utf-8"):
        """ Generates a GraphML XML file at the given path.
        """

        import xml.etree.ElementTree as etree
        ns = "{http://graphml.graphdrawing.org/xmlns}"
        etree.register_namespace("", ns.strip("{}"))
```

```
# Define type for node labels (string).
# Define type for node edges (float).
root = etree.Element(ns + "graphml")
root.insert(0, etree.Element(ns + "key", **{
    "id": "node_label", "for": "node", "attr.name": "label", "attr.
    type": "string"
}))
root.insert(0, etree.Element(ns + "key", **{
    "id": "edge_weight", "for": "edge", "attr.name": "weight",
    "attr.type": "double"
}))
# Map Node.id => GraphML node id.
m = {}
g = etree.SubElement(root, ns + "graph", id="g",
edgedefault=directed and "directed" or "undirected")
# Export nodes.
for i, n in enumerate(self.graph.nodes):
    m[n.id] = "node%s" % i
    x = etree.SubElement(g, ns + "node", id=m[n.id])
    x = etree.SubElement(x, ns + "data", key="node_label")
    if n.text and n.text.string != n.id:
        x.text = n.text.string
# Export edges.
for i, e in enumerate(self.graph.edges):
    x = etree.SubElement(g, ns + "edge", id="edge%s" % i,
    source=m[e.node1.id], target=m[e.node2.id])
    x = etree.SubElement(x, ns + "data", key="edge_weight")
    x.text = "%.3f" % e.weight
# Export graph with pretty indented XML.
# http://effbot.org/zone/element-lib.htm#prettyprint

...
tree = etree.ElementTree(root)
tree.write(path, encoding=encoding)
```

The below element tree methods and functionalities are used in the snippet:

1. `ElementTree.Element(tag, attrib={}, **extra)`:
   Creates a new element with the specified tag and attributes

2. `ElementTree.SubElement(parent, tag, attrib={}, **extra)`:
   Creates a new element as a child of the specified parent element

3. `ElementTree.ElementTree(element)`:
   Creates an `ElementTree` object from the specified element

4. `ElementTree.ElementTree.write(file, encoding="us-ascii", xml_declaration=None, default_namespace=None, method="xml")`:

   Writes the element tree to a file, with options for encoding, XML declaration, and method

5. `Element.insert(index, subelement)`:

   Inserts a subelement at the specified position in the parent element

6. `Element.text`:

   Sets or gets the text content of an element

In the provided code snippet, the `xml.etree.ElementTree` module is used to generate a GraphML XML file. The process begins by importing the module and registering the GraphML namespace to ensure proper XML formatting. The root element `<graphml>` is created, and key elements defining node labels and edge weights are inserted. A `<graph>` element is then added as a child of the root, with attributes indicating whether the graph is directed or undirected. The code iterates over the nodes and edges of the graph, creating corresponding `<node>` and `<edge>` elements and adding `<data>` elements to store node labels and edge weights. Finally, the constructed XML tree is written to a file using the `ElementTree.write` method, completing the export process.

Conclusion

Data serialization and persistence are crucial aspects of modern software development, enabling the storage and retrieval of complex data structures. Throughout this chapter, we explored various serialization formats such as JSON, pickle, shelve, marshal, XML, and CSV. Each of these formats has its own strengths and weaknesses, making them suitable for different use cases. However, it is important to exercise caution when parsing untrusted data with any of these modules, as they can pose security risks if not handled properly.

Beyond the discussed serialization formats, Python also offers robust file-handling capabilities and built-in support for SQLite, providing a lightweight and efficient solution for data persistence. Additionally, the dbm family of modules offers a simple interface for key–value storage, similar to GNU DBM. For those seeking alternative formats, external libraries such as PyYAML can be used to work with YAML, offering more flexibility and human-readable data serialization.

CHAPTER 18

Context Managers and Contextlib

In the previous chapter, we explored how to serialize and persist data using formats like JSON, pickle, and other built-in tools—essential when data needs to outlive the program or move between systems.

Now, we shift our focus to context managers—an essential feature in Python for managing resources like files, network connections, and locks in a clean and reliable way. Context managers simplify the process of setting up and tearing down resources by handling these steps automatically. They're most often used with the `with` statement, which ensures that cleanup code runs whether an operation completes successfully or raises an exception. For instance, when we open a file using `with`, Python guarantees that the file is closed properly, even if something goes wrong.

Python's `contextlib` module offers powerful utilities for building and customizing context managers, enabling us to write cleaner and more maintainable code. In this chapter, we'll explore how context managers work, how to create our own, and how `contextlib` helps us use this pattern more effectively.

Context Managers in the Standard Library

In addition to the `contextlib` module, Python comes with several built-in context managers that we can use. Let's take a look at some of the most common ones.

File Handling

When working with files, we want to ensure that they are closed properly after their use to prevent potential file corruption or memory leaks. Python's built-in `open()` function returns a context manager that does this automatically:

© Adarsh Divakaran 2025
A. Divakaran, *Deep Dive Python*, https://doi.org/10.1007/979-8-8688-1261-3_18

```python
with open('my_file.txt', 'w') as f:
    f.write('Hello, world!')
# The file is automatically closed outside the 'with' block
```

Locks for Thread Safety

In multithreaded programs, locks help prevent race conditions when multiple threads access shared resources. Python's threading module provides a Lock class with a context manager interface:

```python
import threading

lock = threading.Lock()

with lock:
    # Access and modify shared resources safely
    # ...
# The lock is automatically released outside the 'with' block
```

Managing Thread Pools

Thread pools are useful for executing tasks concurrently. Python's concurrent.futures module provides a ThreadPoolExecutor that can be used with a context manager:

```python
from concurrent.futures import ThreadPoolExecutor

with ThreadPoolExecutor(max_workers=4) as executor:
    # Submit tasks to the thread pool
    future = executor.submit(some_function, argument)
    # ...
# The thread pool is automatically shut down outside the 'with' block
```

SQLite Database Connection Management

When interacting with databases, we need to establish a connection, perform operations, and then close the connection to release resources. The sqlite3 module allows us to manage database connections using the connect() function, which returns a context manager:

```python
import sqlite3

with sqlite3.connect('my_database.db') as conn:
    # Perform database operations using the connection object
    cursor = conn.cursor()
    cursor.execute("SELECT * FROM tablename")
    results = cursor.fetchall()
# The database connection is automatically closed outside the 'with' block
```

Defining Custom Context Managers Using Dunders

To create a context manager, we need to define a class with two dunder methods: __enter__ and __exit__.

- __enter__(self): This method is called when the execution flow enters the context of the with statement. It typically acquires the resource and returns it.

- __exit__(self, exc_type, exc_value, traceback): This method is called when the execution flow exits the context of the with statement. It handles the cleanup, such as releasing the resource. It also receives information about any exceptions that occurred within the context (through the arguments).

The below code from the *youtube-dl* library shows the definition of the locked_file context manager class:

```python
# File: youtube_dl/utils.py

class locked_file(object):
    def __init__(self, filename, mode, encoding=None):
        assert mode in ['r', 'a', 'w']
        self.f = io.open(filename, mode, encoding=encoding)
        self.mode = mode

    def __enter__(self):
        exclusive = self.mode != 'r'
        try:
            _lock_file(self.f, exclusive)
```

```python
        except IOError:
            self.f.close()
            raise
        return self

    def __exit__(self, etype, value, traceback):
        try:
            _unlock_file(self.f)
        finally:
            self.f.close()

    def __iter__(self):
        return iter(self.f)

    def write(self, *args):
        return self.f.write(*args)

    def read(self, *args):
        return self.f.read(*args)
```

The __init__ method opens a file with the given filename, mode, and encoding. The mode must be 'r', 'a', or 'w' (read, append, or write). The opened file is stored in self.f. The __enter__ method is called when entering the context (the block of code after the "with" statement). It tries to lock the file for exclusive access if the mode is not 'r' (read). If an IOError occurs (e.g., if the file cannot be locked), it closes the file and re-raises the exception. The __exit__ method is called when exiting the context. It tries to unlock the file and then closes it, regardless of whether unlocking was successful or not.

This context manager can be used similarly to the built-in open(), which is used normally for opening files.

```python
with locked_file('example.txt', 'w') as f:
    f.write('Hello, world!')
```

Context Manager Base Classes

The contextlib module comes with abstract context manager base classes—AbstractContextManager and AbstractAsyncContextManager.

AbstractContextManager is the abstract base class for classes that implement object.__enter__() and object.__exit__(). The default implementation for __enter__() returns self, while __exit__() by default returns None. AbstractAsyncContextManager is for classes that implement object.__aenter__() and object.__aexit__() with similar defaults.

The below example from *PyMongo* defines a context manager for managing timeouts by implementing the AbstractContextManager base class:

```python
# File: pymongo/_csot.py

from contextlib import AbstractContextManager
from contextvars import ContextVar, Token

TIMEOUT: ContextVar[Optional[float]] = ContextVar("TIMEOUT", default=None)
RTT: ContextVar[float] = ContextVar("RTT", default=0.0)
DEADLINE: ContextVar[float] = ContextVar("DEADLINE", default=float("inf"))

...

class _TimeoutContext(AbstractContextManager):
    """Internal timeout context manager.

    Use :func:`pymongo.timeout` instead::

      with pymongo.timeout(0.5):
          client.test.test.insert_one({})
    """

    def __init__(self, timeout: Optional[float]):
        self._timeout = timeout
        self._tokens: Optional[
            tuple[Token[Optional[float]], Token[float], Token[float]]
        ] = None

    def __enter__(self) -> _TimeoutContext:
        timeout_token = TIMEOUT.set(self._timeout)
        prev_deadline = DEADLINE.get()
        next_deadline = (
            time.monotonic() + self._timeout if self._timeout else
            float("inf")
        )
```

```
        deadline_token = DEADLINE.set(min(prev_deadline, next_deadline))
        rtt_token = RTT.set(0.0)
        self._tokens = (timeout_token, deadline_token, rtt_token)
        return self

    def __exit__(self, exc_type: Any, exc_val: Any, exc_tb: Any) -> None:
        if self._tokens:
            timeout_token, deadline_token, rtt_token = self._tokens
            TIMEOUT.reset(timeout_token)
            DEADLINE.reset(deadline_token)
            RTT.reset(rtt_token)
```

In this code, the _TimeoutContext class is used to manage timeout settings for a block of code. When the "with" statement is used with an instance of this class, it sets up certain timeout settings before the block of code is run and then ensures those settings are properly cleaned up after the block of code is finished, whether it finishes normally or with an error.

AbstractAsyncContextManager

The below snippet from *CPython* showcases the definition of aclosing, a context manager defined from the AbstractAsyncContextManager base class:

```
# File: cpython/Lib/contextlib.py

class aclosing(AbstractAsyncContextManager):
    """Async context manager for safely finalizing an asynchronously
    cleaned-up resource such as an async generator, calling its
    ``aclose()`` method.

    Code like this:

        async with aclosing(<module>.fetch(<arguments>)) as agen:
            <block>

    is equivalent to this:

        agen = <module>.fetch(<arguments>)
```

```
    try:
        <block>
    finally:
        await agen.aclose()
"""
    def __init__(self, thing):
        self.thing = thing
    async def __aenter__(self):
        return self.thing
    async def __aexit__(self, *exc_info):
        await self.thing.aclose()
```

The aclosing context manager upon exit automatically calls the aclose method of the object supplied to the context manager init.

Decorators for Defining a Context Manager

@contextmanager

The @contextmanager decorator from the contextlib module provides us with an easy way to create context managers without having to write a custom class with __enter__ and __exit__ methods. It lets us create a context manager using a simple generator function (with yield). The code before the yield runs in the setup phase, the yield is where the code defined in the with block runs, and the code after yield runs as the cleanup.

The code snippet from the *transformers* library defines a context manager using the decorator:

```
# File: transformers/benchmark/benchmark.py

from contextlib import contextmanager

@contextmanager
def checkout_commit(repo: Repo, commit_id: str):
    """
    Context manager that checks out a given commit when entered, but gets
    back to the reference it was at on exit.
```

```
Args:
    repo (`git.Repo`): A git repository (for instance the
    Transformers repo).
    commit_id (`str`): The commit reference to checkout inside the
    context manager.
"""
current_head = repo.head.commit if repo.head.is_detached else repo.
head.ref

try:
    repo.git.checkout(commit_id)
    yield

finally:
    repo.git.checkout(current_head)
```

The checkout_commit function takes two arguments: repo and commit_id. commit_id is the commit reference to check out. The function first saves the current head of the repository. If the head is detached, it saves the commit; otherwise, it saves the reference.

Then, it tries to check out the commit specified by commit_id. This is done within a try-finally block to ensure that the original head is checked out again, even if an error occurs. The yield statement yields the control of execution to the code inside the with block.

The finally block gets called when the code from the with block exits, ensuring that the repository is returned to its original state by checking out the original head.

The checkout_commit context manager defined can be used as follows:

```
with checkout_commit(repo, "abc123"):
    # Do something with the repo at commit abc123
    pass
# After this block, the repo is back to its original state
```

@asynccontextmanager

The asynccontextmanager is similar to the contextmanager decorator, with the only difference being it is used with asynchronous context managers (used in async with statements).

The code below from *Ruff* shows an asynchronous context manager:

```python
# File: ruff/scripts/check_ecosystem.py

class Repository(NamedTuple):
    """A GitHub repository at a specific ref."""

    org: str
    repo: str
    ref: str | None
    select: str = ""
    ignore: str = ""
    exclude: str = ""
    # Generating fixes is slow and verbose
    show_fixes: bool = False

    @asynccontextmanager
    async def clone(self: Self, checkout_dir: Path) -> AsyncIterator[Path]:
        """Shallow clone this repository to a temporary directory."""
        if checkout_dir.exists():
            logger.debug(f"Reusing {self.org}:{self.repo}")
            yield await self._get_commit(checkout_dir)
            return

        logger.debug(f"Cloning {self.org}:{self.repo}")
        git_clone_command = [
            "git",
            "clone",
            "--config",
            "advice.detachedHead=false",
            "--quiet",
            "--depth",
            "1",
            "--no-tags",
        ]
```

```
        if self.ref:
            git_clone_command.extend(["--branch", self.ref])

        git_clone_command.extend(
            [
                f"https://github.com/{self.org}/{self.repo}",
                checkout_dir,
            ],
        )

        git_clone_process = await create_subprocess_exec(
            *git_clone_command,
            env={"GIT_TERMINAL_PROMPT": "0"},
        )

        status_code = await git_clone_process.wait()

        logger.debug(
            f"Finished cloning {self.org}/{self.repo} with status "
            {status_code}",
        )
        yield await self._get_commit(checkout_dir)
```

The method clone is defined as an asynchronous context manager. This method is used to clone the repository to a temporary directory. If the directory already exists, it reuses the repository. If not, it clones the repository from GitHub using a subprocess to execute the git clone command. The method is asynchronous; it's designed to handle tasks that can run concurrently in an asyncio context.

The below code is an example usage of the context manager:

```
repo = Repository(org="octocat", repo="Hello-World", ref="master")
checkout_dir = Path("/path/to/checkout_dir")

# Use the clone context manager to clone the repository
async with repo.clone(checkout_dir) as cloned_repo:
    # Do something with the cloned repository
    print(f"Cloned repository: {cloned_repo}")
```

Context Manager as a Decorator

By combining the functionality of context managers and decorators, we can apply the same resource management logic to multiple functions or methods with minimal boilerplate. The ContextDecorator base class from contextlib helps us with the same and allows us to define context managers that can be used as decorators.

The snippet below from *Django* shows a class defined by inheriting from the ContextDecorator class:

```python
# File: django/utils/timezone.py

class override(ContextDecorator):
    """
    Temporarily set the time zone for the current thread.

    This is a context manager that uses django.utils.timezone.activate()
    to set the timezone on entry and restores the previously active
    timezone
    on exit.

    The ``timezone`` argument must be an instance of a ``tzinfo`` subclass,
    a time zone name, or ``None``. If it is ``None``, Django enables the
    default time zone.
    """

    def __init__(self, timezone):
        self.timezone = timezone

    def __enter__(self):
        self.old_timezone = getattr(_active, "value", None)
        if self.timezone is None:
            deactivate()
        else:
            activate(self.timezone)
```

```python
    def __exit__(self, exc_type, exc_value, traceback):
        if self.old_timezone is None:
            deactivate()
        else:
            _active.value = self.old_timezone
```

On using the above-defined `override` class as a decorator, when the function is entered, the `__enter__` method is called, which saves the current time zone and then activates the new one. When the function is exited, the `__exit__` method is called, which restores the old time zone. This is useful when we want to temporarily change the time zone for a specific block of code or function and then automatically have it changed back, no matter how the block or function is exited.

The `override` class defined here can be used as a decorator as well as a context manager, like in the sample snippet below:

```python
# Context manager usage
with override('timezone'):
    # Code here
```

```python
# Decorator usage
@override('timezone')
def my_function():
    # Function code here
```

contextlib.ExitStack()

`ExitStack` is a context manager that allows us to enter and exit multiple context managers in a flexible and dynamic way. Imagine we have several resources to manage, like files, network connections, or locks, and want to handle them all within a single `with` statement. `ExitStack` makes this possible by letting us stack multiple context managers and ensuring they are all properly cleaned up, even if an error occurs.

It allows you to add context managers to the stack at runtime, which is particularly useful when the number of resources you need to manage isn't known until runtime. The below snippet showcases a sample use case where two context managers, `cm1` and `cm2`, are to be entered:

```python
from contextlib import ExitStack

# A demo context manager
class SimpleContextManager:
    def __init__(self, name):
        self.name = name

    def __enter__(self):
        print(f"Entering context: {self.name}")
        return self

    def __exit__(self, exc_type, exc_value, traceback):
        print(f"Exiting context: {self.name}")

# Using ExitStack to manage multiple context managers
with ExitStack() as stack:
    # Enter the first context manager and add it to the stack
    cm1 = stack.enter_context(SimpleContextManager('cm1'))

    # Enter the second context manager and add it to the stack
    cm2 = stack.enter_context(SimpleContextManager('cm2'))

    # Both context managers are now active
    print("Both context managers are active")

# Exiting the with block triggers the __exit__ methods of both context
# managers
```

The below snippet from *Posthog* showcases a real-world example:

```python
# File: posthog/models/person/util.py

def bulk_create_persons(persons_list: list[dict]):
    persons = []
    person_mapping = {}
    for _person in persons_list:
        with ExitStack() as stack:
            if _person.get("created_at"):
                stack.enter_context(freeze_time(_person["created_at"]))
            persons.append(Person(**{key: value for key, value in _person.
            items() if key != "distinct_ids"}))
```

601

```python
    inserted = Person.objects.bulk_create(persons)

    person_inserts = []
    distinct_ids = []
    distinct_id_inserts = []
    for index, person in enumerate(inserted):
        for distinct_id in persons_list[index]["distinct_ids"]:
            distinct_ids.append(
                PersonDistinctId(
                    person_id=person.pk,
                    distinct_id=distinct_id,
                    team_id=person.team_id,
                )
            )
            distinct_id_inserts.append(f"('{distinct_id}', '{person.uuid}',
            {person.team_id}, 0, 0, now(), 0, 0)")
            person_mapping[distinct_id] = person

        created_at = now().strftime("%Y-%m-%d %H:%M:%S.%f")
        timestamp = now().strftime("%Y-%m-%d %H:%M:%S")
        person_inserts.append(
            f"('{person.uuid}', '{created_at}', {person.team_id}, '{json.
            dumps(person.properties)}', {'1' if person.is_identified else
            '0'}, '{timestamp}', 0, 0, 0)"
        )

PersonDistinctId.objects.bulk_create(distinct_ids)
sync_execute(INSERT_PERSON_BULK_SQL + ", ".join(person_inserts),
flush=False)
sync_execute(
    BULK_INSERT_PERSON_DISTINCT_ID2 + ", ".join(distinct_id_inserts),
    flush=False,
)

return person_mapping
```

In the bulk_create_persons function, the ExitStack is used to manage the context of freezing time for each person being created if the created_at field is present in the person's data. The freeze_time context manager from the freezegun library is used to mock the current time. This is useful for testing or for ensuring that the created_at timestamp is consistent with the provided data.

If the _person dictionary contains a created_at key, freeze_time is used to set the current time to the value of _person["created_at"]. By using ExitStack, the code dynamically enters the freeze_time context only if the created_at field is present. This avoids the need for nested with statements or complex conditional logic. The stack. enter_context(freeze_time(_person["created_at"])) line ensures that the time is frozen for the duration of the context managed by ExitStack. Once the block is exited, the time is automatically unfrozen, ensuring that the time manipulation does not affect other parts of the code.

AsyncExitStack

AsyncExitStack is the asynchronous counterpart to ExitStack. It provides the same functionality but is designed for use with asynchronous context managers.

The below snippet from *reflex* exemplifies its usage:

```python
# File: reflex/app_mixins/lifespan.py

class LifespanMixin(AppMixin):
    """A Mixin that allow tasks to run during the whole app lifespan."""

    # Lifespan tasks that are planned to run.
    lifespan_tasks: Set[Union[asyncio.Task, Callable]] = set()

    @contextlib.asynccontextmanager
    async def _run_lifespan_tasks(self, app: FastAPI):
        running_tasks = []
        try:
            async with contextlib.AsyncExitStack() as stack:
                for task in self.lifespan_tasks:
                    if isinstance(task, asyncio.Task):
                        running_tasks.append(task)
```

```
        else:
            signature = inspect.signature(task)
            if "app" in signature.parameters:
                task = functools.partial(task, app=app)
            _t = task()
            if isinstance(_t, contextlib._
            AsyncGeneratorContextManager):
                await stack.enter_async_context(_t)
            elif isinstance(_t, Coroutine):
                running_tasks.append(asyncio.create_task(_t))
        yield
finally:
    cancel_kwargs = (
        {"msg": "lifespan_cleanup"} if sys.version_info >= (3,
        9) else {}
    )
    for task in running_tasks:
        task.cancel(**cancel_kwargs)
```

In the provided code, AsyncExitStack is used to manage the lifespan tasks of a FastAPI application. These tasks are either asyncio.Task instances or callables that return a coroutine or an asynchronous context manager.

Here's a breakdown of the code:

1. The AsyncExitStack is entered using the async with statement. This sets up the context for managing the lifespan tasks.

2. Each task in self.lifespan_tasks is checked. If it's an asyncio. Task, it's added to the running_tasks list.

3. If the task is a callable, it's checked whether it requires the app parameter. If it does, the app is bound to the task using functools.partial.

4. The callable task is then called. If it returns an asynchronous context manager, it's entered using stack.enter_async_context. If it returns a coroutine, a new asyncio.Task is created and added to the running_tasks list.

5. After all tasks have been started, control is yielded back to the caller. This allows the caller to run code while the lifespan tasks are running.

6. When the control flow leaves the context (either normally or due to an exception), the `finally` block is executed. This cancels all running tasks.

Built-In Context Managers from `contextlib.suppress`

The `contextlib.suppress` context manager allows us to temporarily ignore specific exceptions. This can be useful in cases where we know an exception might occur and we do not want the occurrence to interrupt the program execution.

Below is a snippet illustrating its usage:

```python
# File: yt_dlp/cache.py

class Cache:
    ...

    def load(self, section, key, dtype="json", default=None, *, min_
    ver=None):
        assert dtype in ("json",)

        if not self.enabled:
            return default

        cache_fn = self._get_cache_fn(section, key, dtype)
        with contextlib.suppress(OSError):
            try:
                with open(cache_fn, encoding="utf-8") as cachef:
                    self._ydl.write_debug(f"Loading {section}.{key}
                    from cache")
                    return self._validate(json.load(cachef), min_ver)
```

```
        except (ValueError, KeyError):
            try:
                file_size = os.path.getsize(cache_fn)
            except OSError as oe:
                file_size = str(oe)
            self._ydl.report_warning(
                f"Cache retrieval from {cache_fn} failed ({file_size})"
            )
    return default
```

In the code, `contextlib.suppress(OSError)` is used to ignore `OSError` exceptions that might occur when trying to open the cache file with `open(cache_fn, encoding="utf-8")`. If an `OSError` occurs (e.g., if the file does not exist), the code will not crash, but instead, it will continue to the `return default` line.

closing

The `closing` context manager ensures that an object's `close()` method is called when we are done with it, even if an exception occurs.

The below snippet from *Rust* bootstrapping code illustrates the usage of `closing`:

```
# File: rust/src/bootstrap/bootstrap.py

def unpack(tarball, tarball_suffix, dst, verbose=False, match=None):
    """Unpack the given tarball file"""
    eprint("extracting", tarball)
    fname = os.path.basename(tarball).replace(tarball_suffix, "")
    with contextlib.closing(tarfile.open(tarball)) as tar:
        for member in tar.getnames():
            if "/" not in member:
                continue
            name = member.replace(fname + "/", "", 1)
            if match is not None and not name.startswith(match):
                continue
            name = name[len(match) + 1:]

            dst_path = os.path.join(dst, name)
```

```
    if verbose:
        eprint("  extracting", member)
    tar.extract(member, dst)
    src_path = os.path.join(dst, member)
    if os.path.isdir(src_path) and os.path.exists(dst_path):
        continue
    shutil.move(src_path, dst_path)
shutil.rmtree(os.path.join(dst, fname))
```

Here, `tarfile.open(tarball)` opens the tarball file. Wrapping this statement with `contextlib.closing()` ensures that the file is closed automatically when the processing is done, even if exceptions occur within the `with` block.

redirect_stdout

The `redirect_stdout` context manager allows us to temporarily redirect the standard output (stdout) to a file-like object. This is useful for capturing output or redirecting it to a different stream.

The snippet below from *Perfetto* uses `redirect_stdout` to write to a file:

```
# File: perfetto/tools/extract_linux_syscall_tables

def Main():
    KSRC = "https://raw.githubusercontent.com/torvalds/linux/v6.7/"

    response = urlopen(KSRC + "arch/x86/entry/syscalls/syscall_64.tbl")
    syscalls["x86_64"] = parse_tlb(response.read().decode())

    ...

    dst_file = os.path.join(
        PROJECT_ROOT, "src", "kernel_utils", "syscall_table_generated.h"
    )
    tmp_file = dst_file + ".tmp"

    print("Writing ", dst_file)
    with open(tmp_file, "w") as f:
        with contextlib.redirect_stdout(f):
            print_tables()
```

```
    os.rename(tmp_file, dst_file)

    print("Running clang-format (might fail if depot_tools isn't in
    the PATH)")
    os.system("clang-format -i " + dst_file)

if __name__ == "__main__":
    sys.exit(Main())
```

The above script is used to extract Linux system call tables from the Linux kernel source code and write them to a file. The contextlib.redirect_stdout context manager is used here to redirect the output of print_tables to the file.

Similar to redirect_stdout, contextlib also has contextlib.redirect_stderr, which can be used to redirect the standard error stream.

Use Cases

Context managers are used when reusable setup or cleanup operations are required before working with certain code snippets. We will explore a couple of common context manager use cases in this section.

Timer

Context managers can be defined to track the execution time of code. This can be useful in debugging to track the execution time of a group of statements.

The below snippet from *opencv* shows a timer context manager:

```
# File: opencv/samples/python/common.py

@contextmanager
def Timer(msg):
    print(msg, '...',)
    start = clock()
    try:
        yield
    finally:
        print("%.2f ms" % ((clock()-start)*1000))
```

Patching

Context managers can be used to patch the environment during its execution context. This can be used in testing scenarios or use cases where a temporary modification of behavior is required.

Given below is an example of such a usage from *spacy*:

```
# File: spacy/util.py

@contextmanager
def working_dir(path: Union[str, Path]) -> Iterator[Path]:
    """Change current working directory and returns to previous on exit.
    path (str / Path): The directory to navigate to.
    YIELDS (Path): The absolute path to the current working directory. This
        should be used if the block needs to perform actions within
        the working directory, to prevent mismatches with relative paths.
    """
    prev_cwd = Path.cwd()
    current = Path(path).resolve()
    os.chdir(str(current))
    try:
        yield current
    finally:
        os.chdir(str(prev_cwd))
```

The context manager is used to change the working directory during the execution context of the working_dir context manager.

The below snippet from *Airflow* defines a context manager that patches the environment variables and switches it back when the context block exits:

```
# File: airflow/utils/process_utils.py

@contextmanager
def patch_environ(new_env_variables: dict[str, str]) -> Generator[None,
None, None]:
    """
    Set environment variables in context.
```

After leaving the context, it restores its original state.
:param new_env_variables: Environment variables to set
"""

current_env_state = {key: os.environ.get(key) **for** key **in** new_env_
variables}
os.environ.update(new_env_variables)
try:
    yield
finally:
    for key, old_value **in** current_env_state.items():
        if old_value **is** None:
            if key **in** os.environ:
                del os.environ[key]
        else:
            os.environ[key] = old_value

Conclusion

In this chapter, we've taken a comprehensive journey through the contextlib module and the world of context managers in Python. We explored various built-in context managers like open for file handling and threading.Lock for synchronization, which help manage resources efficiently. We also delved into different methods for defining custom context managers, from the traditional class-based approach with __enter__ and __exit__ methods to the more concise @contextmanager decorator. We touched on advanced tools like ExitStack and AsyncExitStack for dynamic resource management and the ContextDecorator class, which allows context managers to be used as decorators, enhancing code modularity and reusability. Throughout this chapter, we've seen how context managers can simplify resource management, making our code cleaner, more readable, and more reliable by ensuring proper resource cleanup even in the face of errors.

## CHAPTER 19

Abstract Base Classes

In the previous chapter, we explored context managers and the `contextlib` module, learning how to manage resources like files and network connections efficiently using the `with` statement.

In this chapter, we dive into abstract base classes (ABCs)—a powerful tool in object-oriented programming that lets us define common interfaces for related classes. ABCs help enforce consistency by ensuring that all subclasses implement specific methods, making our codebase easier to maintain and reason about.

Python's abc module gives us everything we need to define abstract classes, including the ABC base class and decorators for declaring abstract methods. By using ABCs, we can define method signatures that must be implemented by concrete subclasses, and Python will enforce this contract at runtime. This becomes especially useful in larger projects where multiple classes are expected to follow the same structure or behavior.

Throughout this chapter, we'll see how to define and work with abstract base classes, understand where they fit in Python's class system, and explore real-world use cases where they shine.

abc.ABC and abc.ABCMeta

In the abc module, we have two primary ways to create abstract base classes: `abc.ABC` and `abc.ABCMeta`. While both serve the same purpose, they differ in how we use them to define our abstract base classes.

© Adarsh Divakaran 2025
A. Divakaran, *Deep Dive Python*, https://doi.org/10.1007/979-8-8688-1261-3_19

The `abc.ABC` Class

`abc.ABC` is a helper class that we can use to create an abstract base class simply by inheriting from it. This is the more modern and recommended approach, introduced in Python 3.4.

Here's a simple example:

```python
from abc import ABC, abstractmethod

class MyAbstractClass(ABC):
    @abstractmethod
    def my_abstract_method(self):
        pass
```

The `abc.ABCMeta` Metaclass

`abc.ABCMeta` is a metaclass that we can use to create an abstract base class. This approach was the original method and is still valid, though slightly more verbose:

```python
from abc import ABCMeta, abstractmethod

class MyAbstractClass(metaclass=ABCMeta):
    @abstractmethod
    def my_abstract_method(self):
        pass
```

The key difference between these two approaches lies in how we specify that our class is an abstract base class. With `abc.ABC`, we simply inherit from it. With `abc.ABCMeta`, we specify it as the metaclass. In practice, both approaches achieve the same result: they create an abstract base class that can't be instantiated directly and requires its concrete subclasses to implement all abstract methods.

The `abc.ABC` approach is generally preferred due to its simplicity and readability. It's a shortcut that internally uses `ABCMeta` as its metaclass, providing the same functionality with a cleaner syntax. However, `abc.ABCMeta` can still be useful in more complex scenarios, particularly when we're already dealing with custom metaclasses or need more control over the class creation process. Regardless of which method we choose, the behavior of our abstract base class remains the same. Both approaches will prevent the instantiation of the abstract class and ensure that concrete subclasses implement all abstract methods.

Below is a real-world example from the library *plumbum* using the metaclass approach:

```python
# File: plumbum/colorlib/styles.py

class Style(metaclass=ABCMeta):
    """This class allows the color changes to be called directly
    to write them to stdout, ``[]`` calls to wrap colors (or the
    ``.wrap`` method)
    and can be called in a with statement.
    """

    __slots__ = ("attributes", "fg", "bg", "isreset", "__weakref__")

    color_class = Color
    """The class of color to use. Never hardcode ``Color`` call when
    writing a Style
    method."""

    # These must be defined by subclasses
    # pylint: disable-next=declare-non-slot
    attribute_names: ClassVar[dict[str, str] | dict[str, int]]

    ...

    @abstractmethod
    def __str__(self):
        """Base Style does not implement a __str__ representation. This
        is the one
        required method of a subclass."""
```

For better efficiency, the class Style is defined as a slotted class. Using a metaclass instead of inheriting ensures that the slots of the class Style are not modified by the parent class. However, the current implementation of the ABC class (as of Python 3.13) is also slotted, and there won't be any significant impact if the inheritance method is used in this case to mark Style as an abstract base class.

ABC Method Decorators

The abc module provides decorators that we can use to define abstract methods in our abstract base classes. These decorators help us specify which methods must be implemented by concrete subclasses.

@abstractmethod Decorator

The @abstractmethod decorator is the most commonly used decorator in abstract base classes. It marks a method as abstract, meaning that any concrete subclass must implement this method.

Without implementing these abstract methods, the subclass cannot be instantiated, thereby maintaining consistency and integrity across different implementations.

```
from abc import ABC, abstractmethod

class Parent(ABC):

    @abstractmethod
    def say_hello(self):
        pass

class Child(Parent):

    def say_hi(self):
        print("Hi")

child_obj = Child()
```

When we try to instantiate a subclass that doesn't implement all abstract methods, Python will raise a TypeError. Running the above snippet will raise an error, as shown below:

```
Traceback (most recent call last):
  File ".../abstractmethod.py", line 15, in <module>
    child_obj = Child()
                ^^^^^^^

TypeError: Can't instantiate abstract class Child with abstract method
say_hello
```

The class Child is missing the implementation of the say_hello() abstract method, leading to the error. Note that errors will be raised only when we try to instantiate the child class.

The code works as expected when we implement all abstract methods:

```python
from abc import ABC, abstractmethod

class Parent(ABC):
    @abstractmethod
    def say_hello(self):
        pass

class Child(Parent):
    def say_hello(self):
        print("Hi")

child_obj = Child()
child_obj.say_hello()  # Outputs: Hi
```

The class Parent is abstract and can't be instantiated. If we try to create an instance for the class, a TypeError will be raised:

```python
parent_obj = Parent()
"""
Traceback (most recent call last):
  File ".../abstractmethod.py", line 18, in <module>
    parent_obj = Parent()
                 ^^^^^^^^
TypeError: Can't instantiate abstract class Parent with abstract method
say_hello
"""
```

The below snippet from the library *Serve*, which is used to optimize and scale PyTorch models in production, showcases the usage of @abstractmethod:

```python
# File: serve/benchmarks/utils/benchmarks.py

from abc import ABC, abstractmethod

class Benchmark(ABC):
```

```python
    def __init__(self, execution_params):
        self.execution_params = execution_params
        self.warm_up_lines = 0
        if is_workflow(self.execution_params["url"]):
            self.execution_params["inference_model_url"] = "wfpredict/
            benchmark"

    @abstractmethod
    def warm_up():
        raise NotImplementedError

    @abstractmethod
    def run():
        raise NotImplementedError

    ...
```

The benchmark class is an abstract base class with warm_up() and run() abstract methods. Below is a snippet from the library showing the LocustBenchmark class, which implements the abstract class:

```python
class LocustBenchmark(Benchmark):
    def __init__(self, execution_params):
        self.locust_benchmark_file = Path(__file__).parent / "locust_
        benchmark.py"
        super().__init__(execution_params)

    def warm_up(self):
        locust_cmd = (
            f"locust  -H {self.execution_params['inference_url']}
            --locustfile {self.locust_benchmark_file} "
            f"--headless --reset-stats -u {self.execution_
            params['concurrency']} -r {self.execution_
            params['concurrency']} -i {self.execution_
            params['requests']//10} "
            f"--input {self.execution_params['tmp_dir']}/benchmark/input
            --content-type  {self.execution_params['content_type']} "
            f"--model-url {self.execution_params['inference_model_url']} "
        )
```

```
click.secho("\n\nExecuting warm-up ...", fg="green")

execute(locust_cmd, wait=True)

self.warm_up_lines = sum(1 for _ in open(self.execution_
params["metric_log"]))

def run(self):
    locust_cmd = (
        f"locust  -H {self.execution_params['inference_url']}
        --locustfile {self.locust_benchmark_file} "
        f"--headless --reset-stats -u {self.execution_
        params['concurrency']} -r {self.execution_
        params['concurrency']} -i {self.execution_params['requests']} "
        f"--input {self.execution_params['tmp_dir']}/benchmark/input
        --content-type  {self.execution_params['content_type']} "
        f"--model-url {self.execution_params['inference_model_url']} "
        f"--json > {self.execution_params['result_file']}"
    )
    click.secho("\n\nExecuting inference performance tests ...",
    fg="green")

    execute(locust_cmd, wait=True)
```

We can see in the code that the LocustBenchmark class defines both the warm_up()
and run() abstract methods. The ABC Benchmark acts as a blueprint to define concrete
benchmark classes.

Decorating Class Methods

The @abstractclassmethod decorator was previously used to define abstract class
methods, combining the functionality of @classmethod and @abstractmethod. However,
this decorator has been deprecated since Python 3.3. In modern Python (3.3 and
later), the recommended approach is to use the @classmethod and @abstractmethod
decorators together. This combination achieves the same functionality as the deprecated
@abstractclassmethod decorator.

This combination is useful when we want to define an abstract method that operates on the class itself rather than on instances of the class. Concrete subclasses must implement this method as a class method. This usage will ensure that subclasses provide their own implementation of the class method, maintaining a consistent interface.

The below example from *causalml* shows the definition of an abstract class method:

```python
# File: causalml/inference/meta/base.py

from abc import ABCMeta, abstractmethod

class BaseLearner(metaclass=ABCMeta):
    @classmethod
    @abstractmethod
    def fit(self, X, treatment, y, p=None):
        pass

    @classmethod
    @abstractmethod
    def predict(
        self, X, treatment=None, y=None, p=None, return_components=False,
        verbose=True
    ):
        pass
```

The BaseLearner abstract class defines fit() and predict() as abstract class methods.

Note   The original implementation in the library uses the deprecated @abstractclassmethod decorator. This will still work as it is not removed from Python as of Python 3.13, but it is recommended to use the combination of @classmethod and @abstractmethod to prevent any future breakages.

The class is implemented by the BaseDRLearner class:

```python
# File: causalml/inference/meta/drlearner.py

class BaseDRLearner(BaseLearner):
    """A parent class for DR-learner regressor classes.
```

A DR-learner estimates treatment effects with machine learning models.

Details of DR-learner are available at `Kennedy (2020) <https://arxiv. org/abs/2004.14497>`_ .
    """

```python
def __init__(
    self,
    learner=None,
    control_outcome_learner=None,
    treatment_outcome_learner=None,
    treatment_effect_learner=None,
    ate_alpha=0.05,
    control_name=0,
):
    ...

def fit(self, X, treatment, y, p=None, seed=None):
    """Fit the inference model.
    """
    X, treatment, y = convert_pd_to_np(X, treatment, y)
    check_treatment_vector(treatment, self.control_name)
    self.t_groups = np.unique(treatment[treatment != self.
    control_name])
    self.t_groups.sort()
    self._classes = {group: i for i, group in enumerate(self.t_groups)}
    ...

def predict(
    self, X, treatment=None, y=None, p=None, return_components=False,
    verbose=True
):
    """Predict treatment effects.
    """
    X, treatment, y = convert_pd_to_np(X, treatment, y)
```

```
te = np.zeros((X.shape[0], self.t_groups.shape[0]))
yhat_cs = {}
yhat_ts = {}

for i, group in enumerate(self.t_groups):
    ...

if not return_components:
    return te
else:
    return te, yhat_cs, yhat_ts
```

We can see that the fit() and predict() methods are implemented by the BaseDRLearner concrete class.

Note that the implementation defines the methods fit() and predict() as normal instance methods and not class methods. Python does not enforce that the implementation in the subclass is also a class method. This means a subclass could implement the method as an instance method or class method, and Python would still consider the abstract method requirement fulfilled.

Decorating Static Methods

In modern Python (3.3 and later), the recommended approach to define abstract static methods is to use the @staticmethod and @abstractmethod decorators together. Similar to @abstractclassmethod, Python has the @abstractstaticmethod decorator to define abstract static methods, which has been deprecated since Python 3.3.

We use this decorator combination when we want to define an abstract static method. This is a method that doesn't have access to the class or instance but still must be implemented by concrete subclasses.

Below is an ABC example from the *ludwig* library, which is a low-code framework for building custom LLMs and AI models:

```
# File: ludwig/features/base_feature.py

from abc import ABC, abstractstaticmethod, abstractmethod

class BaseFeatureMixin(ABC):
    """Parent class for feature mixins.

    Feature mixins support preprocessing functionality shared across input
    and output features.
    """

    @staticmethod
    @abstractmethod
    def type() -> str:
        """Returns the type of feature this mixin supports."""
        raise NotImplementedError

    @staticmethod
    @abstractmethod
    def cast_column(column: DataFrame, backend) -> DataFrame:
        """Returns a copy of the dataset column for the given feature,
        potentially after a type cast.

        Args:
            column: Pandas column of values.
            backend: (Union[Backend, str]) Backend to use for feature data
            processing.
        """
        raise NotImplementedError

    ...
```

The type() and cast_column() are defined as abstract static methods.

This class is implemented by the BinaryFeatureMixin class:

 # File: ludwig/features/binary_feature.py

```python
class BinaryFeatureMixin(BaseFeatureMixin):
    @staticmethod
    def type():
        return BINARY

    @staticmethod
    def cast_column(column, backend):
        """Cast column of dtype object to bool.

        Unchecked casting to boolean when given a column of dtype object
        converts all non-empty cells to True. We check
        the values of the column directly and manually determine the best
        dtype to use.
        """
        values = backend.df_engine.compute(column.drop_duplicates())

        if strings_utils.values_are_pandas_numbers(values):
            # If numbers, convert to float so it can be converted to bool
            column = column.astype(float).astype(bool)
        ...
        return column
```

Both the type() and cast_column() are implemented by this concrete class as static methods as specified by the abstract base class. Similar to abstract class methods, Python does not enforce that the implementation in the subclass is also a static method. The decorator acts more like a guideline for developers implementing the class.

Decorating Property Methods

In earlier versions of Python, the @abstractproperty decorator was used to define abstract properties, but it has been deprecated. The modern approach is to use a combination of @property and @abstractmethod. This method allows us to define abstract properties that subclasses must implement, ensuring a consistent property interface across different classes.

The example below from *plumbum* defines multiple abstract properties in the base Path class:

```python
# File: plumbum/path/base.py

from abc import ABC, abstractmethod

class Path(str, ABC):
    """An abstraction over file system paths. This class is abstract, and
    the two implementations
    are :class:`LocalPath <plumbum.machines.local.LocalPath>` and
    :class:`RemotePath <plumbum.path.remote.RemotePath>`.
    """

    CASE_SENSITIVE = True

    @property
    @abstractmethod
    def name(self) -> str:
        """The basename component of this path"""

    @property
    @abstractmethod
    def stem(self) -> str:
        """The name without an extension, or the last component of
        the path"""

    @property
    @abstractmethod
    def dirname(self: _PathImpl) -> _PathImpl:
        """The dirname component of this path"""

    ...
```

These are defined in the concrete LocalPath implementation as seen below:

```python
# File: plumbum/path/local.py

class LocalPath(Path):
    """The class implementing local-machine paths"""

    CASE_SENSITIVE = not IS_WIN32
```

623

```
    @property
    def name(self):
        return os.path.basename(str(self))

    @property
    def dirname(self):
        return LocalPath(os.path.dirname(str(self)))

    @property
    def stem(self):
        return self.name.rsplit(os.path.extsep)[0]

    ...
```

The property method name, dirname, and stem are defined by the concrete LocalPath class adhering to the specification by the Path ABC.

Note that similar to static and class abstract methods, the usage of the @property decorator in implementations is not validated or enforced by Python. It is up to the developer to choose to implement the method as a property in the concrete class.

Subclassing ABCs
Use of `isinstance()` and `issubclass()` with ABCs

ABCs integrate seamlessly with Python's built-in isinstance() and issubclass() functions. These functions work not only with direct subclasses of ABCs but also with virtual subclasses (which we'll discuss shortly).

```
from abc import ABC, abstractmethod

class MyABC(ABC):
    @abstractmethod
    def my_method(self):
        pass

class ConcreteClass(MyABC):
    def my_method(self):
        return "Implemented!"
```

```
obj = ConcreteClass()
print(isinstance(obj, MyABC))  # Output: True
print(issubclass(ConcreteClass, MyABC))  # Output: True
```

This behavior allows us to use ABCs in type checking and ensures that objects adhere to the expected interface.

Multiple Inheritance with ABCs

Python's support for multiple inheritance extends to ABCs as well. We can create classes that inherit from multiple ABCs, combining their abstract methods:

```python
from abc import ABC, abstractmethod

class MyABC(ABC):
    @abstractmethod
    def my_method(self):
        pass

class AnotherABC(ABC):
    @abstractmethod
    def another_method(self):
        pass

class ConcreteClass(MyABC, AnotherABC):
    def my_method(self):
        return "First method"

    def another_method(self):
        return "Second method"

obj = ConcreteClass()

print(isinstance(obj, MyABC))  # Output: True
print(isinstance(obj, AnotherABC))  # Output: True
print(issubclass(ConcreteClass, MyABC))  # Output: True
print(issubclass(ConcreteClass, AnotherABC))  # Output: True
```

When using multiple inheritance with ABCs, we must implement all abstract methods from all parent ABCs to create a concrete class. In the snippet above, ConcreteClass should implement both my_method() and another_method() so that it can be instantiated successfully.

The register() Method: Registering Virtual Subclasses

The register() method of an ABC allows us to register a class as a virtual subclass of an ABC. This means that the class is considered a subclass of the ABC, even if it doesn't explicitly inherit from it. This is useful when we want to retrofit an existing class to be recognized as a subclass of an ABC without modifying its inheritance.

```python
from abc import ABC, abstractmethod

class Vehicle(ABC):
    @abstractmethod
    def drive(self):
        pass

class Boat:
    def drive(self):
        return "Sailing"

# Register Boat as a virtual subclass of Vehicle
Vehicle.register(Boat)

boat = Boat()
print(isinstance(boat, Vehicle))  # Outputs: True
```

In the above code, the class Boat is registered as a virtual subclass of ABC Vehicle. We can see that Boat does not inherit from any classes but still passes the instance check of the ABC Vehicle.

This method is useful for instance checks, but abstract method implementation is not enforced by Python in virtual subclasses. When using .register(), it is the responsibility of the developer to ensure that all the required methods are properly implemented.

We can see a real-world example from the library *plumbum*:

```python
# File: plumbum/cli/progress.py

from __future__ import annotations

import datetime
import sys
import warnings
from abc import ABC, abstractmethod

from plumbum.cli.termsize import get_terminal_size

class ProgressBase(ABC):
    """Base class for progress bars. Customize for types of progress
    bars."""

    ...

    def __len__(self):
        return self.length

    def __iter__(self):
        self.start()
        return self

    @abstractmethod
    def start(self):
        """This should initialize the progress bar and the iterator"""
        self.iter = iter(self.iterator)
        self.value = -1 if self.body else 0
        self._start_time = datetime.datetime.now()

    def __next__(self):
        try:
            rval = next(self.iter)
            self.increment()
        except StopIteration:
            self.done()
            raise
        return rval
```

```
    @value.setter
    def value(self, val):
        self._value = val

    @abstractmethod
    def display(self):
        """Called to update the progress bar"""

    @abstractmethod
    def done(self):
        """Is called when the iterator is done."""
```

We have two classes implementing this ABC:

1. Progress

    ```
    class Progress(ProgressBase):
        def start(self):
            super().start()
            self.display()

        def done(self):
            self.value = self.length
            self.display()
            if self.clear and not self.has_output:
                sys.stdout.write("\r" + len(str(self)) * " " + "\r")
            else:
                sys.stdout.write("\n")
            sys.stdout.flush()

        def __str__(self):
            width = get_terminal_size(default=(0, 0))[0]
            if self.length == 0:
                self.width = 0
                return "0/0 complete"

            percent = max(self.value, 0) / self.length
            ending = " " + (
                self.str_time_remaining()
                if self.timer
    ```

```
        else f"{self.value} of {self.length} complete"
    )
    if width - len(ending) < 10 or self.has_output:
        self.width = 0

        if self.timer:
            return f"{percent:.0%} complete: {self.str_time_
            remaining()}"

        return f"{percent:.0%} complete"

    self.width = width - len(ending) - 2 - 1
    nstars = int(percent * self.width)
    pbar = "[" + "*" * nstars + " " * (self.width - nstars) +
    "]" + ending

    str_percent = f" {percent:.0%} "

    return (
        pbar[: self.width // 2 - 2]
        + str_percent
        + pbar[self.width // 2 + len(str_percent) - 2 :]
    )

def display(self):
    disptxt = str(self)
    if self.width == 0 or self.has_output:
        sys.stdout.write(disptxt + "\n")
    else:
        sys.stdout.write("\r")
        sys.stdout.write(disptxt)
    sys.stdout.flush()
```

2. ProgressIPy

```
class ProgressIPy(ProgressBase):  # pragma: no cover
    HTMLBOX = '<div class="widget-hbox widget-progress"><div
    class="widget-label" style="display:block;">{0}</div></div>'
```

```python
    def __init__(self, *args, **kargs):
        # Ipython gives warnings when using widgets about the API
        potentially changing
        with warnings.catch_warnings():
            warnings.simplefilter("ignore")
            try:
                from ipywidgets import HTML, HBox, IntProgress
            except ImportError:  # Support IPython < 4.0
                from IPython.html.widgets import HTML, HBox,
                IntProgress

        super().__init__(*args, **kargs)
        self.prog = IntProgress(max=self.length)
        self._label = HTML()
        self._box = HBox((self.prog, self._label))

    def start(self):
        from IPython.display import display

        display(self._box)
        super().start()

    ...

    def display(self):
        pass

    def done(self):
        if self.clear:
            self._box.close()
```

Finally, we have ProgressAuto that calls the register method provided by the base class ABC:

```python
class ProgressAuto(ProgressBase):
    """Automatically selects the best progress bar (IPython HTML or text).
    Does not work with qtconsole
    (as that is correctly identified as identical to notebook, since the
    kernel is the same); it will still
```

iterate, but no graphical indication will be displayed.
"""

```python
def __new__(cls, *args, **kargs):
    """Uses the generator trick that if a cls instance is returned, the
    __init__ method is not called."""
    try:  # pragma: no cover
        __IPYTHON__    # noqa: B018
        try:
            from traitlets import TraitError
        except ImportError:  # Support for IPython < 4.0
            from IPython.utils.traitlets import TraitError

        try:
            return ProgressIPy(*args, **kargs)
        except TraitError:
            raise NameError() from None
    except (NameError, ImportError):
        return Progress(*args, **kargs)

ProgressAuto.register(ProgressIPy)
ProgressAuto.register(Progress)
```

In this code, ProgressAuto is designed to select the best progress bar implementation automatically. By registering ProgressIPy and Progress with ProgressAuto, these classes are recognized as subclasses of ProgressAuto without directly inheriting from it. This means that issubclass(ProgressIPy, ProgressAuto) and issubclass(Progress, ProgressAuto) will return True and instances of ProgressIPy and Progress will be recognized as instances of ProgressAuto.

Since ProgressIPy and Progress are virtual subclasses, the system allows for treating these classes interchangeably under the ProgressAuto type. This can be useful for type checks or when dynamically selecting the appropriate progress bar implementation based on the execution environment (e.g., whether running in an IPython environment or a standard terminal).

The __subclasshook__() Method

The __subclasshook__() method provides a way to customize the subclass checking of an ABC. This class method is called by issubclass() to determine whether a class is considered a subclass of the ABC.

By implementing __subclasshook__(), we can define our own criteria for what constitutes a subclass of our ABC. This can be useful when we want to consider classes as subclasses based on their structure (duck typing) rather than their explicit inheritance.

This dunder also affects the instance checks using the isinstance() function. Here is how __subclasshook__ works with isinstance():

- When isinstance(obj, Class) is called, Python first checks if the type of obj is a direct subclass of Class. If it is, isinstance() returns True.

- If the direct subclass check fails, and if Class has a metaclass that implements __subclasscheck__, Python will call Class.__subclasscheck__(type(obj)).

- __subclasscheck__ will then call Class.__subclasshook__(type(obj)).

- If the call returns True, isinstance() returns True.

Below is an example of __subclasshook__ in action:

```
from abc import ABC

class MyABC(ABC):
    @classmethod
    def __subclasshook__(cls, subclass):
        return hasattr(subclass, "my_method") and callable(subclass.
        my_method)

class One:
    def name(self):
        print("One")
```

```python
class Two:
    def name(self):
        print("Two")

    def my_method(self):
        print("Method called")
print(issubclass(One, MyABC))   # Output: False
print(issubclass(Two, MyABC))   # Output: True

obj = Two()
print(isinstance(obj, MyABC))   # Output: True
```

In this code, the MyABC abstract base class has the __subclasshook__ dunder defined. It returns true only if a callable attribute with the name my_method is present in the subclass. Class Two has a my_method() defined and therefore returns true when issubclass(Two, MyABC) is called.

Below is an example of __subclasshook__() usage in the *Rich* library:

```python
# File: rich/abc.py

from abc import ABC

class RichRenderable(ABC):
    """An abstract base class for Rich renderables.

    Note that there is no need to extend this class, the intended use is to
    check if an object supports the Rich renderable protocol. For example::

        if isinstance(my_object, RichRenderable):
            console.print(my_object)

    """

    @classmethod
    def __subclasshook__(cls, other: type) -> bool:
        """Check if this class supports the rich render protocol."""
        return hasattr(other, "__rich_console__") or hasattr(other,
        "__rich__")
```

In this code, the __subclasshook__ method in the RichRenderable class allows RichRenderable to act as an interface for the "Rich renderable protocol" without requiring explicit inheritance. The __subclasshook__ method checks if a class has either the __rich_console__ or __rich__ attribute. If a class possesses one of these attributes, it is considered to implement the "Rich renderable protocol." This approach allows developers to easily integrate objects with Rich's rendering system by implementing specific methods without needing to alter their class inheritance structures.

The below example is from the library *aesara*:

```python
# File: aesara/graph/type.py

class HasDataType(ABC):
    """A mixin for a type that has a :attr:`dtype` attribute."""

    dtype: str

    @classmethod
    def __subclasshook__(cls, C):
        if cls is HasDataType:
            if any("dtype" in B.__dict__ for B in C.__mro__):
                return True
        return NotImplemented
```

In the HasDataType class, the __subclasshook__ method is used to determine if a class can be considered a subclass of HasDataType based on the presence of a dtype attribute. This allows HasDataType to act as a mixin interface without requiring explicit inheritance. Classes that have a dtype attribute can be recognized as implementing this interface, even if they do not explicitly inherit from HasDataType.

The `collections.abc` Module

In the coming sections, we will take a look into some of the ABCs from the collections module. The collections.abc module in Python provides a set of abstract base classes that define common interfaces for collections. These ABCs serve as blueprints for creating custom collection types, ensuring that they adhere to the expected interface and behavior. In previous chapters, we've already explored creating custom list (Chapter 1) and dict (Chapter 3) classes.

The collections.abc module includes many useful ABCs, such as Sequence, Mapping, Set, MutableSequence, MutableMapping, MutableSet, and more. These ABCs provide a standard interface for different types of collections, making it easier to create custom collection classes that behave consistently with built-in types. Now, we'll look at some of the ABCs provided by collections.ABC that can help us define more specialized collection types.

collections.abc.MutableSequence

The MutableSequence ABC defines the interface for mutable sequence types, such as lists. It provides a set of methods that must be implemented by any class that claims to be a mutable sequence, ensuring that the class supports operations like item assignment, deletion, and appending elements.

When we create a custom mutable sequence type, inheriting from MutableSequence ensures that our class implements all the necessary methods for a mutable sequence. This makes our custom class behave similarly to built-in mutable sequences like lists.

The below example showcases an example of a custom class defined by inheriting from the abstract MutableSequence class:

```
# File: colour/io/luts/sequence.py

from __future__ import annotations

import re
from collections.abc import MutableSequence
from copy import deepcopy

from colour.hints import (
    Any,
    ArrayLike,
    List,
    NDArrayFloat,
    ProtocolLUTSequenceItem,
    Sequence,
)
```

```python
from colour.utilities import as_float_array, attest, is_iterable

class LUTSequence(MutableSequence):
    """

    Define the base class for a *LUT* sequence, i.e., a series of *LUTs*,
    *LUT* operators or objects implementing the
    :class:`colour.hints.ProtocolLUTSequenceItem` protocol.

    """

    def __init__(self, *args: ProtocolLUTSequenceItem) -> None:
        self._sequence: List[ProtocolLUTSequenceItem] = []
        self.sequence = args

    @property
    def sequence(self) -> List[ProtocolLUTSequenceItem]:
        return self._sequence

    @sequence.setter
    def sequence(self, value: Sequence[ProtocolLUTSequenceItem]):
        """Setter for the **self.sequence** property."""

        for item in value:
            attest(
                isinstance(item, ProtocolLUTSequenceItem),
                '"value" items must implement the '
                 "ProtocolLUTSequenceItem" '
                "protocol!",
            )

        self._sequence = list(value)

    def __getitem__(self, index: int | slice) -> Any:
        return self._sequence[index]

    def __setitem__(self, index: int | slice, value: Any):
        for item in value if is_iterable(value) else [value]:
            attest(
                isinstance(item, ProtocolLUTSequenceItem),
```

```
                '"value" items must implement the
                 "ProtocolLUTSequenceItem" '
                "protocol!",
            )

        self._sequence[index] = value

    def __delitem__(self, index: int | slice):
        del self._sequence[index]

    def __len__(self) -> int:
        return len(self._sequence)

    def __str__(self) -> str:
        ...

    def __eq__(self, other) -> bool:
        if not isinstance(other, LUTSequence):
            return False

        if len(self) != len(other):
            return False

        return all(self[i] == other[i] for i in range(len(self)))

    def __ne__(self, other) -> bool:
        return not (self == other)

    def insert(self, index: int, value: ProtocolLUTSequenceItem):
        attest(
            isinstance(value, ProtocolLUTSequenceItem),
            '"value" items must implement the "ProtocolLUTSequenceItem"
            protocol!',
        )

        self._sequence.insert(index, value)

    def apply(self, RGB: ArrayLike, **kwargs: Any) -> NDArrayFloat:
        RGB = as_float_array(RGB)

        RGB_o = RGB
```

```
    for operator in self:
        RGB_o = operator.apply(RGB_o, **kwargs.get(operator.__
        class__.__name__, {}))

    return RGB_o

  def copy(self) -> LUTSequence:
      return deepcopy(self)
```

The MutableSequence abstract base class requires the implementation of the following methods:

1. __getitem__(self, index)

2. __setitem__(self, index, value)

3. __delitem__(self, index)

4. __len__(self)

5. insert(self, index, value)

    The concrete class LUTSequence implements all these:

6. __getitem__(self, index: int | slice) -> Any:

    This method is implemented to allow indexing and slicing of the sequence. It directly accesses the internal _sequence list.

    ```
    def __getitem__(self, index: int | slice) -> Any:
        return self._sequence[index]
    ```

7. __setitem__(self, index: int | slice, value: Any):

    This method allows setting items in the sequence by index or slice. It includes type checking to ensure that the added items implement the ProtocolLUTSequenceItem protocol.

8. __delitem__(self, index: int | slice):

    This method allows deleting items from the sequence by index or slice.

9. `__len__(self) -> int:`

    This method returns the length of the sequence.

    ```
    def __len__(self) -> int:
        return len(self._sequence)
    ```

10. `insert(self, index: int, value: ProtocolLUTSequenceItem):`

    This method inserts an item at a specified index in the sequence.
    It also includes type checking for the inserted item.

By implementing these five methods, LUTSequence fulfills the requirements of the
MutableSequence abstract base class. This allows LUTSequence to behave like a mutable
sequence, supporting operations like indexing, slicing, item assignment, deletion, and
insertion.

collections.abc.Iterable

The Iterable ABC represents any object capable of returning its members one at a time.
In Python, an object is iterable if it implements the __iter__() method. By subclassing
Iterable, we signal that our class can be used in for loops, list comprehensions, and
other contexts where iteration is expected.

Below is an example of an Iterable implementation in the *deepsparse* library:

```
# File: src/deepsparse/benchmark/results.py

from typing import Iterable

class BenchmarkResults(Iterable):
    """

    The benchmark results for a list of batched inference runs
    """

    def __init__(self):
        self._results = []  # type: List[BatchBenchmarkResult]

    def __len__(self) -> int:
        return len(self._results)
```

```python
    def __getitem__(self, index: int) -> BatchBenchmarkResult:
        return self._results[index]

    def __iter__(self) -> Iterator[BatchBenchmarkResult]:
        for result in self._results:
            yield result

    @property
    def results(self) -> List[BatchBenchmarkResult]:
        """

        :return: the list of recorded batch results
        """

        return self._results
```

In the code, the BenchmarkResults class implements the Iterable interface. The defined __iter__ returns an iterator over the BatchBenchmarkResult objects stored in the _results list.

collections.abc.Iterator

The Iterator ABC builds on the Iterable interface by adding the __next__() method. An iterator not only supports iteration but also keeps track of the current position during traversal. This allows the iterator to return the next element in the sequence each time __next__() is called until it raises a StopIteration exception.

The below snippet from the *detect_secrets* library implements an Iterator class, BidirectionalIterator:

```python
# File: detect_secrets/audit/iterator.py

from collections.abc import Iterator

class BidirectionalIterator(Iterator):
    def __init__(self, collection: Sequence):
        self.collection = collection
        self.index = -1  # Starts on -1, as index is increased _before_
        getting result
        self.step_back_once = False
```

```python
    def __next__(self) -> Any:
        if self.step_back_once:
            self.index -= 1
            self.step_back_once = False
        else:
            self.index += 1

        if self.index < 0:
            raise StopIteration

        try:
            result = self.collection[self.index]
        except IndexError:
            raise StopIteration

        return result

    def next(self) -> Any:  # pragma: no cover
        return self.__next__()

    def step_back_on_next_iteration(self) -> None:
        self.step_back_once = True

    def can_step_back(self) -> bool:
        return self.index > 0

    def __iter__(self) -> 'BidirectionalIterator':  # pragma: no cover
        return self
```

The __next__ method in BidirectionalIterator implements a unique bidirectional iteration mechanism. It uses an index-based approach, allowing both forward and backward movement through the collection. The method checks a step_back_once flag to determine whether to decrement or increment the index, enabling reverse iteration when needed. It then retrieves and returns the item at the current index, raising StopIteration if the index is out of bounds. The __iter__ method simply returns self, making the object itself iterable and allowing it to be used in for loops and other iteration contexts.

collections.abc.Coroutine

The Coroutine ABC defines the interface for coroutine objects, which are used for asynchronous programming. Coroutines must implement the __await__() method, allowing them to be used with the await expression along with other interface methods like send(), throw(), and close().

While we typically don't subclass Coroutine directly (as coroutines are usually created using async def), understanding this ABC can be helpful when working with asynchronous programming in Python.

The below code from *xmanager* showcases WorkUnitCompletedAwaitable, which is a concrete implementation of the Coroutine ABC:

```python
# File: xmanager/xm/core.py

from typing import Any, Callable, Coroutine

class WorkUnitCompletedAwaitable(Coroutine):
    """Awaitable for work unit completion event.
    """

    def __init__(self, work_unit: "WorkUnit", awaitable: Callable[[], Any])
    -> None:
        self.work_unit = work_unit
        self._awaitable = awaitable
        self._wait_coro = self._wait()

    async def _wait(self) -> "WorkUnit":
        # Coroutine must be created inside of async function to avoid
        # "coroutine ... was never awaited" runtime warning.
        await self._awaitable()
        return self.work_unit

    def __await__(self) -> Generator[Any, None, "WorkUnit"]:
        return self._wait_coro.__await__()

    def send(self, value: Any) -> Any:
        return self._wait_coro.send(value)
```

```
def throw(self, typ, val=None, tb=None) -> Any:
    return self._wait_coro.throw(typ, val, tb)

def close(self) -> None:
    self._wait_coro.close()
```

In the WorkUnitCompletedAwaitable class, the Coroutine abstract base class (ABC) is implemented to provide custom coroutine behavior for handling work unit completion events. The core of this implementation lies in the _wait coroutine method, which encapsulates the actual waiting logic and returns the work unit upon completion.

The __await__ dunder method is the key to making this class awaitable, returning the __await__ of the internal _wait coroutine. This allows the object to be used with the await keyword in async contexts. The send, throw, and close methods are implemented as pass-through calls to the corresponding methods of the internal _wait coroutine. These methods are essential for proper coroutine behavior: send allows values to be sent into the coroutine, throw enables exception propagation, and close provides a mechanism to terminate the coroutine prematurely.

Conclusion

In this chapter, we've explored abstract base classes (ABCs) in Python, a powerful feature that allows us to define abstract interfaces and enforce them in concrete subclasses.

We started by introducing the concept of ABCs and their implementation through the abc module. We examined the two primary ways to create ABCs: using abc.ABC and abc.ABCMeta. We then delved into various method decorators provided by the abc module, which help us define abstract methods and properties. We also explored subclassing ABCs, including the use of isinstance() and issubclass(), multiple inheritance, virtual subclasses through the register() method, and customizing subclass relationships with __subclasshook__(). Finally, we looked at some common ABCs provided by the collections.ABC module.

When to Use Abstract Base Classes

When deciding whether to use abstract base classes, it's important to consider the context of the project. ABCs are beneficial in complex systems where multiple developers are involved, as they enforce a strict interface and prevent the instantiation

643

of incomplete subclasses. However, in smaller projects or situations where flexibility is more critical than strict structure, ABCs might introduce unnecessary complexity. In such cases, it may be more practical to rely on simpler inheritance or composition patterns.

ABCs are useful in the following scenarios:

1.   When defining a common interface for multiple related classes

2.   When we want to ensure that certain methods are implemented by subclasses

3.   In large projects or libraries where maintaining a consistent API is crucial

4.   When we need to provide a clear contract for other developers to follow

When to Avoid Abstract Base Classes

While ABCs are powerful, they're not always the best solution:

1.   In small, simple programs where the added complexity isn't justified

2.   When flexibility is more important than rigid structure

3.   If we are working with duck typing and don't need strict method enforcement

ABCs vs. Protocols

We have discussed protocols in Chapter 11 on typing. It's worth comparing ABCs with protocols, another feature in Python for defining interfaces:

1.   ABCs use inheritance and are checked at runtime, while protocols use structural subtyping and can be checked statically with type checkers.

2. ABCs can prevent the instantiation of incomplete implementations, while protocols are more flexible but don't enforce implementation at runtime.

3. ABCs can use `register()` for virtual subclasses, while protocols automatically consider any matching class as a subtype.

We must go with ABCs when we need runtime checks and method enforcement and prefer protocols when we want more flexibility and static type checking.

CHAPTER 20

Packaging

In the previous chapter, we explored abstract base classes and how they help define and enforce interfaces in our code.

Now, we turn our attention to packaging—an essential step in making our Python projects reusable and shareable. Packaging is what allows us to distribute our code so others can install and use it with ease. It also enables us to take advantage of libraries built by the Python community, helping us avoid reinventing the wheel.

In this chapter, we'll walk through the core concepts of Python packaging. We'll look at how packaging has evolved, examine the tools available today, and go over the best practices for creating and publishing a Python package. Whether you're building a library, CLI tool, or application, understanding packaging is a key step toward making your work more accessible and maintainable.

PyPI

PyPI, short for the Python Package Index, is the central online repository for Python packages. It's the place where Python developers from around the world share their packages, making them easily accessible to everyone.

PyPI's main purpose is to make it simple to discover, download, and install Python packages. It hosts a vast collection of packages covering a wide range of functionalities, from web development and data science to system administration and more. We can search for packages directly on the PyPI website or use command-line tools like `pip` to find and install them.

For testing purposes, PyPI also offers **TestPyPI**. TestPyPI is a separate instance of PyPI that allows developers to upload and test their packages without affecting the main PyPI repository. This is useful for trying out the packaging and publishing process, ensuring everything works as expected, before making a package publicly available on the main PyPI. It's considered best practice to first publish to TestPyPI to catch any issues before a public release.

© Adarsh Divakaran 2025
A. Divakaran, *Deep Dive Python*, https://doi.org/10.1007/979-8-8688-1261-3_20

History

As we explore the history of Python packaging, we'll see how it has evolved to meet the growing needs of the Python community.

In the early days of Python, packaging code was a challenging task. Developers often had to manually manage their code and dependencies, leading to inconsistencies and difficulties in distribution. The need for a standardized approach became evident as the Python community grew and projects became more complex. This necessity paved the way for the development of tools and standards that would streamline the packaging process.

Egg Files

One of the first significant advancements in Python packaging came with the introduction of **egg files**. Eggs were an early attempt to create a standard packaging format for Python. They were designed to bundle Python projects into a single, easily distributable archive. Eggs aimed to make it easier to share code by packaging a Python project along with its metadata, allowing for easier distribution and installation of Python packages, including dependencies.

Historically, to create an egg file, we might have used the `setuptools` library (which was developed alongside eggs). A basic command to create an egg distribution would look something like this, run from the project's root directory containing `setup.py`:

```
python setup.py bdist_egg
```

This command would generate an egg file in the `dist` directory. To install an egg file, we could use `easy_install`, a tool associated with egg files:

```
easy_install mypackage.egg
```

However, egg files had their limitations. They weren't always consistent across different platforms, and they didn't solve all the problems related to dependency management. For instance, they were not compatible with all Python tools and could be difficult to manage. As the Python ecosystem evolved, the need for a more flexible and robust packaging format became evident, leading to the eventual decline of egg files in favor of more advanced solutions.

Distutils

Distutils, short for distribution utilities, was a significant step forward in standardizing Python packaging. Introduced as a standard library module, Distutils provided a framework for packaging Python projects, making it easier to distribute and install them. It offered features such as building and installing packages, managing dependencies, and creating distribution archives.

Using Distutils, we would typically write a `setup.py` file to describe the package. To build a source distribution using Distutils, we would run

```
python setup.py sdist
```

This command would create a source distribution (e.g., a `.tar.gz` file) in the `dist` directory. To install a package from a source distribution created by Distutils, we would navigate to the directory containing `setup.py` and run

```
python setup.py install
```

Despite its contributions, Distutils had its shortcomings. It lacked some features needed for modern Python development, such as easy specification of development dependencies. As Python continued to evolve, it was eventually removed in Python 3.12 to make way for more modern tools.

Wheel

The **Wheel** format is a significant milestone in the packaging history. Introduced in PEP 427, whcels have become the standard for distributing Python packages, offering numerous advantages over previous formats.

Wheels, with their `.whl` extension, are essentially ZIP files containing all the files needed for a Python package. They're designed to be more efficient and reliable than previous distribution formats, addressing many of the shortcomings we encountered with eggs and source distributions.

To build a wheel file, we would typically use `setuptools` or the `wheel` package itself. Assuming we have a `setup.py` file, we can create a wheel using

```
python setup.py bdist_wheel
```

This command will generate a `.whl` file in the `dist` directory. To install a wheel file, we use `pip`:

```
pip install mypackage-1.0-py3-none-any.whl
```

Or, more commonly, `pip` automatically handles wheels when installing from PyPI or local directories:

```
pip install mypackage
```

`pip` prefers wheels if available, making the installation process faster.

Wheels have significantly improved the Python package installation process. They eliminate many of the issues we used to face with compiling packages from source, especially on platforms without proper build tools. For pure Python packages, wheels ensure that the installation process is as simple as copying files to the right location.

pyproject.toml

The **pyproject.toml** file was introduced by PEP 518 and further defined by PEP 621. `pyproject.toml` represents a major step forward in standardizing and simplifying Python project configuration.

`pyproject.toml` has become a central component in modern Python packaging, serving as a configuration file that facilitates the building and packaging of Python projects. It provides a standardized way to define build system requirements and project metadata, allowing various tools to interoperate seamlessly. Modern build tools use it to build packages.

For example, to build a source distribution and a wheel from a project with a `pyproject.toml` file, we can use the `build` tool:

```
# Install the `build` tool
pip install build
```

```
# Build the package using the tool
python -m build
```

This command will read the `pyproject.toml` file to determine the build backend and build the distributions.

Similarly, `pip` uses `pyproject.toml` when installing packages to manage build requirements:

```
pip install .
```

When we install a project using `pip` and a `pyproject.toml` is present, `pip` will use it to handle the build process, ensuring a consistent and standardized build environment.

By using `pyproject.toml`, we address several limitations of the previous `setup.py` and `setup.cfg` approach. It's a static, declarative file, eliminating security concerns associated with executing `setup.py`. It provides a single, standardized location for all project configurations. Its format (TOML) is more readable and less error-prone than the mix of Python code and INI-style configuration used previously.

Looking to the future, `pyproject.toml` is set to become the standard for Python project configuration. As more tools adopt and support for it, we can expect to see a more unified and streamlined packaging experience across the Python ecosystem.

Tools

In this section, we explore several tools that can be used for packaging Python projects. Each tool offers unique features that cater to different aspects of packaging and project management.

Setuptools

Setuptools stands as a foundational tool in the Python packaging ecosystem. It significantly expands upon the capabilities of the older Distutils, offering a more feature-rich and flexible approach to packaging Python projects. For many years, Setuptools has been the go-to choice for developers looking to create and distribute Python packages, and it remains highly relevant today.

Setuptools also provides robust mechanisms for **customizing the build process**. Through the `setup.py` script, we have fine-grained control over how the package is built, installed, and distributed. This script allows us to specify package metadata, declare dependencies, include data files, and even define custom installation routines.

Here are some of the major commands we commonly use with Setuptools:

```
# Install setuptools
pip install setuptools
```

To create a **source distribution** (sdist), which is an archive containing the project's source code, we can run

```
python setup.py sdist
```

This command packages the project into a source archive (like a `.tar.gz` file) that can be distributed and built on various systems.

To create a **wheel distribution**, the preferred binary distribution format, we can use

```
python setup.py bdist_wheel
```

This command builds a wheel file (`.whl`), which is generally faster and more reliable to install than source distributions, especially for packages with compiled extensions.

Setuptools can be configured using either the traditional `setup.cfg` file or the modern `pyproject.toml` file. While `setup.cfg` provides a declarative way to specify package options, `pyproject.toml` is becoming the standard for build system configuration in Python projects.

Here's a basic example of a `pyproject.toml` file configuring Setuptools as the build backend:

```
[build-system]
requires = ["setuptools"]
build-backend = "setuptools.build_meta"

[project]
name = "my_package_example"
version = "0.1.0"
description = "A simple example package using Setuptools"
authors = [{ name = "Your Name", email = "you@example.com" }]
```

In this `pyproject.toml`, we specify that Setuptools is the build backend and define some basic project metadata like the name, version, description, and author.

Setuptools is particularly well-suited for projects that require a high degree of customization in their build process or have complex package structures. Its flexibility and wide adoption within the Python community make it a powerful tool for packaging Python projects.

Flit

Flit is a lightweight tool designed for building and publishing Python packages. It emphasizes simplicity and ease of use, making it an excellent choice for smaller projects or those new to packaging.

One of the key design principles of Flit is to minimize configuration. It relies heavily on the pyproject.toml file for project metadata and build instructions, reducing the need for a separate setup.py or setup.cfg file in most cases. This declarative approach simplifies project setup and makes it easier to understand and maintain the packaging configuration.

Here are some of the **major commands** we can use with Flit:

```
# Install flit
pip install flit
```

To initialize a new project with Flit, we can use the flit init command. This command will guide us through creating a basic pyproject.toml file with essential project metadata:

```
flit init
```

To build distributions (both source distributions and wheels) of the package, we use the flit build command:

```
flit build
```

This command generates the distribution files in the dist directory, ready for uploading to PyPI or other package indexes.

To publish the package to PyPI, Flit provides the flit publish command. This command securely uploads the package distributions to PyPI:

```
flit publish
```

Flit also supports local installation for development purposes. To install the package for local development, we can use the flit install command:

```
flit install
```

This command installs the package in a way that's suitable for development, similar to `pip install -e .` with Setuptools. Flit is configured primarily through the `pyproject.toml` file. Here's a basic example of a `pyproject.toml` file for a Flit-managed project:

```
[build-system]
requires = ["flit_core >=3.2,<4"]
build-backend = "flit_core.buildapi"

[project]
name = "my_simple_package"
authors = [{name = "Your Name", email = "you@example.com"}]
version = "0.1.0"
description = "A very simple example package managed by Flit"
requires-python = ">=3.8"
```

In this `pyproject.toml`, we specify `flit_core` as the build backend and define basic project metadata like name, authors, version, and Python requirements. Flit uses this information to build and package the project.

The below is a `pyproject.toml` file of Django-ninja, a project that uses Flit for package building:

```
[build-system]
requires = ["flit_core >=2,<4"]
build-backend = "flit_core.buildapi"

[tool.flit.metadata]
module = "ninja"
dist-name = "django-ninja"
author = "Vitaliy Kucheryaviy"
author-email = "ppr.vitaly@gmail.com"
home-page = "https://django-ninja.dev"
classifiers = [
    "Intended Audience :: Information Technology",
    "Intended Audience :: System Administrators",
    "Operating System :: OS Independent",
    ...
]
```

```
requires = ["Django >=3.1", "pydantic >=2.0,<3.0.0"]
description-file = "README.md"
requires-python = ">=3.7"

[tool.flit.metadata.urls]
Documentation = "https://django-ninja.dev"
Repository = "https://github.com/vitalik/django-ninja"

[tool.flit.metadata.requires-extra]
test = [
    "pytest",
    "pytest-cov",
    "pytest-django",
    "pytest-asyncio",
    "psycopg2-binary",
    "mypy==1.7.1",
    "ruff==0.5.7",
    "django-stubs",
]
doc = ["mkdocs", "mkdocs-material", "markdown-include", "mkdocstrings"]
dev = ["pre-commit"]
```

...

In the workflow file (GitHub actions), the flit publish command is used to publish the built package to PyPI.

```
name: Publish

on:
  release:
    types: [published]
  workflow_dispatch:

jobs:
  publish:
    runs-on: ubuntu-latest
```

```
steps:
  - uses: actions/checkout@v3
  - name: Set up Python
    uses: actions/setup-python@v5
  - name: Install Flit
    run: pip install flit
  - name: Install Dependencies
    run: flit install --symlink
  - name: Publish
    env:
      # FLIT_USERNAME: ${{ secrets.FLIT_USERNAME }}
      # FLIT_PASSWORD: ${{ secrets.FLIT_PASSWORD }}
      FLIT_USERNAME: __token__
      FLIT_PASSWORD: ${{ secrets.PYPI_TOKEN }}
    run: flit publish
```

Flit is well-suited for simple, pure Python projects where ease of use and minimal configuration are desired. If the project is primarily Python code without complex build steps or platform-specific extensions, Flit can provide a very efficient and straightforward packaging experience.

Poetry

Poetry is a comprehensive tool for dependency management and packaging. It provides a unified interface for managing dependencies, virtual environments, and publishing packages, making it a popular choice for modern Python projects. One of Poetry's standout features is its sophisticated dependency resolution. It employs a robust algorithm to resolve complex dependency trees, ensuring compatibility and preventing conflicts. Poetry also automatically generates a lock file (poetry.lock), which precisely records the versions of all dependencies, including transitive ones. This lock file is crucial for achieving deterministic builds, ensuring that everyone working on the project uses the exact same dependency versions.

Poetry's command-line interface (CLI) is designed to be intuitive and user-friendly, making common tasks like adding dependencies, building packages, and publishing to PyPI straightforward.

Here are some of the major commands we will use with Poetry:

```
# Install Poetry
pipx install poetry
```

To **create a new project**, Poetry offers the poetry new command. This command scaffolds a new project directory with a basic structure and a pyproject.toml file:

```
poetry new my-poetry-project
cd my-poetry-project
```

To **initialize Poetry in an existing project**, we can use poetry init. This command interactively guides us through creating a pyproject.toml file:

```
poetry init
```

To **add dependencies** to the project, we use the poetry add command. Poetry automatically updates the pyproject.toml file and resolves dependencies:

```
poetry add requests
```

To **install dependencies** based on the pyproject.toml and poetry.lock files, we use the poetry install command. This command also creates a virtual environment if one doesn't exist:

```
poetry install
```

To **activate the virtual environment** managed by Poetry, we can use poetry shell. This command opens a new shell session within the project's virtual environment:

```
poetry shell
```

To **run Python scripts or commands** within the Poetry environment without activating the shell, we can use poetry run:

```
poetry run python my_script.py
```

To **build distributions** (both source distributions and wheels) of the package, we use the poetry build command:

```
poetry build
```

To **publish the package to PyPI**, Poetry provides the `poetry publish` command. This command streamlines the publishing process, handling metadata and uploads:

```
poetry publish
```

Poetry uses the `pyproject.toml` file for configuration, but with its own specific structure under the `[tool.poetry]` section. Here's a basic example of a `pyproject.toml` file for a Poetry-managed project:

```
[tool.poetry]
name = "my-poetry-package"
version = "0.1.0"
description = "An example package managed by Poetry"
authors = ["Your Name <you@example.com>"]
readme = "README.md"
license = "MIT"

[tool.poetry.dependencies]
python = "^3.8"
requests = "^2.28"

[tool.poetry.dev-dependencies]
pytest = "^7.0"

[build-system]
requires = ["poetry-core"]
build-backend = "poetry.core.masonry.api"
```

In this `pyproject.toml`, we define project metadata, dependencies under `[tool.poetry.dependencies]`, and development dependencies under `[tool.poetry.dev-dependencies]`. Poetry uses this information to manage the project.

The below `pyproject.toml` file is from Skyplane, a cloud data migration tool, which uses Poetry for packaging:

```
[tool.poetry]
name = "skyplane"
packages = [{ include = "skyplane" }]
version = "0.3.2"
```

```
description = "Skyplane efficiently transports data between cloud regions
and providers."
authors = ["Skyplane authors <skyplaneproject@gmail.com>"]
license = "Apache-2.0"
homepage = "https://skyplane.org/"
repository = "https://github.com/skyplane-project/skyplane"
documentation = "https://skyplane.org/"
readme = "README.md"
include = ["skyplane/data/*"]

[tool.poetry.dependencies]
python = ">=3.7.1,<3.12"
boto3 = ">=1.16.0"
cachetools = ">=4.1.0"
cryptography = ">=1.4.0"
pandas = ">=1.0.0"
paramiko = ">=2.7.2"
questionary = ">=1.8.0"
requests = ">=2.23.0"
rich = ">=9.0.0"
sshtunnel = ">=0.3.0"
typer = ">=0.4.0"

...

[tool.poetry.extras]
aws = ["boto3"]
azure = ["azure-identity", "azure-mgmt-authorization", "azure-mgmt-
compute", "azure-mgmt-network", "azure-mgmt-resource", "azure-mgmt-
storage", "azure-mgmt-quota", "azure-mgmt-subscription", "azure-
storage-blob"]
gcp = ["google-api-python-client", "google-auth", "google-cloud-compute",
"google-cloud-storage"]
ibm = ["ibm-cloud-sdk-core", "ibm-cos-sdk", "ibm-vpc"]
scp = ["boto3"]
```

```
all = ["boto3", "azure-identity", "azure-mgmt-authorization", "azure-
mgmt-compute", "azure-mgmt-network", "azure-mgmt-resource", "azure-
mgmt-storage", "azure-mgmt-subscription", "azure-storage-blob",
"google-api-python-client", "google-auth", "google-cloud-compute", "google-
cloud-storage", "ibm-cloud-sdk-core", "ibm-cos-sdk", "ibm-vpc"]
gateway = ["flask", "lz4", "pynacl", "pyopenssl", "werkzeug"]
solver = ["cvxpy", "graphviz", "matplotlib", "numpy"]

[tool.poetry.dev-dependencies]
pytest = ">=6.0.0"
pytest-cov = ">=2.10.0"
pytest-xdist = ">=2.0.0"
black = "^23.1.0"

[build-system]
requires = ["setuptools", "poetry-core>=1.2.0"]
build-backend = "poetry.core.masonry.api"

[tool.poetry.scripts]
skylark = "skyplane.cli.cli:app"
skyplane = "skyplane.cli.cli:app"
```

Given below is the workflow file for the library, which first publishes the library to test PyPI after each GitHub release:

```
# File: .github/workflows/poetry-publish.yml

name: poetry-publish
on:
  release:
    types: [published]
  workflow_dispatch:

jobs:
  publish-test-pypi:
    runs-on: ubuntu-latest
    steps:
      - uses: actions/checkout@v1
      - name: Set up Python 3.8
```

```yaml
    uses: actions/setup-python@v4
    with:
      python-version: 3.8
- name: Install Poetry
  run: curl -sSL https://install.python-poetry.org | python3 -
  --version 1.5.1
- name: Cache Poetry virtualenv
  uses: actions/cache@v1
  id: cache
  with:
    path: ~/.virtualenvs
    key: poetry-${{ hashFiles('**/poetry.lock') }}-${{
    hashFiles('pyproject.toml') }}
    restore-keys: |
      poetry-${{ hashFiles('**/poetry.lock') }}-${{
      hashFiles('pyproject.toml') }}
- name: Set Poetry config
  run: |
    poetry config virtualenvs.in-project false
    poetry config virtualenvs.path ~/.virtualenvs
    poetry config repositories.test-pypi https://test.pypi.
    org/legacy/
    poetry config pypi-token.test-pypi ${{ secrets.TEST_PYPI_API_
    TOKEN }}
- name: Install Dependencies
  run: |
    poetry install -E gateway -E solver -E aws -E azure -E gcp
    poetry run pip install -r requirements-dev.txt
- name: Build package
  run: |
    export SKYPLANEVERSION=`poetry version | awk 'END {print $NF}'`
    echo "gateway_version = '$SKYPLANEVERSION'" > skyplane/gateway_
    version.py
    poetry build
```

```
    - name: Publish package (dry run)
      run: poetry publish -r test-pypi --dry-run
    - name: Publish package
      run: poetry publish -r test-pypi
```

publish-pypi-dev:

  •••

publish-pypi:

  •••

Poetry is well-suited for projects where **dependency management is a primary concern** and for developers who appreciate a **comprehensive, all-in-one tool** for Python project management. Its focus on ease of use, robust dependency resolution, and streamlined workflows make it a popular choice for modern Python development.

Hatch

Hatch is a modern tool for managing Python projects, offering capabilities for environment management, packaging, and versioning. It aims to simplify the development workflow and provide a seamless experience for developers.

Furthermore, Hatch offers features for automatic versioning, which can be a significant time-saver when managing project releases. Its extensible plugin system allows for customization and extension of its core functionalities, adapting to diverse project needs.

Here are some of the **major commands** we will use with Hatch:

```
# Install hatch
pipx install hatch
```

To **create a new project**, Hatch provides the hatch new command. This command sets up a new project directory with a basic structure and necessary configuration files:

```
hatch new my-hatch-project
cd my-hatch-project
```

To **run commands within a Hatch-managed environment**, we use the hatch run command. This is useful for executing tests, scripts, or any other commands within the project's isolated environment:

```
hatch run python my_script.py
```

Or this is useful specifically for running tests:

```
hatch run test
```

To **build distributions** (both source distributions and wheels) of the package, we use the hatch build command:

```
hatch build
```

To **publish the package to PyPI**, Hatch offers the hatch publish command, simplifying the release process:

```
hatch publish
```

Hatch also provides commands for managing environments directly. To **create a new environment**, we can use hatch env create:

```
hatch env create
```

Hatch relies on the pyproject.toml file for project configuration. Here's a basic example of a pyproject.toml file for a Hatch-managed project:

```
[build-system]
requires = ["hatchling"]
build-backend = "hatchling.build"

[project]
name = "my-hatch-package"
version = "0.1.0"
```

In this pyproject.toml, hatchling is specified as the build backend, and basic project metadata is defined. Hatch uses this file to manage the project's build process and other configurations.

Marimo, a Python notebook library, uses Hatch for packaging. Its pyproject.toml is shown below:

```
[build-system]
requires = ["hatchling"]
build-backend = "hatchling.build"

[project]
name = "marimo"
```

```
description = "A library for making reactive notebooks and apps"
dynamic = ["version"]
# We try to keep dependencies to a minimum, to avoid conflicts with
# user environments;we need a very compelling reason for each
dependency added.
# Dependencies should have lower bounds, which should be as loose as
possible.
dependencies = [
    # For maintainable cli
    "click>=8.0,<9",
    # code completion
    "jedi>=0.18.0",
    ...
]
readme = "README.md"
license = { file = "LICENSE" }
requires-python = ">=3.9"
classifiers = [
    "Operating System :: OS Independent",
    "License :: OSI Approved :: Apache Software License",
    ...
]

[project.scripts]
marimo = "marimo._cli.cli:main"

[project.urls]
homepage = "https://github.com/marimo-team/marimo"

[project.optional-dependencies]
sql = [
    "duckdb>=1.0.0",
    "polars[pyarrow]>=1.9.0",
    "sqlglot>=23.4"
]
```

```
[tool.hatch]
installer = "uv"

[tool.hatch.build.hooks.custom]
path = "build_hook.py"

[tool.hatch.version]
path = "marimo/__init__.py"

[tool.hatch.build.targets.sdist]
include = ["/marimo"]
artifacts = ["marimo/_static/", "marimo/_lsp/", "third_party.txt", "third_
party_licenses.txt"]
exclude = ["marimo/_smoke_tests"]
force-include = { "build_hook.py" = "build_hook.py" }

[tool.hatch.build.targets.wheel]
include = ["/marimo"]
artifacts = ["marimo/_static/", "marimo/_lsp/", "third_party.txt", "third_
party_licenses.txt"]
exclude = ["marimo/_smoke_tests"]
force-include = { "build_hook.py" = "build_hook.py" }

[tool.hatch.envs.test]
extra-dependencies = [
    "hypothesis~=6.102.1",
    # For server testing
    "httpx~=0.27.0",
    "matplotlib~=3.9.2",
    "pytest~=8.3.4",
    "pytest-timeout~=2.3.1",
    "pytest-codecov~=0.6.1",
    "pytest-asyncio~=0.25.2",
]

[[tool.hatch.envs.test.matrix]]
python = ["3.9", "3.10", "3.11", "3.12"]

...
```

The GitHub action file uses hatch build and hatch publish commands to build and upload the package to PyPI:

```
# File: .github/workflows/release-marimo-base.yml

name: Publish marimo-base release

# release a new version of marimo-base on tag push
on:
  push:
    tags:
      - '[0-9]+.[0-9]+.[0-9]+'
  workflow_dispatch: {}

env:
  TURBO_TOKEN: ${{ secrets.TURBO_TOKEN }}
  TURBO_TEAM: marimo
  REGISTRY: ghcr.io
  IMAGE_NAME: marimo-team/marimo

jobs:
  publish_release:
    name: 📤 Publish release
    runs-on: ubuntu-latest
    defaults:
      run:
        shell: bash

    steps:
      - name: 🛑 Cancel Previous Runs
        uses: styfle/cancel-workflow-action@0.12.1

      - name: ⬇️ Checkout repo
        uses: actions/checkout@v4

      - name: ◯ Install Hatch
        uses: pypa/hatch@install

      - name: Adapt pyproject.toml to build marimo-base
        run: ./scripts/modify_pyproject_for_marimo_base.sh
```

```
- name: 🗔 Build marimo-base
  run: hatch build --clean

- name: 🗔 Validate wheel under 2mb
  run: ./scripts/validate_base_wheel_size.sh

- name: ☁ Upload to PyPI
  env:
    HATCH_INDEX_USER: ${{ secrets.PYPI_USER }}
    HATCH_INDEX_AUTH: ${{ secrets.PYPI_MARIMO_BASE_PASSWORD }}
  run: hatch publish

- name: ☁ Upload to TestPyPI
  env:
    HATCH_INDEX_USER: ${{ secrets.TEST_PYPI_USER }}
    HATCH_INDEX_AUTH: ${{ secrets.TEST_PYPI_MARIMO_BASE_PASSWORD }}
  run: hatch publish --repo test
```

Hatch is particularly well-suited for developers who are looking for a **modern, feature-rich tool** that can grow with their project's complexity. Its extensibility and comprehensive feature set make it a strong contender for managing Python projects of various sizes and types.

Twine

Twine is a utility for publishing Python packages on PyPI. It's the recommended tool for uploading distribution packages as it provides a secure and straightforward way to interact with package indexes.

Twine is not a full-fledge package management utility similar to the ones we discussed previously. Its main use is to publish the already built packages to PyPI.

Here are some of the **key features** of Twine:

- *Secure uploads*: Twine enforces HTTPS for all communication with PyPI, safeguarding against man-in-the-middle attacks and ensuring secure credential transmission.

- *Distribution format support*: It supports uploading both source distributions (`sdist`) and wheel files (`.whl`), giving us flexibility in how we package the project.

- *Pre-upload checks*: Twine includes a check command that helps us validate the distribution files before uploading, catching common errors in package metadata or structure.

- *TestPyPI support*: It easily allows us to upload to TestPyPI, a separate instance of PyPI used for testing package uploads without affecting the live PyPI index.

Here are some of the **major commands** we will use with Twine:

```
# Install twine
pip install twine
```

Before uploading, it's always a good practice to **check the distribution files** using the check command:

```
twine check dist/*
```

This command will validate the package metadata and README format, helping us catch potential issues before publishing.

To **upload the package to TestPyPI** for testing, we would use the upload command with the `--repository-url` option:

```
twine upload --repository-url https://test.pypi.org/legacy/ dist/*
```

This command uploads all files in the dist directory to TestPyPI.

Once you're confident with the package and ready to **publish to the main PyPI repository**, we can use the upload command without the `--repository-url` option:

```
twine upload dist/*
```

Twine also supports different methods for providing PyPI credentials. We can **provide credentials directly** in the command, although this is generally discouraged for security reasons:

```
twine upload -u pypi_username -p pypi_password dist/*
```

A more secure approach is to use a **.pypirc configuration file** or environment variables for authentication. Twine will automatically look for credentials in these locations.

To see **what files Twine would upload without actually uploading**, we can use the --dry-run option:

```
twine upload --dry-run dist/*
```

This is useful for verifying the upload process before making changes to PyPI.

If we need to **remove a specific version of the package from PyPI** (yank it), Twine provides the yank command:

```
twine yank my-package==1.0.0
```

Best practices when using Twine:

- *Always test on TestPyPI first*: Before publishing to the main PyPI, upload the package to TestPyPI to ensure everything works as expected.

- *Securely manage PyPI credentials*: Avoid hardcoding credentials in scripts or command lines. Use environment variables or a .pypirc file with appropriate permissions.

- *Use* twine check *before uploading*: Validate the distribution files to catch errors early.

The below GitHub action file showcases the use of Twine by Allure-Python, a pytest plugin:

```
name: release allure python
run-name: Release ${{ github.ref_name }} by ${{ github.actor }}

on:
  release:
    types: [published]

jobs:
  deploy:
    runs-on: ubuntu-latest
```

```
  steps:
  - uses: actions/checkout@v4

  - name: Set up Python
    uses: actions/setup-python@v5
    with:
      python-version: '3.x'

  - name: Install dependencies
    run: |
      python -m pip install --upgrade pip
      pip install setuptools wheel twine

  - name: Build and publish
    env:
      TWINE_USERNAME: ${{ secrets.PYPI_USERNAME }}
      TWINE_PASSWORD: ${{ secrets.PYPI_PASSWORD }}
    run: |
      pushd allure-python-commons-test
      python setup.py sdist bdist_wheel
      twine upload dist/*
      popd

      pushd allure-python-commons
      python setup.py sdist bdist_wheel
      twine upload dist/*
      popd

      pushd allure-behave
      python setup.py sdist bdist_wheel
      twine upload dist/*
      popd

      pushd allure-nose2
      python setup.py sdist bdist_wheel
      twine upload dist/*
      popd

      pushd allure-pytest
```

```
python setup.py sdist bdist_wheel
twine upload dist/*
popd

pushd allure-pytest-bdd
python setup.py sdist bdist_wheel
twine upload dist/*
popd

pushd allure-robotframework
python setup.py sdist bdist_wheel
twine upload dist/*
popd
```

Here, the package is built using Setuptools and is pushed to PyPI using Twine.

Best Practices

In this section, we delve into the best practices for packaging Python projects, focusing on organization, security, and efficient management to ensure high-quality, maintainable, and distributable code.

__init__.py Files in Python Packages

The __init__.py files' presence in a directory signals to Python that the directory should be treated as a package, allowing for modular code organization and namespace management.

__init__.py serves several key purposes within a Python package:

- *Package initialization and setup*: The most fundamental role of __init__.py is to act as the package's initializer. When a package is imported for the first time in a Python session, the code within its __init__.py file is executed. This provides an opportunity to perform setup tasks that are necessary for the package to function correctly. Common initialization tasks include

- Setting up package-level logging configurations. For instance, we might need to configure a logger that is used by all modules within the package.

- Initializing package-level variables or constants that are intended to be accessible throughout the package.

- Loading configuration files or environment variables that the package relies on.

- Performing checks for required dependencies or environment conditions.

- *Namespace management and definition*: `__init__.py` plays a vital role in defining the package's namespace. It controls what names are directly available when the package itself is imported. This is achieved through several mechanisms:

  - *Selective imports*: We can import specific modules, subpackages, or objects (like classes, functions, or variables) from within the package's modules into the `__init__.py` file. These imported names then become directly accessible under the package's namespace.

  - For example, if `mypackage.module1` contains a class `ClassA`, importing it in `__init__.py` like `from .module1 import ClassA` allows users to access it as `mypackage.ClassA` instead of the more verbose `mypackage.module1.ClassA`. This can significantly improve the usability and readability of the package for end users.

  - *Defining* `__all__`: The `__all__` list, defined within `__init__.py`, is a powerful tool for controlling what names are exported when a user performs a wildcard import using `from package import *`. By listing specific names in `__all__`, we explicitly define the public interface of the package when using wildcard imports. This is crucial for maintaining a clean and predictable API, as it prevents internal modules or helper functions from being inadvertently exposed to users through wildcard imports. It's generally considered good practice to define __all__ in __init__.py to clearly document and control the package's public API.

- *Implicit namespace packages and the role of* __init__.py: Since Python 3.3, implicit namespace packages were introduced, which technically allow directories to be treated as packages even without an __init__.py file, especially if they are spread across multiple locations on sys.path. However, even with implicit namespace packages, including an __init__.py file, even if it's empty, is still highly recommended for several reasons:

  - *Clarity and explicitness*: The presence of __init__.py explicitly marks a directory as a Python package. This makes it immediately clear to anyone reading the project structure that the directory is intended to be a package, improving code readability and maintainability.

  - *Enabling package-specific functionality*: If we ever need to add package-level initialization code, define __all__, or perform selective imports to shape the package's namespace, we will need an __init__.py file. Starting with an empty __init__.py from the outset provides a placeholder and makes it easier to add these functionalities later as the package evolves without requiring structural changes to the package.

Example: __init__.py in Action

Consider a package named mypackage with the following structure:

```
mypackage/
    __init__.py
    module1.py
    module2.py
    subpackage/
        __init__.py
        module3.py
```

The mypackage/__init__.py file might contain

```
# mypackage/__init__.py
from .module1 import ClassA
from .module2 import function_b

__all__ = ['ClassA', 'function_b']

import logging
logging.basicConfig(level=logging.INFO)
logging.info("mypackage initialized")
```

In this example

- `from .module1 import ClassA` and `from .module2 import function_b` make `ClassA` and `function_b` directly accessible as `mypackage.ClassA` and `mypackage.function_b`.

- `__all__ = ['ClassA', 'function_b']` specifies that only `ClassA` and `function_b` will be imported if a user does `from mypackage import *`.

- The logging configuration and the `logging.info` statement demonstrate package-level initialization code that runs when `mypackage` is first imported.

Best Practices for __init__.py

- *Keep it concise*: While `__init__.py` can contain initialization code and namespace definitions, it's generally best to keep it relatively concise. Complex logic is usually better placed within dedicated modules. Overly complex `__init__.py` files can slow down package import times and make the package structure harder to understand.

- *Explicitly define `__all__`*: If we intend to control the public API of the package, we should always define `__all__` in the `__init__.py`. This makes it clear which names are intended for public use and helps prevent accidental exposure of internal parts of the package.

- *Use relative imports*: When importing modules or subpackages within the package in __init__.py, use relative imports (e.g., `from .module1 import ...`, `from .subpackage import ...`). Relative imports are more robust to changes in the package's installation location and are generally considered best practice within packages.

- *Consider an empty __init__.py*: If the package requires no initialization code and we are not explicitly shaping the namespace through selective imports or __all__, an empty __init__.py is perfectly acceptable and often recommended for clarity, especially for simple packages. It explicitly marks the directory as a package without adding unnecessary code.

By effectively utilizing __init__.py, we can create well-structured, easy-to-use, and maintainable Python packages.

Code Organization: Structuring Packages for Clarity and Maintainability

Organizing the Python package effectively is as crucial as writing clean code. A well-thought-out directory structure and consistent naming conventions significantly enhance the readability, maintainability, and scalability of the package.

A logical and consistent directory structure provides a roadmap for developers to navigate the codebase, locate specific modules, and understand the overall architecture of the package. A poorly structured package, on the other hand, can lead to confusion, increased development time, and a higher likelihood of introducing bugs.

Consider the following aspects when designing the package's directory structure:

- *Logical grouping of modules*: Organize the code into directories and subdirectories based on functionality or domain. This principle of separation of concerns should guide our directory design. For instance, if we are developing a package for image processing, we might have subdirectories for modules related to image loading, filtering, feature detection, and format conversion. This logical separation makes it easier to find and work with specific parts of the package.

For example, in an ecommerce package, we might structure directories like this:

```
ecommerce_package/
├── __init__.py
├── catalog/              # Modules related to product catalog
│                             management
│   ├── __init__.py
│   ├── products.py
│   └── categories.py
├── orders/               # Modules for order processing and
│                             management
│   ├── __init__.py
│   ├── orders.py
│   └── payments.py
├── users/                # Modules for user accounts and profiles
│   ├── __init__.py
│   ├── accounts.py
│   └── profiles.py
└── utils/                # Utility modules used across the package
    ├── __init__.py
    └── helpers.py
```

- *The src layout—best practice for source code*: A highly recommended practice for structuring Python packages is to use a src layout. In this structure, we place the actual package source code within a src directory at the top level of the project. This approach offers several advantages, particularly in preventing import-related issues during development and testing.

```
my_package/
├── src/
│   └── my_package/  # Actual package source code resides here
│       ├── __init__.py
```

```
|         ├── module1.py
|         └── module2.py
├── tests/           # Tests are kept separate
├── docs/            # Documentation files
├── pyproject.toml   # Build system configuration
└── README.md        # Project description
```

- *Benefits of the* src *layout*:

  - *Avoids top-level import confusion*: When the package code is directly at the project root, we can sometimes run into import issues, especially when running scripts from within the project directory. Python might add the project root to sys.path, leading to potential conflicts if the package name clashes with other installed packages or standard library modules. The src layout avoids this by clearly separating the source code from the project's root directory. During development, we would typically add the src directory to the PYTHONPATH or use development tools that handle this automatically, ensuring that the package is imported correctly as my_package and not as a module within the project root.

  - *Clear separation of concerns*: The src layout visually separates the source code from other project-related files like documentation, tests, and build configurations, making the project structure cleaner and easier to understand.

  - *Improved testability*: With the src layout, it becomes more straightforward to configure the testing environment to specifically target the source code within the src directory, ensuring that tests are run against the correct version of the package.

- *Dedicated directories for tests and documentation*: It is a standard and highly recommended practice to keep the tests and documentation in separate top-level directories, typically named tests and docs, respectively.

  - tests *directory*: All test-related files should reside in the tests directory. This separation makes it easy to locate and run tests

677

and keeps test code from cluttering the source code directory. Within the `tests` directory, we should mirror the structure of the source package to some extent. For example, if we have `my_package/module1.py`, the corresponding tests might be in `tests/test_module1.py`. Using a consistent naming convention for test files (e.g., prefixing with `test_` or suffixing with `_test`) is also beneficial for test discovery tools.

– `docs` *directory*: Place all documentation files within the `docs` directory. This typically includes the project's API documentation (often generated using tools like Sphinx), tutorials, and any other documentation. A common practice is to use a documentation generator like Sphinx, which can take reStructuredText or Markdown files in the `docs` directory and generate nicely formatted HTML or PDF documentation.

Most of the popular packages follow these code organization best practices. For example, Flask has `src/flask` as the root for package files. Django has the package files in the `/django` directory. Both of these libraries have other folders like `docs`, `tests`, `examples`, etc. in their project root, which are supporting components not core to the package functionality.

By adhering to these principles of code organization, we can create Python packages that are not only functional but also easy to navigate, understand, and maintain over time.

Managing Private Python Packages for Internal Use

Private Python packages are essential for organizations that need to share code internally without making it publicly accessible. These packages facilitate code reuse, standardize internal tools, and ensure that proprietary code remains secure. Unlike public packages available on PyPI, private packages require careful consideration of hosting, access control, and distribution mechanisms.

Private packages serve several critical purposes within organizations:

- *Secure code sharing*: The primary reason for using private packages is to securely share code within an organization. This is crucial for proprietary algorithms, internal libraries, or tools that should not be exposed to the public.

- *Code reusability and consistency*: Private packages promote code reuse across different projects within the organization. By packaging common functionalities, teams can avoid redundant development efforts and ensure consistency in how certain tasks are performed. This leads to more efficient development cycles and reduces the risk of inconsistencies and errors.

- *Standardization of internal tools*: Organizations often develop internal tools and libraries that are essential for their operations. Packaging these tools as private packages ensures that they are easily distributable, versioned, and consistently used across different teams and projects. This standardization simplifies maintenance and updates.

- *Dependency management for internal projects*: Just as public packages manage external dependencies, private packages help manage dependencies within internal projects. By breaking down large internal systems into smaller, packageable components, we can create a more modular and maintainable architecture.

- *Compliance and regulatory requirements*: In some industries, regulatory compliance mandates that certain code and data handling processes remain strictly internal. Private packages help organizations meet these requirements by ensuring that sensitive code is not inadvertently exposed.

Hosting Options for Private Packages

Choosing the right hosting solution is crucial for managing private packages effectively. Several options are available, each with its own set of features and trade-offs:

- *Private repositories (e.g., GitHub, GitLab, Bitbucket)*: Using private repositories offered by platforms like GitHub, GitLab, or Bitbucket is a straightforward approach, especially if the organization already uses these platforms for version control.

- – *Pros*: Easy to set up if we are already using these platforms. Leverage existing access control mechanisms of the repository platform. Version control is built-in.

- – *Cons*: Primarily designed for source code, not specifically for package distribution. Installation typically involves direct access to the repository, which might not be ideal for all deployment scenarios. Require users to have access to the repository.

To install a package directly from a private repository using `pip`, we can use the following format, embedding credentials in the URL (use with caution and consider security implications):

```
pip install git+https://<username>:<password>@github.
com/<user>/<private-repo>.git#egg=<package-name>
```

For enhanced security, especially in CI/CD pipelines, consider using access tokens or deploy keys instead of passwords directly in URLs.

- *Self-hosted PyPI servers (e.g., Artifactory, devpi)*: For a more dedicated package management solution, consider setting up a self-hosted PyPI server. Tools like Artifactory and devpi are designed for managing binary artifacts, including Python packages.

  - – *Pros*: Designed specifically for package hosting and distribution. Offer fine-grained access control, package versioning, and search capabilities, and often include features like caching and proxying of public PyPI. Can be integrated with CI/CD pipelines for automated package publishing.

  - – *Cons*: Require setting up and maintaining server infrastructure. Can be more complex to configure initially compared with using private repositories. May incur additional costs depending on the chosen solution.

To install packages from a self-hosted PyPI server, we would typically configure `pip` to use the server's index URL. This can be done using the `--index-url` option when using pip:

```
pip install --index-url http://<your-private-pypi-server>/
simple <package-name>
```

- *Cloud-based private package registries*: Several cloud providers offer managed private package registry services, which can simplify the setup and maintenance of a private package repository. Examples include Azure Artifacts, AWS CodeArtifact, and Google Artifact Registry.

  - *Pros*: Managed services reduce operational overhead. Integrate well with cloud provider ecosystems. Often offer scalability, security, and compliance features.

  - *Cons*: May incur cloud service costs. Vendor lock-in might be a consideration.

`pyproject.toml` and Private Packages

Classifiers and the Special "Private :: Do Not Upload" Classifier

Classifiers are like tags that we add to our Python project's metadata. They help categorize the project on package indexes like PyPI. Think of them as labels that describe different aspects of the project, making it easier for people to find and understand what the package is all about.

We can specify classifiers in the project's configuration files, such as `setup.cfg` or `pyproject.toml`. Here's an example of a list of classifiers:

```
classifiers = [
  # Project maturity level
  "Development Status :: 4 - Beta",

  # Intended users of the project
  "Intended Audience :: Developers",
  "Topic :: Software Development :: Build Tools",

  # Supported Python versions (for display/search only, not installation enforcement)
  "Programming Language :: Python :: 3",
  "Programming Language :: Python :: 3.6",
  "Programming Language :: Python :: 3.7",
  "Programming Language :: Python :: 3.8",
```

```
  "Programming Language :: Python :: 3.9",
]
```

What Classifiers Do

- *Categorization and discovery*: Classifiers help users find the package on PyPI when they are browsing or searching. For example, someone looking for "build tools" or packages compatible with "Python 3.9" can use classifiers to filter their search.

- *Metadata, not installation enforcement*: It's important to know that while we can list supported Python versions as classifiers, this is only for informational purposes on PyPI. Classifiers *do not* prevent users from installing the package on unsupported Python versions.

There's a specific classifier designed to prevent accidental uploads of packages to PyPI:

```
"Private :: Do Not Upload"
```

If we include this classifier in the project's configuration, PyPI will *always reject* any attempt to upload the package. This is a straightforward way to ensure that packages intended for private use are not mistakenly made public on PyPI.

Optional Dependencies with "Extras"

Optional dependencies allow package developers to offer extended functionality without forcing users to install dependencies they might not need. This approach makes packages more lightweight, reduces installation overhead, and provides users with the flexibility to choose only the features they require. "Extras" are the mechanism in Python packaging used to define and manage these optional dependencies.

Consider a Python package that offers a range of functionalities, some of which depend on external libraries that are not essential for the core features of the package. For example, a data analysis library might have core functionalities for data manipulation but also offers optional features like

- *PDF report generation*: This might depend on libraries like reportlab or PyPDF2.

- *Advanced plotting*: This could rely on libraries such as matplotlib or seaborn.

- *Integration with specific databases*: Support for certain databases might require database-specific drivers like psycopg2 for PostgreSQL or mysqlclient for MySQL.

If these dependencies were mandatory, every user installing the base package would also have to install all these extra libraries, even if they only needed the core data manipulation features and not, for instance, PDF report generation. This would lead to

- *Bloated installations*: Users would end up installing libraries they don't use, increasing disk space usage and potentially slowing down installation processes.

- *Dependency conflicts*: Introducing more dependencies increases the risk of version conflicts with other packages in the user's environment.

- *Unnecessary overhead*: For users with limited resources or specific deployment environments, minimizing dependencies is often crucial.

Optional dependencies, managed through "extras," solve these problems by allowing package developers to declare these additional dependencies as optional features. Users can then choose to install only the extras they need, keeping their environments clean and efficient.

Defining Extras in `pyproject.toml`

With modern Python packaging tools that use pyproject.toml, such as Poetry, Flit, and PDM, optional dependencies are defined in the [project.optional-dependencies] section of the pyproject.toml file.

```
[project]
name = "mypackage"
version = "1.0.0"
dependencies = [
    "core-dependency>=1.0",
```

```
    # ... other core dependencies
]

[project.optional-dependencies]
pdf = [
    "reportlab>=3.5",
    "PyPDF2>=1.4"
]
plot = [
    "matplotlib>=3.0",
    "seaborn>=0.10"
]
database-postgres = [
    "psycopg2-binary>=2.8"
]
database-mysql = [
    "mysqlclient>=1.4"
]
dev = [
    "pytest>=6.0",
    "flake8>=3.8",
    "tox>=3.20"
]
docs = [
    "sphinx>=3.0",
    "sphinx-rtd-theme>=0.5"
]
```

The structure is similar to extras_require when using setup.py. Extra names are defined as keys under [project.optional-dependencies], and the values are lists of dependencies. Note that in pyproject.toml, extra names should use hyphens instead of underscores (e.g., database-postgres instead of database_postgres).

Installing Packages with Extras

Users can install a package with specific extras using `pip` by appending the extra names in square brackets after the package name. Multiple extras can be specified, separated by commas.

```
# Install the base package only (core dependencies)
pip install mypackage

# Install the package with the 'pdf' extra
pip install mypackage[pdf]

# Install the package with both 'pdf' and 'plot' extras
pip install mypackage[pdf,plot]

# Install the package with all defined extras
pip install mypackage[all]

# Install development dependencies (using the 'dev' extra)
pip install mypackage[dev]

# Install documentation dependencies (using the 'docs' extra)
pip install mypackage[docs]
```

When we install a package with extras, `pip` will resolve and install both the core dependencies and the dependencies specified for the selected extras.

Below is the `pyproject.toml` file of the Flask framework with multiple extras defined:

```
[project]
name = "Flask"
version = "3.2.0.dev"
description = "A simple framework for building complex web applications."
readme = "README.md"
license = {file = "LICENSE.txt"}
maintainers = [{name = "Pallets", email = "contact@palletsprojects.com"}]
classifiers = [
```

```
    "Development Status :: 5 - Production/Stable",
    "Environment :: Web Environment",
    "Framework :: Flask",
    ...
]
requires-python = ">=3.9"
dependencies = [
    "Werkzeug>=3.1",
    "Jinja2>=3.1.2",
    "itsdangerous>=2.2",
    "click>=8.1.3",
    "blinker>=1.9",
    "importlib-metadata>=3.6; python_version < '3.10'",
]

[project.urls]
Donate = "https://palletsprojects.com/donate"
Documentation = "https://flask.palletsprojects.com/"
Changes = "https://flask.palletsprojects.com/changes/"
Source = "https://github.com/pallets/flask/"
Chat = "https://discord.gg/pallets"

[project.optional-dependencies]
async = ["asgiref>=3.2"]
dotenv = ["python-dotenv"]

[project.scripts]
flask = "flask.cli:main"

[build-system]
requires = ["flit_core<4"]
build-backend = "flit_core.buildapi"

...
```

Flask ships with async and dotenv as extras as seen from the pyproject.toml file.

By effectively using optional dependencies and extras, we can create more user-friendly, efficient, and maintainable Python packages that cater to a wider range of use cases and user needs.

Automating Package Deployments with CI/CD

Automating the deployment process for Python packages is crucial for efficient software development and release management. Continuous Integration (CI) and Continuous Deployment (CD) pipelines streamline the journey from code commit to package release, ensuring consistency, reducing manual errors, and accelerating the delivery of new features and updates.

Implementing CI/CD for Python packages offers numerous benefits:

- *Increased efficiency and speed*: Automation significantly reduces the manual effort involved in testing, building, and publishing packages. This speeds up the release cycle, allowing for more frequent updates and faster delivery of new features and bug fixes to users.

- *Improved consistency and reliability*: Automated pipelines ensure that every package release follows the same predefined steps, minimizing human error and inconsistencies. This leads to more reliable and predictable releases.

- *Early detection of issues*: CI pipelines automatically run tests whenever code changes are made. This allows for early detection of bugs and integration issues, preventing problems from propagating further down the development lifecycle.

- *Enhanced code quality*: By automatically running linters, code formatters, and static analysis tools in the CI pipeline, we can enforce code quality standards and maintain a consistent codebase.

- *Faster feedback loops*: Automated testing and deployment provide rapid feedback to developers on the impact of their changes. This quick feedback loop is essential for iterative development and continuous improvement.

- *Simplified rollbacks*: In case of issues with a new release, automated deployment systems often facilitate quick rollbacks to previous versions, minimizing downtime and impact on users.

- *Reduced risk*: Automation reduces the risks associated with manual deployments, such as configuration errors, missed steps, or inconsistent environments.

Example: GitHub Action Workflow for PyPI Release

Below is a GitHub action workflow for automatic PyPI release. The pipeline gets triggered on GitHub release events for the repository:

```
name: Publish to PyPI # Workflow name
on: # Trigger conditions for the workflow
  release: # Trigger on GitHub release events
    types: [created] # Trigger only when a new release is created
jobs: # Define jobs to be executed
  deploy: # Job name: deploy
    runs-on: ubuntu-latest # Run job on Ubuntu latest runner
    steps: # Steps within the job
      - uses: actions/checkout@v2 # Step: Checkout code
        # Uses the 'actions/checkout@v2' action to checkout the
        repository code
      - name: Set up Python # Step: Set up Python environment
        uses: actions/setup-python@v2 # Uses 'actions/setup-python@v2'
        action
        with: # Configuration for 'actions/setup-python@v2'
          python-version: '3.x' # Set up Python 3.x
      - name: Install dependencies # Step: Install build dependencies
        run: | # Run shell commands
          python -m pip install --upgrade pip # Upgrade pip
          pip install build # Install 'build' package for building
          distributions
      - name: Build package # Step: Build distribution packages
        run: python -m build # Run 'python -m build' to create wheel and sdist
```

```
- name: Publish package # Step: Publish to PyPI
  uses: pypa/gh-action-pypi-publish@27b31702a0e7fc50959f5ad993c78deac
  1bdfc29 # Uses 'pypa/gh-action-pypi-publish' action
  with: # Configuration for 'pypa/gh-action-pypi-publish'
    user: __token__ # Username for PyPI (always '__token__' when
    using API token)
    password: ${{ secrets.PYPI_API_TOKEN }} # Password: PyPI API
    token from GitHub secrets
```

Key aspects of this workflow:

- *Trigger*: The workflow is triggered when a new release is created in GitHub. This is a common practice to tie package releases to GitHub releases.

- *Check out code*: The `actions/checkout@v2` action checks out the code from the repository, making it available to the workflow.

- *Set up Python*: The `actions/setup-python@v2` action sets up a Python environment on the runner, ensuring Python is available for subsequent steps.

- *Install dependencies*: It upgrades `pip` and installs the `build` package, which is necessary for building Python distribution packages.

- *Build package*: The `python -m build` command uses the `build` package to create wheel (`.whl`) and source distribution (`.tar.gz`) files in the `dist/` directory.

- *Publish package*: The `pypa/gh-action-pypi-publish` action is used to securely publish the built packages to PyPI.

  – *Authentication*: It uses a PyPI API token stored as a GitHub secret (`PYPI_API_TOKEN`). **Never hardcode API tokens or passwords directly in workflow files.** GitHub secrets provide a secure way to store sensitive information. We need to create a PyPI API token and store it as a secret in the GitHub repository settings.

- – *Username*: The user is set to __token__ when using an API token for PyPI authentication.

Enhancements and best practices for CI/CD pipelines:

- *Comprehensive testing*: Expand the testing stage to include various types of tests (unit, integration, doctests), test different Python versions, and test on different operating systems if cross-platform compatibility is important. Use tools like tox to automate testing across multiple environments.

- *Semantic versioning (SemVer) and version management*: Implement a strategy for automatically determining the next package version based on semantic versioning principles and commit history. Tools like semantic-release can help automate version bumping and release note generation.

- *Changelog generation*: Automate the generation of changelogs based on commit messages to provide users with clear release notes.

- *Pre-release checks*: Add stages for pre-release checks, such as verifying that all tests pass, code quality metrics are met, and documentation builds successfully before proceeding with the actual release.

- *Rollback strategy*: Define a rollback strategy in case a new release introduces critical issues. This might involve automatically reverting to the previous version in the package registry or providing instructions for users to downgrade.

- *Security scanning*: Integrate security scanning tools into the CI pipeline to detect potential vulnerabilities in dependencies or the package code itself.

- *Monitoring and alerting*: Set up monitoring and alerting for the CI/CD pipeline to be notified of build failures, deployment issues, or other anomalies.

- *Environment variables and secrets management*: Use environment variables and secrets management systems provided by the CI/CD platform to securely handle sensitive information like API tokens, passwords, and credentials. Avoid hardcoding these values in pipeline configurations.

- *Idempotency*: Ensure that the deployment scripts and processes are idempotent, meaning they can be run multiple times without causing unintended side effects. This is important for reliability and recovery in case of failures.

In addition to GitHub actions, most hosted Git solutions and cloud platforms provide their own CI/CD mechanisms that can be used to automate the testing, building, and release of Python packages. By implementing robust CI/CD pipelines, we can significantly improve the efficiency, reliability, and quality of Python package releases, enabling faster releases and better user experience.

Version Management

Effective version management is critical, especially for packages intended for distribution and reuse. A well-defined versioning scheme communicates the nature and scope of changes in each release to users, ensuring compatibility, facilitating updates, and fostering trust in the package.

Versioning provides several key benefits for Python packages:

- *Compatibility communication*: Version numbers clearly signal the type of changes introduced in a new release. Users can quickly understand whether an update is a minor bug fix, a new feature addition, or a potentially breaking change that requires code adjustments.

- *Dependency management*: Versioning is essential for dependency management. When one package depends on another, version constraints ensure compatibility. For example, a package might specify that it requires `mypackage >= 1.2.0, < 2.0.0`, indicating compatibility with versions 1.2.0 and above, but not version 2.0.0 or later, due to potential breaking changes.

- *Release tracking and history*: Version numbers provide a clear history of package releases. Users can easily track changes over time, refer to specific versions, and understand the evolution of the package.

- *Reproducibility*: Versioning ensures reproducibility. By specifying exact package versions in project requirements, developers can recreate consistent environments and avoid issues caused by unexpected updates.

Semantic Versioning

Semantic versioning (SemVer) is a widely adopted versioning scheme that uses a three-part version number: **MAJOR.MINOR.PATCH**. It provides a clear and standardized way to communicate the type of changes in each release.

- *MAJOR version (X in X.Y.Z)*: Increment the MAJOR version when we make **incompatible API changes**. This indicates that the new version is not backward-compatible with previous major versions. Users upgrading to a new major version should expect to potentially need to modify their code to adapt to the API changes. Examples of major changes include

  - Removing or renaming public functions, classes, or modules

  - Changing the expected input or output formats of functions or methods in a way that breaks existing usage

  - Significant architectural changes that fundamentally alter how the package is used

- *MINOR version (Y in X.Y.Z)*: Increment the MINOR version when we add **functionality in a backward-compatible manner**. This means that new features are introduced without breaking existing API contracts. Users can upgrade to a new minor version without needing to change their code, and they can optionally take advantage of the new features. Examples of minor changes include

  - Adding new functions, classes, or modules to the public API

  – Introducing new features that extend the package's capabilities
     without altering existing functionality

  – Adding new optional parameters to existing functions or methods

- *PATCH version (Z in X.Y.Z)*: Increment the PATCH version when we
  make **backward-compatible bug fixes**. Patch releases are intended
  for correcting issues without introducing new features or breaking
  existing functionality. Users can safely upgrade to a new patch
  version to benefit from bug fixes without any risk of code breakage.
  Examples of patch changes include

  – Fixing bugs that cause incorrect behavior or crashes

  – Improving performance without changing the API

  – Updating documentation or comments

  – Addressing security vulnerabilities that do not affect the API

Example scenarios of version bumps:

- *Bug fix in a function*: Version changes from 1.2.3 to 1.2.4 (PATCH
  increment).

- *Adding a new, non-breaking feature*: Version changes from 1.2.3 to
  1.3.0 (MINOR increment).

- *Removing a deprecated function*: Version changes from 1.3.0 to 2.0.0
  (MAJOR increment).

Pre-release versions: Semantic versioning also defines conventions for pre-release
versions (e.g., alpha, beta, release candidate). These are typically indicated by appending
a hyphen and a pre-release identifier to the version number, such as `1.0.0-alpha.1`,
`1.0.0-beta`, and `1.0.0-rc.2`. Pre-release versions signal that the release is not yet stable
and may contain bugs or API changes.

Alternative Versioning Schemes

While semantic versioning is widely recommended, there are alternative versioning
schemes that might be suitable in specific contexts such as **zero versioning (ZeroVer)**
or **calendar versioning (CalVer)**.

Tools for Automated Versioning

Manually managing version numbers can be error-prone and tedious. Several tools can automate version bumping and release management:

- bump2version: bump2version is a popular Python tool specifically designed for automating version number updates in projects. It can

    - Update version strings in project files (e.g., setup.py, pyproject. toml, __version__ variables).

    - Commit the version changes to version control.

    - Create tags for releases.

    - Support various versioning schemes, including SemVer.

    - Be configured through a .bumpversion.cfg file.

Example usage with bump2version:

```
bump2version patch      # Increment patch version (e.g., 1.2.3 -> 1.2.4)
bump2version minor      # Increment minor version (e.g., 1.2.3 -> 1.3.0)
bump2version major      # Increment major version (e.g., 1.2.3 -> 2.0.0)
bump2version release    # Remove pre-release suffix (e.g., 1.0.0-beta
                          -> 1.0.0)
bump2version --dry-run  # Test version bump without making changes
```

- semantic-release: semantic-release is a more comprehensive tool that automates the entire release process based on semantic commit messages. It can

    - Analyze commit messages to determine the type of version bump (major, minor, patch).

    - Automatically bump the version number.

    - Generate changelogs based on commit messages.

    - Publish releases to package registries.

    - Create GitHub releases and tags.

> semantic-release enforces a specific commit message format
> (e.g., using prefixes like feat:, fix:, BREAKING CHANGE:) to
> determine the appropriate version increment.

Below is an example of an open source release action using the semantic-release tool:

```
# .github/workflows/semantic-release-python.yml
name: Semantic Release

on:
  push:
    branches:
      - master

jobs:
  release:
    runs-on: ubuntu-latest
    concurrency: release

    steps:
    - uses: actions/checkout@v2
      with:
        fetch-depth: 0

    - name: Python Semantic Release
      uses: relekang/python-semantic-release@master
      with:
        github_token: ${{ secrets.GH_TOKEN }}
        repository_username: __token__
        repository_password: ${{ secrets.PYPI_TOKEN }}
```

When the main branch receives a push, this workflow bumps the version according to the commit message. For example, a commit with message fix: bug in profile API will result in the release of a new patch version.

Testing Packages

Testing is not just an optional step but an integral part of the Python packaging process. Rigorous testing ensures that the package functions as expected, is free from critical bugs, and provides a stable and reliable experience for users.

Comprehensive testing offers numerous benefits for Python packages:

- *Bug detection and prevention*: Testing helps identify and eliminate bugs early in the development cycle before they reach users. This reduces the likelihood of unexpected errors, crashes, or incorrect behavior in production environments.

- *Ensuring functionality*: Tests verify that the package's features and functionalities work as designed and meet the intended requirements. This ensures that the package delivers its promised value to users.

- *Regression prevention*: As we develop and modify our package, tests act as a safety net to prevent regressions. They ensure that new changes do not inadvertently break existing functionality.

- *Code quality and maintainability*: Writing tests encourages better code design and modularity. Testable code is often cleaner, more organized, and easier to maintain. Tests also serve as living documentation, illustrating how different parts of the package are intended to work.

- *Confidence in releases*: Thorough testing builds confidence in the package releases. When we know that the package is well-tested, we can release new versions with greater assurance and reduce the risk of introducing issues for users.

- *Facilitating collaboration*: A comprehensive test suite makes it easier for teams to collaborate on a package. Tests provide a shared understanding of the package's behavior and help prevent integration issues when multiple developers contribute.

- *Supporting refactoring and evolution*: Tests enable safe refactoring and code improvements. We can confidently make changes to the codebase, knowing that tests will quickly reveal if any existing functionality is broken.

Types of Testing for Python Packages

A robust testing strategy typically involves different levels and types of testing:

- *Unit testing*: Unit tests are the foundation of a good testing strategy. They focus on testing individual units of code in isolation. A "unit" is usually a function, method, or class. The goal of unit testing is to verify that each unit performs its intended task correctly, independently of other parts of the package.

  - *Benefits of unit testing*:

    - *Pinpoint bugs*: Unit tests help quickly identify the source of bugs by isolating them to specific units of code.

    - *Fast feedback*: Unit tests are typically fast to run, providing rapid feedback during development.

    - *Detailed verification*: They allow for detailed verification of specific code behaviors and edge cases.

    - *Code design improvement*: Writing unit tests often leads to better-designed, more modular, and testable code.

  - *Tools and frameworks*: Python offers excellent testing frameworks for unit testing, primarily

    - `unittest` *(built-in)*: Python's built-in unit testing framework provides a structured way to organize tests using test cases and test suites.

    - `pytest` *(external)*: A popular and powerful third-party testing framework. `pytest` is known for its simplicity, discoverability of tests, rich plugin ecosystem, and excellent error reporting. It is often preferred for its more concise syntax and advanced features.

  - *Example (using* `pytest`*)*:

```python
# mypackage/math_utils.py
def add(a, b):
    """Adds two numbers."""
    return a + b
```

697

```
# tests/test_math_utils.py
from mypackage.math_utils import add

def test_add_positive_numbers():
    assert add(2, 3) == 5

def test_add_negative_numbers():
    assert add(-2, -3) == -5

def test_add_mixed_numbers():
    assert add(5, -2) == 3

def test_add_zero():
    assert add(0, 7) == 7
```

- *Integration testing*: Integration tests go beyond unit tests to verify the interactions between different components or modules of the package. They ensure that these components work correctly together as a whole. Integration tests are crucial for catching issues that arise from the way different parts of the package are integrated.

  – *Benefits of integration testing*:

    - *Verify component interactions*: Integration tests ensure that different parts of the package communicate and collaborate correctly.

    - *Detect interface issues*: They can uncover problems with interfaces between modules, data flow issues, and incorrect assumptions about component behavior.

    - *Test complex scenarios*: Integration tests can simulate more realistic use cases and complex workflows that involve multiple components working together.

  – *Example (conceptual)*: If the package involves data processing and storage, an integration test might verify that the data processing module correctly interacts with the data storage module to save and retrieve data as expected. This would involve testing the flow of data between these modules and ensuring that the integration points are working correctly.

- *Doctests*: Doctests are tests embedded directly within the docstrings of Python code. They are a simple way to test code examples in the documentation and ensure that the examples are not only correct but also up to date. Doctests are useful for verifying basic functionality and providing executable documentation.

  - *Example*:

    ```python
    def multiply(a, b):
        """Multiplies two numbers.

        >>> multiply(3, 4)
        12
        >>> multiply(-1, 5)
        -5
        """
        return a * b
    ```

    Python's doctest module can run these tests and verify that the output matches the expected output in the docstring.

- *Property-based testing*: Property-based testing (e.g., using hypothesis) is an advanced testing technique where we define properties that the code should satisfy for a wide range of inputs, rather than writing tests for specific input values. The testing framework then automatically generates many different inputs and checks if the properties hold true. This can uncover edge cases and unexpected behaviors that might be missed by traditional example-based tests.

Environment Testing with **tox**

tox is a powerful tool for automating testing across multiple Python environments. It allows us to define different testing environments with specific Python versions and dependencies and run the tests in each environment. This is crucial for ensuring that the package works correctly across different Python versions and dependency configurations that users might be using.

- *Benefits of using* tox:

- *Cross-Python version testing*: Easily test the package against multiple Python versions (e.g., Python 3.6, 3.7, 3.8, 3.9, etc.) to ensure compatibility.

- *Isolated environments*: tox creates isolated virtual environments for each test run, preventing dependency conflicts and ensuring clean test environments.

- *Automated test execution*: Automates the process of setting up test environments, installing dependencies, running tests, and reporting results.

- *Customizable environments*: We can define custom test environments with specific dependencies and configurations in the tox. ini configuration file.

- *Integration with CI/CD*: tox is commonly used in CI/CD pipelines to automate testing as part of the build and release process.

- tox.ini *configuration*: The tox.ini file in the root of the project defines the test environments and configurations for tox.

```
# tox.ini
[tox]
envlist = py39, py310, py311 # List of environments to test
(Python versions)

[testenv]
deps =
    pytest # Test dependencies for all environments
    pytest-cov # Example: code coverage plugin
commands =
    pytest --cov=mypackage --cov-report=term-missing {posargs}
    # Test command
```

- *Explanation of* tox.ini:

  - [tox]: Section for general tox settings

    - envlist = py39, py310, py311: Defines the list of environments to be created and tested. Here, it specifies

Python 3.9, 3.10, and 3.11. tox will look for interpreters named python3.9, python3.10, and python3.11 in system's PATH.

- [testenv]: Section for test environment settings that apply to all environments unless overridden

  - deps = pytest\n pytest-cov: Specifies dependencies to be installed in each test environment. Here, it installs pytest and pytest-cov (a pytest plugin for code coverage). Dependencies are listed one per line.
  - commands = pytest --cov=mypackage --cov-report=term-missing {posargs}: Defines the command to run in each test environment.

    - pytest: Runs the pytest test runner

    - --cov=mypackage: Enables code coverage measurement for the mypackage package

    - --cov-report=term-missing: Configures code coverage to report missing lines in the terminal

    - {posargs}: Allows passing additional arguments to the test command from the command line (e.g., tox -- -k test_specific_feature)

- *Running tests with* tox: To run tests using tox, simply navigate to the root directory of the project (where tox.ini is located) in terminal and run the command

tox

tox will then

1. Create virtual environments for each environment listed in envlist (e.g., py39, py310, py311).

701

2. Install the dependencies specified in deps for each environment.

3. Execute the command specified in commands in each environment.

4. Report the test results for each environment.

    We can also run tests for a specific environment:

```
tox -e py39 # Run tests only in the 'py39' environment
```

Security Considerations

Security is a critical aspect of Python packaging. Ensuring that packages are secure protects users from potential vulnerabilities and maintains the integrity of the Python ecosystem. This section details essential security considerations and practices for Python package developers.

Auditing Dependencies with Safety

Regularly auditing the project's dependencies for known security vulnerabilities is a proactive security measure. safety is a tool specifically designed for this purpose.

- *Installing safety*: safety can be easily installed using pip:

  ```
  pip install safety
  ```

- *Checking for vulnerabilities*: To check the project's dependencies for vulnerabilities, navigate to the project directory (where requirements.txt or pyproject.toml is located) and run

  ```
  safety check
  ```

  safety will scan the dependencies against a database of known vulnerabilities and report any it finds, along with severity levels and remediation advice. We can also specify a requirements file directly:

  ```
  safety check -r requirements.txt
  ```

- *Integrating safety into CI/CD*: For continuous security monitoring, integrate `safety` checks into the CI/CD pipeline. This ensures that every build and release is automatically checked for dependency vulnerabilities, allowing us to catch and address issues early in the development cycle.

Best Practices for Secure Packaging

Beyond specific tools, adopting general best practices is crucial for maintaining secure Python packages.

1. *Keep build tools and dependencies up to date*: Regularly update packaging and build tools (like `setuptools`, `pip`, `build`, `twine`) and project dependencies. Outdated tools and dependencies may contain known vulnerabilities that can be exploited.

2. *Use virtual environments*: Always develop and build packages within isolated virtual environments. This practice prevents conflicts between project dependencies and system-wide packages, and it helps ensure reproducible builds.

3. *Be cautious with dependencies*: Carefully evaluate each dependency that is included in the project. Only add dependencies that are truly necessary, and prefer well-maintained, reputable packages. Be wary of including dependencies simply because they are convenient; each dependency introduces potential security risks.

4. *Regularly update and patch dependencies*: Establish a process for regularly reviewing and updating the project's dependencies. Stay informed about security updates and patches for the libraries that we use, and promptly apply these updates to minimize vulnerability windows.

5. *Utilize static security analysis tools like* `bandit`: Incorporate static security analysis tools like `bandit` into the development workflow. `bandit` scans Python code for common security vulnerabilities, such as injection flaws, hardcoded credentials, and more.

```
pip install bandit
bandit -r ./src
```

Running `bandit` against the package source code helps identify potential security issues before they make it into the packaged releases.

6. *Implement proper access controls for private repositories*: If we are using private package repositories, we must ensure that we have robust access controls in place. Restrict access to only authorized users and use strong authentication mechanisms to protect private packages from unauthorized access and distribution.

7. *Be mindful of package contents*: Carefully review the contents of the package before release. Avoid including sensitive information, unnecessary files, or development artifacts in the distribution packages. Only include the code and resources that are essential for the package's functionality.

Handling Security Vulnerabilities

Despite best efforts, security vulnerabilities may still be discovered in packages. Having a plan for handling these vulnerabilities is essential for responsible package maintenance.

1. *Prepare a fix quickly*: As soon as a security vulnerability is reported or discovered, prioritize preparing a fix. This may involve patching the vulnerable code, updating dependencies, or implementing other necessary security measures.

2. *Release a new version with the fix*: Release a new version of the package that includes the security fix. Follow semantic versioning to clearly communicate the nature of the release (e.g., a patch release for a security fix).

3. *Consider yanking affected versions from PyPI*: If the vulnerability is severe and could pose a significant risk to users, consider yanking the affected versions from PyPI. Yanking removes the releases from public visibility, preventing new installations of the vulnerable versions.

```
pip install twine
twine yank mypackage==1.0.0
```

Use the `twine yank` command carefully, as it can disrupt users who are already relying on the yanked versions. Communicate clearly with the user base before and after yanking a release.

4. *Communicate clearly with users*: When a security vulnerability is discovered and addressed, communicate clearly and transparently with the users. Provide details about the vulnerability, its potential impact, the fixed version, and the steps users should take to update. Use channels like release notes, security advisories, and community forums to disseminate this information.

By diligently implementing these security considerations and practices, we can significantly enhance the security posture of our Python packages, protect the users, and contribute to a more secure and trustworthy Python ecosystem.

Conclusion

In this chapter, we have explored the landscape of Python packaging, understanding its critical role in the development and distribution of Python projects. We began by exploring the historical context, where early challenges in packaging led to the development of tools and standards that have shaped the modern packaging ecosystem. By looking into the evolution from egg files to the versatile Wheel format and the introduction of the `pyproject.toml` file, we have seen how Python packaging has matured into a robust and efficient process. These advancements have provided developers with powerful tools and methodologies to ensure their projects are well-organized, easily distributable, and maintainable.

As we conclude, it's essential to emphasize the importance of adhering to best practices and security considerations in packaging. A well-packaged Python project not only simplifies the installation process for users but also ensures that the code is secure and reliable. By utilizing tools like Setuptools, Poetry, and others and implementing practices such as semantic versioning, testing, and dependency auditing, we can create packages that stand the test of time.

## CHAPTER 21

Dependency Management

In the previous chapter, we explored Python packaging—how to prepare our code for distribution so others can install and use it easily.

Building on that foundation, this chapter focuses on *dependency management*—the process of handling external libraries and packages that a project depends on. These dependencies play a critical role in adding functionality and improving development speed without reinventing the wheel.

Despite its importance, dependency management is often an afterthought until it causes problems. Poor management can lead to version conflicts, security vulnerabilities, and unpredictable behavior across environments. On the other hand, proper dependency management keeps our projects stable, secure, and easy to maintain.

But managing dependencies isn't always straightforward. We often face challenges like

- Keeping track of multiple package versions

- Resolving conflicts between incompatible packages

- Ensuring compatibility with specific Python versions

- Maintaining consistency between development and production environments

In this chapter, we'll dive deep into Python's ecosystem for dependency management. We'll cover virtual environments, version specifiers, deterministic builds, and the tools that make managing dependencies more predictable and less painful.

Virtual Environments

Virtual environments are essential for creating isolated environments for each project. This isolation ensures that dependencies for one project do not interfere with those of another, preventing version conflicts and maintaining a clean development

707

© Adarsh Divakaran 2025
A. Divakaran, *Deep Dive Python*, https://doi.org/10.1007/979-8-8688-1261-3_21

environment. They allow us to create isolated spaces for individual projects where we can install and manage dependencies without affecting our system-wide Python installation or other projects.

Virtual environments work by creating a copy of the Python interpreter and its core libraries in a separate directory. When we activate a virtual environment, it adjusts our system path to use this isolated Python installation.

Let's look at how we can create and use a virtual environment using Python's built-in venv module:

```
# Create a new virtual environment
python -m venv myproject_env

# Activate the virtual environment
# On Windows:
myproject_env\Scripts\activate
# On macOS and Linux:
source myproject_env/bin/activate

# The prompt will change to indicate the active environment
(myproject_env) $

# Install packages as needed
pip install package_name

# Deactivate the virtual environment when done
deactivate
```

When working with projects, a new independent virtual environment should be created and activated before dependencies are installed.

Managing Python Versions

As Python evolves, new versions are released with new features, improvements, and sometimes breaking changes. Managing multiple Python versions becomes crucial when

- We need to maintain projects that use different Python versions.

- We want to test our code across various Python versions.

- We're transitioning a project from an older to a newer Python version.

The default Python installers obtained from `python.org` are guaranteed to be installed independently without interfering with existing Python versions. We can then create a virtual environment by choosing a base interpreter from any of the Python versions installed in the system.

Also, there are tools like `pyenv` that can help us manage multiple Python versions. It allows us to install and switch between multiple Python versions effortlessly.

Here's a quick overview of a few `pyenv` commands:

```
# Install a specific Python version
pyenv install 3.13.0

# Set a global Python version
pyenv global 3.12.1

# Set a local Python version for a specific project
cd myproject
pyenv local 3.12.5

# Check the current Python version
pyenv version

# List all available Python versions
pyenv versions
```

We can integrate `pyenv` with virtual environments to create a powerful workflow:

1. Use pyenv to install and select the desired Python version for our project.

2. Create a virtual environment using that specific Python version.

3. Activate the virtual environment and install project dependencies.

Deterministic Builds

Deterministic builds ensure that our projects build and run the same way every time, regardless of the environment. This consistency is crucial for reliability and reduces unexpected behavior in production environments.

In the context of Python projects, deterministic builds mean that given the same source code and dependencies, we can recreate the exact same environment and build output every time. This consistency is crucial for several reasons:

1. *Reproducibility*: Anyone can recreate the development environment exactly as intended.

2. *Debugging*: It's easier to track down and fix issues when we know exactly what versions of dependencies we're working with.

3. *Collaboration*: Team members can work with identical environments, reducing system-specific issues.

4. *Deployment*: We can ensure that our production environment matches our development and testing environments.

However, achieving truly deterministic builds can be challenging. Dependencies may have their own dependencies (called transitive dependencies), and without proper management, these can lead to inconsistencies. Some packages might not specify exact versions for their dependencies, leading to potential variability.

In the coming sections, we will explore a few techniques for avoiding potential dependency issues across environments.

Dependency Specifiers

Dependency specifiers allow us to define which versions of a package our project can use. By specifying version ranges in our requirements, we can ensure compatibility while still allowing for some flexibility in updates. Dependency specifiers follow the guidelines originally set out in PEP 440. Currently, the standard is maintained by the Python Packaging Authority (PyPA) and is available online in the Python Packaging User Guide (`https://packaging.python.org/en/latest/specifications/dependency-specifiers/`). This standardization ensures that all Python packaging tools interpret version numbers and constraints consistently.

Let's break down some common version specifier formats:

1. *Exact version*: `==X.Y.Z`

   - *Example*: `==3.7.2` (only accepts version 3.7.2)

2. *Greater than or equal to*: >=X.Y.Z

    – *Example*: >=2.1.0 (accepts 2.1.0, 2.1.1, 2.2.0, 3.0.0, etc.)

3. *Less than*: <X.Y.Z

    – *Example*: <4.0.0 (accepts 3.9.9, 3.8.0, 2.0.0, etc., but not 4.0.0 or newer)

4. *Compatible release*: ~=X.Y.Z

    – *Example*: ~=2.2.3 (accepts 2.2.3, 2.2.4, and 2.2.10, but not 2.3.0 or 3.0.0)

    – ~=2.2 (accepts 2.3, 2.4, and 2.10, but not 3.0 or 3.0.1)

5. *Version exclusion*: !=X.Y.Z

    – *Example*: !=1.3.5 (accepts any version except 1.3.5)

We can also combine these specifiers for more precise control:

requests>=2.20.0,<3.0.0

This means "use any version of requests from 2.20.0 up to, but not including, 3.0.0." Here are some best practices for using version specifiers:

1. *Be as specific as necessary*: If your project works with a specific version, it's often safest to pin to that exact version.

2. *Use ranges for flexibility*: When you're confident about compatibility (e.g., in libraries following semantic versioning), use ranges to allow for minor updates and bug fixes.

3. *Avoid overly broad specifiers*: Using just >= without an upper bound can lead to unexpected breaking changes.

4. *Consider semantic versioning*: Many projects follow semantic versioning (MAJOR.MINOR.PATCH). In this case, ~=2.1.0 would allow patches (2.1.1, 2.1.2, etc.) but not minor or major updates.

5. *Update regularly*: Regularly review and update your dependencies to benefit from bug fixes and security patches.

6. *Test thoroughly*: When changing version specifiers, always test the project thoroughly to ensure compatibility.

Locking Dependencies

Version locks are necessary to achieve truly deterministic builds. Version locks include the exact versions of the dependencies (including transitive dependencies). By locking the versions, we can ensure that the same versions are used every time we build our project. This prevents unexpected issues caused by updates or changes in dependencies. Tools like `pip freeze` help us generate a `requirements.txt` file with pinned versions, ensuring consistency across environments.

- `pip freeze > requirements.txt`: Generates a `requirements.txt` file with the current environment's package versions

- `pip install -r requirements.txt`: Installs packages from a `requirements.txt` file (with exact versions specified), ensuring the same versions are used

Other tools, such as Pipenv or Poetry use a lock file for deterministic builds. A lock file is a detailed record of all direct and transitive dependencies in a project, including their exact versions. Tools like Poetry, Pipenv, and pip-tools generate these lock files, which typically have names like `poetry.lock`, `Pipfile.lock`, or `requirements.lock`.

Benefits of using lock files include

1. *Exact replication*: Every dependency is pinned to a specific version.

2. *Faster installations*: The resolver doesn't need to calculate dependencies each time.

3. *Conflict prevention*: Lock files catch and prevent dependency conflicts early.

4. *Auditability*: It's easier to review and track changes in dependencies over time.

We will explore these tools in the coming sections.

Tools

There are various tools available to help us manage dependencies effectively. Here, we will explore some of the most popular ones and their key features.

pip

pip is the default package manager for Python, allowing us to install, update, and manage packages easily. Starting from Python 3.4, pip comes as a part of the standard Python installation.

Let's look at some essential pip commands:

```
# Install a package
pip install package_name

# Install a specific version
pip install package_name==1.2.3

# Upgrade a package
pip install --upgrade package_name

# Uninstall a package
pip uninstall package_name

# List installed packages
pip list

# Show details about a package
pip show package_name

# Install packages from a requirements file
pip install -r requirements.txt
```

When we use pip to install a package, it goes through a process called dependency resolution. Here's how it works:

1. Pip reads the package's metadata to determine its dependencies.

2. It then checks if these dependencies are already installed.

3. If not, it tries to find versions of these dependencies that are compatible with each other and with the package we're installing.

4. This process continues recursively for all dependencies and their sub-dependencies.

5. Once pip has figured out a set of packages that satisfy all requirements, it proceeds with the installation.

This process can sometimes lead to conflicts, especially in complex projects with many dependencies. That's where `pip check` comes in handy:

```
pip check
```

This command verifies that all installed packages have compatible dependencies. If there are any issues, it will report them, helping us identify and resolve conflicts.

Being the default package manager, `pip` is immensely popular. However, it lacks features such as the ability to automate the generation of lock files.

If we need to manually replicate the currently installed packages into another environment, we can use pip freeze to generate a frozen requirements.txt file. `pip freeze` gives us the requirements with the exact installed versions in the current environment. We can write that to a file using `pip freeze > requirements.txt` to generate versioned requirements, e.g.:

```
pip install flask
pip install django

pip freeze > requirements.txt

pip check # No broken requirements found.
```

The generated requirements file will contain exact version specifiers as seen below:

```
asgiref==3.8.1
blinker==1.8.2
click==8.1.7
colorama==0.4.6
Django==5.1.2
Flask==3.0.3
itsdangerous==2.2.0
Jinja2==3.1.4
MarkupSafe==3.0.2
sqlparse==0.5.1
tzdata==2024.2
Werkzeug==3.1.1
```

We can use this requirements file to install the exact same requirements in a new environment. This method is commonly used in smaller projects to create deterministic builds.

pip-tools

pip-tools is a set of command-line tools that extend pip's functionality, primarily focusing on generating and managing requirements files. It's particularly useful for creating deterministic builds.

Key commands of pip-tools:

1. *pip-compile*: The `pip-compile` command lets you compile a `requirements.txt` file from your dependencies specified in either `pyproject.toml`, `setup.cfg`, `setup.py`, or `requirements.in`.

2. *pip-sync*: Ensures that the virtual environment matches exactly what's specified in the requirements.txt. This command installs the necessary packages specified in the compiled requirements file.

Here's how to use pip-tools:

```
# Install pip-tools
pip install pip-tools

# Create a requirements.in file with your top-level dependencies
echo "requests" > requirements.in

# Compile the requirements.txt file
pip-compile requirements.in

# Sync your environment with the compiled requirements
pip-sync requirements.txt
```

pip-tools helps bridge the gap between pip's simplicity and the need for more robust dependency management.

Consider the `requirements.in` file as seen below:

```
flask
requests
```

When compiled using `pip-compile`, it generates a `requirements.txt` file as seen below:

```
#
# This file is autogenerated by pip-compile with Python 3.11
# by the following command:
#
#    pip-compile
#
blinker==1.8.2
    # via flask
certifi==2024.8.30
    # via requests
charset-normalizer==3.4.0
    # via requests
click==8.1.7
    # via flask
colorama==0.4.6
    # via click
flask==3.0.3
    # via -r requirements.in
idna==3.10
    # via requests
itsdangerous==2.2.0
    # via flask
jinja2==3.1.4
    # via flask
markupsafe==3.0.2
    # via
    #    jinja2
    #    werkzeug
requests==2.32.3
    # via -r requirements.in
urllib3==2.2.3
    # via requests
werkzeug==3.1.1
    # via flask
```

The compiled requirements specify the exact versions of our dependencies and transitive dependencies. This will help us create deterministic environments.

To remove a package, we can delete the same from the `requirements.in` file and run `pip-compile` again. When looking to upgrade the package versions, `pip-compile --upgrade` can be used, which will switch to the latest stable version of the packages.

The below GitHub action workflow file from Microsoft's responsible-ai-toolbox library showcases the usage of pip-tools in CI/CD environments:

```
name: CI rai_core_flask

on:
  push:
    branches: [main]

jobs:
  ci-rai-core-flask:
    strategy:
      # keep running remaining matrix jobs even if one fails
      # to avoid having to rerun all jobs several times
      fail-fast: false
      matrix:
        operatingSystem:
          [ubuntu-20.04, ubuntu-latest, macos-latest, windows-latest]
        pythonVersion: ["3.8", "3.9", "3.10", "3.11"]

    runs-on: ${{ matrix.operatingSystem }}

    steps:
      - uses: actions/checkout@v4

      - name: Set up Python ${{ matrix.pythonVersion }}
        uses: actions/setup-python@v5
        with:
          python-version: ${{ matrix.pythonVersion }}

      - if: ${{ matrix.pythonVersion == '3.8' || matrix.pythonVersion == '3.9'
        || matrix.pythonVersion == '3.10' || matrix.pythonVersion == '3.11' }}
        name: Setup tools for python gte 3.8
```

```
    run: |
      python -m pip install --upgrade pip
      pip install --upgrade setuptools
      pip install --upgrade "pip-tools<=7.1.0"

  - name: Pip compile
    run: |
      pip-compile requirements-dev.txt -o requirements-dev-comp.txt
      cat requirements-dev-comp.txt
    working-directory: rai_core_flask

  - name: Upload requirements
    uses: actions/upload-artifact@v3
    with:
      name: requirements-dev-comp.txt
      path: rai_core_flask/requirements-dev-comp.txt

  - name: Install dependencies
    run: |
      pip-sync requirements-dev-comp.txt
    working-directory: rai_core_flask

  - name: Install package
    run: |
      pip install -v -e .
    working-directory: rai_core_flask

  - name: Run tests
    run: |
      pytest -s -v --durations=10 --doctest-modules --junitxml=junit/
      test-results.xml --cov=rai_core_flask --cov-report=xml --cov-
      report=html
    working-directory: rai_core_flask
```

...

Here, the workflow uses `pip-tools` to

1. Generate exact dependencies for different Python versions (3.8-3.11).

2. Test the package across multiple operating systems.

3. Ensure reproducible builds and tests.

pipenv

`pipenv` is a tool that combines `pip` and `virtualenv`, providing a seamless way to manage dependencies and virtual environments. It simplifies the process of creating and managing virtual environments and automatically generates a `Pipfile` and `Pipfile.lock` to lock dependencies.

Key features of Pipenv:

1. Automatic virtual environment management

2. Dependency resolution and lock file generation (`Pipfile.lock`)

3. Security vulnerability checking (`pipenv check` command)

```
# Install Pipenv
pip install pipenv

# Initialize a new project
pipenv --python 3.9

# Install packages
pipenv install requests

# Activate the Pipenv shell
pipenv shell

# Run a script in the virtual environment
pipenv run python my_script.py
```

Pipenv's `Pipfile` and `Pipfile.lock` provide a more modern and comprehensive approach to dependency management compared with traditional requirements.txt files.

Below is an example of installing a package using pipenv:

```
(3.11venv) > pipenv install requests
Courtesy Notice:
Pipenv found itself running within a virtual environment,  so it will
automatically use that environment, instead of  creating its own for any
project. You can set
PIPENV_IGNORE_VIRTUALENVS=1 to force pipenv to ignore that environment and
create  its own instead.
You can set PIPENV_VERBOSITY=-1 to suppress this warning.
Creating a Pipfile for this project...
Pipfile.lock not found, creating...
Locking [packages] dependencies...
Locking [dev-packages] dependencies...
Updated Pipfile.lock (ed6d5d614626ae28e274e453164affb266947
55170ccab3aa5866f093d51d3e4)!
To activate this project's virtualenv, run pipenv shell.
Alternatively, run a command inside the virtualenv with pipenv run.
Installing requests...
Installation Succeeded
To activate this project's virtualenv, run pipenv shell.
Alternatively, run a command inside the virtualenv with pipenv run.
Installing dependencies from Pipfile.lock (51d3e4)...
All dependencies are now up-to-date!
Upgrading requests in  dependencies.
Building requirements...
Resolving dependencies...
Success!
```

pipenv can create a virtual environment if it does not exist. It can also install the dependencies in requirements.txt files, convert them to Pipfile, and output the Pipfile.lock file.

The above output will produce a Pipfile, as seen below:

```
[[source]]
url = "https://pypi.org/simple"
verify_ssl = true
```

```
name = "pypi"

[packages]
requests = "*"

[dev-packages]

[requires]
python_version = "3.11"
```

Running `pipenv install` generates a `Pipfile.lock` with the exact same requirement versions installed in the current environment.

Below is a `Pipfile.lock` generated by installing the `requests` library:

```
{
    "_meta": {
        "hash": {
            "sha256": "ff88c6939e3090788e917cfdecf1af872168b83c880
            3457853061495493b5a71"
        },
        "pipfile-spec": 6,
        "requires": {
            "python_version": "3.11"
        },
        "sources": [
            {
                "name": "pypi",
                "url": "https://pypi.org/simple",
                "verify_ssl": true
            }
        ]
    },
    "default": {
        "certifi": {
            "hashes": [
                sha256:922820b53db7a7257ffbda3f597266d435245903d80737e34f
                8a45ff3e3230d8",
```

```
                "sha256:bec941d2aa8195e248a60b31ff9f0558284cf01a52591ceda73
                ea9afffd69fd9"
            ],
            "markers": "python_version >= '3.6'",
            "version": "==2024.8.30"
        },
        ...
        "requests": {
            "hashes": [
                "sha256:55365417734eb18255590a9ff9eb97e9e1da868d4ccd6402399
                eaf68af20a760",
                "sha256:70761cfe03c773ceb22aa2f671b4757976145175cdfca038
                c02654d061d6dcc6"
            ],
            "index": "pypi",
            "markers": "python_version >= '3.8'",
            "version": "==2.32.3"
        },
        "urllib3": {
            "hashes": [
                "sha256:ca899ca043dcb1bafa3e262d73aa25c465bfb49e0bd9dd5d59
                f1d0acba2f8fac",
                "sha256:e7d814a81dad81e6caf2ec9fdedb284ecc9c73076b62654547c
                c64ccdcae26e9"
            ],
            "markers": "python_version >= '3.8'",
            "version": "==2.2.3"
        }
    },
    "develop": {}
}
```

To replicate the same environment, the pipenv sync command should be used. It installs the same requirement version specified in the lock file in the executed environment.

Below is a workflow file from JQ, a command-line JSON processing library that showcases Pipenv usage in CI/CD environments:

```yaml
# File: jq/.github/workflows/website.yml
name: Update website
on:
  push:
    branches:
      - master
    paths:
      - 'docs/**'
concurrency: website
permissions:
  contents: write

jobs:
  website:
    runs-on: ubuntu-latest
    steps:
      - name: Checkout code
        uses: actions/checkout@v4
        with:
          fetch-depth: 0
      - name: Setup Python
        uses: actions/setup-python@v5
        with:
          python-version: '3.11'
          cache: pipenv
      - name: Install pipenv
        run: pip install pipenv
      - name: Install dependencies
        run: pipenv sync
        working-directory: docs
      - name: Update website
        run: scripts/update-website
      - name: Commit changes
```

```
    run: |
      if ! git diff --quiet; then
        git add --all
        git config user.name 'github-actions[bot]'
        git config user.email 'github-actions[bot]@users.noreply.
        github.com'
        git commit -m 'Update website'
        git push origin gh-pages
      fi
```

Here pipenv is used to replicate the pushed environment dependencies using the sync command.

pdm

PDM is a tool that provides a modern and easy way to manage dependencies and projects.

Key features of PDM:

- Supports PEP 621 project metadata (pyproject.toml)

- Lock file generation for deterministic builds

- Virtual environment management support

Basic PDM usage:

```
# Install PDM
pip install pdm

# Initialize a new project
pdm init

# Add dependencies
pdm add requests

# Install dependencies
pdm install

# Run a script
pdm run python my_script.py
```

724

The pdm init command initializes the project using an interactive wizard. It allows the user to choose from different Python versions present in the system. The command bootstraps a project by creating a pyproject.toml file, src directory, tests directory, readme file, etc. It can be used to build packages as well as manage normal applications.

Below is a pyproject.toml generated by pdm-init:

```
[project]
name = "pdm-project"
version = "0.1.0"
description = "Default template for PDM package"
authors = [
    {name = "Adarsh D", email = "adarshdevamritham@gmail.com"},
]
dependencies = ["requests>=2.32.3"]
requires-python = "==3.11.*"
readme = "README.md"
license = {text = "MIT"}

[tool.pdm]
distribution = false
```

Installing the requests library generates the below pdm.lock file.

```
# This file is @generated by PDM.
# It is not intended for manual editing.

[metadata]
groups = ["default"]
strategy = ["inherit_metadata"]
lock_version = "4.5.0"
content_hash = "sha256:18ae299931cbf788151c0ca0553315b61b22f5a01443a26471f
e89e196127a7c"

[[metadata.targets]]
requires_python = "==3.11.*"

[[package]]
name = "certifi"
version = "2024.8.30"
```

```
requires_python = ">=3.6"
summary = "Python package for providing Mozilla's CA Bundle."
groups = ["default"]
files = [
    {file = "certifi-2024.8.30-py3-none-any.whl", hash = "sha256:922820b53d
    b7a7257ffbda3f597266d435245903d80737e34f8a45ff3e3230d8"},
    {file = "certifi-2024.8.30.tar.gz", hash = "sha256:bec941d2aa8195e248
    a60b31ff9f0558284cf01a52591ceda73ea9afffd69fd9"},
]

...

[[package]]
name = "requests"
version = "2.32.3"
requires_python = ">=3.8"
summary = "Python HTTP for Humans."
groups = ["default"]
dependencies = [
    "certifi>=2017.4.17",
    "charset-normalizer<4,>=2",
    "idna<4,>=2.5",
    "urllib3<3,>=1.21.1",
]
files = [
    {file = "requests-2.32.3-py3-none-any.whl", hash = "sha256:70761cfe03
    c773ceb22aa2f671b4757976145175cdfca038c02654d061d6dcc6"},
    {file = "requests-2.32.3.tar.gz", hash = "sha256:55365417734eb18255590
    a9ff9eb97e9e1da868d4ccd6402399eaf68af20a760"},
]

[[package]]
name = "urllib3"
version = "2.2.3"
requires_python = ">=3.8"
summary = "HTTP library with thread-safe connection pooling, file post,
and more."
```

```
groups = ["default"]
files = [
    {file = "urllib3-2.2.3-py3-none-any.whl", hash = "sha256:ca899ca043dcb1
    bafa3e262d73aa25c465bfb49e0bd9dd5d59f1d0acba2f8fac"},
    {file = "urllib3-2.2.3.tar.gz", hash = "sha256:e7d814a81dad81e6caf2ec9f
    dedb284ecc9c73076b62654547cc64ccdcae26e9"},
]
```

To update packages, the `pdm update` command can be used. Packages can be removed using the `pdm remove` command.

PDM supports organizing dependencies into logical groups through its dependency group feature. We can define separate groups like "dev" or "test" in the `pyproject.toml`, making it easier to manage different sets of dependencies for various development stages. Dependencies can be installed selectively by group, which helps keep development environments lean and purpose-specific.

Consider the below `pyproject.toml` file:

```
[project]
dependencies = ["requests"]  # Production dependencies

[project.optional-dependencies]
extra1 = ["flask"]           # Optional dependency group 1
extra2 = ["django"]          # Optional dependency group 2

[dependency-groups]
dev1 = ["pytest"]            # Development dependency group 1
dev2 = ["mkdocs"]            # Development dependency group 2
```

The commands installs the dependencies as illustrated below:

- `pdm install`: Installs all groups locked in the lock file

- `pdm install -G extra1`: Installs prod deps, dev deps, and "extra1" optional group

- `pdm install -G dev1`: Installs prod deps and only "dev1" dev group

- `pdm install --prod`: Installs prod only

The below dockerfile from *xiaomusic* showcases an example of PDM usage at the time of building the application for production:

```
FROM hanxi/xiaomusic:builder AS builder
ENV DEBIAN_FRONTEND=noninteractive
RUN pip install -U pdm
ENV PDM_CHECK_UPDATE=false
WORKDIR /app
COPY pyproject.toml README.md .
COPY xiaomusic/ ./xiaomusic/
COPY plugins/ ./plugins/
COPY xiaomusic.py .
RUN pdm install --prod --no-editable

FROM hanxi/xiaomusic:runtime
WORKDIR /app
COPY --from=builder /app/.venv /app/.venv
COPY --from=builder /app/xiaomusic/ ./xiaomusic/
COPY --from=builder /app/plugins/ ./plugins/
COPY --from=builder /app/xiaomusic.py .
ENV XIAOMUSIC_HOSTNAME=192.168.2.5
ENV XIAOMUSIC_PORT=8090
VOLUME /app/conf
VOLUME /app/music
EXPOSE 8090
ENV TZ=Asia/Shanghai
ENV PATH=/app/.venv/bin:$PATH
ENTRYPOINT [".venv/bin/python3","xiaomusic.py"]
```

In the dockerfile, the command `pdm install --prod --no-editable` installs only production dependencies (excluding development dependencies) in a non-editable mode, making it ideal for deployment environments where development tools aren't needed.

uv

uv is a relatively new, extremely fast Python package installer and resolver written in Rust. It aims to replace most of the current dependency management tools by offering the same features with minimal changes, providing good speedup, thanks to Rust. It can also be used as a drop-in replacement for pip, offering significant speed improvements.

uv can be installed globally using installers provided on the official uv site (`https://docs.astral.sh/uv/getting-started/installation/`) or via pip (`pip install uv`).

Key features of uv:

- Extremely fast package installation and resolution

- Compatible with existing requirements.txt and pyproject.toml files

- Can generate lock files for deterministic builds

The below commands show uv usage as a `pip` replacement:

```
# Install uv
pip install uv

# Install packages
uv pip install requests

# Install from requirements.txt
uv pip install -r requirements.txt

# Generate a lock file
uv pip compile requirements.txt -o requirements.lock
```

When `uv pip` is used instead of `pip`, the speed improvement is usually significant, often several times faster. The speed improvement comes from `uv pip`'s parallel dependency resolution, concurrent downloads, and caching, along with its Rust-based implementation that handles package installation more efficiently. uv's speed can significantly improve workflow efficiency, especially for projects with many dependencies.

In addition to being a pip replacement, uv provides a comprehensive toolkit for Python environment management, dependency handling, and package distribution.

It can

- Install Python.

- Generate a pyproject.toml file.

- Manage dependencies.

- Generate lock files.

- Build and publish packages.

Below are some other uv commands:

```
# Install Python and create virtual environment
uv python 3.11.5
uv venv

# Initialize project and manage dependencies
uv init                    # Generate pyproject.toml
uv add fastapi             # Add packages
uv add pytest --dev        # Add dev dependencies
uv remove requests         # Remove packages
uv lock                    # Generate lockfile
uv sync                    # Install from lockfile
```

Below is a uv.lock file generated after installing the requests library:

```
version = 1
requires-python = ">=3.11"

[[package]]
name = "certifi"
version = "2024.8.30"
source = { registry = "https://pypi.org/simple" }
sdist = { url = "https://files.pythonhosted.org/packages/b0/ee/9b19140fe82
4b367c04c5e1b369942dd754c4c5462d5674002f75c4dedc1/certifi-2024.8.30.tar.
gz", hash = "sha256:bec941d2aa8195e248a60b31ff9f0558284cf01a52591ceda73ea9a
fffd69fd9", size = 168507 }
```

```
wheels = [
    { url = "https://files.pythonhosted.org/packages/12/90/3c9ff051203803
    5f59d279fddeb79f5f1eccd8859f06d6163c58798b9487/certifi-2024.8.30-py3-
    none-any.whl", hash = "sha256:922820b53db7a7257ffbda3f597266d435245903
    d80737e34f8a45ff3e3230d8", size = 167321 },
]
```

•••

```
[[package]]
name = "idna"
version = "3.10"
source = { registry = "https://pypi.org/simple" }
sdist = { url = "https://files.pythonhosted.org/packages/f1/70/7703c2968563
1f5a7590aa73f1f1d3fa9a380e654b86af429e0934a32f7d/idna-3.10.tar.gz", hash =
"sha256:12f65c9b470abda6dc35cf8e63cc574b1c52b11df2c86030af0ac09b01b13ea9",
size = 190490 }
wheels = [
    { url = "https://files.pythonhosted.org/packages/76/c6/
    c88e154df9c4e1a2a66ccf0005a88dfb2650c1dffb6f5ce603dfbd452ce3/idna-3.10-
    py3-none-any.whl", hash = "sha256:946d195a0d259cbba61165e88e65941f16e9
    b36ea6ddb97f00452bae8b1287d3", size = 70442 },
]

[[package]]
name = "requests"
version = "2.32.3"
source = { registry = "https://pypi.org/simple" }
dependencies = [
    { name = "certifi" },
    { name = "charset-normalizer" },
    { name = "idna" },
    { name = "urllib3" },
]
```

```
sdist = { url = "https://files.pythonhosted.org/packages/63/70/2bf7780ad
2d390a8d301ad0b550f1581eadbd9a20f896afe06353c2a2913/requests-2.32.3.tar.
gz", hash = "sha256:55365417734eb18255590a9ff9eb97e9e1da868d4ccd6402399ea
f68af20a760", size = 131218 }
wheels = [
    { url = "https://files.pythonhosted.org/packages/f9/9b/335f9764261e915
    ed497fcdeb11df5dfd6f7bf257d4a6a2a686d80da4d54/requests-2.32.3-py3-none-
    any.whl", hash = "sha256:70761cfe03c773ceb22aa2f671b4757976145175cdfc
    a038c02654d061d6dcc6", size = 64928 },
]

[[package]]
name = "urllib3"
version = "2.2.3"
source = { registry = "https://pypi.org/simple" }
sdist = { url = "https://files.pythonhosted.org/packages/ed/63/22ba4ebfe743
0b76388e7cd448d5478814d3032121827c12a2cc287e2260/urllib3-2.2.3.tar.gz",
hash = "sha256:e7d814a81dad81e6caf2ec9fdedb284ecc9c73076b62654547cc64ccdca
e26e9", size = 300677 }
wheels = [
    { url = "https://files.pythonhosted.org/packages/ce/d9/5f4c13cecde6239
    6b0d3fe530a50ccea91e7dfc1ccf0e09c228841bb5ba8/urllib3-2.2.3-py3-none-
    any.whl", hash = "sha256:ca899ca043dcb1bafa3e262d73aa25c465bfb49e0bd9d
    d5d59f1d0acba2f8fac", size = 126338 },
]

[[package]]
name = "uv-demo"
version = "0.1.0"
source = { virtual = "." }
dependencies = [
    { name = "requests" },
]

[package.metadata]
requires-dist = [{ name = "requests", specifier = ">=2.32.3" }]
```

It can also act as a replacement for pip-tools using the below commands:

- uv pip compile: Compile requirements into a lock file.

- uv pip sync: Sync an environment with a lock file.

The workflow file from *Jurigged* showcases the usage of uv in a CI environment:

```yaml
name: Python package

on:
  push:
    branches: [ master ]
  pull_request:
    branches: [ master ]

jobs:
  lint:
    runs-on: ubuntu-latest
    strategy:
      matrix:
        python-version: ['3.12']
    steps:
    - name: Check out the code
      uses: actions/checkout@v3
    - name: Set up uv
      uses: hynek/setup-cached-uv@v2
      with:
        cache-dependency-path: uv.lock
    - name: Pin Python version
      run: uv python pin ${{ matrix.python-version }}
    - name: Lint check
      run: uvx ruff check
    - name: Check formatting
      run: uvx ruff format --check

  test:
    runs-on: ubuntu-latest
    strategy:
```

```yaml
    matrix:
      settings:
      - python: '3.9'
        coverage: false
      - python: '3.10'
        coverage: false
      - python: '3.11'
        coverage: false
      - python: '3.12'
        coverage: true
  steps:
  - name: Check out the code
    uses: actions/checkout@v3
  - name: Set up uv
    uses: hynek/setup-cached-uv@v2
    with:
      cache-dependency-path: uv.lock
  - name: Pin Python version
    run: uv python pin ${{ matrix.settings.python }}
  - name: Sync dependencies
    run: uv sync --all-extras
  - name: Test with pytest
    if: ${{ !matrix.settings.coverage }}
    run: uv run pytest tests/
  - name: Test with pytest and coverage
    if: ${{ matrix.settings.coverage }}
    run: uv run pytest --cov=src --cov-report term-missing tests/
  - name: Verify coverage
    if: ${{ matrix.settings.coverage }}
    run: uv run coverage report | tail -1 | egrep "TOTAL +[0-9]+ +0 +100%"
```

In the file

- `uv python pin <version>`: Sets the specific Python version for the environment

- `uvx ruff check`: Runs linting using Ruff (shorthand for `uv run ruff check`)

- `uvx ruff format`: Checks code formatting with Ruff

- `uv sync --all-extras`: Installs all dependencies, including optional extras from a lock file

- `uv run pytest`: Executes pytest within the uv environment

- `uv run coverage`: Runs coverage commands in the uv environment

While tools like Pipenv and pip-tools serve their purpose well, uv offers a compelling alternative for Python project management. Its significant performance improvements in package installation and dependency resolution, combined with a straightforward command interface, make it valuable for projects where build times matter.

Dependency Conflicts

Dependency conflicts occur when different packages require different versions of the same dependency. These conflicts can cause issues in our projects, leading to errors and unexpected behavior.

To go deeper into a dependency issue, we can utilize the `pipdeptree` library. It is a tool that helps us visualize the dependency tree of our project. It provides a clear overview of all dependencies and their versions, making it easier to identify and resolve conflicts.

Key features of `pipdeptree`:

1. Displays dependencies in a tree-like format

2. Highlights conflicting dependencies

3. Can generate output in JSON format for further processing

4. Can visualize dependencies as real graphs using Graphviz

Here's how to use pipdeptree:

```
# Install pipdeptree
pip install pipdeptree

# Display dependency tree
pipdeptree
```

```
# Show only conflicting dependencies
pipdeptree --warn silence

# Generate JSON output
pipdeptree --json-tree
```

The below requirements can generate a conflict when installed:

```
flask==3.0.3
jinja2==2.11.3
```

pip successfully installs both with a warning that the dependencies are conflicting.

The pip check command can be run to detect dependency conflicts, which produces the output flask 3.0.3 has requirement Jinja2>=3.1.2, but you have jinja2 2.11.3.

Running pipdeptree on the same environment generates the below output, which is a bit more detailed:

```
Warning!!! Possibly conflicting dependencies found:
* Flask==3.0.3
 - Jinja2 [required: >=3.1.2, installed: 2.11.3]
------------------------------------------------------------------------
Flask==3.0.3
├── blinker [required: >=1.6.2, installed: 1.8.2]
├── click [required: >=8.1.3, installed: 8.1.7]
│   └── colorama [required: Any, installed: 0.4.6]
├── itsdangerous [required: >=2.1.2, installed: 2.2.0]
├── Jinja2 [required: >=3.1.2, installed: 2.11.3]
│   └── MarkupSafe [required: >=0.23, installed: 3.0.2]
└── Werkzeug [required: >-3.0.0, installed: 3.1.1]
    └── MarkupSafe [required: >=2.1.1, installed: 3.0.2]
pipdeptree==2.23.4
├── packaging [required: >=24.1, installed: 24.1]
└── pip [required: >=24.2, installed: 24.3.1]
setuptools==65.5.0
```

Pipenv also comes with a command to detect conflicts. The below output will be generated by running `pipenv graph --json`:

```
[
    {
        "package": {
            "key": "flask",
            "package_name": "Flask",
            "installed_version": "3.0.3"
        },
        "dependencies": [
            {
                "key": "blinker",
                "package_name": "blinker",
                "installed_version": "1.8.2",
                "required_version": ">=1.6.2"
            },
            {
                "key": "click",
                "package_name": "click",
                "installed_version": "8.1.7",
                "required_version": ">=8.1.3"
            },
            {
                "key": "itsdangerous",
                "package_name": "itsdangerous",
                "installed_version": "2.2.0",
                "required_version": ">=2.1.2"
            },
            {
                "key": "jinja2",
                "package_name": "Jinja2",
                "installed_version": "2.11.3",
                "required_version": ">=3.1.2"
            },
```

```
        {
            "key": "werkzeug",
            "package_name": "Werkzeug",
            "installed_version": "3.1.1",
            "required_version": ">=3.0.0"
        }
    ]
},
...
]
```

By using tools like `pipdeptree`, `pip check`, etc., we can identify and resolve dependency conflicts more easily, ensuring our projects remain stable and predictable.

Security in Dependency Management

When managing dependencies, security should be at the forefront of our minds. Malicious actors often target package ecosystems, and Python's popularity makes it an attractive target. Let's explore some key security concerns and how to mitigate them.

Typosquatting Attacks

Typosquatting is a type of attack where malicious actors publish packages with names very similar to popular packages, hoping developers will accidentally install them due to typos, e.g.:

- `requests` (legitimate) vs. `reqeusts` (potential typosquat)

- `beaulifulsoup` (legitimate) vs. `beautifulsoup4` (legitimate) vs. `beautifulsoup5` (potential typosquat)

To protect against typosquatting

1. Double-check package names before installation.

2. Use a requirements file or lock file to specify exact package names.

3. Consider using tools like `safety` to check for known malicious packages.

Supply Chain Attacks

Supply chain attacks occur when an attacker compromises a legitimate package or its distribution channel. This can happen if a package maintainer's account is hacked or if a mirror site is compromised. To mitigate supply chain attacks

1. Use package hashes in your requirements file (we'll discuss this more in the next section).

2. Regularly update dependencies to get security patches.

3. Use private PyPI mirrors for critical projects.

4. Consider using tools like `pip-audit` to check for known vulnerabilities in your dependencies.

Auditing Dependencies

In this section, we will explore some tools and techniques to audit and secure our dependencies.

Pip-audit

The `pip-audit` tool, maintained by the Python Packaging Authority (PyPA), scans Python environments and requirements files for known vulnerabilities. It leverages the Python Packaging Advisory Database (PyPI Advisory) to identify security issues in installed packages, making it an official, community-supported solution for dependency security scanning.

```
# Install pip-audit
pip install pip-audit
```

```
# Audit your dependencies
pip-audit
```

To check the command, we can install an outdated version of Django (`pip install django==4.1`) and run `pip-audit`. It produces a result like below:

```
Found 9 known vulnerabilities in 1 package
Name    Version ID                  Fix Versions
------  ------- ------------------- -------------------
django  4.1     PYSEC-2022-304      3.2.16,4.0.8,4.1.2
django  4.1     PYSEC-2023-13       3.2.18,4.0.10,4.1.7
django  4.1     PYSEC-2023-12       3.2.17,4.0.9,4.1.6
django  4.1     PYSEC-2023-61       3.2.19,4.1.9,4.2.1
django  4.1     PYSEC-2023-100      3.2.20,4.1.10,4.2.3
django  4.1     PYSEC-2023-222      3.2.23,4.1.13,4.2.7
django  4.1     PYSEC-2023-225      3.2.21,4.1.11,4.2.5
django  4.1     PYSEC-2023-226      3.2.22,4.1.12,4.2.6
django  4.1     GHSA-rrqc-c2jx-6jgv 4.2.16,5.0.9,5.1.1
```

We can use pip-audit in CI environments or as a pre-commit hook to ensure that our dependencies are checked frequently.

Safety

The safety package by PyUp.io is a security tool that checks installed dependencies against a comprehensive database of known vulnerabilities. It offers both a free community database and a commercial database with additional security advisories.

The initial setup requires signing up to use the command, and the package comes with additional proprietary offerings also.

```
# Install safety
pip install safety
```

```
# Check installed packages for known security issues
safety scan
```

Running the safety scan command on an environment with an outdated Django version produces the below output:

```
Dependency vulnerabilities detected:
```

📝 requirements.txt:

```
django==4.1 [19 vulnerabilities found, including 1 critical severity
vulnerability]
```

Update django==4.1 to django==4.2.16 to fix 19 vulnerabilities, including 1
critical severity vulnerability ⬡
Versions of django with no known vulnerabilities: 5.1.3, 5.1.2,
5.1.1, 5.0.9
Learn more: https://data.safetycli.com/p/pypi/django/
eda/?from=4.1&to=4.2.16

Hash-Checking Mode to Secure Dependencies

Pip's hash-checking mode allows us to verify that the packages we're installing haven't
been tampered with. By including hashes in our requirements file, we ensure that pip
will only install packages that exactly match these hashes. This security measure protects
against supply chain attacks and man-in-the-middle attacks by verifying the integrity of
each package, ensuring that what you install matches exactly what was published by the
package maintainer.

While using pip, hashes can be specified in requirements.txt, and pip install
validates them before installation.

A requirement can be specified along with hashes seen below:

django==4.1 --hash=sha256:031ccb717782f6af83a0063a1957686e87cb4581ea61b47b
3e9addf60687989a

The tools such as uv, pipenv, and pdm have hash checking enabled by default. pip-
tools does not do this by default, but adding a --generate-hashes option to pip-
compile adds package hashes to the requirements.txt file generated.

Here's how to generate and use hashes with pip-tools:

Generate a requirements file with hashes:

pip install pip-tools
pip-compile --generate-hashes requirements.in

The requirements.txt will now include hashes:

requests==2.26.0 \
--hash=sha256:b8aa58f8cf793ffd8782d3d8cb19e66ef36f7aba4353eec859e74678b0
1b07a7 \
--hash=sha256:c6c942b9a55c844f8584d8ba1e481ba4735bfdb0293b76a77eb65f0
0c3fa77ae

Install packages using the requirements file:

```
pip install -r requirements.txt
```

Pip will now check the hash of each downloaded package against the provided hashes, refusing to install if there's a mismatch.

By implementing these security measures, we significantly reduce the risk of introducing vulnerabilities or malicious code into our projects through dependencies. Remember, security in dependency management is an ongoing process that requires vigilance and regular maintenance.

Conclusion

In this chapter, we explored the critical aspects of dependency management in Python, highlighting its importance in maintaining stable, secure, and maintainable projects. We've seen how virtual environments provide isolated spaces for our projects, allowing us to maintain separate sets of dependencies for different applications. Additionally, managing different Python versions becomes seamless with tools like pyenv, which allow us to switch between versions effortlessly, ensuring compatibility and reducing conflicts.

We also explored the concept of deterministic builds, emphasizing the importance of version locks in achieving consistent and reliable project builds. By locking dependency versions, we ensure that our projects run with the same set of libraries every time, minimizing unexpected behaviors and simplifying debugging and testing. Version specifiers further allow us to define acceptable version ranges for our dependencies, providing a balance between stability and flexibility. We explored a range of tools, including pip-tools, pipenv, pdm, and uv, each offering unique features to enhance our dependency management processes. By utilizing these tools and techniques, we can manage our dependencies effectively, ensuring our projects remain robust, secure, and easy to maintain.

Index

A

© Adarsh Divakaran 2025
A. Divakaran, *Deep Dive Python*, https://doi.org/10.1007/979-8-8688-1261-3

Printed in the United States
by Baker & Taylor Publisher Services